HOUSING, CULTURE, AND DESIGN

HOUSING, CULTURE, AND DESIGN

A COMPARATIVE PERSPECTIVE

SETHA M. LOW
ERVE CHAMBERS

EDITORS

FOREWORD BY AMOS RAPOPORT

upp UNIVERSITY OF PENNSYLVANIA PRESS

PHILADELPHIA

Library of Congress Cataloging-in-Publication Data

Housing, culture, and design: a comparative perspective / Setha M.
Low, Erve Chambers, editors.
    p.   cm.
"Has its roots in two symposia held during 1985 at the annual
meetings of the Society for Applied Anthropology and the
Environmental Design Research Associations"—Intro.
    Includes bibliographies and index.
    ISBN 0-8122-8120-9.   ISBN 0-8122-1271-1 (alk. paper)
    1. Housing—Cross-cultural studies—Congresses.   2. Culture—
Congresses.   I. Low, Setha M.   II. Chambers, Erve.
HD7287.5.H475   1989
307.3'36—dc19   88-15067
                                                        CIP

Designed by Adrianne Onderdonk Dudden

To Leona Chambers and Marilyn Rudley

CONTENTS

Contents

FOREWORD

We are witnessing a major revival of interest in the study of the relation between culture and built form and in the use of cross-cultural approaches to that and other topics. This book is one significant manifestation of that trend.

This revival has different implications for different disciplines. In anthropology it marks a revival of interest in material culture, including built environments in the broadest sense. This is significant because anthropologists have tended to become much less involved with environment-behavior studies (EBS) than have members of other human sciences. For the design professions this interest has two implications. First, it marks a new direction: a concern with users and particularly with differences among groups of users, as well as an implicit acceptance of major differences between designers and users. Second, it marks a revival of interest, but on a more sophisticated level, in such traditional topics as complexity, character, "place," regional and other differences, *genius loci*, and vernacular design. This revival marks a realization that many of these topics and the design goals related to them, which have eluded designers, can be understood and possibly achieved through a rigorous study of the relation between culture and built form.

In such study all types of settings need to be considered because settings form systems. Among such settings, however, *housing* (or dwelling) is the most important because it is a human universal. For that reason the subject of this book is confined to the relation between culture and housing.

In this foreword I will summarize a conceptual framework to this topic, developed over many years in many publications.

Since, typically, discussions about culture and housing tend to emphasize so-called primitive examples, traditional and "exotic" situations (for reasons which I discussed at the 1984 Culture and Built Form Conference at the University of Kansas), I will therefore conclude with some brief remarks beginning to bear on the case of the United States and other complex, developed societies.

Why should *culture* be studied along with housing? Among many possible answers, consider two. First, in any EBS framework culture must play a role, because culture is what makes humans human. Any specific problem in environment-behavior relations (EBR) can be understood in terms of what I call the three basic questions of EBR. Culture can clearly be shown to play a major role in all three.

1 What characteristics of people as individuals, as members of various groups, and as members of a species are significantly related to built form?

2 What effects do what environments have on what sets of people, under what sets of conditions, and why?

3 Given the two-way interaction implied in the first two questions, what mechanisms link people and settings?

Individuals and their experiences are neither sufficient nor useful in either research or design. Subjective variables are central in EBR, but only if they can be generalized. Generalization, however, implies groups. Hence the second reason why culture needs to be considered: culture is what distinguishes groups within our single species. In fact, the presence of many very different groups is a striking characteristic of *Homo sapiens*. Equally striking is the great variety of settings, especially housing. Given the relatively few needs and activities, the extraordinary variety of settings is puzzling. The explanation is culture; in some way, apparently similar needs, even those as simple as cooking, going to the toilet, storing objects, sleeping, or going upstairs, lead to many different solutions and settings. This suggests that in any study of housing not only is culture of central importance but also there is a crucial need for comparative approaches such as cross-cultural studies.

What Is Meant by Culture?

Culture, needless to say, is a complex term; however, several general conceptualizations can be summarized to help clarify it. Three complementary conceptualizations address the question of what culture is, suggesting that it is a way of life typical of a group; it is a system of schemata transmitted symbolically; it is a way of coping with the ecological setting. Three conceptualizations address the question of what culture *does*, suggesting that it acts as a blueprint for assembling components; it gives meaning to particulars; it is that property which defines groups. All of these conceptualizations are relevant, but for our purposes we are less concerned about the nature of culture than with knowing which expressions of cultural differences affect housing; therefore the last of these concepts will be emphasized—culture as the property of groups, which distinguishes among them and identifies them.

What Is Meant by Housing?

Housing is a form of built environment. Various conceptualizations of the term *built environment* have been proposed. Minimally, environments comprise relationships between people and people, people and things, things and things. The design of the environment can, however, be conceptualized as the organization of four variables: space, time, meaning, and communication.

Common to these and all other conceptualizations is the essential point that built environments are more than just hardware. It follows that housing, a particular type of built environment, is also more than just the "dwelling." For our purposes *housing* can be conceptualized in two ways that are complementary rather than conflicting.

First, housing can be conceptualized as *a system of settings* within which certain systems of activities take place. Such a definition is essential for valid cross-cultural comparisons to be made; otherwise noncomparable units may be compared. This system can comprise different settings arranged in different ways, with different linkages and separations. A frequently useful question is, Who does what, where, and when, and including or excluding whom (and why)? The dwelling and its parts are linked to many other settings: in the neighborhood, in the city, and beyond. The system of settings, can, in principle, extend a very long way, but methods exist to establish reasonable limits. The specifics of the systems of settings that constitute housing vary greatly with culture.

Second, housing can be described in terms of environmental quality, comprising the many attributes that characterize the particular system of settings; those can be seen as undesirable, or alternatively, they are sought and chosen (within the constraints operating for any group at any given time). Environmental quality can be conceptualized as comprising four variables: the components; their ranking; their importance in relation to other qualities, needs, or desires which are not part of housing even in the broadest interpretation of the term (as is often true of spontaneous settlements in developing countries); and whether they are positive or negative. The environmental quality of housing can then be described by *an environmental quality profile*.

A Link Between Culture and Housing: Diversity

While culture both is pan-human and distinguishes among different groups, the variety of groups and their settings is most striking; the emphasis must, therefore, be on diversity. This suggests that choice plays a role. Members of different groups *choose* housing; they migrate, buy, or rent. Members of different groups also *design* housing environments (design can be understood as a process of choosing among alternatives), and they also *modify* housing to make it more acceptable or suitable. This diversity of housing is due to its low criticality; that is, there are always many alternative ways of providing for needs, and therefore *wants* can play a major role. Not only are wants different for different groups, but they also change for any given group over time.

Wants help to explain diversity. Behaviors and activities as expressions of wants are significantly more diverse than behaviors and activities as expressions of needs, because the *latent* aspects of activities tend to be the most important. The same manifest or instrumental activity can be carried out in very different ways; it can be associated with others into systems in even more different ways. The meaning of the activity is the most variable. These variable aspects of activities are related to culture, and in addition they explain the striking variety of environments, including housing, particularly when one considers their full range—including preliterate, vernacular, popular, and so on—and when one examines them cross-culturally and over time.

The Nature of Relevant Groups

I take the subject matter of this book to be a subset of EBS. A major problem, both in EBS and in studies of housing is: What are relevant groups? It is useful to begin with the anthropological concepts of *emic* and *etic* criteria. Emic refers to how members of a given group see things, etic to how an outside observer or analyst sees the same things. Research, therefore, always uses etic categories, but one can distinguish between imposed and derived etics. Imposed etics tend not to be useful: they are very ethnocentric and generally tend to invalidate comparative studies. Derived etics, which take into account emics, are essential; considerations such as these provide the rationale for my redefinition of housing as a system of settings briefly discussed above.

Emic categories are applied to groups typically in terms of *perceived homogeneity*, which can be based on very different criteria: race, ethnicity, religion, language, caste, occupation, ideology, and status, among others. The specifics vary with culture. Also, for a group to exist, the existence of social boundaries must be accepted both by group members and by outsiders. Housing itself can and often is used to make and maintain distinctions among groups—an additional factor in housing diversity.

Congruence Between Culture and Housing

Culture and built environments cannot be linked using these terms as they stand; both are too general. It is impossible to analyze the relation between culture and environment or to "design for culture." Greater specificity does not help. To "design housing for culture" is indeed more specific but no easier or more feasible. To consider housing for a given culture is yet more specific but still impossible. While the housing can be understood as a system of settings with a specific environmental quality profile, defining *culture* as the property of groups seems unmanageable. This is because *culture* is both too abstract and too global. It is too abstract in the sense that, as a "blueprint" or set of instructions, it is an ideational concept which is expressed more concretely in social variables, such as social structures, social networks and relationships, roles, institutions, and the like. Hence the commonly used term *sociocultural variables* tends to confuse the issue: social variables can be understood as more concrete expressions of culture. The term *culture* is too global in the sense that, as a theoretical construct, it subsumes many things: in one sense it is shorthand for a vast variety of specifics. Like other global concepts, culture thus needs to be dismantled. A useful way of doing this considers a series of ever-more concrete components of culture: world views, values, life-style, and finally, activity systems. Although world views can be studied, they are still too global and too abstract for our purposes. An examination of values can be useful: the study of environmental preference and choice is explicitly based on values. However, as I will argue below, *life-style* as an expression of values is even more useful. Activity systems have already been discussed.

Both of these approaches, using lower-level, more operational components of culture and emphasizing its more concrete social expressions, make it easier to relate culture to settings. Consider an example. One suggestion for linking culture to housing at the ideational level has been to consider housing as an expression of cognitive categories and domains. As I once put it, environments are thought before they are built. While feasible, this approach is difficult. It has, therefore, been suggested that the concept of expressive space as a stage for cultural behavior be used. The examples used, the Tswana, Navaho, and Australian Aborigines, are all "exotic" in the sense already discussed. Although it may be feasible, albeit difficult, to derive culturally expressive space for the above three groups, it would be much more difficult, if not impossible, to do so for most groups in the United States.

Considering settings as stages for cultural behaviors in their more concrete and lower-level manifestations is much easier. Social variables can be related to systems of settings; activity systems (always considering their latent aspects, including meaning) can easily be related to settings as stages for daily life. This leads directly to congruence between those more concrete and specific manifestations of culture and systems of settings and their desirable (and undesirable) attributes, that is, their environmental quality profiles. It leads directly to congruence with housing as I defined it above.

This result can be extremely useful when designing for specific groups of users. Activity systems, however, are too specific and detailed for the level of analysis which I am discussing here. The most useful component of culture in this context, and as a starting point, which I increasingly advocate, is *life-style*. Nothing precludes the possibility that, with more knowledge, it may become possible to operate at more abstract levels, should that prove necessary or desirable.

Life-Style

Life-style is a clear expression of culture. A useful operational definition is to consider it the result of choices made about how to allocate resources—economic and symbolic resources, effort, time, and so on. It thus expresses and incorporates values: this links it to culture. It also leads directly to activity systems. Since design, like life-style, can also be understood as a choice process, there is a suggestive potential link with built environments, including housing. Also, people as members of groups design, choose, or modify housing to improve congruence with life-style. Since life-style also can be conceptualized as a profile, this provides another potential link with housing (and other environments)—congruence between the life-style profile and the environmental quality profile.

Environments can also be seen as supportive of given life-styles. People try to maximize supportiveness. Three questions can be asked about this: What is being supported? By what is it being supported? How is it being supported? The answer to the first question refers to the components of life-style and their expressions. The answer to the second question specifies the physical units, or the particular systems of settings already described. The answer to the last question specifies various mechanisms: instrumentally supportive elements; latent characteristics such as meanings communicating status or identity; and financial, economic, or physical security.

In all these cases, housing is made congruent with life-style through choice, expressing preferences and values—all ultimately related to culture. For users today, this typically involves choosing among available housing alternatives and within limits set by various constraints. For designers (today or in the past), it involves making design choices congruent with users' life-styles. The effort, whether in designing, moving, buying, renting, remodeling, or furnishing (or changing one's life-style or expectations when none of the above is feasible) is always directed toward making the life-style profile as congruent as possible with the environmental quality profile of that system of settings which constitutes housing. Of course, as described, choice in housing is an *ideal model*. It is distorted by various constraints—resources, knowledge, technology, availability, prejudice, and others. It is often useful to begin with groups that have maximum choice, for example, the rich, and then study effects of various constraints which operate for various groups in various situations, up to the case where the constraints may become dominant and choice minimal.

Two major aspects of housing thus vary with life-style (and ultimately with culture): the nature of the system of settings and its environmental quality profile.

One of the definitions of culture, in terms of a way of life typical of a group (= life-style!!), often involves a notion of ideal human beings leading ideal lives in ideal settings. There is thus some notion of an ideal environment—in our case, an ideal housing environment. This is used to evaluate perceived qualities in making choices. This ideal is typically embodied in an image or schema and is linked primarily to latent aspects: meaning, status, identity, the good life, and so on, that is, wants rather than needs. Housing must, therefore, be considered in terms of such aspects—*housing involves dreams*. Advertisers of housing, for example in the United States, are well aware of that which makes advertisements useful in the study of housing. Moreover, choice is based on an affective, global response. This much less conscious and methodical process is then conceptualized by researchers in terms of various notions, such as matching profiles.

This discussion of dreams, choice, and advertising brings me close to the topic of housing in cultures such as our own in which there are many diverse groups. Such housing is an interesting, most important, and rather neglected topic which I cannot discuss here. The issue of groups, however, which has been central in this foreword, needs to be discussed.

Groups in the United States and in Other Complex, Developed Societies

Large-scale, contemporary, pluralistic societies, such as the United States, raise problems not faced by researchers in those small-scale, traditional, often preliterate societies that were typically studied in culture–built form research or anthropology until fairly recently. This situation has implications which need to be discussed.

Small-scale, traditional societies have tended to be homogeneous. The behavior of their members is fairly constrained, and they have limited choice in behavior, activities, or life-style. While recent research suggests that the extent of such constraints has tended to be exaggerated, and choice rather greater, as a generalization in relation to, say, the United States, it is certainly valid. Housing for traditional societies tends to be homogeneous for any one group, to the extent that settlement forms, dwellings, or parts of them often identify the group or even become symbols of group identity.

The criteria for the identification of such groups (in both emic and etic terms) are relatively clear-cut. It is *relatively* easy to identify preliterate groups such as an Australian Aboriginal tribe (neglecting the arguments in the literature as to whether there are actually tribes—this suggests that my argument is somewhat too strong, although the general point is valid), the Yagua, Navaho, Fang, M'buti, Tswana, Hmong, or whatever. It is also a *relatively* straightforward matter to identify their relationship to housing. This is still true in preindustrial literate societies, those where the housing of most people is traditional vernacular. In those societies the various subgroups are generally highly place-specific, by region (for example, traditional Mexico), particular locale (for example, valleys in Switzerland or Norway), and other aspects of culture (including dialect, activities, costume, and so on, and, related to all those and more, *life-style*). In general, these groups clearly so identify themselves and are so identified by others; any one of those groups also tends to be highly homogeneous and locationally, culturally, and conceptually localized (or localizable). Again, the matter is not always that simple, and difficulties arise. For example, in traditional India, regional and village localization is crosscut by caste links, which means that wider networks play an important role.

The diversity already emphasized is found cross-culturally in studies *across* units (places and groups), not *within* the place or society being studied.

The United States—possibly from its beginning, but certainly now—and also other modern, technologically developed societies are quite different in kind from preindustrial societies. They tend to be large, complex, and hetero-geneous ("pluralistic"). Not only are there multiple groups, but these are both nonlocalized and overlapping: people belong simultaneously to different groups. In the United States, one is a member of the national culture (which is different from, for example, India). Then, one is a member of subgroups within the larger population—ethnic, racial, religious, occupational, ideo-logical, class, stage in life cycle, life-style. Moreover, one can belong to more than one group. There are also individual variations which tend to develop early and persist; hence the importance of cohort effects.

The study of the relation of culture and housing in modern societies is much more complex and difficult than in more traditional societies. More-over, normative constraints on behavior, activities, dress, and so forth—that is, life-style—tend to be relatively weak and have been getting weaker over recent decades. This allows far more choice about how to dress, eat, interact, educate children, behave—or dwell. Resource and other similar constraints are also weaker for most people. Differences *among* groups (individuals shar-ing common characteristics which are sometimes called "aggregates") are still greater than *within* groups—or one could not distinguish among groups or talk about them. However, the variability among individuals within groups is much greater in the United States than in traditional societies. It follows that *individual* differences and choices play a greater role than in more traditional societies. While there is still agreement among individuals within a group, the scatter about a given norm is much greater. Also, the agreement often expresses itself in life-style—which becomes by far the most useful aspect to study as the link between culture and housing. This has implications for housing: first, there should be more variability in dwellings and systems of settings than in traditional groups; and second, more open-endedness is needed to allow adjustments to environmental quality profiles to life-style profiles.

There is thus a great diversity of groups in the United States (and similar places), cross-cutting in complex ways that is not matched by a corresponding diversity of housing environments. There is less *apparent* diversity of housing: differences in housing within the United States are much smaller than differ-ences in African or Asian countries, for example. Also, in the United States the housing variations that do exist tend to be less "extreme," more subtle, although this does not necessarily make them less important. The apparent absence of housing variation, given the much greater apparent variety of life-styles, may be due to a weaker link between culture and housing (and built environments generally). Alternatively, it may be due to constraints rather than choice. If the latter is the case, then the designers' task becomes to broaden this variety or, better, to make it possible. To do so, the relevant groups need to be identified; at the same time the general problem of identifying relevant groups increases.

Another general point greatly affects any discussion of housing in the United States and comparable societies. A major group difference is between designers and users as a whole. (It is the diversity of the latter that I have been discussing.) Since designers tend to be very different from most users, they need to be very careful, particularly about housing—the primary setting for users and closely related to preferences and choices based on *their* ideals. There are major differences in values, interests, ideals, life-style, tastes, and preferences between users as a whole, and designers as a whole. One major difference is that users tend to emphasize associational qualities much more than do designers, who typically emphasize perceptual qualities. When designers do address meaning, it is their own meanings—which tend to be very different. There are also major differences in the ways in which environments are evaluated by insiders and outsiders; *designers are always outsiders.*

In reading the mainstream architectural literature, one would think that buildings (more correctly environments) are produced for other architects. Yet if one asks the apparently trivial (but basic) questions—Why does one build? What are environments and settings for?—one realizes that the settings are for users. *Designers are merely surrogates for users.*

My argument, however, is that users cannot be considered as a whole. They do differ among themselves significantly, and these differences are in some way related to culture. We are thus back where we began. There is a need to study the relation of culture and built form, and it is, therefore, encouraging that this field appears to be so active. Given my long-standing emphasis on this topic, it is satisfying to witness such interest, and I am pleased to welcome this book as a major contribution to the field. I hope that the framework briefly discussed in this foreword will help in reading, integrating, and applying the diverse and fascinating studies in this book. They, and many more like them, are essential, as are their integration and systematization in some conceptual system and (dare one say it?) theory.

I wrote and revised this foreword in Yogyakarta, Indonesia, during two visits as a visiting professor at the Department of Architecture, Gadjah Mada University. During my stay I was working with faculty on research. Living there, one sees the complex interaction of dramatic changes and the persistence of tradition in a country that is already extremely diverse in terms of cultural landscapes, build environments, life-styles, activities, and cultures. As one tries to begin to understand how all these diverse cultures and environments are related and how the changes in life-style will (or should) influence environments, and as one discusses these matters and does fieldwork with one's Indonesian colleagues, it becomes even clearer were that possible, that these issues require the kind of knowledge I have been discussing and which the editors and contributors to this book discuss. Any question about cultural landscapes, settlements, neighborhoods, shops, markets, housing, or any other settings immediately raises these kinds of issues. More abstract subjects such as social networks, territoriality, privacy, the effect of environment on behavior, stress, orientation, cognitive maps—in fact almost all concepts used in EBS—raise questions of cultural variability and cry out for research locally, across Indonesia, and internationally. Any attempt to guide change, development, planning, and design anywhere in appropriate directions (and knowing what "appropriate" means) depends essentially on an understanding of culture–built form relationships.

It seems quite clear, now more than ever before, that culture-environment studies are inevitably at the center of environment-behavior research.

Amos Rapoport

HOUSING, CULTURE, AND DESIGN

INTRODUCTION
ERVE CHAMBERS
SETHA M. LOW

Social scientists, designers, and planners have long recognized a relation between culture and housing. The anthropologist Lewis H. Morgan (1965) published a comprehensive study of American Indian housing in 1881, and nearly ninety years later Amos Rapoport's (1969) study of house form and culture focused our attention on the cross-cultural dimensions of human habitation. Every discipline represented in this book has contributed landmark studies in the area. The sociologist Herbert Gans in his book *The Urban Villagers* (1963) provided insight into the housing and design preferences of an Italian-American neighborhood in New York. Anthropologists have concentrated most of their research on squatter housing and settlement in lesser developed countries (Peattie 1968; Mangin 1970). Psychologists entered housing research primarily through their interest in behavior and environmental design (Altman, Rapoport, and Wohlwill 1980). Architects, historians, city planners, anthropologists, and folklorists have focused our attention on vernacular housing (Glassie 1975; Upton and Vlach 1986) and on the symbolic dimensions of house form (Cooper-Marcus 1977; Perin 1977; Hayden 1984). Planners have examined cultural constructs such as time and space to explore issues related to housing styles (Lynch 1972). These and many other studies have led us over the past few decades to a common interest in the cultural dimensions of house design and to a gradual blurring of the distinctions between our fields of study, as is in evidence with the appearance of several recent collaborative works (Lang 1974; Duncan 1981; Altman and Werner 1985; Saile 1986).

Housing, Culture, and Design: A Comparative Perspective has its roots in two symposia held during 1985 at the annual meetings of the Society for Applied Anthropology and the Environmental Design Research Association. A major aim of these symposia was to examine how the methods and insights of cultural analysis have been integrated into the study of problems related to housing and its design. We also wanted to look at how such concepts as design, culture, and even housing were being used by representatives of different disciplines and professional fields. The potential of interdisciplinary work has become apparent; the danger of such work is that, because our concepts have their bases in differently learned perspectives, we often find ourselves using the same words to mean different things. To understand the issues explored in this book it is important to appreciate the professional and cultural differences that exist between students of culture.

This book is a collection of research and commentary focused on how cultural process, the provision of shelter, and principles of housing design are related. These studies have been organized into four sections that present the sociopolitical, cognitive, symbolic, and interpretive approaches to housing, culture, and design research. One major difference between the contributions is found in the two types of problem focus that can be identified. Some of the articles are most concerned with cultural responses to environment design, while others locate those cultural variables which prompt the creation and provision of housing in particular social settings.

In most contemporary societies, there is a difference between the cultural values, rules, and perspectives of people who design and build housing and those who occupy housing. This "cultural distance" becomes especially apparent when designers work in cultures that are different from their own, or when they design for people who occupy a different social class or economic stratum within their own society. Design failures can result from culturally inappropriate assumptions about the life-styles, needs, and responses of the potential users. Housing design can be improved, however, as many of the chapters in this book indicate, when attention is paid to its cultural appropriateness.

The focus described above provides a basis for understanding why people sometimes reject and often alter the housing spaces that others have designed. The understanding of the cultural dimension of housing is also furthered by exploring the impulses, values, and needs that give rise to the creation and provision of housing by the users themselves. One approach to this study is centered on housing designers as representatives of a mainstream culture and participants in changing attitudes toward the cultural valuation of shelter. In this vein, it is also important to keep in mind that in many countries most housing is not designed by professionals and that, even where it is, shelter is often radically "redesigned" by occupants. Our approach to such issues as "self-help housing" and human resettlement, in which professional designers have often been involved, is improved when we better understand why people respond, often as builders and lay designers in their own right, to such initiatives in the ways they do.

Definitions and Concepts

The concepts used throughout this book—housing, culture, and design—are used in different ways at different times. Rapoport, in the foreword, begins the task of clarifying these meanings, and the following discussion further refines their application.

Design The term *design* is used in two ways in this book. According to the first use, designed things are artifacts of material culture—they are tangible expressions of a culture which appear on the landscape in physical, designed form. Designed environments and landscapes are material culture in the sense that their form is influenced by culture, and the cultural principles of their formation can be understood as a communication system (Rapoport 1982). Design provides information about culture and can be studied as such.

The term *design* is also used in this book to refer to a culture-making process in which ideas, values, norms, and beliefs are spatially and symbolically placed on the landscape to create new cultural forms and meanings. Designed environments can be created by human ecological forces, such as patterns of settlement created by farming techniques and mineral extraction procedures; by direct human intervention based on cultural traditions or historical context, such as vernacular or popular architecture; and by direct, self-conscious professional intervention, such as the design of a high-style building. Design, in this sense, refers to the given form or form-giving properties of the built environment or landscape. Design is a product of environmental relationships and can be studied as such.

Housing The term *housing* is used here in three ways. First, and most simply, housing refers to those physical structures that shelter people in the pursuit of their "private" lives. A house contains a domestic unit, although the constitution of those units can vary widely across cultures and social classes. Concepts of privacy and the arrangements of people within domestic units also vary across cultures.

To study the way people construct meanings around the places in which they live, or the way planners and designers make decisions about the housing needs of others, it is necessary to conceptualize the house as having meanings that transcend the physical boundaries of shelter. For some people, the concepts of house and neighborhood are almost inseparable. Houses represent many activities and human relationships which vary across cultures and which are often not included in the minimal definition of the term *housing*. In the planning and design environment, concepts of housing become mixed with concepts from the sociopolitical context of shelter and with differing criteria of the utility of the house.

These first two definitions of housing correspond to Rapoport's definition of housing, presented in the Foreword, as a "system of settings within which certain systems of activities take place." A third definition is found in Rapoport's description of housing as an "environmental quality profile." This definition adds an evaluative dimension to the study of housing and its components which is important in assessing design practices and housing interventions. The purpose of this book is to present the argument that the evaluation of housing quality must be developed in close association with an understanding of the cultural impulses and constraints that influence our perception of shelter and design variables.

These different meanings suggest that there can be no standard definition of the terms *house* or *housing*, and that in every instance these words must be understood as they relate to a particular cultural context and to the parameters defined for a specific research project.

Culture   The term *culture* is used here in several ways. Each definition provides a different perspective on cultural process and, to a large extent, suggests a different methodology for cultural analysis. Sometimes culture is defined as being constituted solely of observable *social structural patterns* of human behavior. The rules that govern these patterns are often studied through field observations of how people behave. Rules of behavior are collectively described as those social structures, particularly sociopolitical and economic, which order and pattern behavior according to cultural standards. Culture is also sometimes defined as a *cognitive structure*. Here, the researcher studies the emic or "native point of view" through interviews. As in behavioral research, the cognitive structure is most often represented by a set of rules, but these rules are in the mind, encoded in language, and serve as a template of cultural ideas. Culture as behavior and culture as cognition are both conservative definitions in that they generally emphasize constraints on behavior through social structural or consensual rules. The acquisition of culture is differentially learned through language and behavior, and change is reflected in the distribution of normative behaviors and patterns of language use.

Two other definitions of culture, culture as a symbolic process and culture as an interpretive process, emphasize the changing and reflexive qualities of culture. Culture when defined as a *symbolic process* refers to a socially constructed meaning system that can be studied through participant observation. Cultural symbols reflect shared cultural meanings and provide an opportunity to decode and discover those meanings. Culture when defined as an *interpretive process* refers to the study of changing meanings and actions over time through historical and critical analysis. Culture as an interpretive process is in many respects the most recent of the definitions and the most difficult to identify clearly but is used here to suggest that culture is a rapidly changing set of meanings and ideas that are specific to a group of people, a political and economic context, and a historical period. Cultural knowledge is transformed and reproduced through language and symbolic representation but is best interpreted or understood within particular sociopolitical contexts and historical periods. The idea of change is important here—while students of culture usually refer to cultural meanings as they relate to particular societies or groups, the source of interpretive culture is often found in the interaction of culturally distinct peoples.

Each of these definitions adds a layer to the understanding of culture and cultural processes. The contributors to this volume, in their research and analysis, are suggesting from different perspectives that the way people behave, what they think, what they believe and value, and how they interpret the world will influence their response to and creation of shelter and housing environments. Each of these definitions also helps identify the basic areas of research and practice within the field of housing, culture, and design.

Research and Practice in Housing, Culture, and Design

This book is divided into four parts, each of which represents a different dimension of cultural analysis of housing, culture, and design. The term *cultural analysis* is used here to express the complementary nature of cultural understanding and spatial expression. Cultural analysis provides an approach to the interpretation of the interaction between meaning systems, the spatial and social contexts out of which meaning is constructed, and the design interventions that alter both contexts and meanings.

This approach can be applied several ways, as is indicated by the different theoretical and methodological assumptions underlying the contributions to this book. Specifically, cultural analysis includes observational, cognitive, symbolic, and ethnographic methodologies that link the physical environment—house, neighborhood, community, or region—with the cultural codes that lie beneath the surface of spatial configurations, building patterns, and associated meaning systems. Cultural analysis is especially useful to the extent that it helps us understand the relation between concepts of housing, culture, and design and thereby defines the parameters for successful intervention.

In this book, the strategies of cultural analysis are focused on the processes described above—sociopolitical, cognitive, symbolic, and interpretive—as they articulate with problems in housing and design. These different approaches inform the four parts of the book. Part I deals primarily with sociopolitical processes that have a bearing on behavioral problems related to housing and human settlement. Part II focuses on different strategies of cognitive research that reveal how people perceive their housing. Part III focuses on the symbolic dimensions of cultural meaning. Part IV provides illustrations of different interpretations of housing development and design. The introduction to each section elaborates these strategies of cultural analysis and relates these categories to the individual research contributions.

The editors would like to thank Irwin Altman and Amos Rapoport for their support and encouragement during the preparation of this book. Their leadership and commitment to the culture-environment field inspired the development of our comparative and multidisciplinary perspective. We also would like to thank our contributors for their enthusiastic participation in the two working symposia at the annual meetings of the Society for Applied Anthropology and the Environmental Design Research Association that ultimately produced this book. And finally, we are grateful to Jo Mugnolo, assistant director of the University of Pennsylvania Press, for shepherding this book through from its conception to its completed published form.

References

Altman, I., A. Rapoport, and J. F. Wohlwill, eds. 1980. *Human behavior and environment: Advances in theory and research*. Vol. 4, *Culture and environment*. New York: Plenum Press.

Altman, I., and C. Werner, eds. 1985. *Home environments*. New York: Plenum Press.

Cooper-Marcus, C. 1977. *Easter Hill Village: Some sociological implications of design*. New York: Free Press.

Duncan, J., ed. 1981. *Housing and identity: Cross-cultural perspectives*. London: Croom Helm.

Gans, H. J. 1963. *The urban villagers*. New York: Free Press.

Glassie, H. 1975. *Folk housing in middle Virginia*. Knoxville, Tenn.: University of Tennessee Press.

Hayden, D. 1984. *Redesigning the American dream: The future of housing, work, and family life*. New York: W. W. Norton.

Lang, J., ed. 1974. *Designing for human behavior*. Stroudsburg, Pa.: Dowden, Hutchinson and Ross.

Lynch, K. 1972. *What time is this place?* Cambridge, Mass.: M.I.T. Press.

Mangin, W. 1970. *Peasants in cities: Readings in the anthropology of urbanization*. Boston: Houghton-Mifflin.

Morgan, L. H. 1965. *Houses and house-life of the American aborigines*. Chicago: University of Chicago Press. Original 1881.

Peattie, L. R. 1968. *View from the barrio*. Ann Arbor: University of Michigan Press.

Perin, C. 1977. *Everything in its place: Social order and land use in America*. Princeton: Princeton University Press.

Rapoport, A. 1969. *House form and culture*. Englewood Cliffs, N.J.: Prentice-Hall.

Rapoport, A. 1982. *The meaning of the built environment: A nonverbal communication approach*. Beverly Hills: Sage.

Saile, D. G. 1986. *Architecture in cultural change: Essays in built form and culture research*. Lawrence, Kan.: School of Architecture and Urban Design, University of Kansas.

Upton, D., and J. M. Vlach, eds. 1986. *Common places: Readings in American vernacular architecture*. Athens, Ga.: University of Georgia Press.

PART ONE

CULTURE AS A POLITICAL AND ECONOMIC STRUCTURE

COMMUNITY CULTURE, NEIGHBORHOOD POLITICS, AND HOUSING POLICY

Studies of culture as revealed in the political and economic structures of a society examine the behavioral basis of culture as it is expressed in the organization of neighborhood and community groups and in the political and economic patterning of human values, needs, and desires. The rules and norms of behavior, the politics of groups, the economic factors of change, and the dynamics of complex social interactions—all these factors influence our concepts of housing and design. Political and economic structure can be studied both to identify community values and needs that are relevant to new designs or interventions and to explain why a community has certain kinds of housing or a particular spatial and social structural configuration.

The authors of chapters 1—5 critique accepted notions of neighborhood and community by examining the political and economic structure and perceptual basis of what constitutes a neighborhood and its community culture. They emphasize cultural and community-based conflict and point out the combinations of power and powerlessness that often underlie planned intervention and housing policy.

Every chapter in this part underscores the importance of understanding the relation between housing needs on a local or community level and the larger political and economic environments that encompass these needs. Delmos Jones and Joan Turner begin with a case study of factors that threaten the reproduction of urban households and habitats for low-income residents of New York City. They point to an impending housing crisis which, among other factors, threatens to undermine the social and cultural integrity of low-income groups. Graeme Hardie and Timothy Hart describe how a program developed in South Africa to encourage resident ownership of previously state-owned housing was threatened by a long-perpetuated cycle of suspicion and distrust on the part of black tenants. Here, naive assumptions that a seemingly good housing plan will be easily accepted by the people for which it is intended are laid to rest by the realization that client groups do not view such plans in isolation but see them instead within the social context and history of their relationship with a dominant group or class. Ken McDowell describes how government housing initiatives for Canadian native groups have been shaped and altered over time by the changing perceptions of those who make decisions about the cultures and housing needs of these groups. This is the other side of the argument offered by Hardie and Hart—demonstrating that planners and designers are also influenced by the historical and cultural configurations of their time. Edward Robbins's chapter on the recent housing policy in Sri Lanka is especially useful in demonstrating how easily national housing policies are jeopardized by the failure to understand local cultural meanings and by a tendency of housing bureaucracies to distrust and misinterpret local initiatives. Sri Lanka's national effort to improve low-cost housing appears to be most successful in situations where conscientious planners have served as mediators between the housing bureaucracy and local communities. Richard Dent concludes this part with a theoretical discussion of housing gentrification in the United States. He argues that ideological factors play as important a role in the process as do strictly economic factors.

Chapters 1—5 demonstrate that the dangerous tendency to discount the importance of understanding the impact of housing and design policy at the local or community level is widespread throughout the world. They also provide the opportunity to begin to appreciate the complex relations between culture and housing and among policy, planning, and design. The recognition that cultural differences exist and influence our attitudes toward housing and community is just a first step in this direction. As the contributors demonstrate, the cultural and social dimensions of housing are best understood as part of an interactive process in which successful intervention depends in great part upon our ability to resolve breakdowns in communication which have their base in cultural differences.

1

HOUSING AND THE MATERIAL BASIS OF SOCIAL REPRODUCTION: POLITICAL CONFLICT AND THE QUALITY OF LIFE IN NEW YORK CITY

DELMOS J. JONES

JOAN T. TURNER

The relationship between society and the environment is an important aspect of traditional anthropological research (Meggers 1954, 19; Forde 1963). The raw materials of the environment are transformed to satisfy basic needs—food, shelter, clothing, and so on. The transformation of raw material into the necessities of social reproduction requires both organization and effort. In rural societies there is a direct relation between the collective effort of a specific social group and the attempt to supply the necessities of life. Simply put, if a family needed a house they collected the supplies, and, with the help of their neighbors, constructed it.

In urban society there is an indirect relation between collective activities and the attempt to provide and maintain the necessities of social life. As we will demonstrate, however, the collective activity that does take place through the means of neighborhood associations is frequently concerned with the physical necessities of social reproduction. The difference between neighborhood associations and rural villages is that the neighborhood organizations must act indirectly. To achieve results they must apply political pressure to those institutions and agencies responsible for the upkeep and maintenance of the physical environment. There is serious concern about the quality of the environment in many, if not most, areas of New York City. These concerns are not merely based on attractiveness or appearance but are rooted in more basic apprehension about social reproduction.

Social reproduction refers to a set of processes that allows for the maintenance of human life. According to Evers, Clauss, and Wong (1984, 23–24), the maintenance or reproduction of the labor force is the mainstay of any economy and requires the satisfaction of basic needs. They make a distinction between "*primary reproduction,*" the reproduction of labor power and human life in general, and "*secondary reproduction,* the reproduction of the social and economic order in such a way as to ensure either its continued existence as a definite social formation or its propitious transformation" (Evers, Clauss, and Wong 1984, 24). Primary reproduction includes the production of food and its processing, education, household management, and the provision of housing.

It is in the household where the activities of reproduction take place on a day-to-day and generational basis (Dickinson and Russell 1986, 5). Evers, Clauss, and Wong distinguish further between habitat reproduction and household reproduction. Household reproduction is the production of living space. In rural areas where houses are built by villagers with materials they collect themselves, the provision of housing is part of subsistence production. "In urban areas . . . houses may be built by building contractors using wage labor, in which case housing is provided by normal capitalistic production" (Evers, Clauss, and Wong 1984, 25). Habitat reproduction refers to the fact that "a house has to be cleaned, repaired, and maintained in order to provide continuous living facilities." Commonly this is provided through a form of subsistence activity, unpaid labor, "in which the family, especially the women, produce and consume the habitat continuously, very much in the same way as a rural family in a subsistence economy produces and consumes rice, vegetables, and other food stuffs" (Evers, Clauss, and Wong 1984, 25). Clearly, subsistence activities are not the only means whereby the habitat is reproduced. Wallerstein talks about the commodification of everyday life including everything "from the preparation of food, to cleaning and repair of home appurtenances and clothing, to custodial care, to nursing care to emotional repair" (Wallerstein 1984, 21).

The household is the major setting for social reproduction but must have a suitable material context. In simple societies the very location of settlements is determined by the availability of water, a source of fuel, and an adequate means of obtaining food. In complex urban societies these aspects of the physical environment fall under the heading of human services; the responsibility for providing these services is in the hands of public and private agencies. Pynoos, Schafer, and Hartman (1980, 1) call this "the housing bundle," which includes such attributes as neighborhood status, neighborhood characteristics, and quality of public and quasi-public services (schools, garbage collection). "It is this bundle of attributes that members of a household consider when they choose a residence or when they express dissatisfaction with their living arrangements." Much of the conflict that has taken place in cities over the last few decades has been rooted as much in concerns about this set of attributes as about housing itself.

The period 1965–75 witnessed many examples of local community groups organizing in opposition to the planning of city institutions. The most well known of these protests, in Forest Hills and Corona Queens, was over the issue of housing and the material context of housing (see Castells 1983 for a comparative description of such protests). The conflicts revealed a wide gap between the planning process carried out by developers and the city, and the citizens' perception of their own needs. As a result the New York City of the late 1960s was a city whose government was increasingly estranged from its citizenry.

In 1972 political decentralization seemed an appealing solution to many of the problems facing New York and other cities. The goal was to offer an opportunity to the neighborhood residents to voice their opinions on proposed development plans. The 1977 Charter revision divided the city into fifty-nine community districts, each with a population of between 100,000 and 250,000 people. Each community board was comprised of approximately fifty volunteers who were appointed by the borough president and the councilman from the district. Each community board had the power to review and make recommendations on all land-use matters that affected its district. These included changes in the city map, changes in zoning, and approval of housing or urban renewal plans.

This chapter is based on data from a study of four decentralized community boards in New York City. Community board meetings became settings where citizens could voice concerns about quality of life and quality of environment issues. These meetings made it possible to collect information on the structure and function of the community boards as well as information on the kinds of problems being faced by local neighborhoods, and on their attempts to do something about them. Kotler, writing in 1970, observed that neighborhood residents generally organized their own territories to control their institutions in order to serve their own, rather than outside, interests. It is a misconception to assume that this conflict always pitted the neighborhood against the city. The bundle of housing attributes are distributed unevenly, and therefore some segments of the population, and sometimes different segments of the same neighborhood, are afforded more social advantage than others. Although we characterize neighborhood concerns as being related to the material basis of social reproduction and outside concerns more with profit, we also contend that, in this study, segments of the local population had different levels of concerns about social reproduction. This meant that different neighborhoods, and sometimes different segments of the same neighborhood, were often in conflict with each other as well as with institutions of power.

We will explore these issues by looking at two community boards. We will focus on data from one board, on the Lower East Side of New York, and briefly describe a comparable case from a second board in Queens.

The Context   In 1975 new policies were instituted in New York City because of the city's fiscal crisis. The city committed itself to economic recovery by focusing on retaining businesses, encouraging expansion, and attracting new investments.[1] At the same time, programs were designed to attract and retain the white-collar taxpayer by improving the overall "image" and desirability of the city, and by implementing an unofficial policy of "planned shrinkage." Planned shrinkage is the dismantling of services to lower-income communities with the goal of pushing them out of the city (Tabb 1978, 269). Owing to these policies, housing for the city's low-income population became increasingly difficult to obtain. Arson and landlord abandonment increased in the more deteriorated areas of the city and new housing construction was at a virtual standstill. These problems were particularly manifest on Manhattan's Lower East Side.

The Lower East Side of Manhattan is located in the lower, southeastern portion of the Borough of Manhattan.[2] Its northern boundary, 14th Street, forms a clear line of demarcation indicated by the distinctive contrast in housing between the middle-income district to the north and the low- and moderate-income district to the south. North of 14th Street are the well-maintained, tree-lined streets of Stuyvesant Town and Cooper Village, whereas south of 14th Street are the deteriorating tenement buildings and dirty streets typical of aging slums.

Within the past decade, housing shortages and escalating rents throughout Manhattan have caused an increase in the number of young white single or coupled residents, generally without children and with higher incomes, who are finding the Lower East Side a more suitable place to live. The process is commonly referred to as "gentrification." This influx of single middle-class couples has to be viewed in the context of building deterioration and abandonment and planned shrinkage. When buildings are abandoned, lower-income families must move out; when they are remodeled, middle-income families move in.[3]

Housing Abandonment, the Failure of Habitat Reproduction   As noted earlier, habitat reproduction refers to the fact that a house has to be cleaned, repaired, and maintained to provide continuous living facilities. When a building has been abandoned it means that this process has failed. The reasons for this failure are complex. More than the subsistence efforts of household members are required for the habitat to be reproduced. The process of reproduction is beyond the control of most tenants despite the amount of labor that is expended.[4]

Housing abandonment is a widespread phenomenon in New York City. Real estate interests have argued that abandonment and housing decline are caused by tenants, increased costs, rent control, or the aging of buildings. Economic factors, including the movement of capital from the city to the suburbs and to other regions of the country, are more reasonable explanations for abandonment. Industry in its quest for profit sought other, more favorable, areas for investment and was also facilitated by government subsidies. Since housing tends to "follow" the flow of money and jobs, it is not surprising that disinvestment by banks and other financial institutions in New York City's residential real estate followed these capital shifts.

Disinvestment takes many forms. "Redlining," a common practice instituted by banks and insurance companies, is the result of decisions to withhold investment monies in deteriorating neighborhoods. Landlords or prospective buyers are unable to procure mortgage monies, loans, or insurance for property in the designated redlined area. Private disinvestment soon follows the institutional pattern and landlords begin to "milk" their buildings. They continue to collect rents and take tax deductions but at the same time fail to provide adequate services (heat, hot water, maintenance) and barely keep up with real estate taxes and mortage payments. In the final stages of abandonment the landlord simply stops paying the city real estate taxes and leaves the building for the city to take over or ignore. Abandonment of the building by tenants follows the landlord's cutback in services. Through the unofficial policy of planned shrinkage the city has accelerated neighborhood decline by cutting back such services as police and fire protection, schools, hospitals, and transportation. Thus the city acts in concert with market forces by implementing policies that are inimical to the housing needs of poor and low-income people. The city has the power, and the legal obligation, to take title to buildings or vacant lots for nonpayment of real estate tax; this foreclosure process is known as "in rem."

The management of city-owned residential buildings is handled by the Department of Housing Preservation and Development (HPD) under several management programs, while the sale of city-owned buildings is handled by another city agency, the Department of Buildings.

HPD admits to owning 340 buildings throughout the Lower East Side. However, the Department of City Planning in a recent report states the city has acquired ownership of 620 parcels of property—31 percent of all the land and buildings in a designated Neighborhood Strategy Area (NSA)—inhabited largely by Hispanics and blacks and encompassing a total population of 86,276. The Neighorhood Strategy Area represents 51.6 percent of the total population of the decentralized community district under study.

The Sale of City-Owned Property and the Failure of Household Reproduction The disposition of abandoned, city-owned buildings is an issue that concerns different segments of the local population in different ways. While some local residents see the sale of abandoned buildings as a way of improving the neighborhood by attracting a higher class of resident, middle- and upper-middle-income families, others see the problem as a loss of housing for the poor. This conflict was reflected in issues that came before the community board. The community board is mandated to review land use changes that occur in its district. The board was asked to make recommendations to HPD and the Department of City Planning on the disposition of city-owned property. Eighteen months of observations of Housing Committee meetings, community board meetings, and public hearings, as well as interviews with residents of the community and members of local housing organizations, revealed that the disposition of city-owned property, particularly the sale of city-owned property at public auction, was one of the major sources of conflict in this district. The following examples illustrate the situation.

A program for turning abandoned tenement buildings on the Lower East Side into cooperative housing for artists of moderate income was being developed by the city's Department of Housing Preservation and Development. The buildings were part of the city's stock of some nine thousand residential structures abandoned by landlords in tax arrears (*New York Times*, 11 August 1981). The two areas selected for artists housing fall within the Lower East Side's designated Neighborhood Strategy Area. Sixteen burned-out and largely abandoned buildings on East 8th Street were slated for renovation. Local housing groups and the Department of City Planning had already earmarked these buildings for housing construction in preliminary plans. During the late 1960s Action for Progress, a local antipoverty agency, sponsored a housing program that included the Forsyth Street buildings. Action for Progress had a promise from the city to develop the site for low-income families. However, the city reneged on its promise, and the housing construction-moratorium imposed during the Nixon presidency brought housing construction plans to a halt. This plan died along with many others.

On 16 January 1980 at the Lower East Side Community Board's Housing

Committee meeting (Community Board #3 in Manhattan) several people came before the Housing Committee members to request support for a proposal to rehabilitate a city-owned building on Forsyth Street. Mr. P., a spokesman for the group of artists, musicians, and craftsmen, detailed their plans to rehabilitate the building into six to eight cooperative units under HPD's "sweat-equity" program.[5] After the spokesman for this local group finished his presentation, Mr. H., a Community Board #3 Housing Committee member and a former member of the Board of Directors of Action for Progress, explained to the rest of the Housing Committee members why they should not support this group's proposal. Mr. H. explained that he represented a local group that had been working on a comprehensive plan for this site for five years in conjunction with HPD. Mr. H. discussed his project and stated that after it fell through it left a group of two representatives from each building on Eldridge and Forsyth streets, a six-block area which subsequently formed a housing development corporation called the Forsyth Development Corporation. He stated that his group has made its views known on housing programs in the area and that

> we are trying to stop the process of gentrification and other factors that push people out of the area and we do not want to see one building pulled out of our proposal which would break up our comprehensive package. Moreover the buildings in that section are part of the Neighborhood Strategy Area [NSA] proposal and it would be contrary to that proposal to develop individual buildings haphazardly.

Mr. P. questioned the legitimacy of Mr. H.'s group and claimed he had never heard of it. In fact, the Forsyth Development Corporation was not legally incorporated, and hence it was not officially recognized by the city.

To mediate the conflict between Mr. P. and Mr. H., the board passed a motion urging the two parties to meet and try to settle their differences. Several efforts were made by a Housing Committee member to resolve the issue but to no avail. In the meantime, other housing group leaders had heard that HPD was entertaining the idea of developing the Forsyth Street site for artists' cooperative housing.

Most of the housing organization leaders and other community activists operated under the assumption that the city had a hostile stance toward community management of its property. An article in *The Village Voice* (19 May 1980) noted that only fifty-four buildings in the entire area covered by Community Board #3 (including part of Chinatown) had been cleared for tenant ownership. Moreover, the city's proposed budget would cut community management funds from $16.75 million to $14.50 million, and sweat equity from

$2 million to $200,000—enough for one building. Meanwhile, funds for 8-A loans, which benefit private developers, would increase from $5 million to $12 million.

In view of these facts a delegation of housing organization leaders from the Lower East Side met with the assistant commissioner of special housing at HPD. They stated that they would not oppose the artist housing on that site provided that low-income family housing would also be included in the development plans. They reminded the HPD official that there were many local artists on the Lower East Side who would be interested in the proposed artists' cooperatives, and they expressed their concern about outside artists moving into the area and the possible effects of gentrification. In subsequent negotiations between HPD and the local housing organizations, tentative plans were worked out in which artists' housing and low-income family housing would be developed in a joint proposal for the Forsyth Street site only.

On 24 June 1980 at Community Board #3's regular monthly meeting, the assistant commissioner of special housing at HPD asked to present a proposal for a small pilot artist housing project in the Lower East Side. She explained that the Special Housing Unit was created to redevelop city-owned residential buildings for special populations such as senior citizens, the handicapped, and artists. The proposed site for the artists' housing was "a group of six buildings on Forsyth Street." She promised that a "Request for Proposals" (RFP) would be forthcoming and that "Lower East Side artists and artists displaced by urban renewal plans" would "receive priority." The Special Housing Unit was seeking proposals from developers and artists' groups for redevelopment of the building units as co-ops or condominiums to sell within the $40,000–$50,000 range. The program had been suggested by the mayor, and the Department of Housing had been encouraged to push the program because many artists had telephoned to ask how to buy a city building. During this presentation no mention was made of the low-income family housing plans for Forsyth Street.

The local housing organizations and other community activists representing the low-income minority population on the Lower East Side were opposed to what they considered to be an outright public policy of gentrification. Clearly a $40,000–$50,000 unit price was not in keeping with the socioeconomic characteristics of the area. In the subsequent weeks they intensified their efforts to obtain a commitment from the city for the inclusion of the low-income housing.

Representatives of several housing organizations, the locally elected City Council member, and three staff members of the New York City Housing Authority met to survey the Forsyth Street site and evaluate its development potential. As a result of this meeting and other negotiations, a compromise plan was worked out—the Housing Authority would construct 183 dwelling units of low- and moderate-income housing and HPD would develop its artists' cooperative housing. Members of the housing organizations learned, however, that HPD was expanding its plans to develop another site. Another meeting was scheduled between the city's housing commissioner and a delegation of the same local housing organization leaders. They protested the inclusion of the 8th Street site. They declared that this was an outright gentrification policy on the part of the city and, furthermore, it undercut the NSA's proposal for the construction of housing that was designed to meet the needs of the community's residents. They vigorously opposed HPD's plans for 8th Street.

At the July 1980 meeting of Community Board #3 a motion was made by housing organization leaders and board members to oppose the artist housing plans of HPD. This motion was passed by the board, but to no avail. On 11 August 1981 the *New York Times* detailed the city's plans in an article entitled "The Mayor's Lower East Side Story: Tenements into Co-ops." On 4 May 1982, the *New York Times* and the *Daily News* announced the completion of the city's artists' housing projects. No progress was reported on the proposed 183 units of low-income family housing on the Forsyth Street site.

The above example reveals several aspects of the relationships between the parties involved. First, there are the many different interests of the community as revealed by the interactions between local organizations at board meetings; second, there is the position taken by the board; and third, there is the interest of the city that seemed to reflect the interest of housing developers. In the best of all possible situations there would be no difference between the interest of the city and the interest of the community. In this situation, however, the city's concern with fiscal responsibility created a conflict between the desire to provide low- and moderate-income housing and the desire to achieve a profit from the available housing.

The foregoing discussion is not sufficient to give a full picture of the amount of energy that was expended by a large number of people: the committee meetings, the board meetings, the debates, the mobilization of people for meetings, and more. This is only one of many similar issues about housing that came before Community Board #3 around which residents and local organizations had to organize, politicize, and mobilize to protect their interests (see Turner 1984 for a more detailed discussion).

In almost all cases of public auction sales the community board opposed the city's policy. A subcommittee of the Housing Committee has been effective in establishing a monthly meeting with the deputy commissioner of property management of HPD where the district's housing problems are discussed and worked out. Despite these monthly meetings and the united opposition of the board to public auction, periodically the board was asked to approve or disapprove of the sale—for unknown reasons by an unspecified mechanism—an apparently random list of residential, institutional, and commercial buildings and lots. (These lists are compiled by the Department of Real Estate and forwarded to the local community district.) In July 1980 a formal letter was drafted by the community board and sent to the members of the Board of Estimate where final decisions about the sale of property are made. It stated, in part, that Community Board #3 voted unanimously to oppose the sale of in rem properties "as it has done in the past except to neighborhood non-profit organizations wishing to use properties for a constructive residential or organizational purpose." The letter observed that the properties owned by the city "presents a tremendous opportunity to replan and rebuild a neighborhood that serves the housing and social needs of our residents." Instead of taking this approach the city was accused of trying to get rid of the properties "as quickly as possible and for the greater profit." The letter promised that the board would continue to resist the sale of these properties as a profit-making tool.

While the community board was taking this approach, other measures were being taken. A coalition of local housing organizations was formed which called itself the "This Land Is Ours Coalition." The goal of this group was to prevent the auction of buildings to outsiders and to rehabilitate city-owned buildings for low- and moderate-income housing. The This Land Is Ours Coalition has accused the city of attempting to facilitate the gentrification of the area and has called for protest gatherings and marches. Several city-owned buildings had banners strung across their facades that announce: "Speculators Stay Out"; "Not For Sale"; or "This Land Is Ours."

This example, like many others involving city-owned properties, showed that low-income residents of the Lower East Side view city-owned residential buildings as a community resource. For many, housing needs were at a desperate level. Public auctions therefore were seen as threats to the community's residents since few, if any, had the money to compete with "fair-market" bidding. Developers, speculators, and middle-income people were the potential buyers for city-owned property, and for many of them the profit was often more important than the social reproductive function of the household itself. A letter for one real estate agent to perspective buyers stressed the substantial tax saving and estimated a 30% return on the investment. With each sale, lower-income residents were displaced by higher-income groups. Many displaced residents have gone to single-occupancy residences. Others have become homeless. The fact that housing has not been provided for this population denotes a failure of household reproduction.

The Context of Housing in Southeast Queens

The Lower East Side is a center city area characterized by apartment dwellers. There are clear divisions along ethnic, racial, and class lines. Blacks and Hispanics (primarily Puerto Ricans) are concentrated in the most deteriorated, "slumlike" section of the district. In contrast, whites are concentrated in areas that have been rebuilt, often with government subsidies. Much of the conflict over housing in this district sets lower-class minorities against middle-class whites. Southeast Queens is also divided between adequate and inadequate housing, with middle-class homeowners concentrated in one area and lower-income welfare recipients in another. But because this is a predominantly black area, the division is more of a social class phenomenon than a racial or ethnic one. Space does not permit a detailed description of the Queens district. The goal is simply to offer a brief example of another dimension of political conflict over the issue of housing.

According to the 1980 Census, the area encompassed by Community Board #12 in Queens is 77 percent black, 10 percent Hispanic, 9 percent white, and 3 percent other. The median income is $15,000 per household. Unlike the Lower East Side, 82 percent of the dwellings are one- to two-family residences (City of New York 1986), but like the East Side, there are approximately five hundred abandoned buildings. Moreover, in the Queens district, approximately 7.6 percent of the land area consists of vacant lots (City of New York 1986), which is a more serious concern for this community than the problem both communities have with abandoned buildings.

Like many homeowner areas settled by blacks in the last thirty years, this part of Queens was once a white suburb. Although much of the district is composed of homeowners, some of these homeowners are very poor and many of them are on welfare.

What stands out most about the district is the general lack of basic services, such as police protection and proper sewage disposal, and the shortage of stores and adequate transportation. Added to these problems was the fact that the list of projects, beginning with the construction or reconstruction of sewers, streets, and sidewalks, that Community Board #12 annually submitted to the city never appeared on the city's budget.

The community board regularly reviewed proposals from the city. Most proposals were viewed in terms of how they would affect social services. The board rejected a proposal for a drug treatment center because of the social element "it would bring into the community." When a mental hospital was looking for a "group home" for some of its discharged patients, the board also expressed concern about this social element. Board members felt that agencies looked at sites in southeast Queens only because it was a black area. They believed they were becoming the "dumping grounds" for the city's social problems. Adding to this "dumping grounds" perception was the city's tendency to use vacant lots as garbage dump sites.

The availability of vacant lots also attracted developers to southeast Queens. For example, a senior citizen project came before the board on 18 March 1980 for its approval. The sponsors, a local black church, already had federal money for the project. When the board met to discuss the project, a block association adjacent to the proposed project site objected to the development and presented a petition to the board opposing it. The petition noted that the "delivery of services, the quality of life and general welfare of all our neighbors will be threatened by the project."

At the next board meeting the members of the block association turned out in force to press its opposition to the project. One board member, speaking in favor of the project, observed that the board "has an obligation to everyone [in the district] not just one and two family residents."

Members of the block association insisted that they were not opposed to buildings for senior citizens (especially if they were in other parts of the city), but they were opposed to high-rise apartments in their area. They argued that a large building would overload already inadequate sewers. Moreover, "homeowners have rights too, and their rights can't be violated for senior citizens. We will not allow one shovel to be turned." In March 1980, the board decided to oppose the project.

The conflicts that took place in this community board revealed a tremendous concern with the quality of the housing bundle. This concern was also present on the Lower East Side, but there the concern with the provision of housing was much greater because the displacement of the population through gentrification was proceeding at a rapid rate.

In southeast Queens the racial issue is held constant, and therefore the class basis of conflict emerges clearly. This is not meant to minimize racism as an active dimension of the problem of housing but to emphasize the fact that class conflict operates within the framework of race, as well as outside of it. Although the middle-class homeowners of Queens are not equivalent in terms of socioeconomic status to the middle class moving into the renovated buildings on the Lower East Side, they still occupy a differential position with

respect to housing in relation to senior citizens on a fixed income, and therefore they sought to maintain that position through organized pressure.

Conclusion

         The conflicts observed in Queens are rooted in the
same concerns as those observed on the Lower East Side, specifically, the differential access to housing resources. The prominent feature in both cases is
that the provision of housing for one segment of the population infringes on
the privileged position of another segment of the population.

     On the Lower East Side the process of abandonment reflects the failure
of a building to be maintained. Residents of older buildings, normally the
poor, are aware that their building may be the next target of arson and abandonment. They know that they are one step away from homelessness. When
abandoned buildings are renovated they are not for the poor but for those with
a middle-class income who can afford it. The conflict on the Lower East Side
was essentially between these two segments of the population, and much of it
was over the allocation of housing. The gentrification of a neighborhood
promises a higher quality of life for those remaining, and possibly a considerable profit as property values skyrocket.

     The distribution of the scarce and expensive resource of housing has been
instrumental in the formation of what Giddens (1973) has called "distributive
groupings," that is, groups tend to live in residentially segregated and socially
homogeneous neighborhoods, characterized by a distinctive type of housing.
The differential nature of the more affluent and advantaged neighborhoods
provides the residents with material advantages and improved opportunities
for social mobility. According to Shepard (1975), the strategic value of a location is dependent on the place of the site in relation to units such as shopping
centers, industry, sewage plants, and schools. These facilities are provided by
both public and private sectors. If such facilities are absent or less than adequate, the value of the location is reduced. This inevitable reduction in value
explains the concern of the Queens community with the absence of adequate
supermarkets, streets, and sewer systems.

     Local organizations advocate the interests of a specific subpopulation and
try to maintain the physical conditions and social status of their particular
neighborhood. Evers, Clauss, and Wong (1984, 24) define "primary reproduction" as reproduction of labor power and human life, and define "secondary reproduction" as the reproduction of the social and economic order. We
cite this source to suggest, in the context of our material, that each specific

subpopulation wants not only to reproduce human life but also to reproduce a specific life-style. Pynoos, Schafer, and Hartman's notion (1980, 1) of "the housing bundle" includes such attributes as the quality of public and quasi-public services. These attributes must be of a sufficient quality for the reproduction of a given life-style, but much less may be required just for the reproduction of human life. Thus, while some groups are struggling to maintain the material basis of a marginal existence, others are struggling to maintain the material basis of a more privileged life-style.

Castells (1983, 319) refers extensively to the kinds of political actions taken by neighborhood organizations. He concludes that these urban movements are organized around use value, as opposed to the notion of profit, "in which the desirables of space and urban services are distributed according to level of income." We have concluded that this is only partly true, since much of the mobilization on the Lower East Side and in Queens perpetuated the unequal distribution of urban services and, at least on the Lower East Side, represented a reaction to efforts to use housing as a source of profit. Castells goes on to say that urban movements have as their major goals the search for cultural identity, or the maintenance or creation of autonomous local cultures, and more local control, or neighborhood decentralization. Much of the literature on neighborhood mobilization makes it appear that neighborhoods as a collective are mobilizing against outside interest (Boyte 1979, Perlman 1976) and that there is total agreement in the neighborhood on what the interests of the neighborhood are. We can identify the goal to maintain cultural identity, particularly on the Lower East Side, but some of the groups involved were attempting to maintain the material basis for different life-styles (Shepard 1975), and there was a strong class basis to these differences.

The fate of the poor is determined by the outcome of the kinds of local conflicts described in this paper, and these include not only the relationship between the poor and the institutions of power but also the relationship between the poor and others in the local community. Decentralization in New York City seemed designed specifically to emphasize the kind of local conflict related above. Within the context of decentralization the city does not mediate these kinds of conflicts as much as it decides who are the winners and the losers. Each neighborhood, indeed each city block, is encouraged to organize and to apply political pressure to achieve its goals. Heavy emphasis is placed on the act of participation, but the process does not promise results. The results are often negative for minority and low-income individuals. When a group loses out in the final decision the conclusion is that it was not well enough organized, or that it lost to other, better organized groups that had more power and influence to begin with.

We have posited here that housing is an essential requirement for social reproduction. We have not dealt with role relations or the division of labor within the household but with how housing as a material resource is provided in urban society. We have focused on the collective activities of neighborhood organizations and the political and economic context of housing. Within this framework, we have suggested that subsistence activities, which are emphasized in the literature on social reproduction, make little difference; they are insufficient to maintain housing and certainly inadequate to the task of providing housing. It is in this context that we refer to a reproductive crisis.

Large numbers of low-income people are losing the struggle for housing. Even more low-income people, who do have housing, are losing the struggle for an adequate material context. The phenomena of arson, abandonment, and renovation produce homelessness. The tenement dwellers on the Lower East Side, some of them without adequate heat and water, are living in buildings one step removed from abandonment, and they are two steps from being homeless.[6] This is also true of some of the home-owning poor of Queens.

The reproductive crisis, as we are defining it, seems to be worsening. In the 1950s and 1960s most renters spent 20 percent of their income on housing. By the early 1980s, millions were spending more than 50 percent of their income on rent, and the poorest households were paying more than 72 percent for rent (*New York Times*, 16 March 1986). These statistics mean that many low-income families are priced out of the housing market as renters as well as owners.

The provision of housing, or household reproduction, and the maintenance of households, or habitat reproduction, are part of capitalist production for the low-income apartment dwellers on the Lower East Side. When low-income urban households are compared with peasant and tribal households, what stands out is the loss of control in the urban households over various aspects of social reproduction. The peasant household was able to provide through subsistence labor and maintain its own unit and this provided the glue of social interaction within the household. Urban households, however, are dependent on others outside of the household. And what they must have from others they must pay for, and many cannot afford to buy the services they need.

There is another level of this reproductive crisis. In most societies a house is more than a physical structure—it has social and cultural significance. Its very shape is often determined by cultural tradition, and it is saturated with cultural memories. In this sense the household as a physical structure contributes to a sense of historical and cultural continuity. One important manifestation of this concern with physical structure, history, and cultural history is the current interest in historical preservation, the effort to protect historically significant buildings from destruction for urban development. Houses are passed on from generation to generation less frequently now than in the past. They are most often sold for profit, or replaced by newer houses. We suggest that the crisis of family life in the United States, a problem about which there is much current concern, may well be related to the problem of housing.

This paper is based on research supported by grants from the National Institute of Mental Health, MH32095 and MH70524.

Notes

1. City of New York, Office of the Mayor, December 1976, *Economic recovery: New York City's program for 1977–1981*, by Abraham Beame, mayor.
2. This material is taken from the comprehensive plan of Harry Schwartz (assisted by Peter Abeles), "Planning for the Lower East Side" (1973).
3. A letter from a real estate agent to a prospective buyer contained the following:
   Many young people who cannot afford the Upper East side rentals and Soho loft prices are moving in. The seller will give a 15 year self-liquidating mortgage. There are 13 units available; most need only a painting and some kitchen equipment to be easily rented. *There is also a substantial tax saving in the first year. There is an estimated 30% return on this property.*
4. Leavitt and Saegert in a forthcoming book discuss in part tenants who remain in buildings after they have been abandoned by landlords. They deal specifically with the maintenance process and the regaining of control that tenants experience when they are in charge of maintenance.
5. Under this program the basic clearing and any demolition is done by the cooperative investors who invest their labor, which should equal 15 percent of the cost of reconstruction; the mortgage is provided through the Community Development (CD) funds administered by HPD. The city holds the title for five years, during which time payments are made by the investor-tenants.
6. An article in the *New York Times*, 17 November 1986, estimates that there are more than 300,000 people teetering on the edge of hopelessness.

References

Boyte, Harry. 1979. Citizen activists in the public interest. *Social Policy* (Nov.–Dec.), 3–15.
Castells, Manuel. 1975. Advanced capitalism, collective consumption, and urban contributions: New sources of inequality and new models for change. In *Stress and contradiction in modern capitalism: Public policy and the theory of the state*, ed. Leon N. Lindberg, Robert Alford, Colin Crouch, and Clause Offe. Lexington, Mass.: D. C. Heath & Co.
———. 1983. The city and the grassroots. Berkeley and Los Angeles: University of California Press.
———. 1977. *The urban question: A Marxist approach*. London: Edward Arnold.
City of New York. Department of City Planning. 1977. *Planning for housing in New York City*.
City of New York. Office of Management and Budget. Department of City Planning. 1986. *Community district needs: Fiscal year 1986*. Queens.
Dickinson, James, and Bob Russell. 1986. Introduction: The structure of reproduction in capi-

talistic society. In *Family, economy and state: The social reproduction process under capitalism*. New York: St. Martin's Press.

Evers, Hans-Dieter, Wolfgang Clauss, and Diana Wong. 1984. Subsistence reproduction: A framework for analysis. In *Households and the world-economy: Explorations in the world-economy*, vol. 3, ed. Joan Smith, Immanuel Wallerstein, and Hans-Dieter Evers. Beverly Hills, London, New Delhi: Sage Publications.

Forde, C. D. 1963. *Habitat, economy and society: A geographical introduction to ethnology*. New York: E. P. Dutton.

Giddens, Anthony. 1973. *The class structure of the advanced societies*. New York: Harper and Row.

Kotler, Milton. 1969. Neighborhood government: The foundation of political life. New York: Bobbs Merrill.

Meggers, Betty J. 1954. Environmental limitations on the development of culture. *American Anthropologist* 56:801–24.

Mollenkopf, John, and Jon Pynoos. 1972. Property, politics and local housing policy. *Politics and Society* 2(4):407–29.

Perlman, J. E. 1976. Grassrooting the system. *Social Policy* (Sept.–Oct.).

Pynoos, Jon, Robert Schafer, and Chester W. Hartman. 1980. Introduction. In *Housing urban America*, ed. Jon Pynoos, Robert Schafer, and Chester W. Hartman. New York: Aldine.

Leavitt, J., and Susan Saegert. Forthcoming. *The making of community households: Responses to the housing crisis*.

Shepard, Bruce. 1975. Metropolitan political decentralization: A test of the life-style values model. *Urban Affairs Quarterly* 10(3):296–313.

Stauth, Georg. 1984. Household, modes of living, and productive systems. In *Households and the world-economy: Explorations in the world-economy*, vol. 3, ed. Joan Smith, Immanuel Wallerstein, and Hans-Dieter Evers. Beverly Hills, London, New Delhi: Sage Publications.

Tabb, William K. 1978. The New York fiscal crisis. In *Marxism and the metropolis: New perspectives in urban political economy*, ed. William K. Tabb and Larry Sawers. New York: Oxford University Press.

Turner, Joan T. 1984. Building boundaries: The politics of urban renewal in Manhattan's lower east side. Ph.D. diss., Graduate School and University Center, City University of New York.

Wallerstein, Immanuel. 1984. Household structure and labor-force formation in the capitalist world-economy. In *Households and the world-economy: Explorations in the world-economy*, vol. 3, ed. Joan Smith, Immanuel Wallerstein, and Hans-Dieter Evers. Beverly Hills, London, New Delhi: Sage Publications.

2

POLITICS, CULTURE, AND THE BUILT FORM: USER REACTION TO THE PRIVATIZATION OF STATE HOUSING IN SOUTH AFRICA

GRAEME J. HARDIE

TIMOTHY HART

Much of the research that we have undertaken in the field of built form and culture has focused on cultural continuities and changes among black people and the way these are expressed in the built form (Hardie 1981, 1982, 1985). Typically, the thrust of this research has been to see whether traditionally held cultural values still have validity and physical expression in contemporary urban environments. In our research, the term *traditional* has referred principally to the cultural ways and values that existed before contact with whites. A vision of cultural values untainted by alien influences is perhaps attractive to those of us who may see ourselves as advocates and protectors of things traditional, but our work in the crucible of South African black urban areas has revealed how intimately intertwined old and new cultural values have become, and how these have impinged on and in turn have been shaped by political policies relating to the built environment.

The most powerful physical expression of the web of racially discriminatory laws and practices that have come to be known as apartheid is arguably the system of public housing estates for blacks. It is perhaps in these environments that the imprint of apartheid has been most strongly and consistently felt, and it is here that some of the most virulent opposition has been expressed. But policy on the segregated black "townships" has undergone a series of mutations in the decade following the 1976 township riots. The changes that have taken place have been referred to as the "new dispensation" (Lea 1980) and have signaled at least a modification of state control over the residential environment of township people.

In this chapter we examine user reaction to one of the most dramatic state initiatives in the new dispensation: the so-called Big Sale of public housing.

In March 1983, the South African government announced its intention to sell some five hundred thousand houses, mostly in the black townships. At the outset, the sale offered state housing to tenants at prices considerably below replacement costs. Discount incentives were offered to lure early buyers, and the scheme was based on the 99-year leasehold system that had been introduced some five years before the sale (Morris 1981). Under the new tenure system black home buyers were offered a form of tenurial security that in concept at least would facilitate mortgage loan finance (Boaden 1979).

The sale was a key element of a broader move to reduce state involvement in the provision of black township housing, and its objectives were pursued with vigor. Despite the well-orchestrated marketing drive, however, it soon became evident that tenants in public township housing were unexpectedly resistant to the sale. Government sources explained this development by pointing to the shortage of loan finance and the action of political pressure groups as factors retarding the sale, while others singled out low incomes and bureaucratic inertia as major obstacles (Hardie and Hart 1986). These explanations have some validity, and they hint at the complex context in which the campaign to sell public housing in the black townships is set. Using material from group discussions, we attempt to show that resistance to the Big Sale, or to elements that underlie it, is partly rooted in a "township culture" in terms of which policy dispensations are treated with mistrust and cynicism.

User Responses to the "Big Sale" Initiatives

Against the backdrop of the failure of the Big Sale, and having noted the explanations offered, we designed an exploratory research project to investigate specifically subjective township perspectives on and reactions to the Big Sale. The project was not an attempt to validate other versions of the reasons underlying the slowness of the sale. Instead it was a modest effort to uncover black rank-and-file attitudes to, and experiences of, the Big Sale.

Following a series of pilot interviews, we decided to develop a research procedure that would stimulate black respondents to discuss freely their attitudes toward the Big Sale, to reveal fears and rumors, and to recount experiences with the sale or with homeownership in general. As a result of these requirements, a group discussion procedure was adopted (Hardie and Hart 1986). These discussions were arranged with the cooperation of several Witwatersrand companies, and each company was requested to assemble a group of about fifteen employees representing a range of ranks within the company. Names were not recorded, and company officials were asked not to attend the meetings. In all, eight group discussions were convened, and a total of 115 respondents participated (Hardie and Hart 1986).

By basing the group discussions specifically on formally employed black respondents, we deliberately biased the group to include those with a steady income, and therefore those most likely to consider the purchase of state-owned houses a serious option. Because of this rather crude stratification, and against the background of the relatively informal criteria for company and group selection, it cannot be claimed that the responses elicited in the group discussions were representative of any specific black population. It is valid, however, to analyze the qualitatively rich results of the group discussions in the context of the group of respondents, and it is reasonable to propose that some of the deep and often emotional issues exposed are felt by other township-dwellers as well.

We sought to introduce an initial sense of balance to the group discussions by posing two questions: "What are the reasons *for* purchasing a government-owned house?" and, "What are the reasons *for not* purchasing a government-owned house?" Responses were allowed to flow and were recorded on flip charts that were visible to the whole group. The comments reveal an array of attitudes, experiences, and reactions relating to the Big Sale. A selection of these is reproduced below.

Surveys based on questionnaires facilitate a structured and controlled response that contrasts strongly with the material obtained during a flowing and dynamic group session. The group discussions certainly did not suppress controversial or negative sentiments to the Big Sale but allowed these to bubble to the surface in open and sometimes heated discussion. It is in fact a moot point how much black fear, anger, and resentment is concealed behind the brief answers to questions in formal surveys. In counterpoint, however, the "risky shift" possibility of groups endorsing extreme negative viewpoints that may not be held individually must be recognized.

Comments and Themes from the Group Discussions   When the Big Sale was launched, the broad array of welcoming statements (Mabin and Parnell 1983) placed considerable emphasis on the positive objective social and individual ramifications of privatization and access to homeownership, especially among the residents of black townships. Several of the themes that emerged from the group discussions should be familiar to the proponents of home-ownership as important dimensions of residential quality of life, but the comments themselves reveal a township view of homeownership and its often almost unquestioned "benefits" that may be a little surprising.

Comments about security of tenure and independence.   During the group discussions, it became apparent that the major perceived advantage of the government house sale was security. It was clear that feelings of insecurity were fueled by rent increases and by actual or rumored evictions, and that the often expressed imperative to secure an urban base by purchase arose out of a wish to obviate the pressures of an insecure township environment for present and future generations.

> "I felt insecure especially if my husband should die, so I purchased the house to avoid this." In the past a widow without the same urban rights as her husband might well have been forced to leave the rented house and return to a rural area.
>
> "Being a homeowner means that you can't be evicted for nonpayment of the site charge." Defaults on rentals have resulted in the past in many people losing their homes.
>
> "People are thrown out of rented houses, but by buying you can avoid that."
>
> "I bought the house because it could be an advantage to the family as a security. If there are no houses available for them, I could accommodate them." This statement reflects the fears related to the shortage of houses in the urban areas.

Some respondents identified autonomy in decisions about housing as an important adjunct to the perceived security of ownership:

> "You feel more secure if you buy. I have lived in this house as a tenant for twelve years and did not alter because I would have lost on the value of the improvements if I left it. There is no compensation for improvements. Now I have plans in the pipeline."

While a general sense of security and independence were seen to be advantages of ownership by several respondents, the legal and administrative underpinning of township tenure, and of the sale itself, seems to have evoked pervasive confusion and deep mistrust. The 99-year leasehold system, especially, was seen to embody hidden costs, such as the requirement to have the lot surveyed, and was frequently perceived by respondents to offer little guarantee of secure tenure in the long term. Reference is made to administration boards, which until 1986 were the local agents of the state charged with township administration.

"People don't understand the sale. It has not been explained. We don't understand how the houses are costed and the discount procedure."

"There is a problem that when you fill in the forms you are just told to sign, but the forms are not explained and you are not sure what the terms are, how the leasehold works, and how it is renewed."

"We are being robbed here. These people are just getting rich. My friend here lives close to me in a house built at the same time. I paid R 6,000 for my house and he paid R 4,500. How can that be?"

"I have never received a slip saying that I have bought the house, only a receipt of payment."

"I have bought but the house is not registered in my name, so I am still paying rent, having paid for the house."

"When I wanted to buy I got the board to list all the costs. I took this to the bank and received a loan for the amount asked. Then when I went with the check to the board office I was told that I was still R 100 short. I paid this and only received a slip of paper with the board's stamp on it and no description of what it was for."

"I asked the board the price of my house. I was first told R 1,500, and then R 1,200. Now they don't know and say they are still surveying. How can you trust these people?"

"Our company gave a guarantee to the bank which enabled us to obtain a loan. If the building society had given the loan, they would not have given the money until the bond was registered. As yet we don't think our houses are registered in our names, that is why some of us are still paying rent and the board is just holding our money."

"What is the 99-year leasehold? It means that you pay until you die and then your children pay until they die."

"In 1956 my father bought his house for R 500 to obtain a 30-year leasehold. Now in 1986 my mother must buy it again. The government's law changes every year. By the time you reach ninety-nine years you have to pay again."

"We need clarification on the difference between the old system of 30-year leasehold and the present system of 99-year leasehold. What happens at the end of ninety-nine years?"

"There is a problem with the 99-year leasehold. How long will it last? How long will the government last? Will it all get changed again? Will my grandchildren get it? You just can't trust the government's word because they change all the time."

"The government should have thought through what comes first: the land, then the house, and not the other way around. The land is far more important than the house." Under leasehold the land is leased but the house is owned.

"If I die having bought on the 99-year plan and my children don't continue paying the rent, they will lose the house."

"With the 99-year lease you can buy everything but you still have to pay the site rental."

"The government has not reached a conclusion, so the ninety-nine years gives them time to decide on township life and our future."

Comments about finance and defaults.   There appeared to be some confusion and misunderstanding about the complexities of long-term housing finance, but there was a clear sense of unease among some respondents when considering the prospect of repayment periods lasting decades. The ramifications of default were clearly a focus of concern. Against the background of tenancy in mass housing estates, there is little experience of formal housing finance, although short-term credit for automobiles and furniture is familiar.

"Buying a house I can secure a loan. The houses are also sold at a very reasonable price."

"If you take a loan you end up paying so much more for it over many years. I recently bought a car and had a bank loan. Within three years I had paid off the bank, but the house, which did not cost much more, I will be paying for years to come. Why is that? I still don't own it. I much prefer the bank's system to that of the building society."

"The interest charges on the mortgage keep increasing and it doesn't look like I am paying anything off on my loan." In the late 1970s and early 1980s interest rates rose considerably and this added to people's misconceptions of interest. Since these interviews the interest rate has dropped.

"I am not clear what happens when there is a default. Can one be evicted if you own?"

"Even though I have bought I still feel insecure. If you default and someone pays the outstanding amount, they can buy the house."

Comments about inheritance.   Many respondents had specific problems with inheritance. It became clear in the discussion that legal rights of inheritance sometimes clash with traditional social rights.

"Because we are four brothers and two sisters in the house it will give my mother a problem if she buys it. So we are not encouraging her to buy."

"My parents left their rented house to my brother and myself. The board will only let one of us buy it. My brother now has a shop in the homelands, but he doesn't want to lose his urban rights, especially for his children which would happen if he does not maintain an urban base. He won't let me buy for myself, so I have to go on renting."

Comments about investment.   Some respondents who supported the sale did so because they saw investment possibilities in the purchase of discounted state housing. Because of the poorly developed property market in most townships, those underlining the positive aspects of this form of investment frequently had little idea of the potential profits to be made from renting or reselling Sale houses. In fact, some of the group participants were puzzled by the profit claims of others and asked why houses should appreciate in value when most second-hand goods lose resale value. Two comments reflect the investment viewpoint:

> "I know a man who was going to the homeland and who sold his house for R 24,000 having bought it for R 2,000. This could happen to me, but what happens if I die? I don't think that my wife will get the house."

> "It is amazing that although the price is so cheap, the people are still hesitant about buying."

Comments about the cost of owning compared with the cost of renting.   Many respondents felt that there was no clear advantage to owning a house, even given the discounted prices offered in terms of the Sale. Figures cited in group discussions often revealed that owners paid more for the services, a well as having to pay for the installation of water meters, and that this, added to loan repayments and maintenance bills, put owners at a clear disadvantage relative to subsidized renters in similar housing, at least in the short term.

> "Those on 99-year leasehold are paying high money. They must pay for the survey, for the meter and then the costs per month, whereas others pay a flat rate."

> "I am not buying my house because I don't see any advantage in it. If I need maintenance now I can call the board. These houses are old."

> "All you are buying is the bricks. You still have to pay the site rent, and that goes up. And then you pay for the maintenance of the house as well."

> "Before I owned the house I didn't pay separately for water. Now I do, so in fact it costs me more than before."

> "I thought that if I bought I would pay less. But, I am paying more."

A Contextual Interpretation of the
Comments from Group Discussions

The complex body of racial legislation and discriminatory practices underpinning apartheid has several profound manifestations in housing and residential structure. Among these are: (1) the racial segregation of urban residential areas according to the Group Areas Act and related legislation, (2) the containment of black urbanization through influx control measures, and (3) the temporary status of blacks in urban areas outside the so-called homelands.

The "new dispensation" has primarily addressed the third aspect of residential apartheid, acknowledging the permanence of urban blacks and seeking to establish a stable social stratum with vested urban interests. The formal influx control laws were scrapped on 1 July 1986, but residential segregation remains firmly entrenched.

The comments quoted are time bound and reflect the spontaneously expressed views of the 115 respondents who discussed the Big Sale in the sometimes emotionally charged environment of group discussions. At face value, however, the comments show that reactions to homeownership and the associated quality-of-life benefits are mediated by the complex social legacy of life under apartheid in the townships. It is clear, for example, that several respondents felt insecure and saw ownership as a means of putting down roots. Tenant insecurity has to be understood in its peculiar township context; before the reintroduction of leasehold tenure in 1973, the very physical and administrative fabric of black residential areas in "white" South Africa was predicated on the notion of impermanence. The 30- and 99-year leasehold systems heralded the first formal rejection of the myth of impermanence by the South African government, but to date a minority of township residents are homeowners in terms of leasehold tenure. For the majority, the tenants in public housing, eviction is an ever-present possibility. Among the participants in the group discussions, ownership was therefore a perceived strategy to gain control of some aspects of the township residential environment.

Comments about inheritance underline the need felt by some respondents to secure an urban base for their heirs. Against this backdrop failure of the Big Sale seems strange, especially if the security benefits of ownership are popularly accepted. Why should people reject an opportunity to distance themselves from their powerful landlord? A part of the answer may well lie in inadquate incomes, political motivations, and bureaucratic inertia, but the group discussions also reveal an undercurrent of suspicion about the motives underlying the Sale and the regulations and mechanisms that support it.

The 30-year leasehold system was introduced in 1975, having been abolished less than a decade before (Morris 1981). The 99-year leasehold scheme followed in 1977, and freehold title in the townships was given official sanction in 1986. Freehold is the predominant form of tenure in the white residential areas of South African cities. These "reform" moves appear to have been greeted by a significant proportion of our discussants with confusion and mistrust. The confusion is at least in part due to prior poor communication between township residents and local government in the form of administration boards. The mistrust runs far deeper. Some respondents were suspicious of the motives of the state, especially against the background of policy vacillation and the clearly discriminatory tenure packages that were presented as top-down dispensations. An undercurrent of opinion clearly saw successive leasehold dispensations as an imposed indirect tax, especially given the substantial registration and survey costs related to the 99-year system.

Administration boards were created in 1971 and became the front line in the administration and enforcement of residential apartheid in black urban areas. Not surprisingly, the relationship between board officials and black residents has been a troubled one, and this is reflected in some of the comments from the group discussions. Not all of the problems can be attributed to the boards themselves, but because of their powerful and pervasive presence in the townships, it is not entirely unjust that they should bear the brunt of black grievance. Many of the complaints directed by respondents to the boards or other vaguely defined "officials" relate to monetary issues. On the whole, incomes in Soweto are low (Mabin and Parnell 1983), especially by white standards. As a result, householders are acutely aware of cost and react strongly to seemingly unjust taxes, levies, and fees. Complaints about differences in Big Sale prices probably reflect misunderstanding, but there is unconfirmed evidence of bribery among junior officials dealing with Big Sale buyers.

A more pervasive problem has to do with the state housing legacy of the townships. In the 1950s and 1960s, low-cost state housing was provided on a massive scale in black townships throughout South Africa (Hendler, Mabin, and Parnell 1986). Economies of scale enabled the state to build housing to relatively high physical standards at minimal costs. In addition, rents and infrastructure were subsidized, and the subsidization has persisted for decades. In the context of extensive tenant subsidization, new owners of Big Sale houses face massive increases in housing costs, especially where loan repayments replace heavily subsidized rentals and where individually metered water replaces a simple monthly levy. It is not surprising that several respondents questioned the economies of ownership.

Because of a housing policy that was based on tenancy and impermanence, housing markets are in their infancy in the black townships. These markets even now are restricted and operate in an environment where new land for black residential development is difficult to obtain and where formal sources of finance are unfamiliar. For those reasons, many of the participants in our group discussions were unable to speculate on the potential resale value of Big Sale houses and were often fearful of the implications of long-term loan finance. Overarching all of this was a sense of immobility that was partly due to existing overcrowding and the restricted supply of new sites and new houses. Even where profits on resale were noted by respondents, it was clear that few saw residential mobility as a viable proposition.

Conclusion

The Big Sale initiative continues, and there is some recent evidence that the value of sales in black areas is increasing. The fanfare accompanying the Sale and the limited-period incentives offered, however, suggest that state planners did not anticipate a prolonged and arduous campaign. Efforts to privatize township public housing have been a limited success from the point of view of the state, and the new dispensation has been dealt a severe blow. Cheap housing that offers some promise of access to loan finance and investment opportunities, and the added benefits of security, independence, and self-expression, is superficially a quality-of-life deal that is particularly salient in South Africa's black townships. But it is that very township heritage, seen from the politico-cultural perspective of the township dwellers themselves, that appears to have retarded rapid acceptance of the Big Sale. Clearly the state's planners did not reckon with the pervasive mistrust and cynicism of township blacks toward government-initiated housing dispensations or, very simply, with the misgivings and uncertainty about housing markets, formal financing, and permanent tenure among public housing tenants who have had little access to these in the past.

References

Boaden, B. G. 1979. The financial aspects of black homeownership with reference to the new 99-year leasehold legislation. Occasional paper, University of the Witwatersrand, Johannesburg.

Hardie, G. J. 1981. *Tswana design of house and settlement: Continuity and change in expressive space.* Ph.D. diss., Boston University. Ann Arbor: University Microfilms 81-12201.

———. 1982. The dynamics of the internal organization of the traditional tribal capital Mochudi. In *Settlement in Botswana*, ed. R. R. Hitchcock and M. R. Smith, 205–19. Johannesburg: Heinemann Educational Books.

———. 1985. Continuity and change in Tswana's house and settlement form. In *Home environ-*

ment, ed. I. Altman and C. Werner, 213–36, vol. 8 of *Human behaviour and environment.* New York: Plenum.

Hardie, G. J., and T. Hart. 1986. A black perspective of state-owned houses. *Planning and Building Developments,* Mass Housing Supplement (March): 17–20.

Hendler, P., A. Mabin, and S. Parnell. 1986. Rethinking housing questions in South Africa. In *South African Review* 3, ed. and comp. South African Research Service.

Lea, J. P. 1980. The new urban dispensation: Black housing policy in South Africa, post Soweto, 1976. Paper presented to the Conference of African Studies Association of Australia and the Pacific, La Trobe University, Victoria.

Mabin, A. S., and S. Parnell. 1983. Recommodification and working-class home ownership: New directions for South African cities. *South African Geographical Journal* 65:148–66.

Morris, P. M. 1981. *A history of black housing in South Africa.* South Africa Foundation, Johannesburg.

3

HOUSING AND CULTURE FOR
NATIVE GROUPS IN CANADA

KENNETH MCDOWELL

Native groups in Canada are those of aboriginal descent and include status (Indians with treaty rights) and non-status Indians and Inuit (Eskimo). This chapter will deal primarily with status Indians because most of the information that has been written and debated about the clash between those of Euro-Canadian and those of native descent over housing has involved status Indians.

As of 31 December 1970, there were 250,781 status Indians in Canada and approximately two-thirds of them lived on reserves (Central Mortgage and Housing Corporation 1972). Although the proportion of off-reserve Indians is increasing annually, as land claims continue to be settled and as more Indians gain status recognition in the courts, the relation between housing and culture on reserves will likely remain a salient issue, and it is the housing issue on the reserves in Canada that is the major focus of this chapter.

Indian bands are groups of status Indians recognized by the Canadian government "for whose benefit and use land and money have been set aside and held by the government" (Department of Indian Affairs and Northern Development, hereafter referred to as DIAND, 1980). In Canada there are 2,242 separate parcels of reserve land, a total of 10,021 square miles (DIAND 1980). In 1979 the average band size was estimated to be 525. Although this represents a 60 percent increase in band size since 1961, it suggests (1) that the total number of individuals and households in any one location continues to be small, and (2) that uniform Euro-Canadian community planning concepts might not accurately reflect the housing needs or model the way of life of these native groups.

The introduction of comprehensive community planning on reserves is a recent (mid-1970s) effort to increase band control over the planning process. As comprehensive as that planning might be, and as much as it represents a more enlightened approach than what preceded it, it lacks an understanding of the cultural aspects of planning and the historical role that housing has played in maintaining a sense of cultural identity and self-identity in the native communities.

To understand better the problems that currently exist on reserves, we need to draw attention to the dynamic, but sometimes reluctant, role played by the federal government in the native housing situation.

A Historical Perspective

The Indian Act of 1868–69   In the late 1860s, European colonization in Canada resulted in the Indian Act of 1868–69 in which many Indian bands signed treaties for the creation of the reserves. The Indian Act allowed the Department of Indian Affairs "to 'manage the affairs of Indians' in an all-pervasive way" (Beaver 1979, 26), and the government agreed often thereafter to maintain schools for instruction and to encourage farming among Indians. Despite this paternalistic attitude, there was little direct intervention by the government in the affairs of Indians for some eighty years. We suggest, however, that the government's encouragement to the Indians to give up hunting and to adopt farming is a key to understanding subsequent housing issues.

The emphasis in the Indian Act appears to be on the ownership and control of land. The bands were given these lands for the exclusive use of them and their children. The land was good land in the sense that it could sustain the Indians' way of life (hunting and gathering), and the tracts of land were large enough to accommodate the migratory habits of the small bands.

Perceptions of Indians   Imagine for a moment a band of Indians moving seasonally to their trapping or hunting grounds intercepting a migrating herd of caribou. The notion of community was one of kinship ties and living in relation to land resources of water and food. Life was simple and primitive, but more important, it negated the need for the schools and farm community settlement structures familiar to non-natives of European descent. Now superimpose over that image the view that government representatives or missionaries might have had of a group of people that led that kind of life, and it becomes easy to predict the kind of picture of Indian culture that was communicated to the colonists.

> Historical accounts of early contacts with Indian people substantiate the fact that government representatives and missionaries regarded the Indians as savages.

They leave little doubt that the core message transmitted to the indigenous people in the course of their colonization was that their own culture was inferior, even barbaric, and that they should be adopting the more "civilized" ways of the white society. . . . The entire process of "civilization" was to be spearheaded by mission-run schools. . . . By methods of this nature . . . the Indian would be gradually and permanently advanced to the scale of civil society; his migratory habits, and fondness for roaming, would be cured, and an interesting class of our fellow men rescued from degradation. . . .

The aim of all these institutes (mission run schools) is to train the Indian to give up his old ways, and to settle among his white brethren on equal terms and with equal advantage. . . . (JohnMcIntyre, Indian Agent for reserves in Ontario, 1885)

The Government relegated social and educational responsibilities to the missions because "no decent white teachers" could be expected to live under the primitive conditions of Indian life. (Shkilnyk 1981, 7) (The above quotations are as quoted in Simon et al. 1984)

The mission influence on educating Indians had little or no influence on Indian housing. Whether the reason was that those who ran the missionaries accepted the "reality" of primitive living conditions or that they felt housing was outside their sphere of influence is uncertain. Whatever the reason, the lack of commentary about dwellings meant that the subject of Indian housing did not become an issue until the 1950s.

After World War II   As Rose (1980, 16) has noted, "the most important background fact in the Canadian housing experience is that Canada is a federal state." According to the Constitution of 1867, the federal government has responsibility not only for undertaking specific functions but also for discharging residual powers not accorded to the provinces. Housing, in particular, is the responsibility of the provinces, and therefore the housing on reserves is a provincial problem to ignore or deal with as the provincial government sees fit. As a consequence of this, a federal organization for housing development (Central Mortgage and Housing Corporation, now Canada Mortgage and Housing Corporation [CMHC]) whose responsibility was to provide safe and adequate housing for Canadians was to have little direct impact on the affairs of Indians on reserves. When it became apparent after the Second World War that there was considerable disparity between the provinces in how they were dealing with native housing, the federal government exercised its authority with respect to these "residual powers" and created the Indian Affairs Branch. In 1948, a Special Joint Committee of the Senate and House of Commons recommended that "Indian schools for Indians be abolished and that Indian education be placed under the direct and sole responsibility of the Indian Affairs Branch" (Shkilnyk 1981, 16). This meant that while there was a federal agency (CMHC) empowered to look after safe and adequate housing for Canadians, and a federal agency to look after the education of Indians, the issue of non-status Indian housing remained loosely defined as the responsibility of the provinces, which, for many reasons, were not empowered to insure that Indians were living in healthful dwellings.

The War on Poverty   With the expansion of the Indian Affairs Branch into the Department of Indian Affairs and Northern Development (DIAND) in the 1950s and 1960s and the decision by the Canadian government to become involved in the "war on poverty," the belief that Indian culture was at the root of the Indians' problems was replaced by the belief that poverty was at the root of their problems.

> Among many of Canada's Indians, all the classical signs and symptoms of poverty are to be found: under-employment and unemployment, large families, poor health, substandard housing, low levels of education, idleness, and an attitude of despair and defeat. To many Indians in northern settlements, these conditions are the only way of life that exists. They have known no other. They accept poverty as they accept the weather. (J. W. Churchman, director of development, Indian Affairs Branch, as quoted in Shkilnyk 1981, 23)

Modernization Through Improvement   As a developmental agency, DIAND was responsible for engaging in a war to eradicate these poverty conditions. *Modernization* became the buzz word and a description of policy. As economically as possible, DIAND implemented policies to improve physical living conditions on reserves and to provide for native groups the social services available to all Canadians.

Having in hand a program with particular objectives, a belief that when those objectives were achieved the overt signs of poverty would be removed, and the financial backing to implement that program meant that little attention needed to be focused on the history of the people whose lives were going to be improved. Berger (1977, 91) has noted in speaking about Indians that "we have a rich and proud history . . . [and] there is no mention [in schools] of any of our history. . . . Our history and culture has been ignored and shoved aside." At issue here was whether those responsible for implementing modernization of substandard housing saw Indian culture as a barrier to winning this aspect of the war on poverty. To suggest this, as Simon et al. (1984) have done, is to imply that the government made a deliberate effort to eradicate Indian culture. There is little evidence to support this position. I suggest that a more accurate interpretation of history is that either Indians did not resist modernization in the name of preserving their culture or they assumed that their culture would remain in spite of modernization. There are two reasons for this interpretation: (1) Indians had no reason to accept the interpretation of their culture that was being put forward, and (2) it was only after Indians experienced the negative effects of modernization on their culture that the issue of Indian culture was first raised.

Modernization proceeded something like this: a team (or governmental task force) went to a reserve to evaluate the housing situation. They reported finding uninsulated, deteriorating tar paper shacks scattered throughout the "bush." This evaluation team was followed by a construction team that lay out the water and sewage lines and then built prefabricated, low-cost, row house units with indoor plumbing. Families were then encouraged (and enticed with the prospect of running water) to move in.

Within about five years reports began to filter in about how that housing was being "treated" by the dwellers. There were reports that party walls had been removed, that two or three families were living in single-family dwellings, that siding had been removed for fire wood, and more. In essence, the reports suggested that the impoverished culture of Indians does not allow them to know how to appreciate living in "quality" housing.

A common, and erroneous, assumption at this time was that house form and culture go hand-in-hand, that, for a group of people set on mastery over nature, the advancement of the culture is reflected in its notion of housing "standards." The housing that was imposed on the native groups in the modernization effort symbolically acted out the responsibility of the government to permit Indians to participate in this mastery over nature at the individual and community levels. This assumption fails to take into account that for a group of people attempting to live in harmony with their environment, "the land" and not housing is the crucial link. Present-day commentary by native band leaders strongly suggests that the preferred life-style on reserves is one that is shaped by a respect for the attitudes and behaviors of the past. Thus the desire to maintain traditional Indian values on the reserves continues unabated.

It was not until modernization involved the relocation of a tribe to a less suitable site that anyone suggested the possibility that a culture was being destroyed. That is, it was not until the articulate writings of Anastasia Shkilnyk were widely publicized in the 1980s that the issues of Indian housing, Indian community, and Indian culture suggested a different and very disturbing view of what was happening on reserves.

In Shkilnyk's book A *Poison Stronger than Love* (1985), she documents the relocation of the Ojibwa village of Grassy Narrows in 1963 and the subsequent destruction of the tribe's social fabric. Although "modernization" through community relocation was not the norm, her writings brought to public attention (1) the lack of consultation that occurs between community planners and native groups, and (2) the disastrous consequences to a group when they lose contact with their culture. What that culture is and why it does not "fit" into the Euro-Canadian community planners' conceptual framework is the subject to which we turn next.

Implementation of Community Planning Concepts   The most typical modernization approach taken by DIAND was to lay out communities with respect to convenience for sewage disposal and access to electricity and running water. In short, Indians on reserves were offered the opportunity to have water brought to them, instead of their having to carry a bucket down to the lake. The introduction of modern plumbing to the reserves meant, however, that families were encouraged to adopt a living arrangement with respect to their neighbors that was totally foreign to their culture. The initial costs associated with providing these services meant that houses needed to be built in the core area of the community. The words of A. G. Leslie, chief of the Agencies Division, DIAND (1964), express a view that was common during this period:

> It is desired that housing on Indian reserves be on a community planning basis so that all services such as stores, school, etc. will form part of the housing community. Many times in the past, houses have been constructed for the convenience of the individual and when we try to provide roads, water and sewage systems it is a most difficult problem. (Quoted in Shkilnyk 1981, 36)

Planners saw the community in strictly physical terms. They saw the desires of individuals to live in a dispersed pattern as a problem to be overcome in a rational, straightforward, and persuasive manner. While several authors have noted that the building was done without consultation with native groups and without regard to their traditional ways of life (that is, the closest non-kin neighbor was as much as a quarter of a mile away), it could be argued that community planning concepts have always been at odds with individual desires. Whether one is white or Indian, living physically removed from the sight of one's neighbors and having the services of electricity and running water means one must have the financial resources to pay to have those services brought to the dwelling site. Without those financial resources one is forced to live in close physical proximity to others. Consultation with community leaders about what appears to be a rational, logical solution to a problem is thus not an issue.

The salient issue is that Indians were in fact living in a settlement pattern based on a vernacular form of community planning, and that pattern was seen as a fundamental precept of their culture. Simon et al. (1984, 133) point out with respect to the Ojibwa:

> The dispersed pattern is a difficult concept for traditionally trained urban planners to cope with. The settlement pattern is analogous to the density in rural Ontario. House sites should be determined by community members. Infrastructure should be designed after house sites are determined. Technical adjustments should only be made if [the] community feels they will not effect [sic] the social relationships. In general, houses should be spaced far enough apart that neighbours voices cannot be heard.

Implementation of "Good" 1960s Suburban Design   In the 1960s the failure by DIAND to provide a "lasting" solution to housing problems on reserves resulted in an attempt by the federal government, through CMHC, to deal with the problem. CMHC awarded contracts to private developers who professed a sensitivity to the social and cultural problems on reserves. During the predesign phase, planners took one look at the rows of prefabricated and now dilapidated houses on reserves and criticized the Department of Indian Affairs for failing to address the social and cultural problems that this kind of housing presumably created. Their making such criticism reflects the fact that they had their own state-of-the-art solution (in this instance, good 1960s suburban design), such as that by Kennedy and Simonsen (1967), available for implementation. These designers introduced on reserves the idea of either clustering housing around a central green area or building an early form of townhouses. They rationalize that this is an appropriate form of community planning because it respects the social and cultural values of native groups, but they give no indication whatsoever that native groups saw 1960s suburban design as taking native values into consideration. This planning practice, as inappropriate as the practice of planned row housing, still represents, according to Simon et al. (1984), the mainstream of design and implementation of housing for native communities.

Housing Programs   In 1969 active Indian political groups were demanding greater participation in decision making, the government was increasing spending on Indian problems, and Indian bands were assuming more control and responsibility for programs and services. In light of this political climate and the continuous streams of criticism directed toward the government and the housing situation on reserves, it is not surprising that the government was willing to try another approach—that of housing programs. A housing program comes about through federal or provincial legislation. People who qualify are invited to apply, almost always for funds to improve their housing situation. In this situation, individuals or native bands were encouraged to borrow money from the government to build houses on reserves. Before 1970, Indians living on reserves were eligible for three housing programs: The Housing Subsidy Program, Band Administered Programs, and a Canada Mortgage and Housing Corporation mortgage program. A study by Kennedy Smith Associates (1970) (as reported by Simon et al. 1984) found the programs to be ineffective for the following reasons:

(1) The number of units produced was grossly inadequate

(2) The programs lacked flexibility

(3) There was poor co-ordination and integration with other related programs

(4) Lack of native participation in the housing-process

(5) Complaints focused particularly upon poor planning and design without reference to the needs of the occupants with respect to family size, economic values and life style

(6) Failure to employ Native-Canadians in the construction of the dwellings

(7) Substandard housing, built with substandard materials—occasionally houses were left unfinished

(8) Local materials were not used

(9) Houses were located on unsuitable sites or places where people did not want to live

(10) Housing allocations were made by Government officials without regard to the life styles or social structure of the communities

(11) Insufficient funds to furnish the units once completed

(12) Poor communications regarding programs and financial procedures

(13) Problems of housing maintenance were compounded by lack of necessary skills resulting in accelerated deterioration of the housing stock.

DIAND and CMHC received considerable criticism during the 1970s and early 1980s for their role in providing housing on reserves. Rates of illiteracy, alcoholism, and crime on the reserves were many times the national average; overcrowding and misuse of existing housing was seriously depleting the housing stock; and the housing programs were ineffective. The war on poverty being waged on the reserves had not been won, the housing problem was not being solved, and neither technological nor political solutions were working. This period did, however, see the first stirring of recognition of a need for consultation by government representatives with band councils and native leaders in seeking a solution to the problem of Indian community planning. Conspicuously absent in most of the documents written during this period is any discussion of Indian culture.

A Time of Reflection

Site Services   Euro-Canadian plumbing technology solutions implemented in the 1960s to bring running water to individual households on reserves has in the more enlightened 1980s been cast in a somewhat different light:

> The lesson for me has been the appreciation of the misuse of engineering information. Engineers provided a neat, simplistic, technological solution to a complex human problem. The engineers provided their client—the government—with a solution that masked over many fundamental societal problems of which engineers are supposed to be aware. Because the solution looked clear, the decision-makers embraced it. (Gamble 1982, 4–5)

The refusal by some native people to move into new towns built with this technological solution but according to a community settlement pattern foreign to anything they had known forced an emerging recognition of the necessity of dealing with the native culture as a planning issue within the government. For example, E. Rodger, author of "Physical Planning Guidelines for the Native Community" prepared for the Department of Indian and Northern Affairs, states that:

> "special consideration must be given to cultural, social and traditional characteristics which differentiate the community requirements from those of non-Indians" and that the planner, in developing alternative solutions must "identify the nature and extent of physical, environmental, economic, social, and cultural constraints and assets in developing solutions." (Quoted in Simon et al. 1984, 54–55)

Comprehensive Community Planning   The implementation in 1981–82 of comprehensive community planning was an attempt to facilitate Indian band control over the planning process. Funds were allocated to bands for hiring consultants and organizing workshops on community planning. As Wolfe and Lindley (1983, 8) note, the problem that emerged for non-native consultants was that

> few if any professional planners have any understanding of life on reserves, or the intricacies of Indian culture and social relationships. The relationships identified by the professional can only be those which fall within his or her own realm of experience, learning and understanding.

Wolfe and Lindley went on to advocate a three-fold approach to comprehensive community planning: (1) the training of Indian planners and planning assistants, (2) the training of non-Indian planners to fill the gap until such time as Indian planners are available to do the job, and (3) the development of appropriate methods of drawing the community into the planning process. Such an approach is criticized by Simon et al. (1984) because it involves the training of Indians in the prevailing Euro-Canadian planning education process. They suggest, alternatively, a greater understanding of the Indian concept of community, to which we turn next.

The Indian Concept of Community   In contrast to the typical conceptualization of community with its emphasis on a physical network of structures, cultures that engage in migratory hunting and gathering define community in social terms. As Shkilnyk observed at Grassy Narrows (1981, 50):

> Community was not bound by notions of year round residents in a specific village. On the contrary, the "community" was the ebb and flow of families over a territory without exact geographical limits, the movement between winter trapping grounds and summer residence on the old reserve, the alternation between the times of gathering and the times of dispersal. . . . This movement gave community life its ever changing form and character, while other linkages and ties gave "community" its meaning.

While considerable anthropological evidence suggests a dispersed settlement pattern (for example, along a lake shore), the clustering of homes, when it occurred, seems to have been on the basis of kinship ties. A family group would locate themselves approximately a quarter of a mile from other family groups, and within a family group each dwelling would be located to be beyond hearing distance from another dwelling.

The Social, Psychological, and Spiritual Community   The writings of Shkilnyk (1981, 1985) about the Grassy Narrows Reserve and the interviews conducted by Simon and her colleagues with members of the Burwash Native Peoples Project document native peoples' view of community and the physical environment. The social aspects of community are defined by the sharing ethic (in hunting and gathering societies), the family, and the leadership of the community. Traditionally, the family group is the most important source of identity for the Ojibwa people. The reinforcement of identity through symbolic spatial ordering of the community (clustering family groups together) provides a strong sense of identity for the native person. Within most native groups decision making is not the responsibility of either elected leaders or a majority of the community members. Instead, leaders facilitate discussion until a unanimous decision is made.

Native people regard themselves as custodians of the land, which is for their use during their lifetimes and which must be passed on to their children and their children's children. The land (spoken of in a metaphysical sense), its character, and its sacred places determine to what use certain spaces are put. For example, the location of the sacred fire (chosen by the spiritual leader of the community) is conceptually, rather than geometrically, placed in the center of the community.

Present Approaches to Planning and Native Housing

Educating the Planner   An argument can be made for vernacular community planning. When the planner is from another culture, Simon et al. (1984) advocate a derivative of Lynch's (1972) site-planning methodology involving both direct and indirect communication with the client group. Specifically, Simon et al. (1984, 99) see this as a fourfold undertaking for the planner: (1) Developing an understanding of the culture's teachings (mythology, traditions) as a window into the working of the culture; (2) understanding contemporary literature on the planning and design of native communities; (3) interviewing the client with the objective of realizing the "dreams, goals and wishes of the people who will inhabit the community"; and (4) visiting other native communities to validate the teachings, literature, and interviewing information.

On the basis of their use of this strategy, Simon et al. (1984, 115) suggest the adoption of what they call the responsive planning approach:

> The Responsive Approach has two fundamental characteristics:
>   1. Responsive Planning is initiated by the local client group, not by an outside agency.
>   2. Responsive Planning produces minimal incremental plans, not comprehensive or master plans.
>   There are two basic requirements for working in the responsive mode:
>   1. The Responsive Planner acts as a facilitator, not as a director.
>   2. The Responsive Planner learns from the client and adapts to their ways. He or she does not study the client and expect the client to adapt to his or her ways.

Because this approach involves considerable reeducation of the western-trained community planner, the skeptic may wonder how many planners are willing to undergo this training given the relatively small number of Indians interested in living on any one reserve. In addition, the planning student may cast a dubious glance at the potential financial gains to be derived from undertaking the reeducation called for in the four-fold approach combined with the responsive planning approach, unless he plans to work solely with native client groups.

A New Beginning?   We began our account of housing and culture for native groups in Canada by noting the role taken by the government one hundred years ago in managing the affairs of Indians. Neither the federal nor the provincial government seems to have had much interest in becoming involved in the issue of native housing on reserves. A sampling of recent newspaper articles suggests that by Euro-Canadian standards there has been little improvement in native housing over the last one hundred years. A 1985 report by Ekos Research Associates of Ottawa commissioned by the Department of Indian Affairs and Northern Development was reported to have stated:

> 28.8 per cent of reserve housing in Canada was substandard, 16.3 per cent very poor and two per cent beyond repair. It estimates that $200 million [over twice that spent by the government through its on-reserve housing program in 1983–84] would be needed just to restore existing housing to "minimal physical condition standards." (*Star-Phoenix*, 18 July 1985)

Four months before this report was filed, the following report had come out, equally pessimistic in its view of native housing:

> The report suggests policies should not encourage native people to stay on reserves. In paying for construction costs of good housing, the federal Government has "unwittingly created a disincentive (for Indians) to move to areas of economic opportunity." It recommends that only "minimal" standards should guide the construction of housing, and says better [housing] should be paid for by native groups. "Everyone's dream is a private dwelling on a large lot, but it is not a Government responsibility to provide this." (*Globe and Mail*, 18 April 1985)

A considerable portion of the job of housing management for groups living in rural Canada has, in recent years, been turned over to the groups themselves in the form of "self-help" housing through the Rural and Native Housing Division of CMHC. "Self-help" refers not only to housing construction but also to renovation, maintenance, construction management, financial management planning, and advisory or training activities (Middleton 1983). Given the multi-faceted nature of self-help at the individual and group levels, it is difficult to summarize its effectiveness. In psychological terms, however, self-help represents a definite move in the direction of Indian control over Indian destiny, and of the government's being able to disengage itself from the role it has reluctantly played in Indian housing issues. When collective self-help is undertaken, that is, self-help at the community level—which seems to be the preferred approach on reserves—a valuable asset in building individual-community ties on reserves is maintained. Thus, there is a promise of a new beginning in native groups' ability to determine for themselves the kind of housing that fits their culture and environment.

A considerable debt is owed to Joan Simon and her colleagues at Guelph University, Guelph, Ontario, for their paper "A culturally sensitive approach to planning and design with native Canadians" (1984), from which much of the information for this article was taken.

References

Beaver, J. W. 1979. *To have what is one's own.* Ottawa: The National Indian Socio-Economic Development Committee.

Berger, T. R. 1977. *Northern frontier, northern homeland: The report of the MacKenzie Valley Pipeline Inquiry,* vol. 1. A special report prepared by the Canadian Minister of Supply and Services.

Canadian Department of Indian Affairs and Northern Development (DIAND). 1980. *Indian conditions: A survey.*

Gamble, D. C. 1982. Engineering ethics and northern development. Paper presented at Queen's University, Kingston, Ontario, 11 March.

Globe and Mail. 18 April 1985. Drastic cuts proposed in native programs.

Kennedy, A. A., and D. C. Simonsen. 1967. *Housing study: Isolated communities and Indian reserves: Prairie provinces: First stage report.* Winnipeg: Kennedy Smith Associates, August.

Lynch, K. 1972. *Site planning.* Cambridge, Mass.: M.I.T. Press.

Middleton, C. D. 1983. *Self-help components in housing delivery.* Research report prepared for the Canada Mortgage and Housing Corporation, Rural and Native Housing Division, Ottawa.

Rodger, E. 1981. *Physical planning guidelines for the native community: Report.* A special report prepared for the Canadian Department of Indian and Northern Affairs.

Rose, A. 1980. *Canadian housing policies (1935–1980).* Toronto: Butterworths.

Shkilnyk, A. M. 1981. *Government Indian policy and its impact on community life: A case study of the relocation of the Grassy Narrows band.* Ottawa: Department of Indian Affairs and Northern Development.

———. 1985. *A poison stronger than love.* New Haven: Yale University Press.

Simon, J. C., R. R. Forster, T. Alcose, E. A. Brabec, and F. Ndubisi. 1984. *A culturally sensitive approach to planning and design with native Canadians.* Ottawa: Canada Mortgage and Housing Corporation.

Star-Phoenix. 18 July 1985. Indian housing substandard, study reveals.

Wolfe, J., and S. Lindley. 1983. Comprehensive community planning with Canada's first nations: Observations of theory, policy and practice. Paper presented at the 6th Annual Applied Geography Conference, Toronto.

4

CULTURE, POLICY, AND PRODUCTION: MAKING LOW-COST HOUSING IN SRI LANKA

EDWARD ROBBINS

When we look at the culture of housing and its design and production, we need to look at more than the house type and its local context. In the Third World, as well as in our own, housing to a larger and larger extent is as much an outcome of national government and international agency action as it is the result of local activity. National needs and social policy, in addition to national and international political and economic priorities, are an integral part of the culture of housing, particularly low-cost housing. Ignoring the role of government and the large institutional framework of housing only distorts what we know about the culture of housing and prevents us from understanding how, where, and what kind of housing is produced and what it entails and means to its makers and its users.

The effort to produce appropriate low-cost housing in Sri Lanka, a nation dedicated to producing housing on a large scale, illustrates most clearly that the design and production of a cultural artifact, the house, is also the design and production of a cultural practice, the policies and activities that generate housing. In Sri Lanka, the efforts to structure and restructure the design and production of low-cost shelter has had a profound impact on both how housing becomes a social and cultural artifact and the ways the effort to produce housing becomes a part of local and national cultural and social institutions. The story of how Sri Lankans addressed the problem of low-cost housing is the story of how different groups within Sri Lankan society made cultural choices, organized themselves and others, defined their ideological commitments, and began to act within a context of technological, material, and sociopolitical opportunities and constraints.

The critical issues are how and why those concerned with designing low-

cost housing policy and producing low-cost housing in Sri Lanka came to realize, first, that there is a difference between a concern with houses and
a concern with housing, and second, that whereas houses are cultural and
social objects and consumables, housing is a cultural process and a social
activity.

Housing: Background

Housing had little or no place in public policies under
British colonial rule except for certain public officials for whom housing was
provided by the state. In 1941, because of the cessation of building during
World War II, a rent control act became the first law that had to do with housing policy. In 1953, the newly independent government of Sri Lanka did begin to take a more direct role in the provision of housing for the middle and
working classes, but until 1977 the greatest attention to housing was directed
at landlord-tenant relations and the problems of rents, land ownership, and
social equity.

In 1977, under a new government led by the United National Party
(UNP), the emphasis of the government effort directed at housing shifted
from the creation of social policy to direct intervention into the production
and upgrading of housing. The shift from a policy oriented to developing social and economic equity to one of stimulating the housing market and aiding
the various actors in that market by direct production of houses paralleled a
shift from a more socialist to a more market-oriented government. This shift
would later explain other and different directions taken by the UNP on the
issue of housing.

The first major effort by the UNP at direct intervention in the production
of housing was called the 100,000 Houses Program (OHP), and it was directed by the minister of housing, who is now prime minister as well as minister of housing. The direct involvement of a cabinet minister in housing
symbolizes the importance the government then and now has placed on housing and reminds us of the important interpenetrations of the national political
culture with local efforts to build and upgrade housing and settlements—interpenetrations which form a major subtheme in the understanding of housing
design and production in Sri Lanka.

The 100,000 Houses Program

The 100,000 Houses Program, directed by the Urban
Development Authority (UDA) of Sri Lanka, paralleled many such programs
in the Third World. Partly underwritten by various international development

agencies and using western expertise and industrial logics and materials, contractors were hired to build relatively large-scale housing developments. Whereas between 1970 and 1977 the government built and provided only 4,700 units of housing, beginning in 1977 the OHP was to provide 36,000 units constructed directly by government-sponsored contractors.

Settlement upgrading directed at about 50,000 housing units was to be guided by western-trained planners who were put to work surveying and studying the various slums and shantytowns of Colombo.[1] Additionally, 14,000 direct loans for housing upgrading were also given. The net result of the OHP was the construction of a series of "low-cost" houses and projects that created more problems than they were supposed to solve. Problems of cost and allocation and problems with the cultural and social appropriateness of the program developed soon after the program was initiated.

The massive national investment in housing at a rate of 5–8 percent of the GNP was neither sustainable nor appropriate to the problems at hand. The level of investment that the OHP necessitated, given its strategy of production, started to cause inflation. Even if the Sri Lankan government had the means to continue investing such a large amount of the GNP, the large investment would have distorted the economy. The net result would have been economic catastrophe for the very people the government was trying to help with the housing program.

Using contractors to build the houses resulted in housing that was overly rationalized and a building process that was too slow. The UDA had to put out bids and find a contractor. They, in turn, needed to level the land, bring in materials and workers, and build. Such a process was slow, and it was often alienating to the community in which houses were built. Moreover, the emphasis on contractor-built housing ignored the need for incremental shelter and settlement upgrading—a process of no interest to actors caught up in the excitement of large-scale production but often more in keeping with the needs and economic capacity of those to whom the housing program was directed. Even though Sri Lankans had a high propensity to save for housing (10–15 percent of income), contractor-built houses were priced at R 20,000 (about $3,000), too expensive for over 50 perent of the Sri Lankan population and in the long run too costly for the government to subsidize.

Furthermore, contractor-built housing and "planned" upgrading was found to be inappropriate to local-level social and cultural institutions and to the development of any capacity for local settlement initiative and self-help. The process of supplying contractor-built houses and "planned" upgrading was discovered to be much too fragmented. Contractors disregarded traditional modes of building and skilled craftsmen as well as local entrepreneurs, leadership, and social infrastructure. Also, after houses were built, the process of distribution ignored local economic modes of exchange and social practice. If houses were built all at once, as they were of contractors, the issue of allocation became a problem because local needs and the local modes of property allocation were ignored. As the building process was fragmented from the community and the local social and political infrastructure, allocation was left to a process dependent on political patronage, favoritism, and other discordant allocatory procedures. These practices often led to social conflict and, at times, even cultural breakdown.

James Brow, in a study (no date) of a village where thirty new houses were built, points out that the process produced a settlement but probably destroyed a community. The all-at-once process of housing allocation was guided by political party lines, which were insensitive to local caste, class, and social relations. According to Brow, if the process had been more rooted in local culture and based on the local pace of building, allocation might have been handled adequately. If, in addition, the process had been based on some measure of self-help, which might have discouraged those with decent housing from demanding new houses, the impact of the housing program might have been different.

Finally, the materials used to build houses, mostly concrete, were expensive and also inappropriate to their context. In the tropics concrete must be tended to constantly. It mildews, chips, and discolors and keeps heat from escaping. Added to the expense of the material is the necessity for industrial techniques and skills in its production and construction. Furthermore, by using concrete, builders missed an opportunity to develop local industry and employ local skills and local means of building, which not only might have produced more appropriate shelters but also might have improved the local economic infrastructure.

The Redesign of the Housing Program

One of the greatest failings of the OHP was the emphasis it placed on how to provide as many low-cost houses as possible without regard for the way that a house operates within a world of social discourse that is greater than the object itself. A design for building social, cultural, and institutional processes was needed, not a design for producing houses. This approach implied wrenching the concept of design and the culture of designing (as embedded in the bureaucracy and industry concerned with housing) away from its emphasis on the rational production of objects.

The new approach to housing was itself a redesign and might not be considered part of the design of housing in the conventional western and professional sense. The task of providing low-cost housing would involve architecture and industry, but the shift in approach meant that architecture and industry would need to be engaged in the redesign of the cultural and social basis of providing low-cost housing. The question was, Could such a redesign and restructuring of the housing program be accomplished? This issue was what the National Housing and Development Authority (NHDA)—established in 1982 by the prime minister to address housing problems in Sri Lanka—was asked to deal with: the task of rethinking the provision of low-cost housing and settlement upgrading.

Restructuring the Housing Program

The rethinking and eventual restructuring of the low-cost housing program in Sri Lanka was made necessary by the failures of the 100,000 Houses Program and possible by the strong political support of the prime minister, who wanted to make housing a showpiece of his political program. He had decided that housing was an important goal for Sri Lanka both to help solve internal problems and to enhance its international standing (it was he who originally called for the 1987 United Nations Year of Shelter). Success in the area of low-cost housing became important politically as well as socially. The political attention paid to housing was one reason for the appointment in 1982 of a new, energetic, and young group of managers to deal with the housing problem. These new managers were asked to create a new program.

Owing no loyalty to the older 100,000 Houses Program, they were willing and open enough to see its errors and understand the need for a new attitude toward housing. The program they suggested, the 1,000,000 Houses Program (MHP), was to be based on low government investment, minimal levels of direct government intervention, and maximal use of various strategic supports for local and individual initiative.

Political interest and economic necessity combined in the new housing program. The United National Party, ideologically right of center, was attracted by the emphasis on self-help and minimal government intervention. It would give strong support to any program that would lower the general level of government investment.

Moreover, some members of the government saw an opportunity to reframe the relationship of the center to the local settlements. Emphasis on local initiative and local nongovernmental organizations would provide a means for the central government to bypass local political parties in allocating housing supports. This direct access to local actors would increase the power of the executive and decrease the opportunities for corruption by bureaucratic or political middlemen. Direct access to local actors would also be more socially and institutionally appropriate because there would be fewer brokers between the managers of the new program and the local settlements. The MHP slogan "going to the people" was a way of establishing a new cultural design for bureaucratic and productive practice.

With political support for new policies and practices, the managers of the MHP were able to shift the housing program away from the policies of the OHP. The managers decided they had to design, and I emphasize the word *design*, a new way to produce low-cost housing. This new method had to produce as much housing as possible with the lowest possible governmental outlays. Local energies would be harnessed by a redesigned bureaucracy more sensitive to change.

The emphasis on local initiative would bring other dividends to the executive branch of government. It would enable the prime minister to bypass local members of parliament, thus strengthening the prime minister's position. This dividend for some Sri Lankans was the downside of an otherwise positive shift in housing policy for others.

The Process of Redesign: The National Housing Development Authority and the 1,000,000 Houses Program

The story of the housing program after 1983 is the story of a continuous process of design and redesign, of hit-and-run, and of building a way to act and of building an institutional culture rather than a story about building things.

Before any action could be undertaken, the bureaucracy needed to move away from a dependence on academic planning and research, from reliance on contractors, and from an emphasis on houses to an emphasis on action and consideration for local practices. A new ideology was called for. NHDA documents of the period are full of sloganeering. These documents with their calls for a million houses, for learning by acting, and for minimal government intervention and support reveal an agency trying urgently to define and design itself. How successfully they did this remains to be seen although the energy to succeed was, and still is, great.

The NHDA managers decided that they should not assume a definite set of social and economic supports for housing because these supports were neither constant nor passive. The managers also decided they had to examine the conditions under which they would design a housing program. Supports would be defined by the actions of others; that is, local actors would generate housing, but they in turn would be influenced by the actions of the NHDA. Design policy was a way of developing social supports and cultural conditions for local action. Whether or not the NHDA managers consciously accepted this theory, they decided nonetheless that they needed to design a policy that would turn a passive process into an active force by which local energies, skills, and knowledge, along with institutions, would produce housing and further settlement upgrading. Such an approach fitted within the political program of the UNP.

The NHDA team, having decided that it did not want to use old methods and that it did not want to provide houses, had to decide what it did want. The managers concluded that the most critical need was to determine what the problems were with traditional housing. In Sri Lanka there have been several problems with housing in the poorer sectors of society, and these problems vary between the rural and urban context. One critical problem, particularly in urban areas, is the housing infrastructure. Inadequate or nonexistent sewage systems, water supply, toilets, and electrical power are common in the slums and shanty areas. Under the previous housing program, contractors often provided toilets and other infrastructure, but just as often the planners were not sensitive to local needs, either social or technical. Toilets would be provided without adequate sewage or would be placed on main roads where the community could not defend them from strangers. Plumbing was put into four-story apartment buildings but water pressure was too low for it to be used. If urban infrastructure was to be provided, the NHDA had to address both technical and social needs.

Having rejected contractor-built housing, the NHDA managers realized that their emphasis on minimal government intervention meant that they had to rely on traditional local housing as the basis of the 1,000,000 Houses Program. Traditional buildings in the Sri Lankan countryside are made of mud brick, tamped mud, or stone. Mud brick is fine if it has adequate lime-wash exteriors, but mud brick alone will not withstand the annual rains and floods in many areas of Sri Lanka. Traditional dung floors are adequate, but they too can be destroyed by floods. It was found that a mix of concrete in the floors, on the platforms, and three feet around the base of a mud brick building would enable houses to withstand the annual flooding. With only a small investment in nonlocal and nontraditional materials, the NHDA found that it could help provide a house that was less expensive to build but just as practical and habitable (if not more so) as contractor-built concrete houses.

Another problem with traditional houses is the roofing. Traditional roofs are made of coconut and other vegetable fronds. Open hearth fires, which are

most commonly used, ventilate poorly and are a fire hazard in buildings that
have roofs made of fronds. If the kitchen is not in a separate structure, as
is often true with the poor, the problem is considerably worse. When the
NHDA started its study, it found that some people had switched to tin roofing,
but this, though not a fire hazard, does not allow smoke out of the shelter and
intensifies the heat of the tropical sun. One solution to these problems was to
use tile roofs, which breathe and are safe from fire. The problem with tile,
however, is that even though it is a traditional industrial material, it is too
costly for lower-income groups.

The NHDA decided that if small amounts of lime and concrete and larger
amounts of tile, as well as a craftsman's skilled input, were sufficient to construct an improved self-help house, then it could be done with a loan of between R 5,000 and R 7,000, particularly in rural areas. If with this loan people
could use what little savings they had to upgrade the quality of the house design—with wood-carved windows, decorated facades, or a slightly larger than
normal low-cost house—so much the better. A higher quality, safer, healthier,
but locally and culturally appropriate house could be constructed.

There was a hitch, though. The calculation of the cost of construction
assumed that local skilled labor was available and that it could be employed by
local settlements through arrangements that were affordable and appropriate
to the community. This was a crucial assumption in conceiving the design of
the new policy. Local skilled labor, necessary for carpentry and masonry,
would cost less than outside hired labor and in some instances might be hired
in a labor exchange or on a volunteer basis for reasons of religion, community, or kinship. All other labor would be supplied by the family for whom a
house was meant. Unfortunately, in some areas of Sri Lanka, masons and
other skilled craftsmen have been in short supply. Many were working in
Bahrain, Saudi Arabia, and other foreign countries. Where the needed skilled
labor was not available in adequate numbers it had to be generated through
some form of training program. The design of housing was now attached to
the issue of local occupational development.

The cost of construction would also be critically affected by the local
availability of construction materials. Although tile is an indigenous product,
it was no longer manufactured locally in all of Sri Lanka. In some areas, too,
the hardwood for structural frames and windows was also no longer available.
For both tile and hardwood, local manufacturing industries had to be sought
out and developed. The quest for improved housing under the NHDA scheme
became involved with the whole process of local redevelopment and, in the
planners' terms, "community reawakening."

Two interesting strategies, among others, were used to create the necessary material supports for the housing program. They are illustrative of how the NHDA attached housing policy to local social and cultural institutions with an eye toward greater development of the local economy as well as low-cost housing. In one rural community, skilled craftsmen were given support by the *gramodoya mandela*, a local nongovernmental association, through an NHDA grant for development of small-scale industries that were to serve as training centers as well. In one large urban settlement, local small-scale entrepreneurs and craftsmen joined to underwrite the productive efforts of families being given plots on which to build homes using advice and small loans from the NHDA. Both of these cases effectively endorsed the NHDA policy of using locally rooted institutions to provide the basis for the production of low-cost housing.

The key problem that appeared intractable in the 100,000 Houses Program remained—how to allocate new housing effectively without disrupting the local community and how to provide the means to assure that monies would be well spent and that the government would not be financially exhausted by granting loans for housing and upgrading that would not be recoverable. The effective allocation of housing would depend upon a proper understanding of local social cohesion and community relations. Ethnic differences, caste, and class relations and their relation to the organization of place in the local community were important factors that would influence the success of the housing program in any given settlement. Allocation of housing based on an improper analysis of how local social organization and cultural understandings operated might rend a community asunder or, as in one village, lead to a solution whereby new housing was left unoccupied by villagers because the central government was insensitive to local custom. In urban areas, the problem of allocation is also a function of equitable location and property value.

How to allocate housing has to this day remained a problem for the NHDA. In rural areas, the government relied on local people such as the local members of Parliament and chairmen of nongovernmental organizations. Self-help and direct local involvement in the housing process contributed to the reduction of local conflicts. In urban shanty towns, the problem of how to give tenure equitably to land that is unevenly divided still remains. NHDA policy has been to limit each shanty dweller to a specified amount of land, to reallocate land to those who are below the cut-off, and to take away land from those who are above. Problems of value, location, use, proximity to major thoroughfares, and access have not been entirely resolved, and it is not

clear that they will be. Issues of allocation are so deeply rooted in social relations, politics, and social and economic ecology that a simple solution is not
forthcoming. Suffice it to say that, in most instances, local participation has
helped considerably in avoiding the worst of problems.

The issue of loan recovery has been generally more tractable than the
issue of allocation and has served as a test of the ideological commitment of
the NHDA to locally appropriate action. Loan recovery has also been a key
part of the NHDA strategy for mobilizing local energies and local actors to
organize the production and upgrading of housing in the local communities.
The problem of loan recovery thus has become part of the larger problem of
locally appropriate organizing.

Two examples from the rural sector illustrate the use by the NHDA of
appropriate local organizations to underwrite settlement upgrading effectively
and guarantee by NHDA standards a reasonable degree of loan recovery. The
two examples are also illustrations of what an open-ended bureaucratic strategy relying on local initiative meant to the NHDA. The culture of locally
appropriate action needed the support of an open bureaucratic culture in
Colombo. The programmatic notion developed to account for this need for
openness was defined as an "options policy." In the countryside, one major
option the NHDA had for allocating loans and otherwise organizing the housing program was to work with the gramodoya mandelas (GM) and their
chairmen. The GMs are composed of the local nongovernmental organizations. The chairmen of the member groups elect a GM chairman, who is
usually an individual of some local importance, often what has been called a
"culture broker," and who is able to act as an intermediary between local
needs and national programs. In communities that have no such leader, the
NHDA has developed a local leadership training program. Some GM chairmen are motivated by the ideals of Buddhist charity and others by political
aspirations. Whatever the reasons, the energy and skill the GM chairmen provide offer a useful organizational basis for the housing program and have not
been underestimated by various regional directors of the NHDA.

The NHDA assumed that it could make loan monies available to the GM
and that the chairman would distribute these fairly and effectively. It also assumed that because the gramodoya mandelas are small, they would be sensitive to local conditions. If the GM chairman acted unfairly or dishonestly,
he or she would be either defeated for reelection or caught. NHDA managers
also have argued that GM chairmen are usually the most resourceful and
well-connected members of the community. Thus, a housing program is best
left in such hands. The risk was, however, that the NHDA would also be
creating a new power and new form of authority in the community as well.

The GM system has worked well where there has been an active, intelligent, and honest chairman. One particularly successful GM saw to the completion of 250 houses, some training centers for masons and carpenters, an Ayuvedic hospital wing, and a monastery all in less than a year. In this case, judicious and centralized buying, exchange labor, clever use of skilled laborers, and the energies of the GM chairman were central to the success of the project.

What the NHDA has found is that a process that occurs in one community may not be replicable in another. Thus, the program indicates a need for flexibility. NHDA managers found most GMs in rural areas were effective instruments of policy implementation. In some areas where the GMs were not effective, NHDA district managers attempted to reform them. In other areas they decided to shift gears and utilize social and cultural opportunities available in the local community—even if at times such actions challenged bureaucratic policy in Colombo. In Kandy district, for example, a particularly important area of Sri Lanka historically and politically, the importance of caste profoundly affected the capacity of GM organizations to act. GM chairmen were often unwilling to make decisions for fear of being accused of caste favoritism, and so they did what for them was the obvious thing, nothing. This paralysis forced the NHDA district manager to look elsewhere for a local group with which he could work to upgrade housing in the area. What he found was a series of active local Thrift and Cooperative Societies in which poorer groups of the population participated. He used these groups to help allocate and collect loans and to guide the generation of housing.

Thrift Societies are small-scale mutual savings societies which, while informal, are recognized in law. Locally run by the membership, and existing in Kandy for over eighty years, Thrift Societies were the one self-run monetary organization small enough, as well as ethnically and caste specific enough, to be able to allocate loans given to them by the NHDA.

Thrift Societies in Kandy could also organize volunteer labor and labor exchange and hire skilled labor to encourage proper building and expedite the construction of housing in the community. The allocation of loans was based on local and traditional modes of resource provision and was less disruptive of local social relations than the more centralized or bureaucratic modes of resource delivery. Thrifts, it might be added, have so far organized the most efficient programs of house building, loan recovery, and loan reuse of any institution, locally or centrally based.

In urban areas the role of the NHDA was more complex. Groups other than gramodoya mandelas and thrift societies, such as local action groups, leadership clinics, and other alliances of local actors and NHDA officers, had to be developed. In one slum community I visited, for example, NHDA was linked with a Muslim Club. In another, a local UNICEF group might be the crucial link.

In urban areas, the sense of the possible and locally appropriate guided what has been called by the NHDA "action planning." The NHDA found that traditional planners, with their strong emphasis on demographic researches, mapping, and planning, were slow to complete a project. What was needed was a scheme to equalize land distribution and give people land tenure as well as encourage people to upgrade their houses and settlements. The process is imperfect but workable, and the effects realized in new urban infrastructure, improved and new houses, and a community with tenure in their land and homes, has been measured a success by the NHDA. Technical officers from the NHDA work with the urban settlements to develop local skills, expedite the bureaucratic process, and give advice about building. Land tenure and upgrading appear to have given people a greater sense of responsibility toward new infrastructure, specifically, toilets, sewers, and paths, but the results are too new to be complete. Demonstration communities are being developed to examine different ways to create housing and local settlements. Here learning and acting run parallel.

Learning and acting at the same time implies a certain acceptance of spontaneity and risk. Although not at issue for local people building their own housing and upgrading their own settlements, it raises a crucial issue for the NHDA—how to create a bureaucracy that is sympathetic to the process of redesigning and restructuring housing policy as local culture and social conditions demand.

One would like to assume that local actors in self-help housing will be able to organize their communities, allocate resources given by the NHDA, pay back loans, and keep reasonable records. Issues of house construction in urban areas where people have no traditional housing forms or modes for community infrastructure, problems of cost and appropriate use of new materials in both rural and urban areas, where applicable, advice on house construction (the NHDA trusts traditional builders to build desirable and appropriate housing in concert with the family for whom the house is to be built), and other technical, legal, and political issues are not always best dealt with by local groups alone. To deal with these problems and yet remain true to the new ideology of self-help and minimal intervention, the NHDA managers realized that the housing bureaucracy needed to be transformed.

Because bureaucracies are more often committed to inertia than to taking risks, the NHDA designed a program to give more responsibility to district managers and local junior technical officers. These JTOs as they are called, trained as architects and planners, were set up in offices in the local communities. They were set up in local offices for two reasons: to decentralize and thus limit the Colombo bureaucracy, and to put the planners among the people where they could become more sensitive to local needs and realities. It was hoped that as a part of the community, technical officers would begin to identify with local interest and not accept everything they were told from Colombo.

The presence of technical officers in the rural villages and urban slum and shanty areas has had the added benefit of giving local people a sense of the NHDAs commitment and concern. The JTO thus encumbered with the role of good officer can act as a countervailing force to the local GM chairman or other local leader. JTOs can help in the planning of construction and local allocation of funds, and they can represent local interests to the bureaucracy in Colombo. JTOs can offer new possibilities and choices in the design of houses or local settlements and can give advice on costs and materials. They can also inform Colombo of local successes and building strategies. The JTO and district manager system gives more active energy to the NHDA program and symbolizes the NHDA commitment to local housing. While JTOs have been enthusiastic about the program, there still exists resistance to local initiative among part of the government bureaucracy in Colombo.

The chief threat to the 1,000,000 Houses Program I have noted has been the lack of trust by government and international agencies aiding the program in the openness and local spontaneity associated with the program. These agencies still seek to use more instrumental rather than locally derived means to carry out the program. Although in the first year of the 1,000,000 Houses Program over 79,000 houses were either upgraded or built, there were by 1985 signs that the NHDA experiment was being slowed by the use of more traditional, bureaucratic models for dealing with housing problems.

For example, one important international agency looked at the success of the Thrift Societies and immediately wanted to use them as a model for action in the urban areas of Sri Lanka where no such institution exists. The agency ignored local knowledge and experience in its desire to replicate, even in possibly inappropriate circumstances, a model of a system viewed as successful without regard for the context in which it is successful. This international agency ignored the fact that Thrifts work where local cultural understandings and social relationships have embedded notions of mutual saving, cooperation, and trust. Thrifts also assume a narrow cultural, ethnic, and caste alliance or some other traditional cultural mode or institution for social cohesion that is usually lacking in urban areas, particularly those settled recently (and where problems of poor housing exist).

In one newly created model self-help community in Colombo, the size of settlement cluster, location, and specific design issues, important to bureaucracies and easy to model, were found to be less important in defining how well the settlement cluster was organized, managed, and maintained than the social and cultural mix of people in the cluster. The residents of the best managed and best maintained cluster redesigned the way the cluster was used and were able to manage its housing and cluster infrastructure well because, coincidentally, the cluster was settled by a group that had previously lived together and created its own mutual savings society.

Cultural and social issues clearly form the crucible within which houses become the stuff of which everyday life is made. Houses themselves, no matter how well built and designed (and certainly people desire well-built and appropriately designed housing), still are only artifacts and parts of other pieces of the cultural fabric of human settlement.

For the agencies in charge of housing in Sri Lanka to forget this, be they international or national, would endanger the whole programmatic thrust of the 1,000,000 Houses Program and would make of it another version of the 100,000 Houses Program. In the latter case, it was the cost of the house which destroyed the program; in the 1,000,000 Houses Program case reliance on locally inappropriate models would require too heavy administrative costs to run programs grounded more in a bureaucratic culture than local culture.

Conclusion

What we can learn from this case, as the originators of the NHDA experiment have learned, is that to design new low-cost houses it is necessary to confront the conditions under which design occurs. The design of social supports, programs for action, and new modes of practice becomes imperative. So too, does the redesign of the culture and ideology of international experts and government bureaucrats.

The Sri Lankan experience suggests new rules for those dealing with housing as architects, anthropologists, community planners, or housing specialists. It demands new definitions of design and its relation to action and artifact. It also suggests that we need to develop a way to learn from each experience without universalizing the outcome or model of practice in instrumental and bureaucratically attractive terms. We need a sense of the generally shared with a knowledge of the locally specific. This suggests the need to reinvent and rethink how we view the world of housing and what we know houses to be. We need a way to create possibilities, not outcomes, and a way to learn while we act, not act on what we already presume we know.

What we also glean from the Sri Lankan experience is an understanding that housing is a complex world of cultural action and material practices and not merely an artifact. Thus, to think about the design and production of a house is to think about the values, policies, practices, and processes of a culture which, in a sense, gives birth to the house and, in a paraphrase of Louis Kahn, lets housing be what it wants to be.

I would like to thank the MIT/NHDA Design of Housing Program for their support, which enabled me to undertake interviews and hold visits in Sri Lanka during October and November 1985.

Notes

1. In Colombo, the word *slum* normally refers to a more substantial and permanent form of housing than does the word *shantytown*.

References

Brow, J. n.d. Community or settlement: Buildings and their effect. Unpublished manuscript.

5
GENTRIFICATION: THE REDEFINITION OF URBAN NEIGHBORHOOD

RICHARD J. DENT

Gentrification, the word itself and the phenomenon it describes, has become almost a symbol of an era. And the only consensus on the value or impact of gentrification typically emerges relative to its effects on various groups along the socioeconomic spectrum; it can be viewed as either the best or the worst aspect of change to cities today. The variety of terms seen in the corpus of literature to describe this process reflects such a chameleonic view. The term for the phenomenon is transmutable from gentrification in the negative state to neighborhood revitalization in the positive sense. There seems to be no neutral connotation. In placing the word *gentrification* in the title of this chapter, I have already revealed a bias. While a concern for the less fortunate who are impacted by gentrification is not particularly unusual in this type of research, my position that everyone suffers with gentrification, not only the poor, is unique. A goal of this research is to convince others of this perspective.

The term *gentrification* originated in Great Britain, as early as 1963, to label the process by which formerly working-class areas of London were being resettled and transformed by members of higher socioeconomic classes (Hammett and Williams 1980). This process began to reverse a decline in the physical condition of housing stock and public perception of the city. The term *gentrification* was quickly adopted to describe this situation. Since that time, many have realized that the word *gentrification*, with its etymological implication of a wealthy gentry abandoning its manor houses to reclaim the city, is not descriptive of the overall situation. Gentrification is primarily not the realm of the very wealthy. This fact has caused some critics to suggest that such phrases as neighborhood resettlement, neighborhood revitalization, and the like, are more appropriate. Call it what you with—whatever words are ultimately chosen to label the process, it and its impacts are significant on a worldwide basis.

To understand gentrification is to understand the way in which people have traditionally perceived the establishment and evolution of urban neighborhoods, areas that were originally populated by people of the middle or upper socioeconomic classes. As Gale (1984) and others have commented, woven throughout our concept of these neighborhoods is the theme of ultimate decline. For many years, social scientists have shared with the general public a notion that assumes all neighborhoods eventually decline in both physical condition and value with increasing age; such an assumption is usually labeled a "filtering theory." As this decline progresses, the older neighborhood becomes populated by people at the lower end of the economic scale, who replace the original inhabitants. This process has long been viewed as an inevitable feature of most neighborhoods.

Gentrification is the upset of this trend or belief. Since the early 1960s, in many cities what could simply be called reverse filtering began to occur. This consisted of middle- and sometimes upper-income people purchasing, renovating, and moving back into formerly declining urban neighborhoods. Instead of moving "upward" to progressively more affluent areas, these groups began to filter downward to older neighborhoods, originally established in the early twentieth, nineteenth, or sometimes even late eighteenth centuries. This trend, amusing to many at first, began to have a significant impact on many urban neighborhoods.

Gentrification, as stated previously, can be viewed either as detrimental to the overall quality of urban life or as a positive force in cities today. The adoption of either view is usually dependent on what socioeconomic group one chooses to sympathize with as well as what level on the scale of analysis benefit as against cost is assessed. In terms of much of the indigenous population of an urban neighborhood that is in the process of being gentrified, the effects are often disastrous. From the point of view of the resettling population, the gentrifiers, there are distinct social and monetary benefits to be seen. For the city itself, an assessment is more difficult. There are benefits to the city from, among other things, a rising tax base as well as increased commercial and tourist activity. On the other hand, much of the increased flow of revenue into city coffers is drawn down by the cost of services necessary to sustain the displaced who huddle at the artifact's edges. Each of these points deserves some elaboration, albeit brief in this context.

For many inhabitants of a neighborhood in the process of being gentrified, market pressures created by a simple excess of demand over supply of available housing stock starts a cycle over which low- or fixed-income people have almost no control. Working-class owners may be an exception to this trajectory, however much of the indigenous population is typically a renting population. They are, in many cases, displaced when housing units are purchased and either returned to single-family use or renovated and leased for more than the original inhabitants can afford. The demand on this limited supply of housing stock is also exacerbated by investors who arrive to speculate. In the end, the unfortunate are left without housing they can afford in an environment of housing unit restoration, followed by increasing tax rates and high sales or rental costs. This is the negative side of gentrification.

In the terms of the gentrifying population, the picture, at least in the short term, is brighter. By taking some risks, these groups of people often occupy houses and create neighborhoods with a unique social, historical, and architectural ambience. Gentrification often goes hand-in-hand with what is broadly known as the preservation movement. The neighborhoods have an additional advantage of being located within the city, often close to centers of employment, entertainment, and other leisure activities. Potential return on original investment, which need not consist solely of hard capital, is also very high.

For the city itself, the process of gentrification is ultimately a mixed blessing. In many ways this fact has allowed government agencies almost to ignore, in an official sense, the problem. Large or festering problems are addressed through city politics; small or equivocal problems are ignored. Initially, cities welcomed the increasing property value assessments and concomitant tax yield of gentrified neighborhoods within its boundaries. Such a stance is understandable given the financial condition of most cities in recent times. Corresponding with this increased revenue, however, was the need for cities to divert at least some of these monies to provide basic services, such as public housing, welfare, and the like, to a large population that had become destitute and displaced. Gentrifiers themselves, especially in a mature transformed neighborhood, also make demands for increased services and improvements to a decayed infrastructure. In fact, overall one could argue that the balance between increased revenue and increased expenditure is ultimately precarious for a city's treasury.

The foregoing illustrates that gentrification has both a positive and a negative side. In most analyses of the situation to date, researchers choose to focus on the negative impacts on the indigenous population of an urban neighborhood, who become the victims of a process over which they have little control. One can find little fault in social scientists seeking to expose and mitigate these circumstances. Other research on gentrification is essentially value free in viewing it as an almost natural phenomenon. In my research, however, I hope to demonstrate, through an examination of gentrification as a cultural process, that unabated gentrification ultimately does harm to more than only the poor and displaced.

Cultural Perceptions of Neighborhood

At this point, it is appropriate to reveal another bias in my interpretation of the gentrification process. I approach the problem as an archaeologist and anthropologist. As an archaeologist I study material culture and its relationship to people and culture. In my case this relationship typically rests in prehistory, but there is good reason to believe such an analysis can also be undertaken with our own society (see, for example, Rathje 1978; Rathje and Schiffer 1980). It is therefore one of my goals to examine housing literally as an artifact of ourselves.

To accomplish this objective, I draw on the arguments of a classic paper on artifact analysis by Binford (1962). Binford states that an archaeologist, as an anthropologist, should be able to understand artifacts in terms of the different meanings they take on within a society. In short, any object of material culture often assumes different meanings in different contexts. Archaeology thus set off in search of technomic, sociotechnic, and ideotechnic artifacts. Technomic artifacts are objects that are used primarily to cope directly with the environment. Sociotechnic artifacts provide the means of articulating individuals with one another into cohesive social groups. Ideotechnic artifacts have a rather murky functional context in the ideological component of a cultural system. Any single artifact may occupy more than one of these realms; boundaries are not fast. The point is that housing, as an artifact of the gentrification process, is assigned different meanings by different groups of people. Furthermore, people manipulate these meanings in the gentrification process.

The perspective can be applied to housing in an urban neighborhood. To most of the indigenous population of any ungentrified neighborhood, housing simply is a technomic artifact. It provides shelter and refuge from the elements. Often it can also represent a sociotechnic artifact in the sense of reflecting a shared condition and worldview of the inhabitants of a neighborhood. For gentrifiers, housing and a gentrified neighborhood is all this and more.

It is my contention that housing stock and indeed entire neighborhoods are, in the process of gentrification, turned into ideotechnic artifacts of ourselves and our society. Ideology, and by extension ideotechnic artifacts, represents the imaginary relations of individuals to the real relations in which they live, and it operates at a subconscious level (Althusser 1971, 1977). Ideo-

technic artifacts, therefore, are material representations of society concep-
tualizing itself. Many objects are called upon to furnish this service. For
example, the nostalgic dream almost everyone thinks they possess for Mom's
apple pie serves a similar purpose. The ideological component of the pie enters in, however, when we realize that of the many who now dream of Mom's
apple pie, clearly a good many never really liked apple pie, a few more did not
like Mom's apple pie, and some never liked Mom herself. This is ideology
writ large.

Gentrifiers, in this same sense, turn their environment into an ideotechnic artifact of a past of their own creation. For example, a simple late-
nineteenth-century row house two decades ago was shelter to an indigenous
inhabitant of an ungentrified neighborhood. Today this same late-nineteenth-
century structure, now renovated with the obligatory eight-panel stained door
complete with brass pineapple knocker and letter slot, ferns in the window, an
ample supply of Perrier in the refrigerator, and a BMW or Volvo automobile
parked in front, is an ideotechnic artifact. It has been transformed into a
townhouse, and block after block of the same thing is a gentrified neighborhood. To explain why we create ideotechnic artifacts would involve a lengthy
discourse. One of the major reasons in this context, however, is that through
gentrification we create an artifact that ideologically represents, among other
things, a more pure and simple time and thus helps us to rationalize the contradictions of what we perceive to be the present chaos that surrounds us
(MacCannell 1976). Detailed descriptions of this process have been offered by
Middleton (1977) as well as Rowntree and Conkey (1980).

By looking at gentrification in this manner, one can begin to expose the
ways in which material culture is an active agent in the production of social
relations. In the remainder of this chapter, I would like to focus on a more
detailed description of how the gentrification process operates. It is my contention that by understanding this process of creating ideotechnic artifacts one
can see the dangers of gentrification for all, not just the materially unfortunate, and also begin to understand how and why gentrification should be
controlled.

The Gentrification Process

As mapped by various urban planners and sociologists,
the process of gentrification can be broken down into distinct phases. I particularly like the typology offered by Gale (1980) and employ an exegesis of his
research herein. Gale's phases, forming a somewhat evolutionary trajectory,
are referred to here as the pioneer phase (stage one), the frontier phase (stage

two), and the gentrified or resettled neighborhood phase (stage three). These phases or stages can also be further defined according to the risks taken by people in their participation in this process.

There are many urban neighborhoods that contain architecturally and historically significant housing stock occupied by people situated on the lower end of the socioeconomic scale. In this neighborhood, property values are typically low or declining and structures are deteriorating. During the pioneer phase a few "risk-oblivious" households move into what many would uncharitably refer to as this ghetto or slum. Generally these resettlers, almost always single or a childless couple, share a common desire for self-expression or wish to avoid the sense of rejection likely in an attitudinally homogeneous or more conventional neighborhood. These risk-oblivious people all share a propensity to overlook the obvious risks to their person, their property, and their pocketbooks in moving into such a declining environment.

The risk-oblivious residents usually integrate themselves well with the incumbent residents. The incumbent residents actually perceive little, if any, threat from these urban pioneers since their numbers are modest. Also, there is very little displacement, because the dwellings purchased by the newcomers are usually those that become available through abandonment or normal market turnovers. The incumbents therefore show little overt hostility to the pioneers, and both groups often embrace each other with some relish.

Soon other people, through various mechanisms, begin to "discover" the neighborhood in which resettlement has been initiated by the pioneers. The next phase then commences with "risk-conscious" households moving into what is now an urban frontier (stage two). These risk-conscious households are well aware of the chances they take in purchasing and occupying older properties, but they take the chance because both price and investment potential are promising. Another attractive feature of this urban frontier is most certainly the cultural, historical, and architectural characteristics of the neighborhood. Although many of these frontier households complain about their indigenous neighbors' poor property maintenance, lack of respect for public and private property, and incivility, they adjust their routines to minimize vulnerability and try to adopt a tolerant attitude toward matters over which they have little control. An important paradox, however, becomes increasingly evident. Frontier resettlers profess to like a racially or ethnically mixed neighborhood, yet this preference is often in direct conflict with both their economic goals for their property and their sense of security and peace of mind.

At this stage of the gentrification process, the first signs of organized resistance by indigenous residents are also likely to occur. This tension is brought about by the growing rate and effects of immigration of middle- and upper-income people into the neighborhood. Unfortunately, inexorable market pressure engendered by a scarcity of available housing stock starts a process over which many incumbents have little control. They start to be forced out of the neighborhood at an unprecedented rate.

The gentrifiers of the urban frontier also make attempts to organize the neighborhood. The common themes in this effort include protection of the historical identity of the neighborhood, protection of property values, upgrading of public services, improvements of schools, and so on. Often the neighborhood seeks recognition as a historic entity of some sort in an effort to protect its various interests. In this manner, the group also becomes recognized by city officials as an organized interest group that can deliver votes. By the end of this phase, most indigenous renters have been forced out by market pressures, and even those who are fortunate enough to own often eventually succumb to the demands of a historic preserve that legally mandates costly renovation and restoration above barely tolerable stabilization. In a cultural sense, the neighborhood is also no longer attractive to many of the indigenous inhabitants. With almost all of the indigenous population gone, the prestige of the neighborhood becomes well established. During this phase (stage three), people who are risk adverse enter on a very large scale, because they are safe in investing and residing in an area where risks to property and person are not great.

The above characterization is drawn from some very insightful research by Gale (1980). Others have offered similar and sometimes more specific analyses (for example, Henig 1982). No matter how one describes the process, gentrification has taken a neighborhood from the realm of the technomic and moved it into the realm of the ideotechnic. We have seen the trajectory and some of the effects of this process. It is now appropriate to examine more fully just how this transformation is brought about. From this point we are moving beyond most traditional analyses of the gentrification process.

Thompson (1979) uses the term "rubbish theory" to explain how objects of material culture move from, in the terminology of this study, the technomic to the ideotechnic realm. Thompson's research is based on the assumption that our society assigns objects to one or the other of two overt categories: transient or durable. Objects in the durable category increase in value over time and ideally have nearly infinite lifespans, while objects in the transient category decrease in value over time and have relatively finite lifespans. These two categorical objects demonstrate that there is an obvious relationship between our view of the world and our actions in that world. The interesting question about the gentrification process is How does a formerly transient object, such as a simple late-nineteenth-century urban row house, become transformed into a durable object, a late-nineteenth-century townhouse, and hence become a component of a historic gentrified neighborhood?

According to Thompson (1979), there is a third category, one that is covert and is labeled rubbish. The central precept of rubbish theory is that this covert rubbish category is not subject to societal control (see Figure 5.1), and so it is able to provide the path for a seemingly impossible transformation of an object from transience to durability. In an ideal world, a transient object, such as the technomic late-nineteenth-century urban row house, should gradually decline in value and in expected lifespan and then slide into rubbish eventually to disappear in the dust of the wrecker's ball. But in reality, it very often just continues to exist in an almost valueless limbo (rubbish) until it is later discovered, through gentrification, and transferred into durability in the form of a late-nineteenth-century townhouse of a gentrified neighborhood. Its resurrection makes it an ideotechnic artifact and it now takes its place as a part of the crème de la crème of the city's structural landscape and historic patrimony. What kind of mechanism lies behind the transformation of an object from transient to rubbish to durable?

During the pioneer phase (stage one), gentrifiers seem to be on what for lack of better words may be described as a "Bohemian trip." They initiate something they probably had no intention of initiating. In fact, once the neighborhood is completely gentrified it very often loses its original purpose for them and they often must change their life-style or move on. The frontier resettlers (stage two) really start the massive transformation of housing stock from rubbish to durable. In doing this, their goal of living in a socially diverse neighborhood is forfeited as they successfully turn the neighborhood toward durability in their efforts to enhance their investment and way of life.

In the examination of the problem thus far, we see the symptoms and not the causes. It is important to understand why the transformation from transient to rubbish to durable (technomic to ideotechnic) is allowed. Figure 5.2 maps the possibilities for object transfer in three broad types of society. The three types are plotted on x- and y-coordinates defined by the amount of stratification and competition characteristic of each. Regions between these three types represent the amount of manipulation of the meaning of any object typical to each type. It is important to note that the three societal types (caste, class, and egalitarian) should be viewed only as extremes and that they probably never exist in a pure sense in any real social situation. It is a fact, however, that a given society, including our own, periodically can shift in the direction of any of the three types. History, even very recent history, documents such shifts. And I think the diagram tells us something about gentrification.

Since the early 1960s, society seems to have shifted toward the egalitarian extreme on Figure 5.2. This shift has allowed a substantial transformation of objects from the rubbish to the durable category; that is, from technomic to ideotechnic realms. People, most often in the middle range of the socio-economic spectrum, have employed the gentrification process as a mechanism to consolidate economic gain. As socioeconomic class boundaries are relaxed or softened, gentrification is an especially attractive path of movement because it can often be taken with moderate amounts of cash investment, supplemented with personal labor and some risk. In a more exploitive sense, speculators, with ready capital, find the process an attractive return on investment dollars. Whether one is an investor or an individual, the economics of gentrification make sense.

Throughout this chapter I have attempted to illustrate the link between gentrification and history. It is a significant link and a partnership that takes gentrifiers beyond the level of a purely economic species: people who know the cost of everything and the value of nothing. I believe that since the 1960s, the pace of society, the changes it has undergone, and the uncertainties of the era are forces that have turned society toward the past. Gentrification creates a mechanism by which to enter the past. This past is an opiate to the complexities of everyday life; it represents purer and simpler times (MacCannell 1976). While we standardly visit the past as tourists, gentrification allows us quite literally to live in a past of our own creation. It is a reflection of the past serving the present (see Handsman 1977). This paradox affects all of society, and we return to the original argument that gentrification carries dangers for all.

Implications and Solutions

It is now possible to outline all of the problems of and two possible solutions to the gentrification process. I think it is fair to state that every investigator of this phenomenon sees in unabated gentrification at least some danger to the people whose lives are disrupted and at times shattered by this process—much of the population of the original neighborhood. This is the standard argument against encouraging or allowing gentrification. It is a strong argument and one we would do well to heed. In this study, however, I am arguing that there are other dangers in addition to those facing the indigenous population.

If the significant transformation of housing stock from rubbish to durable (technomic to ideotechnic) continues, we will eventually have no durable or ideotechnic category. That is, the durable or ideotechnic category, which is a very necessary category, will begin to dissipate and collapse when it comes to contain everything, yet really nothing. Hence, gentrification will cause history to disappear because everything will be historic and society in general will lose its bearing on the past. Although such an argument may seem rather far-fetched to those who ignore the need for a past, it is valid and signifies the disruption of an important force of rationalization in everyday life. We will live in an environment of sanitized historical ghettos.

Second, even if society has this great a need for so many ideotechnic artifacts of itself, problems of another sort begin to arise. In a mature gentrified neighborhood, property values become astronomical and property taxes rapidly escalate. These results alone cause many of the original pioneers and urban frontier resettlers to abandon a neighborhood they struggled to create. With the gentrified neighborhood firmly established, developers also start to compete for valuable sites in or near the neighborhood, bringing with them architectural monotony (sometimes architectural blasphemy) that further compromises the character of the artifact. Commercialism arrives to exploit a group of established consumers who live within the boundaries of the neighborhood or visitors who come to partake in area activities. Capital facilities, such as new highway construction and rapid transit stations, along with McDonalds, Burger Kings, and complexes of stores offering the items of this new way of life now must be fought. A recent editorial on the op-ed page of the *Washington Post* (March 1985) citing the danger of the entire country's becoming one big chocolate chip cookie emanating from a plethora of small trendy shops is tongue-in-cheek evidence of concern over this problem. On the more serious side, city government must also establish at least some public housing, treatment centers, and the like, to give minimal aid to the destitute. In short, something has been created that eventually loses its original purpose.

Solutions to this gentrification problem have not been forthcoming. It is a problem that will probably continue to defy both regulation and influxes of aid in the traditional manner. In the former case, most gentrification moves forward incrementally and with private money until it reaches some sort of critical mass and creates a problem larger than the sum of its parts. To legislate against private activity, usually individual or family activity, is difficult if not undesirable. In the latter case, sufficient aid to construct new neighborhoods for the displaced seems too massive for most governments to consider seriously and is often doomed to failure anyway. I offer two very direct, radical suggestions based on this study.

First, we could do nothing. It is a contention of this research that the problem may well begin to take care of itself. That is, society today seems to be shifting in terms of the diagram offered in Figure 5.2. It is becoming more stratified, and competition is becoming more intense. As stated above, the boundaries of the durable, rubbish, and transient categories change and crystallize in response to larger forces. Since less competition and stratification allow people to manipulate meanings, more competition and stratification will slow the creation of ideotechnic artifacts and the gentrification process will ameliorate.

Second, we could use regulation or incentive to keep property owners from allowing housing stock to slip into rubbish in the first place. That is, society could legislate transience and thereby maintain housing as a technomic artifact. The key to this solution is to provide intervention before and not after the fact, as we traditionally do. According to this research, aid after gentrification begins does little more than ease the conscience of the more fortunate.

Conclusion

In this chapter I have attempted to show that the gentrification process carries dangers not just to the unfortunate but to us all. I hope that my approach challenges the myth that allows society, if it is willing to forget the poor, to encourage gentrification. I have also made two suggestions about ultimately controlling gentrification. One is that it may control itself, and the other is that if we wish to address the problem directly with regulation or aid, such a solution will only work if the regulation or aid is activated before, and not after, the fact. One solution will save money and the other will not waste it. Both deserve consideration.

Earlier versions of this chapter were read as papers at the University of Maryland, College Park, Anthropology Colloquium, the Middle Atlantic Archaeological Society, and at the Society for Applied Anthropology. Useful comments on this topic have been offered by William Stuart, Michael Agar, Erve Chambers, Nancie Gonzalez, Mark Leone, and Setha Low. I, of course, accept ultimate responsibility for all statements made herein.

References

Althusser, L. 1971. *Lenin and philosophy.* New York: Random House.
———. 1977. *For Marx.* Surrey, Eng.: Unwin Brothers Limited.
Binford, L. 1962. Archaeology as anthropology. *American Antiquity* 28:217–25.
Gale, D. 1980. Middle class resettlement in older urban neighborhoods: The evidence and the implications. *Journal of the American Planning Association* 45:293–304.
———. 1984. *Neighborhood revitalization and the postindustrial city.* Lexington, Ky.: Lexington Books.

Hammett, C., and P. R. Williams. 1980. Social change in London: A study of gentrification. *Urban Affairs Quarterly* 15:12–21.

Handsman, R. 1977. Muddles in the movement: The preservation of masks in Litchfield, Connecticut. *Artifacts* 6:6–9.

Henig, J. R. 1982. *Gentrification in Adams Morgan*. Washington, D.C.: George Washington University Studies.

MacCannell, D. 1976. *The tourist: A new theory of the leisure class*. New York: Schocken Books.

Middleton, I. S. 1977. *A symbolic interaction approach to place meanings in a historic district*. Ann Arbor: University Microfilms 78-4033.

Rathje, W. L. 1978. Le projet du garbage 1975: Historic trade-offs. In *Social archaeology*, ed. C. L. Redman et al., 373–80. New York: Academic Press.

Rathje, W. L., and M. B. Schiffer. 1980. *Archaeology*. New York: Harcourt Brace Jovanovich.

Rowntree, L. B., and M. W. Conkey. 1980. Symbolism and the cultural landscape. *Annals of the Association of American Geographers* 70:459–74.

Thompson, M. 1979. *Rubbish theory: The creation and destruction of value*. New York: Oxford University Press.

transfer

—————— possible

------ unlikely

Figure 5.1. Object categories and possible transfers (from Thompson 1979).

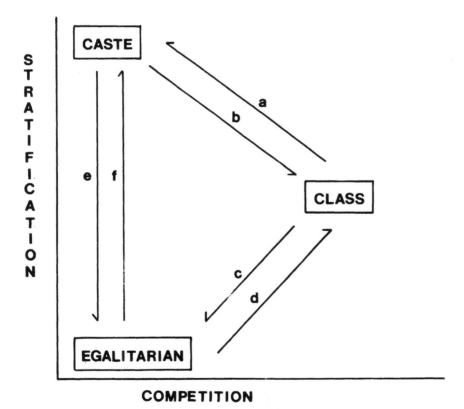

Figure 5.2. Society types and possibilities for object transfers: **(a)** no transfer through rubbish category; **(b)** controlled transfer through rubbish category; **(c)** uncontrolled transfer through rubbish category, durable category disappears; **(d)** emergence of durable category, controlled transfer from rubbish category; **(e)** uncontrolled transfer from rubbish category; **(f)** no transfer from rubbish category (from Thompson 1979).

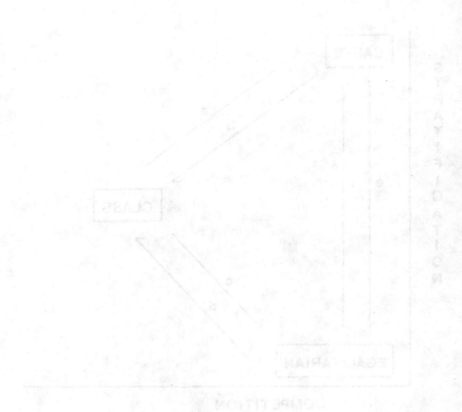

PART TWO

CULTURE AS
COGNITION
PERCEPTION, PATTERN,
AND SPATIAL
STRUCTURE OF HOUSING

The relationships between housing and culture can be studied as a cognitive system composed of rules or codes that govern spatial arrangements. These cultural rules can be conceptualized as a cognitive or structural "map" of the physical environment that determines the appropriateness of spatial relationships and the acceptance of built forms. They might also be seen as sets of contextual, mental attitudes that define sociocultural boundaries. Cognitive research in housing and design has included contextual analyses of vernacular architecture, ethnosemantic studies of design forms and details, perceptual and behavioral analyses of changing environments, and the elicitation of "projections," such as mental maps, which reveal the cognitive structure of an environment.

The chapters in this part focus on case studies of cultural cognition, perception, and behavior. They are linked by the idea that there is a culturally generated cognitive structure expressed in the layout of houses and villages, in the building of tents, and in the perceptions and activities of people who occupy built environments. Part II begins with a theoretical contribution by Roderick Lawrence, who argues that a contextual approach to housing—an approach that decodes the built environment by uncovering cultural rules—produces a more adaptable set of architectural principles for design and housing policy. His approach calls for a high degree of involvement in the design process by future residents. Dennis Doxtater's contribution adds a structuralist perspective to the decoding of spatial patterns. His analysis of an

Andalusian village suggests that the formal structure of cultural spatial domains may develop from an inherent cognitive predisposition, but that the physical settings then lend themselves to sociopolitical manipulation and attributed symbolic meaning. Labelle Prussin's description of Gabra tents employs the process of building or "placemaking"—instead of spatial structure—as the cognitive basis for the creation of nomadic architecture. Each of these chapters emphasizes the use of the domestic environment or the process of the creation of that environment as a map of the underlying sociocultural system.

The last two chapters employ an environmental psychology approach to cognition. Robert Bechtel analyzes the home environment "action patterns" of American families in Alaska and Saudi Arabia, and those of urban Iranian families, to determine optimal spatial requirements in each of these cultural settings. Sidney Brower explores the difference between residents' perceptions of their Baltimore neighborhoods and outsiders' (tourists') perceptions of the same environment, pointing out that knowledge of a place and changing frequencies of behaviors within a setting can change the established cognitive structure of a residential environment.

All of the studies in this part address the problem of determining the cognitive structure of the house or residence within a context of cultural activities and meanings. A cognitive or structuralist approach uncovers the underlying premises, or cultural substrate, that are thought to produce a particular physical form, perception, or activity. Understanding these premises contributes to the design process as well as to an understanding of the generative qualities of culture in the production of the physical environment.

6

TRANSLATING ANTHROPOLOGICAL CONCEPTS INTO ARCHITECTURAL PRACTICE

RODERICK J. LAWRENCE

The construction of a building involves the definition and delimitation of space. Therefore it is important to analyze boundaries that indicate how spaces—here and there, inside and outside, upstairs and downstairs—are separated and linked. The concepts of *boundary, threshold,* and *transition* are useful in examining how different spaces or domains are associated with or demarcated from each other (Lawrence 1986). Moreover, rooms or other kinds of spaces in and around buildings are usually classified, named, and used according to cultural and social conventions. Several social anthropologists (Douglas 1973; Leach 1976) have shown that although the classification of human-made spaces may appear to be arbitrary, this practice usually conforms to a consistent set of rules within a specific society. When objects or events are classified, artificial or conceptual boundaries are introduced to distinguish between "this" and "that." Thus, group "A" is considered to be quite different from everything that is "not A." When human concepts are challenged then the classification of objects and events confronts these situations; for example, earth in the flower or vegetable garden is considered acceptable and natural, whereas if it is brought inside a dwelling unit on shoe heels it is considered unnatural and is classified as "dirt." In this chapter a *code* is defined as the structure of a general set of possibilities for communicating and understanding particular characteristics of human culture. In this sense, architecture has a cultural as well as a pragmatic meaning; architecture therefore encodes cultural and social rules and conventions. A *binary code* is a kind of code that incorporates bipolar opposites, such as the positive/negative values associated with earth and dirt. The term *decoding* is employed here to refer to the analysis of a coded object or events, such as those associated with cooking and eating inside dwellings. The decoding of a domestic environment requires an analysis of all the constituent parts without forgetting their role in the totality of the context in which they occur.

In recent years it has become increasingly common for social anthropologists, other social scientists, and architects to examine extant buildings in terms of a range of cultural and social dimensions (Altman and Werner 1985; Duncan 1981; Lawrence 1987). Many cultural studies of the design of dwellings have focused on the function of rituals during successive phases of the construction process of residential buildings in nonindustrialized societies (Saile 1977, 1985).

It has been much less common for researchers in industrialized countries to analyze the design of dwelling units and residential neighborhoods during the phases of architectural planning and building construction, when fundamental decisions related to the design, meaning, and use of intended buildings are made. The aim of this chapter is to broaden the limited scope of studies of the cultural and social dimensions of dwelling designs. It begins by identifying and discussing some theoretical and methodological principles that can be related to the planning and construction of housing. These principles are illustrated by a study of two medium-density housing projects in Switzerland. This study leads to the development of a conceptual framework for an anthropological interpretation of *privacy* and its impact on the design and use of boundaries, thresholds, and transition spaces between the inside and outside of dwelling units and with respect to the organization of rooms, activities, and objects inside houses. This framework illustrates that dwelling units can be interpreted as structures of affective and spatial dimensions. This interpretation also provides implications for future anthropological studies and architectural practice which are discussed in the concluding section.

Orientations for Research

A dwelling unit, like other kinds of buildings, defines and delimits space. Yet the fact that housing units in the same society have different shapes and sizes and are built with various construction materials suggests that beyond pragmatic functions other factors are of at least equal importance in determining design. For example, one function of the design of dwelling units is to distinguish between public and private domains. The relations between these domains express the administrative, cultural, judicial, and sociopolitical rights of the inhabitants, neighbors, visitors, and strangers (Lavin 1981; Lawrence 1986). The aim of this chapter is to show that dwelling units are more than "a territorial core" (Porteous 1976) by discussing and illustrating a range of anthropological notions. In this respect, a *conceptual approach* will be proposed which includes not only the climatic, geographical, and topographical characteristics of the site of a dwelling unit, but also a range of cultural, sociodemographic, and sociopsychological factors. The study of this complex array of variables as a set of homologous factors raises certain theoretical and methodological problems which can be confronted by examining a range of studies from diverse disciplines.

Some cues for the diversification and reinterpretation of studies of dwelling environments have been published by scholars in different disciplines. For example, some social anthropologists (Hugh-Jones 1979) present lucid ethnographies which show that although the spatial characteristics of domestic architecture in nonindustrialized societies can be described according to the orientation, relative position, and the demarcation of spaces and objects in dwellings, such a description cannot account for the social meaning of household space unless other diverse practices associated with the production and consumption of food, the categorization of animals, kinship rules, and other social conventions are understood. Social historians (Burnett 1978; Daunton 1983) analyze how changes in the morphology, furnishing, and use of dwelling units cannot be dissociated from variations in the social meaning of domestic space and household life which engender changes in the resident's relation to his home. Sociologists (Bourdieu 1977) discuss how the personalization of dwelling units varies with respect to economic, social, cultural, and political factors that impinge upon the life-style of residents. Psychologists (Csikszentmihalyi and Rochberg-Halton 1981) and philosophers (Bachelard 1964; Heidegger 1971) illustrate that the personalization of dwelling units is inscribed not merely in geometrical space and time but also in the subjective "personal world" of the resident and his or her goal-oriented behavior.

In sum, these studies confirm that the design, the meaning, and the use of dwellings are intimately related to a range of cultural, sociodemographic, and psychological dimensions, and that the reciprocal relations between these dimensions ought to be studied in terms of a historical perspective. It is noteworthy that all of these studies are related to extant buildings in different geographical locations. Therefore, these studies are not informative about the intentions and values related to the planning and construction of these dwelling units or about possible changes to the design, meaning, and use of these residential buildings since they were first occupied. This chapter endeavors to overcome this limitation of much contemporary research in this field by examining how the notions derived from a range of studies of extant dwellings can be applied during architectural design practice.

Orientations for Architectural Practice

The opportunity to study the design process leading to the construction and use of a building offers two different contexts for applied design research (Lawrence 1987). First, the design team can translate assumptions, ideals, and values about the interaction between people and their physical surroundings without recourse to numerous people, including the inhabitants, in the design decision-making process. Second, the designers can elicit information that is pertinent to the payout, fabric, and intended use of a new building by incorporating laypeople in the design process. This second option is an important way of generating information, provided that there is a shared language understood by different groups of people. Hence the ideas and values of different groups of people can be identified in specific contexts. Furthermore, this approach accepts that buildings can be attributed several meanings and uses at a specific time by different groups of people, and that the ideas and values of a group or an individual may change through the course of the life cycle.

These principles have important implications for architectural practice and design research. They challenge deterministic interpretations of the interrelationships between people and the built environment. Moreover, they suggest that it is possible to comprehend and design for the inhabitants of specific built environments by using a *contextual* approach that examines the domestic setting and dwelling practices in a complementary way. This approach can be contrasted with the application of design guidelines, patterns, and user needs that are founded on broad generalizations about the design, meaning, and use of buildings. Concurrently, the contextual approach advocated herein refers to a range of notions related to the analysis and comprehension of dwelling practices which define and are defined by a range of cultural, social, and psychological dimensions. These principles can be accommodated and even nurtured by architects and builders, who develop design policies that consider, for example, the polyvalent meanings and uses of dwelling units in terms of the *potential* and *effective* adaptability of the built environment. One example illustrates this point of view.

In the layout of the interior of a dwelling unit there are three generic options for the design of living areas and cooking facilities which are expressed graphically in Figure 6.1 and can be summarized as follows:

1 A demarcated "cellular room" reserved for preparing food, separated from spaces intended for dining and living

2 A demarcated "cellular room" reserved for preparing and eating food, separated from a space for informal living

3 One large room with facilities spatially associated for preparing and eating food and for leisure activities

The alternative layouts that are actually provided vary not only between housing in different cultures (Lawrence 1982a) but also within societies (Goody 1982, Lawrence 1982b) according to the ascribed roles of husband and wife, parents and children, and the stage in the life cycle of members of each household. This finding has important implications for architectural design. First, it indicates that different kinds of room layouts may inhibit or encourage the spatial ordering of domestic activities. Second, it is apparent that beyond the possibilities offered by the design and furnishing of rooms for the spatial and temporal ordering of domestic activities, the way different households organize household chores is related to the age, gender, and socio-economic status of the inhabitants and their interpretation of roles, routines, and rituals. This example illustrates that it is not possible to prescribe where and how often certain kinds of cooking, eating, and leisure activities will occur inside the dwelling unit unless there is prior knowledge of the life-style of the household, and also of the goals and aspirations of its members. On the contrary, the reciprocal relations between the design, meaning, and use of domestic space (and indeed the built environment in general) can be interpreted in terms of one or more of the following codes, elaborated by Lawrence (1987, 158–59):

1. *A code for the classification of activities and space.* The label which is given to an activity encodes that event with a meaning. Similarly, the label given to a room in a house implies a social meaning and use. These significations vary between different cultures, and between different groups of people in the same culture.

2. *A code for the relative position of activities and space.* There is a set of social ideas and images which suggest the location of activities and spaces in the dwelling. Such a code distinguishes between the front and back of the dwelling. This ordering of activities and spaces is extended outside the dwelling to the public realm, particularly in relation to the street.

3. *A code for the association or demarcation of activities and space.* There are customary social systems for the classification of sets of activities and spaces in non-functional terms. Hence the binary oppositions of clean and dirty, day and night, public and private may be used to associate or demarcate domestic activities, and to suggest their position relative to other activities and spaces in a dwelling.

4. *A code for domestic activities which indicates the meaning of one activity* (a food event) *in the total range of domestic activities* (the food system). The significance of a food event suggests not only what food is eaten, how it is embellished, when it is served and who is present at the table, but also where it is served. Hence the greater significance of a food event suggests more embellish-

ment of the food, and more people being present, at a relatively formalized setting.

Unlike laws, or other deterministic interpretations of the interrelation between people and the built environment, these codes enable us to account for and comprehend the polyvalent meanings and functions attributed to the design of the built environment and human activities within the framework of extant architectural, cultural, societal, and behavioral parameters. Moreover, there are also important implications for architectural design practice. In contrast to deterministic interpretations of house planning, the notions of *inherent* and *potential* adaptability can be used in a complementary way to enable the residents to express choices and preferences and to personalize their dwellings; as Pikusa (1983, 62) states:

> The *inherent adaptability* is built into the initial design, giving the occupant choice through intentional ambiguity, within fixed physical constraints of a given plan. . . . The plan characteristics make a wide range of interpretations possible and there is a minimum of design features that would inhibit particular choices of use. *Potential adaptability* can be provided for by various design/construction techniques. Historically, the provision of verandahs, undercrofts, and roof spaces catered well for the potential adaptability, extendability and incremental improvement. More recently, non-structural demountable partitions and movable fittings have been also used in housing design to facilitate easy alterations to suit the changing needs of the users.

This interpretation can be extended beyond the design, meaning, and use of facilities for the preparation and eating of food to include an analysis of all internal rooms and the relation of the dwelling unit to the public realm of the street. The purpose of the remainder of this chapter is to reexamine the concept of *privacy* by understanding how it can and has been applied during the planning of two medium-density housing projects in Switzerland.

What Is Privacy?

The concept of privacy has become a subject of growing concern for architects, town planners, and social scientists, as housing densities in both industrialized and developing countries have increased during this century (Lawrence 1987). Explicit design guidelines for visual and aural privacy in residential areas have been published in several countries. Most of these, however, do not address the fundamental question of what privacy means for people in a particular residential environment or at a particular time, or how attitudes about privacy differ for various groups of people in the same society and also change through the course of history. This limitation may be attributed to a lack of contextual research about the cultural, social, and psychological variables related to the definition of privacy in specific settings. A recent survey by Margulis (1977) shows, however, that some seminal research about the implications of administrative/judicial and behavioral/cultural variables can provide useful guidelines for future research and design policy.

In one important contribution, Altman (1977) examines privacy "as a generic process that occurs in all cultures" but also differs among cultures in terms of "the behavioral mechanisms used to regulate desired levels of privacy." Altman refers to several ethnographical studies in different societies to show that privacy is "a universal process which involves unique regulatory mechanisms." Therefore, from a very general perspective, privacy can be interpreted as being culturally pervasive but, as Altman notes, this perspective is not very informative about kinds of contextually defined mechanisms that are used to regulate social interaction in particular situations. A precise understanding of these mechanisms, which Altman orders in six classes, is necessary to define, design for, and regulate privacy in a specific context at a given time. These six classes of dimensions include, first, a dialectical process involving changes in the degree of accessibility to and separation from other persons; second, a process of controlling social interaction; and third, a nonmonotonic process which seeks an optimal level of interaction with others. Fourth, distinctions between desirable and actual levels of privacy may engender an imbalance resulting in a lack of autonomy or isolation. Fifth, privacy has a dual direction, such that the reciprocal relations between parties ought to be considered. Sixth, privacy applies to various combinations of individuals and groups.

An analysis of diverse interpretations, including that of Altman, enables Margulis (1977, 10) to present a "shared core definition": "Privacy as a whole or in part represents the control of transactions between person(s) and other(s) the ultimate aim of which is to enhance autonomy and/or minimize vulnerability."

From this perspective, privacy serves three main functions (Altman 1977, 68): "the management of social interaction," "the establishment of plans and strategies for interacting with others," and "the development and maintenance of self-identity."

Bearing in mind the functions and contextual definition of privacy, it is important to consider those mechanisms that are used to regulate levels of privacy, including (1) verbal behavior; (2) nonverbal behavior, such as gestures; (3) environmental factors including the definition of personal space and the use of rooms; and (4) cultural and social customs and conventions related to personal behavior and the design of the built environment (Lavin 1981). From this perspective, it can be shown that the architectural, social, and psychological dimensions of privacy regulation are fundamental in daily life. In its essence, privacy regulation entails a dynamic process so that any deterministic formulation of the concept of privacy is unrealistic. Moreover, to control privacy, architectural and behavioral variables ought to operate in tandem if physical and psychological costs—stress, illness, and vandalism, for example—are to be minimized. Following are examples of how this can be achieved.

Designing for Privacy and Personal Control

The preceding principles for anthropological research and architectural practice can be illustrated by a comparative study (Lawrence 1987) of two recent cooperative housing projects in Switzerland. Each cooperative has been formed by laypeople, who have decided to use their resources collectively, coupled with government financial subsidies and architectural expertise, in order to own and build their own homes. Each cooperative appointed an architectural firm to develop a site plan and to participate in the design of the dwelling units. A comparison of the two housing cooperatives is instructive for the following reasons: first, in each project the roles of the architects and the residents during the architectural design process were different; second, there are design policies that impinge upon the intervention of the inhabitants in the design and use of collective and private space.

The first housing scheme, called *Die Bleiche* and designed by Franz Oswald, is a cooperative housing project for thirty-seven households, built at Worb, near the Swiss capital of Bern, in 1981–82. The cooperative members were involved in a prescribed design process, which is comparable to the conventional role of the architect when designing a house for a known client. In this project, communication and decision making were based on discussions between the residents and the architect, who developed sketch plans. The fundamental problem for Oswald was to build with each household in mind, while overcoming the conflict between the addition of individual dwelling units and the necessity for a unified, collective form. To achieve this objective, Oswald proposed a building envelope of parallel party walls either 4.25, 5.25, or 6.25 meters apart, with a uniform depth of 12.55 meters over two or three floor levels, as illustrated in Figure 6.2. Within this building envelope a house could be constructed of any material and have any configuration; even a small independent residence or professional office on one of the three floor levels could be incorporated. The preliminary sketch plans were developed by Oswald in the presence of the residents. Subsequently, Oswald developed the final plans. It is noteworthy that while each house has the same typology, the internal configuration and furnishing of the dwelling units are specific solutions to the unique requirements of each household. In this respect, Oswald adopts an interpretation of typology similar to that of Hertzberger (1977, 150), who states that "in place of prototypes which are collective interpretations of individual living patterns, are prototypes which make individual interpretations of the collective pattern possible . . . such that everyone can bring into being his own interpretation of the collective pattern."

The second housing scheme, called *Les Pugessies*, is also a small housing cooperative which is being constructed in stages at Yverdon, according to the designs of Groupe Y Architects. This project involved the residents in the design process in a relatively nonconventional manner. The architects developed a process of participatory design that is applicable to each member of the cooperative. First, each family recorded its specific requirements (for example, budget, preferred floor area, site, location, relation to the ground, and choice of materials) on an extensive design questionnaire checklist. Second, preliminary sketch plans were developed by the architects in the presence of the residents. Third, these sketches became the basis for an extensive design by simulation process in a spatial simulator which permits full-scale models of the future houses to be simulated, experienced, evaluated, and altered (Lawrence 1980, 1983).

Unlike the residents of Die Bleiche, who had no choice of a house type, each member of this cooperative could choose a house on one, two, or three levels not constrained by party walls, as shown in Figure 6.3.

Although all the stages of Les Pugessies have not been completed, a significant part of the housing cooperatives is now occupied by the residents. The cooperative Die Bleiche was completed and occupied in 1982. Although extensive post-occupancy evaluations of each project in the future will provide useful information, here consideration will focus on these two housing projects as products of design policies related to the active role of the inhabitants and the architects during the architectural design process, and after the occupation of the houses. In particular, given our discussion of the fundamental role of boundaries for the design, meaning, and use of houses and dwelling practices, in general, and with respect to privacy in particular, the following sections will discuss design policies for transitions between the public exterior domain and the private, interior domain of residential environments.

Both housing cooperatives include examples of designing for the critical interface between private/personal and collective/social domains. In Die Bleiche, for example, the inhabitants and their architect agreed on the principle that the boundaries between private and collective external spaces, or between two adjoining private gardens, could be expressed by physical barriers, such as a hedge, a fence, or a screen, and, furthermore, that no one could be prevented from establishing these barriers, even if one party did not want this kind of spatial demarcation. In accordance with this design policy, Oswald established a site plan that permits the development of additional, secondary building structures (for example, "ateliers," storerooms, playrooms) in the private garden adjoining the collective domain. Thus, the residents can modify their own external environment at any time, without encroaching upon the collective space of their neighborhood. In addition, they can employ their preferred materials to achieve their intentions, as shown in Figure 6.4. This fundamental design policy was not an established principle in the planning of Les Pugessies, although it also includes collective and private outdoor spaces; this suggests that the allocation of private and collective domains is considered definitive and will not change in the future. Such an absolute interpretation appears to have been unquestioned by the Groupe Y Architects and the residents. Yet there are already examples of auto-construction by the residents, which, being unofficial, are tolerated after the original construction by the cooperative; for example, the construction of wood stores or sheds for garden utensils has reinforced demarcations between collective and private outdoor spaces, as shown in Figure 6.5. This kind of development is, in essence, very different from the intentional planning for participation at Die Bleiche. Indeed, these two examples briefly show how domestic architecture can embody two different design policies for private, collective, and public domains during an extended time.

In both projects, the cooperative and the architects agreed on the design and administrative principle that the resident could choose the type and size of a limited range of windows and doors for each house. This explicit design policy suggests that the architects did not want an archaic but an ordered facade, the overt face of the collective residential form. On the contrary, the interior of each housing unit is concealed and personal; the residents were free to design and construct what they preferred within the building envelope. In this respect, the importance of previous experiences of residential environments, of the personal, social, and cultural cues (such as heirlooms and archetypes) of known items of furniture, and of domestic rules and routines, particularly those related to the preparation and eating of food, cannot be overlooked.

The diverse kinds of information collected during this study have yielded complementary information about the spatial and the affective characteristics of dwellings which will now be presented with respect to the notion of privacy by a brief discussion of the following themes: transitions between inside and outside the house; the roles of a privacy gradient; relationships between spaces and household activities; the meaning and use of domestic objects.

Transitions Between Inside and Outside the Dwelling

The transition between the exterior and the interior of houses can be simultaneously interpreted as a liaison and separation between public and private, exterior and interior, polluted and nonpolluted, in the anthropological sense of those terms (Leach 1976). This categorical differentiation of external and internal spaces can be extended to include the liaison and separation between spaces inside the dwelling, such as zones for kinds of domestic activities, according to the following binary codes:

inside	female	private	nonpolluted
outside	male	public	polluted

According to this interpretation (Lawrence 1984), the entrance hall has a spatial order and purpose that is explicit and specific. It is intended to regulate the access of people and objects between private and public domains; it is required to control visibility between the exterior and the interior; it is not simply a space to store umbrellas and coats but a place where personal appearance can be controlled; it is not just a passage between exterior and interior spaces but a space where people other than guests (the postman, salesman, and so on) can be received. The role of the entrance hall is a fundamental spatial component in the regulation of visual access between public and private domains: all exterior shared space beyond the entrance door of each dwelling unit is freely accessible and visible, whereas the private interior space is neither freely accessible nor visible. Moreover, whereas the external spaces are profane, the dwelling is sacred, because the entrance hall not only controls access and visibility between these two domains but, from an anthropological perspective (Douglas 1973), also regulates polluted matter. In sum, the entrance hall is an ambiguous space, neither public nor private, neither sacred nor profane, which is attributed a spatial form and ritual functions to inhibit unwanted matter from contaminating the home.

The preceding discussion considers the transition from the public, exterior domain of residential areas to the private interior spaces of the dwelling in terms of an underlying pattern. In this sense, the design of a dwelling is a setting in which the residents create their daily household life and establish contacts with the larger community. How people do this is dependent not solely on the spatial characteristics of homes but also on other factors, including the inhabitants' goals and intentions and past residential experience. The presence of both implicit and explicit regulations for the use of space are related to sociopsychological factors, which transform the residential environment from a "spatial backcloth" into an affective setting endowed with personal values and meaning. Altman et al. (1981) show that both kinds of regulations, which can be in a state of flux for a long time, help define the quality of transitional zones.

The Roles of a Privacy Gradient

A topological analysis of five house plans at Les Pugessies reveals that a privacy gradient structures the position of interior spaces, leading from the most accessible, social, and displayed nearest the entrance hall, to the most private, least accessible, and unseen farthest from the vestibule. This ordering of rooms can be studied by examining the position of the entrance hall relative to the central public courtyard and the private gardens or outdoor spaces located on the periphery of this residential development. Given that the "front door" and entrance hall are always directly accessible from the public court (not the private outdoor areas), it is evident that a consistent gradient exists from the most public to the most private rooms inside each house. The relative positions of the entrance hall to the other rooms of five houses are shown in Figure 6.6. This figure illustrates that although there is no direct correlation between the nominal distance between the rooms in each house, there is an underlying structure that enables the position of rooms to be considered with respect to the desired degree of privacy envisaged by the residents. In sum, the parents' bedroom has consistently been envisaged as the most private room, in contrast to the toilet directly accessible from the entrance hall, which is specifically intended for house guests. This spatial organization is the exact opposite of that found in Australian houses, which commonly include the parents' bedroom adjacent to the front door, where guests are usually invited to leave their coats (Lawrence 1987).

Although the privacy gradient presented here can locate the position of rooms relative to the public realm of the residential environment, it does not explicitly define the spatial relations between rooms, that is, whether they are accessible only from a circulation corridor or whether there is sequencing of spaces or changes of level between them.

Relationships Between Spaces and Household Activities

This study reveals that the spatial location of domestic activities conforms to the way domestic chores are commonly classified, located, and interrelated. Beyond the boundaries of those spaces intended for cooking, eating, and leisure activities, the residents have expressed a clear distinction between the design of rooms for diurnal and those for nocturnal uses. Although there may be one (or two) large spaces in which cooking, eating, and leisure activities occur juxtaposed, in contrast there consistently is a strict, demarcated, cellular plan form for those spaces in which sleeping or ablutions are located; in this study it is even rare for children to share a bedroom.

This division in the ordering of domestic space illustrates not only a strict opposition between spaces for diurnal and spaces for nocturnal use but also whether these spaces are intended for private/personal or collective/household activities. The following binary code expresses the connotation of interior spaces:

cellular plan form	nocturnal use	personal activities
"open" plan form	diurnal use	collective activities

The origin of this spatial code is not clear. This ordering of home interiors was rarely debated during the design process. Moreover, it does not stem directly from present residential experience in flatted dwellings and contradicts the customary arrangement and use of space in previous homes. Here one hypothesis is presented to account for the design of the future homes according to this pattern. For those families who participate in the design of their new home (especially those who rent a government-subsidized flat), there is a preoccupation with eliminating the faults of a present (and perhaps previous) residence. One of the most common defects of contemporary flats is the lack of acoustic privacy from adjoining dwellings. In some cases, this defect has been a principal reason for constructing one's own home. The current flats of all but one couple are located in large buildings containing rented units that have a cellular arrangement of all rooms. As the couples change their social rank from tenants to owner-occupiers their intentions include moving from "noisy, unpleasant, poorly maintained" residential environments to better quality dwellings. One way to do this is by living in a residential complex of much lower density. Another way is by eliminating the cellular arrangement of rooms or their distribution on only one floor level, both of which are common characteristics of flats (but not of houses) in Switzerland.

This interpretation, coupled with the previous discussion of the privacy gradient and how domestic roles and routines are embodied in domestic space organization, shows that there is no deterministic relationship between spatial form, room area, and the location of household activities. Concurrently, at a psychological level, a house that simultaneously emancipates the residents from the defects of previous dwellings and synthesizes the positive features of these and other homes becomes an important vehicle for the expression of sociopsychological meaning. The psychological investment in home design is an important criterion for planning residential environments and is a means of personal dialogue. In essence, this research shows that the materialization of the design of a dwelling embodies a *psychological project* or goal that may be strictly personal or shared by members of the household. Thus, spaces and objects acquire symbolic connotations because of the polyvalent meanings different people in the same household at the same time attribute to them. It is important to consider in the relationship between an individual and his or her home not only personal values and preferences but also compromises (perhaps conflicts), because houses are invariably shared domains which reflect consensus decisions, particularly in those rooms that are not reserved for personal use. In sum, this study shows that if *codes* related to nocturnal and diurnal classifications are used to discuss the spatial definition of rooms, then there are important differences in the designs of rooms intended for food preparation and eating activities that reflect different values and practices and whether the housewife is solely responsible for chores in the kitchen or is supported by other members of the household (Lawrence 1982b).

Meaning and Use of Domestic Objects

Beyond an analysis of domestic space organization as proposed here, the location and use of household objects and the meanings endowed in them should not be overlooked when home interiors are analyzed from an anthropological perspective.

During the design process and the subsequent interviews with some residents, it was noted that the position of household objects may have a direct relation to the furnishing of the present flat or a previous residence of the inhabitants. In some cases, there was a constant association between specific items of mobile furniture and the layout of particular rooms. For example, the location of a desk in a spare bedroom in a mock-up of a house is similar to its position in the spare bedroom of the residents' present flat. In other cases, however, there is no similarity between the two furniture layouts. In the majority of simulated houses, the residents designed the kitchen by adjusting the position and dimension of existing appliances, work surfaces, and storage spaces of the kitchen in their present residence. In both of these cases specific items of furniture were used as *reference elements* to control the simulated design of the future house. In this sense domestic objects are attributed a pragmatic function in assessing the shape and size of rooms, and the position of windows and doors (Lawrence 1983).

Apart from this pragmatic value, this study has shown that domestic objects are endowed with symbolic meaning. The examples of a staircase and the recurrent inclusion of heirlooms in the simulated houses have been discussed elsewhere (Lawrence 1982b). These kinds of objects evoke past residential experiences for the inhabitants. They have unique, personal associations and meanings that can only be grasped by comprehending the residential biography of the inhabitants. However, unlike Csikszentmihalyi and Rochberg-Halton (1981), who failed to consider the social connotation of domestic objects, this study illustrates the interaction between personal and social values and meanings. The fireplace is but one example. The hearth is the archetypal symbol par excellence of the domestic realm that has acquired a social connotation in diverse cultures since antiquity and is still extant in contemporary societies (Bachelard 1964b). The provision of both fireplaces and central heating in all the houses ably illustrates this, but there is also evidence that the inclusion of a hearth reflects its value as a status symbol. The fact that flatted dwellings for low- or middle-income wage earners rarely or never include a fireplace suggests that it acts as an index of the social value of a dwelling unit and the social rank of its occupants. Such indexes can be analyzed according to the following principle: domestic objects (and those activities associated with them) are endowed with meanings that are illustrative of their connotation and use in the total range of household wares and activities. In sum, this research indicates that household objects can be classified as one of the following three indexes:

1 *Construction indexes* that are fixed, such as doors, windows, roofs, or structural features, and serve as reference elements to appraise the size and shape of rooms for pragmatic reasons, such as the furnishing of rooms
2 *Domestic indexes* that are mobile, such as pieces of furniture, that are probably heirlooms or items with a special significance (at least for one member of the household), and that are referred to throughout the design-by-simulation process
3 *Socio-cultural indexes*, such as fireplaces, which are included in the design of houses primarily for their symbolic value, not their practical usefulness

The objects in these sets of indexes can be distinguished from mundane objects that have no symbolic meaning for the members of the household.

Synthesis

The study of the transition between inside and outside the house, the relations between spaces and household activities, and the location and use of domestic objects reported here shows that an anthropological analysis of dwellings should account for both the physical/spatial and the affective/symbolic characteristics of domestic space, objects, and activities. Nonetheless, it has been common for studies of house planning to ignore the affective meaning of spatial relations, room shape, and position, and for studies of the psychological or sociological meaning of furniture layouts frequently to abstract interior decoration from the morphological structure and geographical context of the house. This conceptual dichotomy between the spatial and the affective characteristics of dwellings has inhibited the development of a thorough comprehension of dwelling environments and exacerbated "the applicability gap" between academic research and design practice (Lawrence 1987).

It is appropriate, therefore, that this chapter conclude with a request for the redefinition and diversification of current research and design practice. It has presented and illustrated certain theoretical and methodological principles for the analysis of domestic environments. The preceding discussion shows that dwellings are like a seamless web of affective and spatial considerations that form an interactive whole. For this fundamental reason predictive "models" of furniture layouts and activity patterns (as espoused in much modern housing practice) cannot be employed as resources for design because they misrepresent the inherent nature of domestic life. Knowledge and information about the design, meaning, and use of dwellings can only be derived from a relative, rather than an absolute, model of household life. This model also has direct implications for the translation of anthropological concepts into architectural design practice. This chapter also has illustrated how the chasm between architects and laypeople can be reduced by the formation of housing cooperatives and empathic design policies. Moreover, it shows that when architects and laypeople collaborate in the design of residential environments the discourse is inextricably related to design policies and that, therefore, the expertise of the architect is of crucial importance. Two fundamental principles should be considered by the architect during the design process. First, How can the specific requirements, including the conflicting preferences between building users, be resolved by employing the structural and service components of buildings, and known items of furniture, as design cues to generate unique solutions rather than by relying on preestablished housing stereotypes? Second, How can the specificity of each home be accommodated with the social or communal requirements of residential environments, given that collective form is not merely the addition of individual house dwelling units?

In conclusion, it is suggested that the task of the architect in a housing project is to establish precise design parameters. These parameters include the definition of typological space that enables the residents to participate actively in the design of their homes. This policy ought to be contrasted with the recurring notion that a minimal definition of building structure will provide a maximum degree of liberty for the resident. Given this principle, the architect will have redefined not only his role but also that of the building user in the research and design processes. Furthermore, the role of the architect, the researcher, and the resident will be redefined during both the design process and studies of residential environments.

Conclusion

This chapter has presented theoretical and methodological principles that researchers and designers can employ in their work. These principles, however, are not intended as ultimate formulas that will eliminate difficult decisions by tabling solutions. Instead, they are intended as part of a framework for ongoing research that does not ignore the complexity of the subject of inquiry. In addition, these principles are not meant to challenge the role of the researchers or designers but to enhance their professional acumen. Even if the architect does not consider these principles during the elaboration of building plans the future resident will use them nonetheless to assess a design proposal that was formulated with different criteria. It is important that the dialogue between laypeople, academic researchers, and architects develops an understanding of how different individuals value these parameters and how they ought to be interpreted during the architectural design process and during studies of extant domestic environments.

References

Altman, I. 1977. Privacy regulation: Culturally universal or culturally specific? *Journal of Social Issues* 33(3):66–84.

Altman, I., A. Vinsel, and B. Brown. 1981. Dialectical conceptions in social psychology: An application to social penetration and privacy regulation. In *Advances in experimental social psychology*, vol. 14, ed. L. Berkowitz, 107–60. New York: Academic Press.

Altman, I., and C. Werner, eds. 1985. *Home environments.* vol. 8, *Human behavior and environment: Advances in theory and research.* New York: Plenum Press.

Bachelard, G. 1964a. *The poetics of space.* New York: Orion Press.

————. 1964b. *The psychoanalysis of fire.* Boston: Beacon Press.

Bourdieu, P. 1977. *Outline of a theory of practice.* Cambridge: Cambridge University Press.

Burnett, J. 1978. *A social history of housing 1815–1970.* Newton Abbot, U.K.: David and Charles.

Csikszentmihalyi, M., and E. Rochberg-Halton. 1981. *The meaning of things: Domestic symbols and the self.* New York: Cambridge University Press.

Daunton, M. 1983. *House and home in the Victorian city.* London: Edward Arnold.

Douglas, M., ed. 1973. *Rules and meanings.* Harmondsworth: Penguin Press.

Duncan, J., ed. 1981. *Housing and identity: Cross-cultural perspectives.* London: Croom Helm.

Goody, J. 1982. *Cooking, cuisine and class: A study in comparative sociology.* Cambridge: Cambridge University Press.

Heidegger, M. 1971. Poetry, language, thought. London: Harper & Row.

Hertzberger, H. 1977. Architecture for people. *Architecture and Urbanism* 75:124–52.

Hugh-Jones, C. 1979. *From the Milk River: Spatial and temporal processes in Northwest Amazonia.* Cambridge: Cambridge University Press.

Lavin, M. 1981. Boundaries in the built environment: Concepts and examples. *Man-Environment Systems* 11(5/6):195–206.

Lawrence, R. 1980. The simulation of domestic space: Users and architects participating in the architectural design process. *Simulation and Games* 11(3):279–300.

———. 1982a. Domestic space and society: A cross-cultural study. *Comparative Studies in Society and History* 24(1): 104–30.

———. 1982b. A psychological-spatial approach for architectural design and research. *Journal of Environmental Psychology* 2(1):37–51.

———. 1983. Laypeople as architectural designers. *Leonardo* 16(3):232–37.

———. 1984. Transition spaces and dwelling design. *Journal of Architectural and Planning Research* 1(4):261–72.

———. 1986. *Le Seuil franchi: Logement populaire et vie quotidienne en Suisse romande, 1860–1960.* Geneva: Georg Editeur.

———. 1987. *Housing, dwellings and homes: Design theory, research and practice.* Chichester: John Wiley.

Leach, E. 1976. *Culture and communication: The logic by which symbols are connected.* Cambridge: Cambridge University Press.

Margulis, S., ed. 1977. Privacy. *Journal of Social Issues* 33(3): special issue.

Pikusa, S. 1983. Adaptability: Designing for functional adaptability; a lesson from history. *Architecture Australia* 72(1):62–67.

Porteous, D. 1976. Home: The territorial core. *Geographical Review* 66(4):383–90.

Saile, D. 1977. Making a house: Building rituals and spatial concepts in the Pueblo Indian World. *Architectural Association Quarterly* 9(2/3):72–81.

———. 1985. The ritual establishment of home. In *Home environments,* vol. 8, *Human behavior and environment: Advances in theory and research,* ed. I. Altman and C. Werner, 87–111.

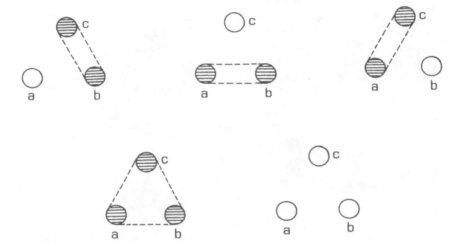

Figure 6.1. Graphic representation of how food preparation, eating, and living activities can be spatially ordered inside the house. **(a)** living area, **(b)** dining area, **(c)** cooking area.

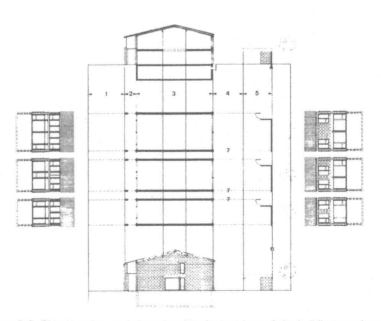

Figure 6.2. Plan, section, and view showing the typology of the building envelope for the housing units in Die Bleiche, designed by Franz Oswald: **(1)** front garden zone, **(2)** balcony zone, **(3)** depth of housing unit, **(4)** back garden zone, **(5)** expansion strip, **(6)** limit between private and communal space, **(7)** lateral boundaries between neighbors.

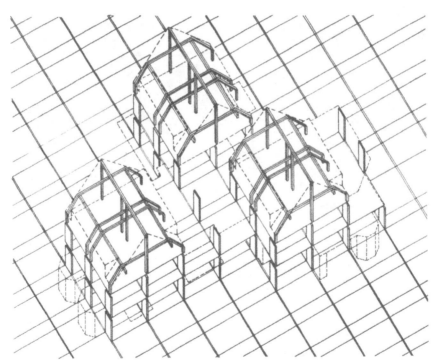

Figure 6.3a. Plan of the housing units in Les Pugessies, designed by Groupe Y Architects.

Figure 6.3b. View of the housing units in Les Pugessies.

Figure 6.4. View of the definition of boundaries and the use of different materials in the outdoor spaces of two adjoining dwelling units at Die Bleiche.

Figure 6.5. An illustration of the makeshift use of the outdoor space adjoining some dwelling units at Les Pugessies.

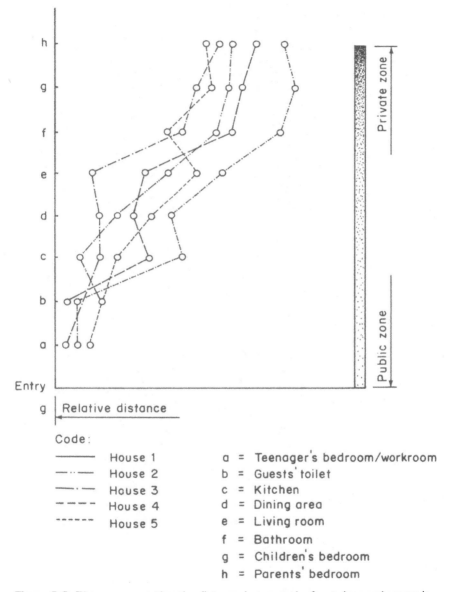

h
g
f
e
d
c
b
a

Entry

Private zone

Public zone

g | Relative distance

Code:

——————— House 1
— · · — House 2
— · — House 3
— — — House 4
- - - - - House 5

a = Teenager's bedroom/workroom
b = Guests' toilet
c = Kitchen
d = Dining area
e = Living room
f = Bathroom
g = Children's bedroom
h = Parents' bedroom

Figure 6.6. Diagram presenting the distance between the front door and rooms inside the house, and their classification as "public" or "private" by five households.

7

"CULTURAL SPACE" AS A
NEEDED RESEARCH CONCEPT
IN THE STUDY OF HOUSING
CHANGE: THE WHITE PUEBLOS
OF ANDALUSIA

DENNIS DOXTATER

Traditional societies change on several levels of analysis as they evolve through contact with, incorporation with, or outright domination by outside and more complex systems. To varying degrees most levels have been considered with respect to housing, for example, the economic, technical, psychological, social, cultural, and even architectural as a separate form of "vernacular" understanding. While it may be easier to separate these aspects of life in contemporary societies, in more traditional groups, all aspects can maintain a high degree of almost systematic integration—in part through the maintenance and appropriation of symbolic culture. Ritual, myth, and other forms of expression are seen, primarily, not as forms of explanation or classification of the world but as integrating, sociopolitical manipulations of highly emotional sets of symbols. I have argued before that the physical spaces of dwellings, settlements, and larger landscape in these societies constitute fundamental means of developing and ritually manipulating these basic expressive meanings (Doxtater 1984). Here I suggest that because the analysis of the formalities of cutural space has generally been lacking in the research of the traditional to contemporary housing continuum, it has been difficult to appreciate the highly important, systematic contribution of symbolically defined dwelling and community spaces to the whole, or much less to begin to understand the effect as these sociocultural entities evolve.

This may at first appear to be a somewhat belated "structuralist" approach that recalls the popularity of the term fifteen years ago. As applied to symbolic expression, structuralism attempted to disclose the way symbolic "objects" were associated within some overall, often very complex "text," such as myth, a work of art, or a piece of architecture. It was essentially the *positional* rela-

tionship between symbols of a text that was assumed to provide the best understanding of its larger expressive meaning. The big problem with structuralist
approaches, and certainly one reason for their apparent decline in fashion,
was always the difficulty of clearly relating patterns of symbol connections
with real social forms and processes. After all, one could only assume that
connecting and transforming oppositional structures were really operational
in the mind of each member of these primitive or traditional societies.

One way to structure symbols, is to position them in space. From time to
time anthropologists and other researchers discovered wonderful, formal patterns of symbolism in the layout of dwellings, villages, and conceptions of
natural landscapes, but these spatial examples were regarded as just additional
examples of expressive texts in one of many media. And while structuralism
seemed ubiquitously applicable to expressive texts of whatever kind, one often
had the feeling that language texts were in many instances regarded as most
fundamental. Many examples can be found in which the structural patterns
of a verbal origin myth are held to be secondarily reflected in other more
"concrete" texts, such as pottery graphics or dwelling and village layout.

It is unfortunate that there has been no special consideration given to
spatial contributions to structuralism. There are at least three aspects of spatial symbolism that seem to justify the present persistence with the so-called
structuralist approach. First, space, more than most other texts, is immediately
integrated with or influenced by social reality. It is lived in, consciously and
unconsciously manipulated in close regard to social others, and probably
evolved from socially important higher order forms of territoriality. Second,
space is able to position symbolic objects in many media, in comparison with
certain medial limitations of other texts, including language. It is therefore
more wholistic, comprehensive, or all-integrating. Third is the cognitive sa-
lience of space, or perhaps a structural predisposition of mental processing of
spatial information, mapping, direction, mnemonics, and so on. Simply put,
if the aim of expressive symbolism is extensive, long-term association, consisting of both structure and affective power, the best means may be to attach
symbolic content to the places we inhabit. Empirically, if one finds cultural
patterns of positional symbols in the physical layout of places, then the opera-
tionality of structuralist assertions—its usefulness or link with social life—
seems at least intuitively more convincing than making the same assumptions
of structure in, for example, a mythic text.

What, finally, are we looking at when we find structuralist formalities in
the layout of more traditional places? Certainly it is more than just the facades
of buildings or the details of adorning artwork—that is, more than just symbolic objects per se. Instead, it is, by definition, a positional organization of

these symbols of many media into distinguishable areas which we may call "domains." The emotional power or content of domains comes from the attached symbols. These symbolic places are utilized, that is, emotionally "turned on," by entering, occupying, denying, or otherwise controlling, during everyday and more specifically ceremonial events. The purpose is social influence or legitimization. The often very formal structure between domains is essential not only to the definition of all groups involved but also to these processes of manipulation, often involving actual movement, hence the ubiquitous "oppositions" between domains, either dominant/subordinate or complementary, and the usefulness of positions of "threshold." The structure can certainly become complex, including linear, diagonal, vertical, and concentric oppositions.

Even the structures of separate places, such as dwelling, village, and landscape, may be isomorphic, though at different scales. The meanings of domains of different sites and scales are most often coordinated though general notions of symbolic direction or the most abstract spatial structure of "cosmos." The coordination between different symbolic sites, as for example when the meaning of one "northern" domain at one site and perhaps scale is associated with the "northern" meaning of some other, provides powerful symbolic association useful in the ritual processes of the society. It is the independence of cosmos from actual physical symbolic settings that makes sociopolitical manipulation possible. Things on the ground and their usage may be altered while still legitimized by the power of that symbolic, directional cognitive map in the mind. Research must investigate both how long cosmos remains intact in evolving societies and how the symbolic physical settings and their use have been manipulated during this process.

The Andalusian Pueblo

The brilliant white clusters of dwellings indigenous to much of the Mediterranean area have been influential in the work of many accomplished architects, including Le Corbusier, Sert, Kahn, Rudolph, Moholy-Nagy, Doxiadis, and Moshie Sadfie. To this list of renowned designers must be added the thousands of unknown architects and students, and the millions of dedicated tourists who for one price or another have instinctively focused their cameras on these architectural attractions. One may simply admire the photographs in Sert's *Ibiza* (1967), Goldfinger's *Villages in the Sun* (1969), Rudofsky's *Architecture Without Architects* (1964), or the *National Geographic* (1972). Even through books or magazines, these precious gems of the Aegean and Balearic Islands, Spanish Andalusia, and southern Italy leave

the viewer impressed by an intuitive sense of well-being, coherence, or reassuring timelessness. Yet these and similar adjectives of praise accompanying
the usually photographic essays remain primarily descriptive rather than ex-
planative. Goldfinger testifies to the elusiveness of explanation when he writes
of "the great anonymous builders of the Mediterranean who made it so easy to
photograph, so reasonable to believe, yet so mystical to interpret" (1969, 6).

Two aspects of the white Mediterranean village seem particularly appealing to architects and others from our diverse, high-tech, contemporary milieu.
First, the forms, colors, volume, textures, spatial mystery, or "perceptual" aspect of the physical environment are inherently and perhaps universally interesting as distinct from learned expressive "associations" of cultural space (see
Rapoport 1970). Second, the sense of well-being and coherence probably results from an intuitive understanding of the balance between individual expression of the dwelling unit as it ecologically adapts to the terrain and the
overall statement of the white, unified village as a whole. We will return to
this often remarked about ideal relation between community and individual.
For now, however, it is interesting to note that while both these aspects of the
physical form, the "perceptual" and the "ecological," are analytically accurate, they are primarily meanings understood by those outside the culture.
These popular impressions do not attempt to map the expressive cultural
space and its relationship to ongoing life, a largely subconscious, internal
ethos of the villagers. In terms of a strictly perceptual analysis and the related
architectural emulation of this sort of ecological housing environment, there
is a great deal more than meets the photographic eye.

In seeking to convince the reader of the need for an enlarged research
paradigm in housing and housing evolution, I chose the Andalusian example
of the white Mediterranean village because of my fieldwork in one such site,
Mijas, and the availability of social science literature on the subject (though
the Greek record is large as well). Particularly important is a recent anthropological monograph on Andalusian village ritual.

In describing the Andalusian pueblo, use of the word *village* is mislead-
ing; it connotes a peasant population with a sacred relationship to agricultural
land and an intrinsic subservience to ruling classes and cities. The tightly
clustered Andalusian community obtains populations of several thousands
compared with peasant nodes of a few hundred. The "Andaluz" guard no love
for the land, even though they must earn their pesetas from it; they sharply
distinguish their "villages" from the agricultural surroundings. The political
relationship between these communities and the national structure, as exemplified by periodic civil disturbances, can only be described as anarchistic.

We have perhaps a last vestige of that ideal and possibly historical urban form, the Greek city. One anthropological source on Andalusia, J. A. Pitt-Rivers, suggests that in fact the Greek word *polis* far more nearly translates "pueblo" than any English word (1971, 31). Most important is the political aspect of this translation. The Andalusian pueblo, like its Greek ancestor, achieves a status rare in urban social organization—it is egalitarian. This refers primarily to the smaller, more isolated pueblos of several hundred to a few thousand residents, not to the larger, more economically integrated "agro-towns" studied by other anthropologists, such as Gilmore (1976). (For an explanation of this problem of comparing the social organization of Andalusian pueblos or towns, see Corbin 1979.)

The pueblo's material equality undoubtedly stems from its often severe economic limitations of day-laboring on larger farms owned by outsiders. The population is geographically isolated in a semi-arid mountainous region supporting only a meager dry-farming economy. Yet the pueblo's ecological adaptation remains extremely stable, even systematic, principally because of an observed stigma against seeking status through accumulation of the scarce material resources. There is, in effect, nothing to do with surplus money inside the pueblo. A person can buy small pieces of property but must later divide it equally among his heirs. There are no expensive sports, no regular entertaining in the home, no competition in conspicuous waste (Pitt-Rivers 1971, 61). Even today, when money has been made on increasing tourism from the coast, we find a tendency to redistribute wealth either through losing in the lotteries or through local generosity. A small number of "important" individuals of the pueblo, such as smaller landowners, government officials, teachers, and some merchants, stand out amongst the citizens. Yet if they live in the pueblo they must observe the manners and customs of not distinguishing the self by such symbols as dress or dwelling, in contrast to the large landowners, provincial or national politicians, or the military aristocracy, who live elsewhere.

Thus it is easy to see how outsiders immediately sense this egalitarian balance, between individual and community, in the expression of the physical setting. The pueblo maintains a perceptual sameness of dwellings through the custom of whitewashing inside and out and through its contiguity of individual units. Proximity to the central plaza or height relationships may not be used as a means of social distinction, as they are in the larger agrotowns described by Gilmore (1977), where the wealthy "senoritos" occupy the center, a middle-class the concentric area around the center, and a lower-class the periphery. Ritual practices suggest that even this larger situation may be an example of formalized cultural space, though not identified as such by Gilmore. Given the lack of such immediately apparent sociospatial patterns in the smaller pueblos of which Pitt-Rivers and others speak, and in the absence of specific research on cultural space, the assumption has been that at more egalitarian levels village form is determined much more by ecological and topological necessity than by the need for formal ritual or religious spaces.

Indications of Cosmos and Cultural Space in the Smaller Pueblos

Particularly in traditional egalitarian societies with limited resources—those of some complexity attached to a relatively stable agricultural setting—is it necessary to provide the formal religious or ritualistic means by which to moderate competitive or aggressive tendencies among individual (usually familial) units. Thus we would expect extensive spatio-symbolic patterns in the smaller pueblos of Andalusia and elsewhere in the Mediterranean, much to the contrary of the ecological and perceptual simplicity of conventional images of the white villages. Given the existing literature which describes primarily a social, economic, and technical continuum from the small Andalusian pueblo to the moderate-sized agrotown, to the largest regional cities such as Ronda, the research opportunity exists to begin to map the effect of change on the role of "housing" in broad sociocultural systems. But to do so we must begin with basic notions about the systematic contributions of cultural space, or cosmos, in its most comprehensive traditional form. While the term *cosmos* is often here used synonomously with *cultural space*, by definition cosmos refers primarily to the abstract directional and cognitive structure, and cultural space generally refers to the actual physical settings which are both symbolic and structured. Both are part of the same phenomenon.

Frequently observed aspects of cosmos are the two sets of symbolically opposed directions which when placed at 90-degree angles to each other comprise some sort of quadrapartite or "cardinal" conception of space (for a typical example, see Doxtater 1981). In addition to direction axes one often finds "concentric" opposition in space, often at several different scales. In many such intact societies at least, one set of cosmic directions seems to be something of a "power" axis, given its opposition between dominant spirits of the other world and subordinate humans of this world. The real psychological power of the opposition comes from the association of physical death with the human condition. Such effect is produced by the actual symbols of spatially opposed domains of cultural space, such as the Christian church domain of nave and human physical death, as opposed to the altar and spiritual rebirth. In addition to the set of directions commonly labeled "Life/Death," the other axis usually found in cosmic patterns is something often identified with the gloss "Male/Female," which also occurred in the Christian church as men sat on one side and women on the other. In distinction to the power axis, this opposition relationship often seems much more complementary than hierarchical. Whereas the impact of the power axis is the fearful position of contact with the other world that it provides, for example, the threshold between Christian church altar and nave where ritual climax occurs, Male/Female axes appear to signify relationships between groups, at and beyond the family union of male and female (see again Doxtater 1981). Usually these are social statuses that must be legitimized or otherwise maintained by the intersecting power of the "major" axis—making contact with the power of the spirit world—during calendrical or passage rites. The essence is not symbolic power, but symbolic designation of those human alliances that are maintained by the power axis. Given the fundamental alliance aspects of most marriages, the Male/Female designation makes sense in this respect. More will be said below about relationships between men and women in Andalusia and whether this prevalent and frequently investigated social opposition relates to the so-labeled categories of cultural space.

In the pueblo of Mijas, near Malaga, we have an enticing indication of these cardinal aspects of cosmos, the two sets of directional oppositions, power and alliance (see Figure 7.3). Contrary to the Catholic cosmos where the Spirits are to the east, Mortality to the west, Male to the south, and Female to the north, in Mijas at least, the power axis runs north-south, and the alliance east-west. Since the two early Christian churches and a chapel of Mijas had three different orientations and originally very modest decor, it is assumed that they reflected not primarily the larger Catholic cosmos, but some more indigenous pattern. The urban form of Mijas runs linearly approximately east-west, parallel to the contours of the relatively steep foothills which run up eight kilometers or so from the sea. The apparent power axis runs perpendicular to the pueblo form with its east-west road connecting to other pueblos in the region. High above the center of the pueblo, on the crest of the hill overlooking the pueblo, sits the small calvary chapel facing south, the object of ritual visits and processions by way of an approximately north-south pedestrian way of the same name which originates in the center of the pueblo. Roughly opposite and below the pueblo to the south or seaside is the cemetery. Thus it appears that this pair of sites forms a typical power opposition which we may designate "North/South," "Above/Below," "Spirit/Human" in recognition of the obvious references to spiritual things in the chapel on the top of the hill and to human mortality in the actual burial ground below.

According to local lore, two chapels were built along the east-west axis of the pueblo at the time when the Spanish reclaimed the village from the Moors. Dedicated to the saints of King Ferdinand and Queen Isabella, respectively, the male chapel (San Sebastian) lies to the east and the Female (Santa Maria) lies to the west. From the point of view of the power axis and calvary chapel, the Male/Female positions indicated by the king's and queen's chapels are consistent with the probable cosmic pattern of Male being to the right hand as one faces the all-powerful direction of the spiritual world, the direction of the calvary chapel entrance to the north. It is also probably significant that the east-west chapels face each other along the major linear road of the pueblo, an apparent indication of reverence for some more indigenous cosmos, largely ignoring the Catholic definition of cardinal space which requires a constant western orientation of church entrance.

Begging the question, for the moment, of how these spatial, symbolic structures become useful in the actual manipulation of daily and ceremonial behavior, and generally the overall maintenance of equality of a society of limited means, I must also comment on the probability of "concentric" oppositions which participate as well in Andalusian cultural space. At the largest scale, Pitt-Rivers's accounts of folklore define a clear opposition between attributes used to describe people of one's own pueblo and attributes used to describe usually a nearby and specific other pueblo in which the people are less honest, less handsome, less resourceful, less desirable as marriage partners, and so on. Spatially, the natural agricultural area around each pueblo is its *termino* (geographical district associated with a pueblo). Probably the pueblo inhabitant has a cultural spatial concept for a roughly concentric termino. We would also expect physical markers, or threshold elaboration, as well as indications in folklore of where the termino of one's pueblo meets that of the opposite other. Another possibility might be some directional concept, say of the east-west alliance set, which might become prominent in ritual activities between these two concentrically defined pueblos.

At the next smaller scale, an unquestionably strong opposition is expressed between the white urban form of the pueblo and the green agricultural area surrounding the pueblo and reaching to the edge of the termino. Although the abruptness of the white clustered form of the pueblo is perceptually striking to the outsider's eye, it is probably more indicative of an internally conceived threshold between architectural and natural domains of this second concentric opposition. Ecologically we should remember that the people of the pueblo do not usually own or otherwise strongly identify with the agricultural land on which they work.

Next we arrive at what must also be an important distinction of cultural space, the opposition between the dwelling itself and the street or plaza. This may be concentric in the sense that some orientational rule may exist or may have existed that accommodates the necessary placement of dwellings on both sides of both east-west and north-south streets. Conceptually, dwellings might "surround" streets or plazas, just as the agricultural area surrounds the pueblo as a whole. Certainly there exists much threshold articulation between the architectural domain of the dwelling and the "natural" domain of the street. Like the edge between pueblo and agricultural area, the whitewash of the dwelling facade cleanly meets the formerly cobbled street as part of this threshold expression.

Finally, at the smallest scale, the dwelling itself contains two distinct places undoubtedly related to the overall scheme of cultural space. The interior mass of the dwelling's interior spaces may constitute a domain opposite the courtyard generally behind the property. The architectural portion of the dwelling appears to surround the natural or open area of the courtyard in a similar expression of concentric opposition. The interior portion of the dwelling contains a larger living/dining room adjacent to the street, and sleeping rooms on the inside, both below and above. The courtyard is a place for animals, cooking, washing, baking, and other activities conceptually distinct from living inside. In addition to this possible concentric opposition at this level, we would fully expect the dwelling, in its universally predicted microcosmic manifestation, to express also the cardinal aspects of cosmos—the directional sets of power and alliance which conform to some orientation rule about the street and pueblo. For a rare but brief structuralist account of the interior of a Mediterranean dwelling, see Hinschon's article about a more contemporary urban Greek house (1981), which unfortunately is not shown to have logical relationships to symbolic structures at larger scales, unlike our present purpose of illustrating the larger systematic aspects of various sites to cosmos. Tentatively, we might identify the concentric oppositions at all four spatial scales as being between "Culture" and "Nature," perhaps the most pervasive structure described by symbolic anthropologists. The diagram of Figure 7.4 identifies characteristics of the concentric, spatial oppositions which appear to define them as belonging to, or even being fundamental to, these core Andalusian conceptions of that which is Cultural and Natural. Nature (Other Pueblo, Agricultural Area or Termino, Plaza and Street, and Courtyard) represents places and activities that are closer to the self-interested, often biological motivations of individuals or family units, which if left unchecked would obviously limit the size, complexity, and durability of sociocultural organization. Thus Culture (My Pueblo, the Urban Pueblo Form, the Dwelling, and the Interior Living Portion of the Dwelling) relates to things, particularly symbols and structure, which must be socially created, maintained, and manipulated in order to control and redirect the energies of Nature.

Certainly the foregoing sketch of cardinal and concentric aspects of cosmos can only suggest the barest of hypotheses about the probability that some such patterns of cultural space existed in at least the smaller of the Andalusian pueblos. This hint of cosmic structure or cultural space remains only superficially defined in terms of actual meanings of directions and domains, and vague about the dynamics of everyday and ritual appropriation of such. We can, however, go somewhat further with the help of other literature and initial fieldwork. Yet my intent here, again, is only to identify possibilities and therefore to promote inclusion in larger research strategies.

The Apparent Oppositions of Community/Identity and Male/Female

A recurrent problem in the study of the meaning of more traditional housing is the methodological and theoretical distinction between the dwelling as a family *territory* and the dwelling as a true *microcosmos* defined by cultural space. As a territory, the family home obviously displays degrees of identity in relationship to the larger community. To some observers this is seen as a continuum from the very contemporary situation where distinctiveness and strong identity are immediately paramount, communicated through extravagant personalization of facade, size of territory, and the like, to the very traditional culture where all decoration and form are dictated by the greater community. Again, although a commonality in facade, detail, and color—such as one immediately sees in the Andalusian pueblos—may represent a general inhibition against the display of unequal wealth, this is not its only level of meaning or even its most important. While the idea that dwelling display represents the dialectic between family and community (as in Gauvain et al. 1983) may become increasingly accurate as cultural space disintegrates through contact and change, it is still primarily an idea based on territorial display or the enforced absence of such.

The term *territoriality* does not seem to describe places that are given their meaning by their structural, cosmic reference to other symbolic places. This idea certainly requires much greater consideration than this chapter has place for; still, it probably can be accepted that territoriality involves a more political, even day-to-day set of relationships between, in this case, family and neighbors or larger community. In a territorial image of dwelling, the force that controls family display and identity is primarily the practical necessity to remain on good terms with one's neighbors, on whom one may at some time have to depend. Much in the concept of "limited good"—from the anthropology of peasant societies—is also applicable to family territory. The expression of one person's gain through a better dwelling, or facade, would be seen as another's loss, hence the idea of limited good or wealth.

As another aspect of a territorial view, the interior of the dwelling is seen as a place where the family members have greatest control, contrary to the social scrutiny and potential gossip associated with behavior in community places. Here again the atmosphere of dwelling as territory is immediately political with respect to community others and can be linked with relatively conscious, even "ethological," motivations for social advantage and personal privacy.

In the cosmically intact society, however, the dwelling is first of all frequently the primary developmental and ritual setting for the entire cultural system. The microcosm contains the most powerful, ramifying cultural codes. Its appearance and content is always highly constrained by community ritual acts, the best example of which are construction and consecration rituals (see Saile 1977). It is probably true that in smaller, egalitarian societies one of the principal ritual purposes the dwelling microcosm performs is the maintenance of the egalitarian condition itself through communal control and dominance of individual families. Although this may be similar to the reasons for the dwelling-community dialectic of territoriality, and politically effective as well in the long run, both the means and extent are different. In the society defined by cultural space, the symbolic, structural (cosmic) relationship between communal spaces and family spaces provides the power behind the ritual presentation of ideal social forms—not the daily politics of notions of limited good. Furthermore, the territorial processes are not very effective at maintaining, for example, egalitarian relationships across entire societies. Most territorial uses of the family dwelling probably tend to occur when large-scale external and essentially acultural forces of economy and politics, whether colonial or simply national, replace the traditional concept of cosmos and its cultural spaces. But this is a huge question, the explanation of which can only emerge from a broadened research paradigm that includes and formulates the relationship between theoretically distinct cultural space and territoriality. While this may turn out to be a continuum, the relationship between increasing individual territoriality and traditional cosmos seems to be much more antithetical, even antagonistic. In the smaller pueblos of Andalusia, where things may be changing rapidly, we at least have fairly recent evidence of somewhat describable and presumably effective cultural space.

Not only were things given meaning by cosmic concepts of space, but that very structure may have specifically referred to those human motivations most associated with personal or family territories. Much of what has been labeled "Nature" in the pueblos, that is, personal politics, gossip, competition for and display of wealth, seems also to describe basic aspects of territoriality. Yet, interestingly for our present discussion, Nature domains proscriptively exclude the architectural dwelling at one scale and the overall urban form at another. The pueblo society thereby recognizes the inherent symbolic, structural, and cosmic, that is, the Cultural importance of these architectural places. Behavior within is to be primarily motivated by symbols and structure, whereas activities are recognized as being motivated by essentially individual, even territorial, principles. The essence of dwelling in such societies is not territorial but cosmic. The idea of personalization for identity does not occur in a situation defined by cultural space; as a concept, personalization only occurs in the absence of such unified conceptions of symbolic space, as dwelling and perhaps community shift to a more territorial mode.

Completely absent in any strictly territorial paradigm of the relationship between community spaces and family spaces is the frequent ritual usage of the dwelling or aspects of such for communally motivated purposes. From the rites associated with the construction of a dwelling in a cosmically intact society to calendrical rituals and rites of passage, typically some microcosmic domain defined as Culture or Spirit is reserved *within* the dwelling for the use of actual or spirit members of the community. While the Andalusian dwelling has yet to be "structurally" mapped, it is highly unlikely that no such provisions would be made. Aside from formally defined ritual occasions for community entry into the dwelling, there is very little entertaining of friends and even relatives in the dwelling of pueblo Andalusians. Such manipulative usage of the family domain seems to be more related to the territorial continuum between community and individual, where the politics of entertaining friends and relatives runs parallel to the tendency to display status with building form and detail.

In the dwellings and pueblos of Mijas, even the casual tourist may observe what is probably a formal rather than a territorial relationship between family and community. The typical daytime street or plaza activity consists of an intensity of children playing; women gossiping, mopping the street (which may be primarily pedestrian), whitewashing, reprimanding children, planting flowers, burning charcoal pots; men gossiping near the bars, loading or unloading burros, laying bricks; men and women weaving; and citizens generally coming and going. The family dwellings front directly on the narrow streets without any yard, fence, or other form of setback. Throughout the day and even into the freezing twilight hours of winter, the front door of the dwelling remains open when people are home. The family dining table and early evening dinner appears only a few feet inside the major dining/living room, in full view of those in the street.

This could be interpreted as a communal means of enforcing an extreme territorial prohibition against personalized interiors and activities—which do not occur in these dwellings. More relevant, however, might be a formal, cultural interpretation which sees the phenomenon as an expression of the important concentric opposition between family dwelling and public street. According to this interpretation, daytime is the period in which the Culture of the family living room and dwelling is played off against the Nature of the street activities. The open threshold is an articulation of both the timing and relationship of the opposition at this particular scale. Only at nighttime, as the dwelling normally becomes most microcosmic (aside from particular ritual times), is the door closed, thus emphasizing the internal opposition between rooms and courtyard. In this tentative symbolic interpretation, the living room during the day is associated primarily with things usually considered communal; the reference is more to the principles and structure of the culturally defined family paradigm. Compared with the informal individual and often political activities of the street, the family dining activity is very formal or Cultural.

In the social literature on Andalusia, the relationship between men and women is a topic of considerable attention, often overlapping the distinction or presumed opposition between community and family. According to ethnographers such as Driessen (1983) and Brandes (1981), for example, a wealth of myth and ritual surround what can only be described as an antagonistic, personally charged tension between the sexes in these seemingly tranquil villages. To Driessen, the basis for men's antifemale jokes, stories, and other expressive behavior, lies in the actual socioeconomic threat from women to the marginal, day-laboring existence of the men, especially as women increasingly enter the labor market (this may be more true as pueblos become larger agrotowns). Brandes, on the other hand, makes less of an attempt to explain this irrational behavior which to him is not directly linked to any actual economic or physical threat. Here this fascinating expressive phenomenon may have some unknown ecologically founded reason; or it may be part of larger Mediterranean, even Moorist, attitudes; or, most appealing to Brandes, it may have a largely psychological basis in universal male-female relationships.

Driessen, as part of his description of the expressive or ritualistic, implies that men's places—the bars and street—represent a formal, symbolic opposition to women's places—the dwellings. This analysis, however, seems much more driven by territorial than cosmic or cultural ideas. No formal spatial elements or activities are described; nor is the microcosmic aspect of the dwelling or its relationship to larger scales ever mentioned. Territories are quite simply assumed to be working on the cultural level; in reality, however, we have examples only of somewhat segregated men's and women's places, though men often use areas of the dwelling, such as the courtyard, and women frequent the street. This supposed territorial pattern coincides with basic assumptions of male-controlled community and female-controlled family. The entire notion of the women's place being the family home, in distinction to the wider public space of men, is probably more a territorial, even contemporary assumption. Even in traditional Arabic societies, where women are highly sequestered in the dwelling, that "family" space still contains domains of men and community that are contextual in terms of cosmos and other cultural space.

Certainly male-female relationships remained largely undefined in terms of some possible logic of cultural space in the Andalusian pueblo. The expression of antagonism must have some basis in real sociopolitical or economic purpose. It would be tempting to add the male and female labels to the several scales of probable concentric oppositions suggested for the pueblo, that is, Male as Culture and Female as Nature. A very interesting discussion of this tendency appears in Ortner's article on the topic (1974), though spatial expression of these categories receives no specific attention in this work. Like Brandes, in his emphasis on some sort of almost purely psycho-expressive need, Ortner, in her explanation of the relationship between men and women, relies primarily on a presumed inherent need of society. Human groups seem destined to distinguish things that are Cultural, symbolic "artifacts" which must be developed, maintained, and expressively appropriated in the control of those things that are individual, biological, entropic, or Natural. Because women's biological roles as mothers and nestmakers place them experientially closer to Nature, Ortner considers the symbolic link between Nature and Female to occur almost universally. Dominance and superiority of men (Culture) over women (Nature) necessarily results because of the inherent need for Culture to control Nature. Although such a view may approach a hypothesis for the expressed dialectic of Andalusian men and women, it does not quite fit the sketched outlines of cardinal and concentric aspects of the pueblo cosmos.

Concentrically it seems incomplete and perhaps unnecessary to label Other Pueblo, Termino, Street, and Courtyard as "Female," while My Pueblo, the Urban Pueblo Form, the Dwelling, and the Dwelling Interior are "Male." It does seem true that these Cultural domains are or should be dominant over the places associated with Nature. One's pueblo must be better than the other pueblo; the village must also be seen as dominant over the competitive, potentially unequalizing potential of day-labor in the surrounding agricultural termino. In contrast to the often assumed maleness and communal aspects of public street or plaza distinguished from the femaleness of family dwelling is the permanence and stability of Culture expressed in the white architectural dwelling, like the entire pueblo form itself, in opposition to the more spontaneous, political experiences of the street as Nature. One can readily see the cultural superiority of interior dwelling rooms over the courtyard as primarily a place of domestic labor and animals. In this sense then, Other Pueblo, Termino, Street, and Courtyard cannot be seen as particularly Female any more than their opposites can be labeled Male. Yet the basic Culture/Nature application is useful.

Considering the possible cardinal axes mentioned, the question immediately arises about whether the dominance and subordinance of the power directions, between Spirits and Humans, is part of the conceptions of Culture and Nature expressed concentrically. Or for that matter, what is the relationship to the so-called alliance axis labeled "Male/Female" primarily by the locations of the two chapels in the pueblo of Mijas. These answers, as well as much better evidence on which to base the definitions and labeling of both concentric and axial domains, can only come from detailed ethnographies that map the cultural spaces and their everyday or ritual activities. One unique and relatively recent work, by Francisco Aguilera, focuses on ritual in the smaller Andalusian pueblo. Unfortunately his account of ritual structure and social process in Santa Eulalia (1978) again does not specifically map the cultural space or associated cosmic concept, but only refers verbally to general pueblo locations and orientations in ritual processions. Still, the work does establish without a doubt that formalities of cultural space do exist in village forms long admired for more immediately understood reasons.

Aguilera's study of Santa Eulalia (the patron saint for the area in which the pueblo of Almonaster sits at the center) verifies the presence of cultural formalities of space, perhaps a cosmos. It is clear from the description of rites of passage (baptism, communion, military registration, marriage, and death) that the dwelling is not essentially a female or family territory. Portions of all these rituals involve community members participating in some domain of the dwelling, whether it be a communion reception or a wake, both presumably in that formal living/dining room opposite the street. Aguilera spends much of his text on major calendrical ritual. These annual celebrations are seen as a means of influencing social relationships:

> There is a constant and pressing need for an institutionalized mechanism for the salutory release of tension and for the reverification of group identity and structure which has the potential for reintegrating the group. . . . Because the chan-

neling of energy into the physical and emotional preparations that lead up to the rituals ensures, as do the group activities of the rituals themselves, that people are participating in a highly charged individual state and group atmosphere which leaves no participant untouched by the depth of social and ideological meaning and emotion aroused, the festival cycle serves as a check upon those social conflicts which might be harmful to the community and to reenforce the elemental strength of the corporate bond. (Aguilera 1978, 50, 53)

At Easter, three separate but sequentially linked rituals occur, each of several days' duration, each with its extremely elaborate preparations. The whole complex spans over a month. The first, Semana Santa, treats the basic values and identities of Catholicism and is orientated toward the individual; the second, the Crosses, expresses a competitive opposition between two halves of the town, and the third, Santa Eulalia, stresses the all-encompassing commonality and solidarity of the entire pueblo and region. All three rest on the organizational activities of brotherhood groups.

The frequent references to spatial position during these events are stimulating but frustrating because no overall spatial context or map is provided. The image of Christ used in the Semana Santa procession is kept in the small rural chapel, *ermita*, on the western margin of town. The pueblo of Almonaster apparently has a large church near a central plaza and two smaller churches or chapels in each of the western and eastern portions of the pueblo, much like the layout of Mijas. We are told that in the major church, men and women sit in separate sections, though we do not know to what directions these conform, or the general orientation of churches or chapels. All three of the Easter rituals involve processions that begin at some customary place outside the pueblo in the natural termino. Typically they make one or more circuits of the pueblo, then at some later point a feast or picnic, *gira*, is held once again at some traditional place out in the countryside. A particularly striking example of this probable expression of concentric domains, for example, Pueblo/Termino, is the pilgrimage to the ancient natural site in the region dedicated to the patron saint Santa Eulalia. If Semana Santa is a form of ritual death of the individual, focused on the larger church, then Santa Eulalia may represent the communal antithesis as numerous participants party through the night at this essentially natural setting. One cannot be immediately certain how to interpret this in terms of the concentric oppositions between Pueblo (Culture) and Termino (Nature).

Cardinal axes of power are at least intuitively present in these rituals. Key or central positions occur in the procession, usually in or in front of a church or chapel, where one senses that contact has been made with the spiritual world, thus legitimizing some aspect or actors of the ritual. The reader cannot determine what the cosmic directions of such encounters might be, even though, like Mijas, Almonaster lies below an imposing mountain with mentioned ritual significance—a conceptual North perhaps? The east-west alliance aspects of the pueblo become clear in the spatial opposition along that axis between halves of the town during the festival of the Crosses. This is a ritual processional competition between two brotherhoods whose allegiance is to the two chapels of the eastern and western areas of the pueblo. Each brotherhood prepares and practices extensively at a small meeting room in its domain of the town. The competitive processions themselves begin again at traditional places outside the pueblo, one on the east and the other on the west, then focus on the now highly decorated chapels of their domains. Finally, reference is made to the entire town and the major church in the center. Unlike the east-west expression in Mijas, the two ritually important chapels in Almonaster give no immediate indication of attached Male or Female meaning through their saints, although much in the processional chants, decoration, and *Mayordomo-Mayordoma* (master and mistress of ceremonies) parade relationship suggests ubiquitous male-female overtones. Thus we are left with a curious and perhaps convincing sense of the presence of cultural space, probably logically unified by cosmic meanings of direction.

Concluding Assumptions: Toward an Understanding of Pueblo Cultural Space

Pitt-Rivers was correct in his regard for the importance of the physical aspects of the pueblo:

> The social structure is founded upon an evaluation of physical proximity which not only orders the grouping within it . . . but also runs through every aspect of its culture from the conventions which govern its manners to its ethical principles or its evaluation of space or time. (1971, 209)

And though Aguilera's description (1978) of actual ritual moves the notion of "physical proximity" much closer to the expressive realities of cultural space or cosmos, the pieces remain to be put together. Somehow the enduring quality of these pueblos is largely dependent on the ritual manipulation of energies of spatially structured symbolism. This conclusion is based on the assumption that, given a coherent and powerful conception of cosmos in the minds of the inhabitants, the daily and ritual movement through coordinated domains in the architecture and settlement patterns is one of the most effective means of "turning on" or mobilizing this expressive affect. Furthermore, only through the shared cosmic conceptions of space can the systematic linkages be made between groups and levels of the society.

The picture we begin to see of the pueblo ethos speaks of the importance of the opposition between Culture and Nature. From the individual's point of view, there appear to be two principles by which one's activities may be judged and ritually influenced. There may be a sort of competition between these two previously defined modes of relationship: either the controlling effect of social or symbolic structure, or the spontaneous, self-interested motivations of individuals. I believe that such an internal competition looms particularly large for men of the society. In contrast to Ortner's view that men are some-how biologically and naturally unconstrained and are therefore free for cultural endeavors, I believe that men are also biologically disposed, particularly in terms of individual aggression. Logically, the inherent physically and territorially aggressive aspects of men's nature represent a greater potential danger to social order than do the aspects of women's nature. It is also logical to assume that if male aggression is the greater cultural threat, then it may be incumbent for men themselves to create symbolic culture to curb aspects of their own selves, hence the acknowledged male preoccupation with and control of most expressive activities.

In the pueblos of Andalusia, lacking as they are the actual or potential ownership of productive land, the greatest threat to the unequal distribution of wealth and power—to men—is the natural resource of women and children. Assuming that an attractive, fruitful woman and many, particularly male, children represent a sort of medium of competition, then we would expect the symbolic tendency of human culture to expressively define this potentially disruptive aspect as Nature. Also defined would be ways and behaviors of controlling these relationships, or Culture. Thus we might understand the formalized antagonism identified by Driessen (1983) and Brandes (1981) not as sentiments directed at women as individuals and wives but at men's natural, potentially disruptive views of women and eventual children as the primary competitive currency.

Also understandable is the elaborate process of courtship in the pueblo. Once a *novio* (intended marital partner) is chosen through a very short selection process, the ensuing courtship normally lasts from eight to ten years! During this time the girl remains openly virtuous. For her the competitive aspect is at this point critical; her reputation is ruined simply by a rejection at any phase of the courtship. Although the male competition would seem to be keenest prior to an acceptance by the female, he must nevertheless continue to perform not so much in relation to his friends as to the girl's parents. Perhaps as many as two thousand hours are spent in nightly visits in the culturally defined front room of the girl's house, always with other members of the family (Price and Price 1966, 309). Although courtship may be regarded as the crucial competitive arena, the resulting children, beginning with the first year of marriage, provide a continuation of competitive objects for both parents. The visible regard of the father for his offspring is particularly unusual.

The concentric oppositions at several scales of real places represent a more continuous, even daily, conception which associates real social behavior with the two *principles* of behavior, Culture and Nature. The activities of the Other Pueblo, Termino, Street, and Courtyard, for example, are in principle opposed to those of My Pueblo, the Urban Pueblo Form, the Dwelling, and the Dwelling Interior. Presumably, though in part generated by men for men, these meanings reflect the behavior of women as well, particularly in regard to competitive behaviors of courtship and child bearing. This would be an essentially static conception were it not for the more dynamic and ritualistic aspects provided by the axes of power and alliance. Certainly one can only suggest, at this point, how axial conceptions may interface with the concentric. It is as if the major oppositions between Culture and Nature—which may be largely philosophical, moral, or otherwise normative meanings devoid of powerful emotions—require the manipulation of more linearily dynamic, axial conceptions that are more purely symbolic or emotive. The meanings of life, death, maleness, and femaleness, while often identified with Cultural and Natural aspects of ritual, seem nevertheless to be on a more primary level. Perhaps it is the specific and axial expressions of ritual which when superimposed over the continuous concentric definitions provide the means of maintaining, heightening, or even reversing the affective charge of the overall principles and activities of behavior.

Often, the power of the spirit world will be associated during ritual with the concentric domains of Culture, thus providing its dominance. Male/Female symbolism is less clear. Although it does not seem necessary to associate the meanings of Male and Female with the concentric oppositions, some essential meaning of alliance does seem useful in the invigoration of static, concentric ideas of Culture and Nature. To many anthropologists, the primary semantic of male-female relationships is generally marriage and specifically the alliance that it creates. But still, alliance represents a less affective form of symbolism than that of the power axis. We could, however, reduce alliance and Male/Female meanings to human competition, which brings it to a much more inherent level. Certainly in the Andalusian pueblo, Male/Female expressions are primarily competitive. How these axial meanings superimpose with the concentric Culture/Nature oppositions remains to be seen.

Finally, it is possible to redefine the outsider's territorial meaning of a white contiguous pueblo. White is Culture, with its expressive opposite of Nature, the color and black of surrounding agricultural termino, streets and plazas, and courtyards. The architectural pueblo and dwelling are in this sense eternal, while the living things within it must eventually die. Since women are the source of dangerous competition, Nature, it is only fitting that women are particularly expressive of the fact that the fruits of competition, individuals and individual families, will biologically die, thus proving the superiority of Culture. In contrast to the white eternal continuity of Pueblo exists the custom of *luto* (mourning). Virtually all middle-aged and older women dress completely in black, along with many younger women and girls. Few examples, if any, may be found of greater duration or adherence to this death-related ritual; if a woman's father dies, for example, she must dress in black for a period of six to eight years!

Beginning as the brightly colored *novia* of the courtship period, the woman will eventually wear black for the better part of her life. While participating in both aspects of the Culture/Nature opposition, in Andalusia, too, women are extremely significant from an expressive male's point of view. Spatially, in keeping with the almost universal female symbolism of the liminal threshold, it is the Andalusian woman who whitewashes the dwelling to the exact edge of the street, which like the expression of dress, maintains the edge between the two conceptions. The symbolism of black and white cannot be understood in terms of immediate territorial observations, but only as part of some yet to be defined cultural structure of Andalusian space.

In overview, what is the effect of externally introduced social, political, and economic changes on the almost systematic contribution of such probable cultural space? At what point in the evolution of national "development" are spatially structured symbolic meanings ignored, replaced by more "territorial" processes, or generally broken apart? If this happens very early in the process of economic and national modernization, then this point is moot. If, however, concepts of cosmos continue to influence the content and structure of places, in spite of external changes in form—remember Hirschon's contention of some such phenomena in a contemporary urban setting (1981)—then the term *housing* in reference to the dwelling cannot be applied independent of the meanings and relationships of other cultural spaces. Only by enlarging the research paradigm to include the cultural level—of spatial structure, not just symbols—can we begin to formulate questions not only about how people in traditional cultures dwell but also about how expressive culture itself has evolved as human space changes historically.

References

Aguilera, F. E. 1978. *Santa Eulalia's people: Ritual structure and process in an Andalucian multicommunity.* New York: West Publishing Co.

Brandes, S. 1981. Like wounded stags: Male sexual ideology in an Andalusian town. In *Sexual meanings*, ed. Ortner and Whitehead. London: Cambridge University Press.

Corbin, J. 1979. Social class and patron-clientage in Andalusia: Some problems of comparing ethnographies. *Anthropological Quarterly* 52:2.

Doxtater, D. 1984. Spatial opposition in non-discursive expression: Architecture as ritual process. *Canadian Journal of Anthropology* 4:1.

———. 1981. Thursday at a crossroads: The symbolism, structure, and politics of "center" in the old Scandinavian farm culture. Ph.D. diss., University of Michigan.

Driessen, H. 1983. Male sociability and rituals of masculinity in rural Andalusia. *Anthropological Quarterly* 56:3.

Gauvain, M., I. Altman, and F. Hussein. 1983. Homes and social change: A cross-cultural analysis. In *Environmental psychology: Directions and perspectives*, ed. Feimer and Geller. New York: Praeger.

Gilmore, D. 1976. Class, culture, and community size in Spain; the relevance of models. *Anthropological Quarterly* 49:86–106.

———. 1977. The social organization of space: Class, cognition, and residence in a Spanish town. *American Ethnologist* 4:3.

Goldfinger, M. 1969. *Villages in the sun*. New York: Praeger.

Hirschon, R. 1981. Essential objects and the sacred: Interior and exterior space in an urban Greek locality. In *Women and space*, ed. S. Ardener. London: Billing and Sons.

Ortner, S. B. 1974. Is female to male as nature is to culture? In *Woman, culture, and society*, ed. Rosaldo and Lamphere. Stanford: Stanford University Press.

Pitt-Rivers, J. 1971. *People of the Sierra*. Chicago: University of Chicago Press.

Price, R., and S. Price. 1966. Noviazgo in an Andalusian pueblo. *Southwestern Journal of Anthropology* 22:3.

Rapoport, A. 1970. Symbolism and environmental design. *International Journal of Symbology* 1:3.

Rudofsky, B. 1964. *Architecture without architects*. New York: Doubleday.

Saile, D. 1977. Making a house: Building rituals and spatial concepts in the Pueblo Indian world. *Architectural Association Quarterly* 9.

Sert, J. L. 1967. *Ibiza*. Barcelona: Ediciones Poligrafa.

Figure 7.1. The Andalusian pueblo.

Figure 7.2. The east (above) and west (below) chapels of Mijas: San Sebastian and Santa Maria.

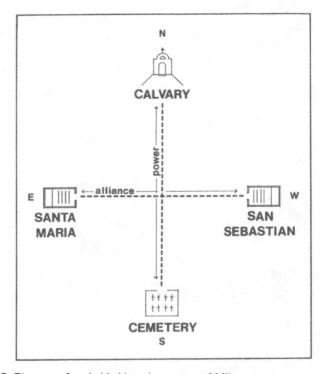

Figure 7.3. Diagram of probable historic cosmos of Mijas.

Figure 7.4. Scales of possible concentric oppositions in Andalusian cultural space.

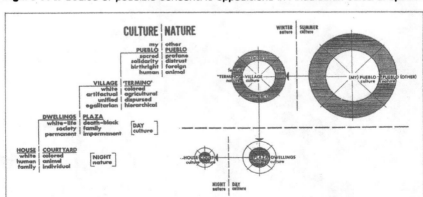

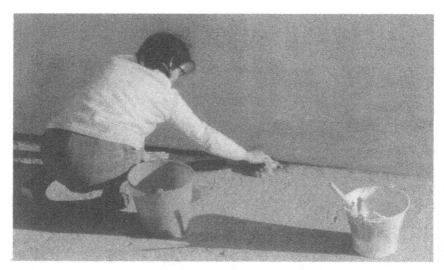

Figure 7.5. Woman's role of whitewashing dwelling facade.

Figure 7.6. Andalusian children.

Figure 7.7. The opposition in black and white.

8

THE ARCHITECTURE
OF NOMADISM:
GABRA PLACEMAKING
AND CULTURE

LABELLE PRUSSIN

The architecture of nomadism—in contrast to the "monumental" and "permanent" architectures associated with "civilization" and urbanization and even in contrast to the vernacular architectures of sedentary, rural populations—has always been considered temporary and ephemeral. Rarely has it engaged the attention of the observer or the concern of the scholar. To be sure, transhumant architectures imply portability, but they are not temporary in the disposable sense. Building components—reused, reassembled, and inherited from one generation to the next, from one occasion to the next—are just as permanent as those associated with fixed or stationary structures, whether one cites contemporary geodesic domes and tensile surface envelopes or traditional woven black tents, sewn leather tents or bent wooden armatures laid over with mats. The concept "temporary" is not synonymous with "transient"; the concept of "permanent" is distinct from "stationary." There are temporary building structures that remain fixed in space and permanent building structures designed and intended to be moved from place to place. Sites remain fixed in space while the built environment that occupies them may be portable.

Murdock's World Ethnographic Sample (1957, 664–87) reveals that close to 25 percent of the African rural cultures he lists are still transhumant to some degree. The Maures, the Tekna, the Tuareg, the Fulbe, the Tubu, the Sorko, and the Saghawa in the west; the Kababish and the Baggara in the northeast; the Borana, the Gabra, the Samburu, the Rendille, the Turkana, and the Somalis in the east are only some of these nomadic cultures. Classifications of nomadism and nomadic boundaries in space, however, are difficult to define and demarcate. Some peoples lead a seminomadic existence, alternating between seasonal movement and fixed agricultural settlements. Others combine hunting with pastoralism or fishing activities. In many groups, one part of the community resides in a fixed location and the other part moves with the herds.

In addition to ethnographic nomadic populations, there are different kinds of pilgrimages (such as the *hajj* undertaken by Muslim believers), annual ritual congregations (such as the Fulbe *koumen* and the Gabra *kolompte* celebrations), and long-term military excursions and raids, all of which generate a politicoreligious, "establishment" architecture based on translocation. Historical references remain meager, but illustrations on early Roman mosaics and accounts of African military campaigns, renderings on the Tassili frescos in southern Algeria, references to the "tent-cities" of Ethiopian capitals, and accounts by early European and Muslim voyagers all suggest a rich, yet to be researched, resource.[1]

Nomadic life-styles presuppose a transportable building package, easy to dismantle and reassemble, pliable, transportable in its entirety, and with its weight and building technology adapted to the available means of transport— human porterage, draft or pack animal, truck or boat. Nomadic life-styles also presuppose the need for multi-use artifacts made of nonfragile, light-weight materials in the form of containers that can be easily suspended and remain intact when in continuous motion. Mobility is inherent in the repetitive building cycle and in the transportation process. Many of the building components used in construction as well as the repertoire of structural and applied artifacts can be and are recombined into saddles, litters, and palanquins to facilitate movement in time and space. As a consequence, the architecture of nomadism has neither beginning nor end, only transformations. It is a process possessing a unique set of formal and behavioral properties. Together, these properties suggest an aesthetic quality quite discrete and distinct from that of sedentary populations. This discussion of Gabra architecture in northern Kenya is one attempt to understand that nomadic aesthetic and the nature of "placemaking" in its culture.

The Physical Context of Gabra Culture

The image of Kenya that most of us carry in our heads has been shaped—if not by *Out of Africa*—by travelers', settlers', and tourists' accounts of the game parks and verdant highlands that make up the southern half of the country. The northern half, with its featureless Great Rift Valley and its salt-laden Chalbi desert seems, by contrast, to be an arid and barren wasteland. Nevertheless, it is the habitat of large populations of nomadic and seminomadic pastoralists, including the Gabra for whom it is a varied source of herbage and game (Figure 8.1). Although many hypotheses have been advanced about their origin and the history of their transhumance, the present-day Gabra rangelands extend from Marsabit Mountain (an extinct volcano) in the south to the Megado Escarpment in the north at the Ethiopian border, from Lake Turkana in the west to the Marsabit-Moyale international trunk road in the east.

The unending expanse of desert topography consists of various natural features: gravel patches, vast saltpans, and thick volcanic ridges are interspersed with bush growth and many species of acacia, commiphora, wild sisal, and asparagus. The horizon line is interrupted by the Ngaso plains in the south and the Dida Galgala plains in the north and punctuated only by the Hurri hills in the northwest.

Annual rain on the desert plain, a bare 8 inches, falls during two brief seasons: there is a long, heavy rain between April and June, and a short light rain between October and November. It rains heavily on Marsabit Mountain, but the desert receives only occasional, concentrated downpours. During the short vegetal growth period, the glistening white surface sands are blanketed with a soft, translucent green haze of miniscule feathery leafbuds and struggling blades of grass. The lack of water almost seems to shape tree profiles into an impluvium, funneling each droplet of water into the core of their trunks.

In early December the fierce northeast trade winds from the Arabian Peninsula bring with them an increasingly hot, dry season, and in March the southeast trade winds begin to sweep across the Indian Ocean ushering in the long rains. These winds, their velocity uninterrupted by topographic profiles, strongly influence settlement patterns and building forms. The north-south alignment of camps, the arrangement of camel kraals, the orientation of openings, and most striking of all, the reinforcement of the east side of the armature tent are all measures of human response to and mediation with the east winds.[2]

The Gabra are camel herders, in contrast to their linguistic relatives the Borana cattle herders.[3] Like many other pastoral societies they also herd goats, but camel husbandry forms the mainstay of their economy. It is the key to their subsistence and existence. Camels constitute the major subject and object of not only their music but also of their daily and ritual life. The seemingly formless and ephemeral acacia-bush fences that enclose and contain their animals are actually formidable: they are environmental necessities that protect animals from destructive winds, predators, and until recently, raiding parties. The kraal (*moonaa gaalaa*) is always located on the eastern side of the camp (*il boruu*), because camels are very sensitive to noise and easily startled

(Figures 8.2 and 8.3). The windward location reduces the chance of stampedes which might result from human noise emanating from the adjoining houses. Each camel kraal has at least two openings, a single *balbala* for people which always faces west toward the house (*man dasse*) and one or more *kara* for camels, depending upon how many related households are sharing the enclosure.

Fences, which define the enclosure, are not only crucial to existence; they are also fundamental to religious and social life. They communicate the owner's worth to the world around him since within them he keeps his most valued possessions—his camels. The fenced enclosure defines the male domain: only men may enter to milk the camels. But at the same time, the camel kraal is also the setting for the enactment of ritual behaviors associated with the marriage ceremony and the creation of a new house. The fences do more than enclose space; they create the boundaries that define the categories used by Gabra to deal with the world.

Myth and reality also reinforce each other in the orientation of house openings. Entrances invariably face west—a logical response to the strong east winds. But the Gabra also told us their entrances face west so they can look out toward Mount Kulal, which they also call *haanqu*; it is also the name of a tree which grows on the mountain. As a consequence, the daily patterns of movement echo two major axes in space, much like the cardinal directions of the ancient Roman camp, which were also imposed onto the natural features of the environment (Figure 8.4).[4]

Although the fences of the kraals—defining the male domain—are left behind with each move, the *man dasse* and all its furnishings—the female domain—is always transported to the new site. Departure leaves few visible remains: the stones of the hearth, the perimeter stones from the base of the domed armature, and an occasional broken, no longer usable artifact are the only material, archaeological remains to testify to the fact that a site was formerly occupied (Tallam 1984). The scarcity of natural resources, the limited labor time available to exploit them, and the arduous effort needed to collect them all help explain the imperative to reuse, maintain, and recycle every material artifact. The only natural resources are perennial grasses, sparse stands of acacia and commiphora trees, and animal hides.

Apart from the materials needed for the construction of the armature tent with its inner lining and outer cover, Gabra material culture consists mainly of carved wooden and woven containers used to carry and store milk, water, fats, and when available, meat. Pottery is almost nonexistent. The traditional clay cookpot used in both ritual and daily life is being rapidly displaced by metalware purchased in the urban markets of Marsabit and Maikona. The few other metal objects, such as tools and jewelry, are commissioned from the Konso blacksmiths. While most wooden containers and utensils are carved by Gabra men, the indispensable ones used to collect and store water and milk, such as the *butte*, the *goddaa*, the *gorffa*, the *chicho*, and the different types of house mat or *dasse*, are woven and plaited by the women. Gabra women possess remarkable knowledge of the strength, performance, and availability of each subspecies of flora in the desert and great skill in maximizing the structural potential of each. The choices and selections they make are evident in the rich lexicon used in designating their resources and in describing the techniques and processes essential to transforming them. Collecting and processing the fibers used in house and container manufacture entails long expeditions by search parties of women and a few old men during the year and requires a sophisticated knowledge of regional botany.[5]

These search parties will often be compelled to remain camped at collection sites for several weeks to locate the asparagus roots (*erggamsaa*) and the wild sisal (*algee*) and prepare them for transport. The preliminary processing, extending over several weeks, is done on site, so a return trip is also necessary. Both the manufacture of woven containers and mats and the repetitive reconstruction of the *man dasse* are restricted to married women, but observation of and participation in the various creative processes begins when babies still rest on thir mothers' backs and continues through prepubescence, because young girls participate in the collection and preparation of the raw materials. Thus, the transmission of knowledge and skills is a continuous, participatory experience, like a lifelong apprenticeship. The repertoire of skills involves not only the skills to create many different kinds of containers but also the skills to create containers to contain containers—all culminating in the construction and reconstruction of the *man dasse* itself. The same skills and the same limited raw materials are utilized in each related undertaking; together, they coalesce into the nomadic placemaking process.

Gabra Marriage

The creation of a new house, including the residential container and its accompanying furnishings—as opposed to its recreation at each successive location—evolves directly out of the rituals and behaviors associated with marriage. The noun for the armature tent, or house of mats (*man dasse*), is linguistically related to the verb for marriage. When the Gabra talk about a marriage, they say *min fuud'aa* or *man fuud'aa*, "we are building a house." Although the events that constitute a marriage process actually extend over a long period and involve negotiations and exchanges both before and after the wedding, it is the four-day *min fuud'aa* ceremony that establishes the synonymous relationship between house and marriage, as the following paraphrased description illustrates (Tablino 1978). This description is central not only to an understanding of Gabra nomadic moral and aesthetic values, but also to an understanding of the universal nature of placemaking.

Once the marriage has been agreed upon by the two families involved, the bridegroom's family moves to join the bride's camp and await the appearance of the new moon of a propitious month.[6] During the week before the four-day ceremony, wooden framing members and tanned hides destined for the house armature are anointed with fat to make them "smart and shining." The fat from animals slaughtered during this week is referred to as *man duuba*, used "to anoint the house."

The evening before the start of the four-day *min fuud'aa*, four elders and four mothers of female children from the bride's camp gather at the *kara* of the bridegroom's father's kraal. Each of the mothers carries her own special walking stick and a branch of the madera tree. Two of them carry full milk containers (*chichos*). Welcomed at the *kara* by the bridegroom's father, the entire group enters his kraal, moves through it, exits at the *balbala*, and, proceeding to the *kara* of the bride's father's kraal, takes up the same position and is greeted by him. The entire group then moves through his kraal in the same sequence and proceeds on to the bride's mother's house. The four mothers insert the branches of the madera tree and their walking sticks into the top of the house dome and, with the others, enter for a ritual evening meal, carrying the two containers full of milk.

On the morning of the first day, two women from the bridegroom's camp carry two *chichos* of milk, a special container of fat, and a camelskin for the marriage bed from his mother's house along the same line of travel established the evening before. They are followed in procession by the bridewealth (*garata*), which consists of: first, an ox or ram; two men each carrying a length of cloth; two women each carrying her walking stick, a male child, and a milk container; and a camel weighted down with milk containers; and second, the father's own contribution, three camels (two male and one female) taken out through the *balbala* of his kraal. These, accompanied by the bridegroom and three elders, head up the procession, moving through the *kara* into the kraal of the bride's father, who, in the company of three elders, greets him. In the evening, the procession of participants, having left the bridewealth in the kraal, returns in reverse order through the kraals to the bridegroom's mother's house.

On the morning of the second day, the bridegroom with the help of four companions collects some branches of the *acacia tortilis* tree (*d'addacha*),

used in all Gabra ceremonies, and with these he inscribes the circle of the
new *mana* inside his father's kraal, using one of the framing posts (*kaala*) of
the bed to establish the radius.[7] Meanwhile, the women from the bride's camp
dismantle her mother's house. The bent arches and the mats that will be
transferred to the new house are put aside while those that will be used to
rebuild the mother's house are left on the ground. Again, in procession, the
women carry the used materials into the bride's father's kraal. Combining
them with those that were anointed the previous week, they construct a new
mana inside the kraal. Then, immediately dismantling it, they carry both old
and new material into the bridegroom's father's kraal and deposit it within the
circle demarcated by the bridegroom. He then anoints the house by pouring
milk and a mixture of fried coffee beans and butter fat (*bunna*) around
the inscribed perimeter and on the house material. Immediately afterward,
the women reconstruct the armature tent on its now sanctified site, while the
bridegroom looks on.[8] In the evening, he builds a new fire inside the house
with the help of four companions and a pair of firesticks (*uchuma*) which his
mother has presented to him, and then he resumes his place to the right of the
balbala on the outside. Having put up the new house, the women from the
bride's camp return to the site of the original house and rebuild it—now reduced in size since part of the material has gone into the new bride's house.
Mothers' houses become progressively smaller with the marriage of each
daughter.

The third and fourth days of the *min fuud'aa* involve the preparation of
the bride, her processional and presentation to the groom along the same line
of travel described above, the positioning and hanging of the primary furnishings (the *chichos* and the *barchuma*), and finally the consummation of the
marriage act.[9]

Ideally, the newly created house remains standing inside the kraal for a
month. When it is dismantled, the house material is loaded on two camels
and the new wife rides the third, carrying a baby boy. When the camels are
unloaded the baby is returned to its mother and the *mana* is rebuilt adjacent
to neighbors in the bridegroom's camp.

Pitching the *Man Dassa*

The first step in building the *mana* is to construct the
primary arch on the east face of the armature (*uttubaa borro*) using two bent
poles (Figure 8.5).[10] This arch is of primary structural import (the surface it
defines, when reinforced by its six vertical members or *rarak*, helps resist the
eastern tradewinds), and it establishes the conceptual "head" of the house.

People always sleep with their heads toward the *borro* and their feet toward the west. The *borro* is the backdrop for marriage negotiations and the first sexual encounters of the newlyweds. It designates the place where children are born and where women "bathe." The Matcha Oromo, culturally and linguistically related to the Borana, recite a blessing when this arch is erected which eloquently expresses the symbolic importance of the *borro* for all Oromo-speaking peoples, the Gabra included (Bartels 1983, 296):

Oh my *boru*, be a *boru* that is firm and upstanding,
A *boru* that does not fall down,
A *boru* where children are born,
Where people sleep and keep in good health,
A *boru* where sons marry
And where daughters are given in marriage.
O *Waka* [God], keep all evil people and everything evil away from this *boru*,
Make it for us a *boru* of peace.

The next two steps in the structural sequence are to set up the arch of the *uttubaa balbala*, which defines the entrance, and to tie two cross arches (*mosar*) horizontally perpendicular to them. Together these increase wind resistance and define the four sides of the house circle in relation to the cardinal directions. For the Gabra, the "right" side is always on the north and the secondary poles and arches are installed moving from right to left.[11] Once the basic frame is established, two more *mosar* are added as part of the buildup of arches (*dediyee*) in both directions. At the same time, a perimeter of stones is wedged in at the base of these arches to stabilize them.

As the basketlike armature takes form, the bedpoles (*kaala*), four for each bed (*sirrir*), are put into position in the northeast and southeast quadrants of the house circle. The *kaala*, the *sirrir*, and the weight of people and artifacts suspended from the *borro* all contribute to structural stability on the east side.

Next, a wainscot (*goola*) made of camel or cow skins, or both, is hung on the interior to line the *uttubaa borro*. Ideally, camel skins are hung on the right, north, "men's" side, and cow skins on the left or south side of the *borro*. These skins in turn serve as the wall lining for the ritual containers and other accoutrements: all together, these are called the *elel'aan*. The exterior covering of the armature is laid up simultaneously with the wainscot. Traditionally, five layers of matting were laid up, perpendicular to each other, again rotating from right to left and recalling the two major axes of the armature frame, but these mats or *dasse* are being rapidly replaced today by substitute materials ranging from European cloth to burlap sacking, polyethylene sheets, and even scraps and sheets of cardboard. As the mats are tied into place with sisal and camel-skin ropes, the architectural container takes shape.

The *manno* is brought in and set at the base of the *borro* over a depression in the floor between the left and right sleeping places and on axis with the *balbala*. The incense burned in the depression fumigates both the woman's body (she squats over the *manno*) and the house environment. The *manno*, an openwork armature dome woven of bent arches and tied with camel-skin thongs, is a miniature of the *man dasse*: the arches are laid up in two directions, three on a side, and skillfully tied, again echoing the two major axes in space of the *man dasse* itself.

Other containers and family possessions are moved in while the woven screens (*korbbo*) are anchored to the interior support poles (*kaala*). The *korbbo*, one on each side, are placed precisely along the diameter of the house circle, dividing it into two halves and creating a physical and visual barrier between the public (*badaa*) and private (*dingaa*) hemispheres. The three hearth stones (*sesuma*) are then set in place in the left quadrant, and the two large water storage containers (*butte*) in their carrying frames (*chanchala*) are set down in the right, northeast quadrant. The carrying frames are essentially an inverted *manno*, engaging the same geometry and technology as the *man dasse*. Finally, the stools to sit on—the *barchuma*, the husband's singular symbol of masculinity, and the *kara*, the stool most often used by children and women—are brought in. These operations in the building process are all a repetition of the ritual building sequence that first unfolded in the marriage ceremony.

Striking and Transporting the House

The pitching and striking of the nomadic domicile are inextricably linked by the loading, transporting, and unloading process to create a sense of continuity in the placemaking process over space and through time. In the striking of the residential container, the order in which things are disassembled is the inverse of the order in which they are then reassembled on the pack camels. Thus, the cognitive system that categorizes and regulates the organization of technological behavior, that creates its "style," is repetitively reinforced. The overture to dismantling the *man dasse* is made by the husband when he strikes it with his walking stick (*ulle*), his ceremonial symbol of authority. Immediately afterward, his wife, to whom the *man dasse* belongs, begins to untie the ropes holding down the mats. Layers are removed in sequence, spread on the ground, rolled into bundles, and tied one by one. Neighboring women join in to help when necessary. The *dediyee* are untied and pulled out, the *mosar* are taken down, the *uttubaa* and *kaala* are brought out and set aside, and then the *korbbo* are untied. While the *manno* and the two *butte* are removed, the interior wainscot of skins is taken down and all that finally remains standing within the ring of stones are the *borro* wall and the two ritual *chichos* hanging from it. During this entire dismantling process, the men of the camp squat at the sidelines, indulging in banter with the working women.

While the dismantling proceeds, three camels that will serve as the pack animals are brought over. The skins that had covered the beds and those that had served as the wainscot are placed on the camels' backs as padding for the litter frames, which are constructed in turn by reassembling the bed rails and houseposts into a crossframe (four poles for each camel). The pairs of curved tied bundles of *mosar* and *dediyee* are wedged into the angle created by the parallelogram of the intersecting poles. The house partitions are wedged in at the front and bent over to meet the curving arches above, creating a moving shelter for old women, young children, and baby goats to ride in. Thus, the armature tent is sweepingly transformed into a litter-palanquin—again a container for people and household goods.

The transformation entails both an inversion of form and a reduction in volume. Like all pack animals, the camel is bisymmetrical along its spinal axis, and the art of loading depends primarily on achieving a balance of weight between the two sides. The difficulty of gaining this balance is forcefully illustrated by the strength required to fasten the litter to the camel. The litter must also be manipulated to accommodate the hump. As a result, the four quadrants of the armature dome are contracted, fanlike, into a straight line, and the major structural elements are linked, their curvature in balanced opposition. Thus, the exigencies of loading and transporting "place" further reinforce—or perhaps help explain—the spatial geometry of the house form itself.

The Meaning of Space

This detailed description of the Gabra marriage ceremony and house construction and reconstruction emphasizes the way meanings attached to marriage become synonymous with meanings attached to "house" or to "place." The house and its basic, critical furnishings are inherent in the gift exchange; they move through the same sequences of ritual space as the participants in the ritual. Building process and marriage performance are simultaneously enacted on the same stage. The nomadic building process, by virtue of its recurrence, renews symbolically the meanings attached to the marriage performance with each pitching sequence. The dismantling and its reenactment in reverse suggests not only a polarity and a heightened complementarity between the sexes but also a balanced equilibrium in space which the zoomorphy of the pack animal further enhances. During the wedding ritual, movement within the kraals is always along the east-west axis because of the location of kraals and their openings. Movement between the houses follows a north-south axis. The spatial order created by these two axes of movement is emphasized within the *man dasse* by the placement of furnishings and the consequent behaviors associated with them, as well as by the technology of house construction and the manufacture of the artifacts that constitute the furnishings.

The material creation of order within the *man dasse* recalls a suggestion made by Leach (1976, 54) that the more featureless the context of territorial space is, the more tightly prescribed the "model" of behavioral categories will be. Gabra interior space is divided into precisely four quadrants, in such a way that predictable social and technical activities can be carried out in each of them. North is associated with men and south is associated with women in and beyond the house. Public space is on the west and private space is on the east. Furthermore, the very form of the various household furnishings and the processes used in their creation recall a similar geometry. (See Prussin [1987] for a detailed description of container construction.)

The idiom of enclosure or containment emerges prominently in the creative process of Gabra placemaking. A container is a receptacle, a formed or flexible covering for the storage, packing, and shipment of both people and goods. Implicit in the definition is the creation of a volume by a set of real (or imagined) walls. Within this volume of space, human codes and behaviors assume, for the Gabra, an awareness of the symmetries of the human body and project them onto the asymmetries of topographic space. The more featureless the context of topographic space and the more hostile the territorial space, the greater, it seems, is the psychological need to articulate the enclosure and emphasize the containment.

A container, to be accessible, must have an opening, and the Gabra acknowledge the binary complementarity of inside/outside that a threshold formally conveys by the generic term *balbala*. *Balbala* is the word for the intricately worked openings of woven containers, the single opening into the *man dasse*, and the "people" entrance to the *moonaa gaalaa*. It is also the word for a Gabra descent group. These many uses emphasize not only the juxtaposition of social and spatial fact but also the essence of continuity. Since the interior is so much a woman's domain, one might ask if the intensity of interior elaboration within a contained and controlled space could be considered a gender-discrete aesthetic preference.

In addressing the subject of granaries in West Africa, some years ago (1972) I suggested that those material facilities which a culture implicitly or explicitly acknowledges as essential to its viability become imbued with the greatest meaning. They are the expressive symbols of the cultural aesthetic. If one can consider the nomadic container equivalent to a granary among sedentary populations, as I believe one can, then contained space forms an implicit component of the cultural aesthetic of the Gabra.

Frequently acknowledged but rarely investigated is the fact that Gabra women, like women in most nomadic cultures, traditionally have carried responsibility for creating, erecting, maintaining, and striking the domicile. As we have suggested, almost all property associated with it is in their hands and of their making. Thus, a nomadic woman spends the major part of her working day, every day, on domestic activities within or close to the walls of her bounded domicile. Her travel away from home, other than when the entire community is on the move, is often associated with the collection of the raw materials necessary to the fabrication of domestic artifacts. In contrast, the primary economic activities of her male counterpart involve more frequent movement further from the immediacy of the residential space. Even when on the move, a Gabra woman spends most of her time either beside or atop the camels and their litters—which are the collapsed house. Almost all of her activities are carried out exclusively in the company of other women. Most of her verbal communication is about domestic activity, moving activity, and house-building activity. At the same time, the words for human actions, such as the marriage behaviors, also refer most frequently to homemaking. As Illich explains:

> The body in action, with its movements and rhythms, its gestures and cadences, shapes the home as something more than a shelter, a tent or a house. . . . Rare are the words that designate human actions—the verbs—that do not also refer to homemaking. In vernacular cultures, dwelling and living coincide. With gender-related tools, oriented by a gender-specific meaning, vernacular life weaves a gendered cocoon . . . the house, at once building and family, links men and women to their possessions. (1982, 118–19)

In the Gabra nomadic architecture, therefore, it is the whole of a woman's personality that is involved in the creation of dwelling. The mind, the body, the senses, and memory are all brought to bear on the architectural creative act. The essential notion of architectural anthropomorphy, which is common to vernacular architectures in ethnographic societies, can be more specifically related to the gender-specific realm. The Gabra *mana* is the ultimate expression of identity with the woman's body and her primary procreative role. Thus, it is not only social space and social labor that lie at the basis of Gabra placemaking. These ultimately relate back to the biological fact of birth, and marriage as its agency. "A man without a wife is a man without a house" is a proverb found in numerous nomadic cultures, including the Gabra.

Men herd camels but women build houses. If the *moonaa gaalaa* is a focal point of the masculine sphere, then the *man dasse* is a focal point of the feminine sphere. Thus, the recurrent mounting and striking of the *man dasse* adjacent to the kraals communicates more than the existence of a complementarity among the two gender-discrete spatial domains; it suggests the weaving of a symbolic and behavioral thread among the two families involved in the marriage ceremony.

The Nomadic Placemaking Process

The process of placemaking as we have described it for the Gabra women involves individuals in the process of building and rebuilding the envelope of shelter and the artifacts within it. Involvement has two critical aspects: control and memory or continuity. Control and continuity for the Gabra women are the same thing: both are in the hands of the same individual. But, what are some of the specific mechanisms that contribute to control and continuity?

Maintenance Meaning in the built, nomadic environment is generated through personalization and maintenance—by taking possession of, or controlling, by creating and changing the material artifacts that constitute the domicile. Despite our Western perception of limited resources and technologies, the Gabra *mana* provides the woman with maximum freedom to manipulate her own, immediate domestic environment. Moving beyond the focus of this chapter, one could compare this freedom to manipulate the domestic environment within the boundaries of the tent to the almost exclusive control by men over the external environment, over the cattle and their patterns of transhumance—the real property investment of the social unit and the balance within the gender realm. Although we have not dealt with the nature of real property, it is a factor of major importance in any consideration of gender-related aspects of economic control within society, and it merits additional analysis.

Maintenance and renewal is reinforced by the recurrent, repetitive, and reproductive mounting and striking of the domestic container. The renewal process, unlike sedentary vernacular housing, is inherent in the creative process itself, as we have shown for the Gabra *mana*. The creation of a new *mana*, at the marriage ceremony, establishes the continuity by bringing together some old, some new. The old, or used material brings with it the meanings which have accrued to it over time. Every mounting or striking of the *man dasse* constitutes a creative event, and the event coalesces into a formalized system, associated with and expressive of the emotionally charged ritual of birth, rebirth, renewal, marriage, and so on, in which it participated as the setting or stage.

Thus, maintenance has a wider dimension in the nomadic context than in other vernacular residential contexts. The transportability and the reconstruction at each stage of a transhuman migration involves the creative act anew. Each time a Gabra woman re-erects the poles or *uttubaa*, the bent frames or *dediyee* of her *man dasse*, she renews, through tactile stimuli, the social and biological events of her existence. An analogy is the poetic distinction between using a mechanical grinder and a mortar and pestle for grinding coffee, cited by Douglas and Isherwood (1979, 73). In the first instance, the product is an impersonal powder, in the second, bodily skills are involved and "out of the mortar comes not mere dust, but a gritty powder pointing straight to the ancient lore of alchemy and its potent brews." The housecleaning responsibilities in the Western world provide another parallel. The polishing of brass candlesticks renews, as does the oiling of wooden utensils and furniture. Creating the patina becomes part of the placemaking process. A contrast with the Western world makes this point even more clearly evident: which of us has not experienced a breakdown in the process of house cleaning and maintenance at the approach of a moving date?

Memory   Maintenance through repetitive behavior is closely related to memory. In a recent exposition on environmental and cognitive structures, Greenwald defined memory:

> A cognitive structure is a knowledge structure or memory. Knowledge structures exist not only inside the head. Many outside-the-head structures—not just obvious ones such as books or computers—can function as memories. . . . If memory is defined more generally as the deposition of records that may subsequently be deciphered, then we can recognize that people use a great variety of external media in mnemonic fashion—that is, as legible records. (1981, 535)

The repetitive behavior in which Gabra women engage in building their houses, assembling their tents anew at each new site, is akin to the "container memories" and "restorage strategies" that we use in organizing the drawers of dressers and shelves of refrigerators. The dresser drawer or refrigerator space has no internal structure to dictate where we put objects. Instead, we use "restorage strategies" and memory to repeatedly put the same objects in the same places after each shopping. In like manner, when the Gabra woman arrives at a new site, she uses a "reconstruction strategy" in which the architectural and artifactual components serve as mnemonic devices to recreate the place that she has just dismantled. These cognitive structures involved in maintenance and recurrent behaviors are further reinforced by associated ritual behaviors involved in birth, marriage, and death—all staged within the container of *man dasse*.

In the traditional nomadic domicile, the container is composed of many small, aggregate elements, designed for portability and assembled into a composite whole. Each of these small-scale elements could be viewed as a semi- or nonfixed feature or cue assembled through the mechanism of a "memory container." These increments require less major investment of materials and labor at any one time than do equivalent sedentary constructions. They are easier to manipulate separately, to maintain individually, and hence to exercise control over. They are equivalent to the movable furnishings within a sedentary household space.

If one applies the concept of "dwelling" as living in the traces that past living has left (Illich 1982, 118), then the traces left by past living are essentially semi- or nonfixed features of the built environment, that is, the equivalent of domestic goods. All that is left when a nomadic camp moves is at best a set of stones marking a circle or a set of hearthstones. The site quickly reverts to deserted, desert space with little trace of previous occupation. The traces left by past living are rarely found on the landscape. Past living persists only within the confines of what has been transported from one site to the next. Constancy and continuity are therefore concentrated within, and bounded by, the moving container.

The nomadic environment is one in which constancy through time is maintained despite changes in space and location. Even though its parts may travel disassembled, the domicile, gender-bound, moves as a total, self-contained entity. On the move, old women and young children travel in a small replica of the domicile, a palanquin composed of the same structural members used in creating the *man dasse*, thus further reinforcing, through repetitive experience of a fixed spatial pattern, the cognitive structure of the interior space forms, sealed against a "hostile" exterior and enhancing a system of internal orientation.

Transhumance, as a way of life, concentrates the Gabra woman's focus on a "moving center," spatially enclosed. Leach (1976, 53–54) has suggested that the more barren the reality of territorial space is, the more its inhabitants will strive to elaborate an ideal conceptual model of its very opposite. He further observes that the rigidity and elaboration of interior nomadic space might well result from the need for a sense of security in "knowing where you are," in fulfillment of some deep psychological need. Experientially, once defined, a closed container itself encourages a more rigid organization of space and consequently a system of more tightly prescribed behaviors within the defined architectonic volume. The Gabra *man dasse*, as a container for a carefully articulated way of life, appears to echo the ideal model of symmetry and balance that is part of basic Gabra moral values and aesthetic.

The rigidity of spatial organization in *man dasse* interiors finds a corollary in the intensity of decorative elaboration of its interior. Color and surface detail reflect the intensity of confinement of daily domestic activity, but they also appear, at the same time perhaps, to be a psychological response to the barren, hostile landscape without. Implied is a gender-related propensity for the enrichment of interior space.

Tools   Among the Gabra, as among other nomads, the processing of materials necessary to the creation and maintenance of the domicile, and the fabrication of artifacts which are part of that creation, takes place, for the most part, within the domicile container or in its immediate environs. Whether the task be basket making or tanning, mat weaving or rope making, the spatial setting for architectural and artifactual creativity is located within the same container with which the end product is destined to become integral. Within their tents, women create the components of new tents. The immediate proximity of models to follow also facilitates the mnemonic process. The tools of production themselves become "gendered" because even though they sometimes are fabricated by the opposite sex, they become, through usage, associated with women's work. They are housed among her things and they "belong" to her. Through repeated usage, the tool itself becomes associated with a particular set of social relationships in a given place.

Techniques   Identity with, or sense of place, is further reinforced by using the same techniques that are required for the creation and maintenance or reproduction of the domestic container and for the creation/production of clothing. And as we described above, furnishings which are integral with the domestic envelope involve technologies that are the same as or similar to those used for the envelope itself. The same basketrylike technique is used to construct both the armature of the *man dasse* and the armature of the *manno* and the *butte* carrier or *chanchala*. The same tanning process used to fabricate the lining for the tent and its ties is used to fabricate leather wearing apparel and leather containers.

Furthermore, and as a consequence of nomadism itself, the same components that constitute the domicile are converted into the transport systems so that continuity with materials is maintained from one site to the next. As a consequence, associative iconographies and graphic symbols are often woven and worked into the spatial metaphors that surround the body itself, the furnishings close by, and by extension, the tent envelope itself. The term *balbala* illustrates this continuity.

Materials   The materials of construction are themselves evocative of a child's early tactile experiences associated with well-being. They provide a continuity in sensory experience that further enhances memory and the cognitive structure. Since the site of women's work for much time is within the house envelope, the mother-child relationship is experienced, for several years at least, in a small, enclosed, "women's" world, in association with the production and maintenance process itself. While on the move, young children travel inside the palanquin atop the camel created by the bent members and the lining of the *man dasse*. Thus, the form and spatial experience is reinforced by the porterage system which houses the child on journeys from one site to the next.

What, after all this, is the relevance of this study of Gabra placemaking to the architectural historian who seeks to understand the built environment, or the professional architect who is currently concerned with shaping it? The reader may well conclude that the data and discussion merely reinforce our perception of the negative aspects of placemaking, that is, its gender subordination. The primary benefit of this study, however, lies in extrapolating aspects that are applicable to the increasing number of alternative life-styles in society-at-large, many of which are assuming new "nomadic" dimensions, and in realizing that these aspects may well be universal. The Gabra experience suggests to us that the placemaking process involves control over (decision making), identity with (meaning), and continuous involvement through repetitive behaviors (memory).

Culturally encoded models of the real and ideal domicile are gender related and gender discrete. Whereas in Western cultures and in most non-Western traditional sedentary cultures these encoded models often reflect masculine values, in traditional nomadic societies where women are the primary "placemakers," the models reflect feminine values. These values find expression in the furnishings, the iconography of interior spaces through the manipulation of their surfaces, and the interior orientation of closed space. It is those elements that one can retain control over that constitute the symbolic expressive elements of placemaking.

Pilot study fieldwork among the Gabra and the Borana between September and November 1985 was funded by the National Science Foundation. The grant proposal focused on the study of women as placemakers in the nomadic context. It was our intent to document both the nature of placemaking and the recursive behaviors associated with building technology in the hope that an analysis of how the structure of architecture and the structure of language co-vary might provide some insight into placemaking processes.

The success of this preliminary exploration was due in great measure to the generosity with which those more familiar with Gabra culture shared their knowledge: Dr. Aneesa Kassam, Fathers Paul Tablino and Lambert Bartels, and Hussein Yusuf at Marsabit. I would also like to extend my thanks to the Catholic Fathers at Maikona, Marsabit, and Maralal for their hospitality, and to my co-investigator, Professor Carol Eastman, for help in recording vernacular terms.

A detailed description of containers and their manufacture appears in African Arts *(February 1987). Although the concept of "container" was originally suggested in Torry (1973), the ideas embodied in this paper are in many ways an extension of several themes introduced in Prussin (1986).*

Notes

1. See, for example, Charles LeCoeur, 1937, Les "Mapalia" Numides et leur survivance au Sahara," *Hesperis* 24(1–2):29–46; Henri Lhote, 1959, *The search for the Tassili Frescoes* (New York: E. P. Dutton); Richard Pankhurst, 1983, The tents of the Ethiopian Court, *Azania* 18: 181–95; Ibn Battuta, 1929, *Travels in Asia and Africa*, trans. H. A. R. Gibb (London: R. M. MacBride), passim. Also see Therese Prechaur-Canonge, 1962, *La View rurale en Afrique romaine d'apres les mosaiques* (Paris: P.U.F.)

2. The vaguely curved but essentially linear layout of Gabra camps is unique. Other northern Kenyan nomadic populations arrange their camps in circular settlements. Seasonal displacements alternate between wet season hill flanks and dry season plains, and the Gabra occupy two types of residential units: main camps in which family nucleii live, and satellite or dry-stock camps. Main camps shift every four to five weeks, but satellite camps, consisting primarily of young men herding in a network of makeshift enclosures and adjoining windscreens, shift more frequently.

3. The Gabra speak a dialect of Boran, part of an extensive family of Eastern Cushitic tongues. They belong to the group of Oromo cultures, traditionally called Galla by others. Of the five clans that comprise Gabra society, two claim direct descent from the Borana and the others claim some affinity with the Rendille and the Somalis.

4. This primary orientation toward the natural features of the environment recalls the importance of Mount Olympus in classical mythology and the ways other ethnographic populations have used myths of origin to legitimize and categorize their positions in space.

5. In contrast to other northern Kenyan pastoral peoples who often use gourds to collect and store food and water, the Gabra (as well as the Borana and Somalis) manufacture their containers out of wood and plant fibers or out of tanned hides. The intrinsic relationship between collection, preparation, and storage of foods and the manufacture of material artifacts including houses and containers is strikingly evident in Torry's description of the Gabra "task repertoire" (1973, 133–38).

6. Among the Gabra, marriage and other rituals or *sorio* occur only during particular months and only on days considered propitious. The *min fuud'aa* always begins between the twelfth and fourteenth day of the rising moon. See Torry (1973) and Robinson (1985) for the social and historical implications of the Gabra version of the lunar calendar.

7. The length of the *kaala* is established by a person's height. Therefore the radii and consequently the height of Gabra houses initially vary little. Two other measures are used: the length from the elbow to the tip of the middle digit, called *dundum*, and the length from the thumb to the middle digit of the outstretched hand, called *tarku*. These anthropomorphic measures are reminiscent of medieval European measures of length.

8. During the building process, the bridegroom always sits on his personal stool (*barchuma*) with a *chicho* of milk on his knees, on the north, right side of the house entrance (*balbala*).

9. Early on the third day, women from the bride's camp collect her from a friend's house (with whom she slept the night before). When she is heavily anointed with fat, dressed in the traditional goatskin dress (*gorffoo*) with her hair combed and braided with a wooden comb (*filaa*), a bridal veil (*agogoo*) on her head, a *chicho* on her back, and her *siigee* in hand, she is blessed by her father. Then, accompanied by the women, she follows the previous processional sequences from her mother's house through the two kraals to join the groom at the *balbala* of the new house. A *gorffa* is placed in the middle of the threshold. Both step over it and enter the house. The *barchuma* is handed in, the *gorffa* is removed and everyone enters. Then the two *chichos* (his and hers) are hung on the east, inside wall (*borro*) of the house. Bride and groom, each accompanied by a close friend, remain within, mute, until the end of the fourth day, when the new wife prepares an evening meal to complete the four-day ceremony. Conversation between them can then begin.

10. The terms for the cardinal directions are as follows: east: *il boruu*, west: *iladu*, north: *mirge*, south: *bita*. It is my impression that *uttubaa* is more than a term for post; it implies support. The eastern half of the house is called *d'iibuu* or *dingaa*; the latter is also a term used by the Borana. When asked the words for building elements, Gabra often responded instead with the names for specific species of wood or plant fibers. These responses suggest that research into Gabra ethnobotany may prove most revealing for a further understanding of the importance of the building process in Gabra placemaking.

11. This primary structure is not unique to the Gabra. The Borana of the Garissa region on both sides of the Tana River and the Somalis use a similar system of basic construction (Anderson 1978; Chailley 1952; Drake-Brockman 1912). The pre-eminence of right (*dextrous*) over left (*sinistre*) has been considered at some length in Needham (1973). Right-hand preference is a fact of both nurture and nature.

References

Anderson, Kaj B. 1978. *African traditional architecture*. Nairobi: University of Nairobi Press.

Bartels, Lambert. 1983. *Oromo religion*. Berlin: Dietrich Reimer.

Chailley, M. 1952. L'habitation à la côte Française des Somalis. *Bulletin IFAN* 14(4):1490–1511.

Drake-Brockman, R. E. 1912. *British Somaliland*. London: Hurst.

Douglas, Mary, and Baron Isherwood. 1979. *The world of goods*. New York: W. W. Norton.

Greenwald, A. G. 1981. Environmental and cognitive structures. In *Meaning and behavior in the built environment*, ed. Broadbent, Hunt, and Llorens. New York: Wiley & Sons.

Illich, Ivan. 1982. *Gender*. New York: Pantheon.

Leach, Edmund. 1976. *Culture and communication*. Cambridge: Cambridge University Press.

Murdock, George Peter. 1957. World ethnographic sample. *American Anthropologist* 59:664–87.

Murdock, George Peter. 1959. *Africa: Its people and their cultural history*. New York: McGraw-Hill.

Needham, Rodney. 1973. *Right and left*. Chicago: University of Chicago Press.

Prussin, Labelle. 1972. West African mud granaries. *Paideuma* 18:144–49.

———. 1986. *Hatumere*. Berkeley and Los Angeles: University of California Press.

————. 1987. Gabra containers. *African Arts*, February 1987.

Robinson, Paul Wesley. 1985. Gabbra nomadic pastoralism in nineteenth and twentieth century Northern Kenya. Ph.D. diss., Northwestern University.

Tablino, Paolo. 1978. The traditional celebration of marriage among the Gabbra of Northern Kenya. *Africa* (Rome) 33(4):568–78.

Tallam, K. C. Arap. 1984. Ethnoarchaeology of the Gabbra. Master's thesis, University of Nairobi.

Torry, William I. 1973. Subsistence ecology among the Gabra. Ph.D. diss., Columbia University.

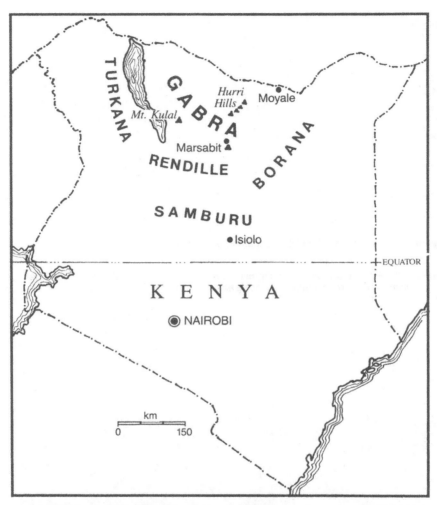

Figure 8.1. Map of Kenya showing the location of some of its nomadic populations in the northern half of the country.

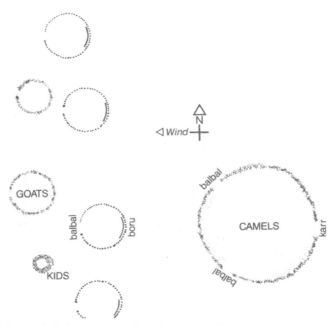

Figure 8.2. Partial plan of a Gabra encampment (*ollaa*).

Figure 8.3. Part of a Gabra encampment outside Maikona, northern Kenya. The *acacia* branch and stone fences of the kraals, located behind the houses, can be seen on the left.

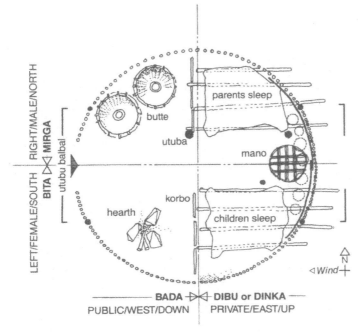

Figure 8.4. Plan of a Gabra *man dasse*.

Figure 8.5. Framing diagram of a Gabra armature.

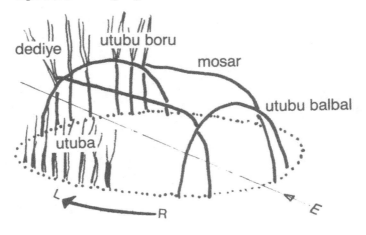

9

BEHAVIOR IN THE HOUSE: A CROSS-CULTURAL COMPARISON USING BEHAVIOR-SETTING METHODOLOGY

ROBERT B. BECHTEL

Environmental psychology (and its parallel, environmental anthropology) seems to have been founded on the premise that a fundamental relationship exists between behavior and its environmental context. This relationship is such that while the environment does not entirely determine the behavior, it has a significant influence, and the behavior, in turn, influences the environment. This interaction sets up a dynamic process by which behavior and environment are constantly influencing and changing each other.

Human behavior in the housing environment is one of the most studied aspects of environment and behavior research. Bechtel and Srivastava (1978) discovered 1,305 published accounts investigating relationships of behavior to housing design. One of the earliest studies (Festinger et al. 1951) discovered that friendship patterns in an apartment complex are related to location in the apartment building. Those people located in the middle apartment had more acquaintances than those living on the ends. Friendship patterns were related to the amount of social contact. People living in the middle apartments passed by more residents than those on the ends.

In this chapter, I will discuss a study that compares four housing environments in three somewhat different cultural settings. The study emphasizes behavior inside the dwelling as opposed to outside. Three settings are essentially North American expatriates in extreme climates (two in Alaska, one in Saudi Arabia), and the fourth setting is urban Iran in the days of the shah. Using similar behavior measures for each area, I will discuss the interaction between the physical design and the behavioral response. The essential question is whether significant cultural differences emerge by these comparisons or whether there are findings that can be related to design and climatic influence across cultures. Given the juxtaposition of geographical and cultural variables, there could be many reasons to expect either predominance. By the mid 1970s when these data were collected, housing construction techniques and design in industrial cities around the world had become so similar that if one espouses environmental influence it would be expected the similar designs would impose similar behaviors across cultures and climates. This study can be seen as an exploration into whether there is evidence for such an influence, or whether culture and climate overcome the physical influences of house design. The behavior setting technique is particularly suited to such a study because it measures both qualitative and quantitative aspects of daily behavior.

The Alaskan Studies

The first attempt to go "inside the house" with behavior setting technology was the series of studies done in Alaska for the Cold Regions Research and Engineering Laboratories (CRREL), a laboratory under the United States Army Corps of Engineers. Work was done mainly under contract No. DAAG-17-73-C-0104 and is reported in detail in CRREL special report No. 76-10 titled *The Temporary Environment*. Four different phases comprised the work period which stretched from 1972 through 1976.

It is hard for the average person living in more temperate climates to imagine the problems of living that exist in a colder environment like Alaska. The problems stem not only from the colder temperature but also from the contrasts between daylight and night in summer and winter, the dryness that the cold makes and the relative isolation that is experienced when people from a temperate climate move to Alaska.

At one time when I got off the plane in Fairbanks the outside temperature was minus 43° Fahrenheit. At that temperature the cold against the skin is experienced as a searing pain that subjectively first feels like a burn. The armed services have coined a catch-phrase to instruct their troops on the danger of the cold. The phrase is "30-30-30," to remind each soldier that at 30° below zero in a thirty-mile-an-hour wind, flesh freezes in thirty seconds. But of course the temperature goes below minus 30°, and an old prospector's tale relates that you can tell when it is too cold to go outside by opening the door and spitting on the ground. If the spit freezes before it hits the ground, it is at least minus 50° and too cold to venture out. I can testify from personal experience that when it is minus 60°, the nostril hairs freeze at the first breath.

The horror stories of what the climate does to a car are many. Materials that are useful in temperate climes become liabilities in Alaska. The average car heater is just not up to the job. Winterizing a car involves motor oil that looks as thin as kerosene. Ordinary brake and transmission fluids will not do and batteries must be continuously heated by electric blankets when the car is not in use. Frost shields are required for windows. During one winter at a central Alaska Air Force station, three fire engines were lost merely by being driven out of the garages into the sub-zero cold. Each time some new item that had been overlooked froze and burst. It goes without saying that no one rides *outside* a fire engine in the Alaska winter.

Military requirements are that no man goes on a trip alone and that reports are made by radio at various checkpoints until the destination is reached.

Houses fare no better than cars. The most serious problem is condensation and dryness. The cold makes the air so dry that the relatively humid interior of a house sets up a vapor pressure that will push all of the paint off the walls in a winter season. This is true even through cement block. The only defense against this vapor pressure is an absolutely waterproof vapor barrier on the inside of the insulation. Yet even a pinhole in the vapor barrier will produce a grapefruit-sized area of peeled paint by spring.

The hazards of condensation inside the house are not to be neglected. Since attics and rafters are often colder than the rest of the house, the water condenses on them and provides an ice cave in winter and a rainfall in spring. Since the climate is so dry, humidifiers are often a necessity. Small children especially are more subject to upper respiratory infections because of the dryness. Otitis media, a middle-ear infection, is endemic. But the humidifiers exacerbate the condensation problems.

"Frost boils" collect at the sites where nails have been driven through wood even though a half inch of wood remains below the nail. Looking at the inside of an attic one can see the location of each roofing nail driven through the shingles marked by one of these frost boils.

The extreme climate of Alaska forces certain design changes on most buildings. In addition to the obvious factors such as greater insulation and thermal panes, there is also the arctic entrance, which is an added vestibule, giving the house two separated doorways so that one can be closed before the other is opened. A well-designed arctic entrance will also provide a grate in the floor for scraping off snow, and a place for hanging heavy parkas.

Isolation comes about by a combination of cold, darkness, and the necessity to "suit up" for the cold. The average housewife, when confronted with dressing two or three children in parkas, sweaters, mittens, boots, and hoods, and then starting and warming the inside of the car, often decides not to go out at all. Since, in the past, children who were left in a car while their mother shopped froze or were asphyxiated, military rules do not allow children to be left in the car while their mother shops. Thus they must also be brought in, disrobed, clothes hung up, and then suited up all over again to go out.

Both the darkness during winter and the constant daylight in summer contribute to people's problems. Residents often complain of the depression resulting from the darkness and a lack of energy and motivation. The worst month seems to be February, because the holidays are over and the expectations of spring are not yet realized. Some people report sleeping twelve hours a night during this period. This also seems to be the peak period for psychiatric disturbances, suicide attempts, and marital breakups.

By contrast, in the summer months of near total daylight, many people report sleeping fewer hours and some need blackout curtains to sleep properly.

One of the most successful ways to deal with the isolation and depression of winter is to have wives work. This simple remedy has proven successful in far north locations such as Nanisivik (Bechtel and Ledbetter 1980).

The above discussion is only a sample of the many flavors of conditions in the far north. The interactions of these and other factors make for a more different life style than one would at first imagine. It is critical to understand that these elements have an even greater impact on the temporary government employees than they do on native Alaskans. The native Alaskan has had time to adapt to many of these conditions and takes them for granted. The attitude of the more transient government or industrial employee is that he or she is there for only a relatively short time and need not bother to adjust completely.

Methods   The behavior-setting survey of families in federal government installations in Alaska was an attempt to derive data that would help design better housing for cold regions. Two major types of environments were compared, the smaller communities where families were housed in relative isolation and the larger army base community where more amenities were available.

In the smaller installations, the Federal Aviation Agency (FAA) maintained services to assist local airports in navigation, landing, and air rescue operations. These facilities often included a control tower, fire station, navigational beacons, and weather stations. The families live in the quarters for periods of up to eight years before rotation to the lower United States. Most housing is single family but some are apartments and duplexes. Figure 9.1 shows a typical view of FAA houses. Four sites in Alaska were studied: Cordova, on the southern coast of Alaska, fifteen miles from the town of Cordova; Gulkannon, ten miles from the town of Glennallen in central Alaska; Kotzebue, on the west coast of Alaska and next to the town of Kotzebue; and Murphy Dome, about thirty miles northwest of Fairbanks in north-central Alaska. A total of forty-two housing units was studied by combining all four sites. This was virtually 100 percent of all families not on leave.

The contrasting site was Fort Wainwright, adjacent to Fairbanks, Alaska, where about 1,145 families were living in houses at the time of the study. From a random sample of 51 families, 40 completed the interviews of the behavior-setting survey. The remaining 10 families were on vacation or special duty, and one family was inaccessible. Figure 9.2 shows typical housing at Fort Wainwright.

Part of the purpose of the behavior-setting study was to experiment with random sampling of families instead of doing a survey that covered every family unit for a year as was the tradition with earlier Barker studies. The findings were expressed in terms of action patterns of behavior for the sampled families, number of hours in various activities, and in other ecological measures such as general richness index, autonomy, and children's activities.

Action Patterns   Barker (1968) used action patterns to mark off the general types of behavior that take place in a community. An action pattern is recorded as the amount of time spent in the activity in hours per person. The total hours in any action pattern are used as percentages of the total occupancy time in the house. For example, if four people live in a house, they have a total occupancy time potential of 8,760 × 4 because there are 8,760 hours in a year. However, sleeping time is not counted as occupancy time, and vacations, trips to the store, walks, and other activities outside the house are all subtracted from the total time available. What remains is the total time spent in the house by each person for a year. Including visitors, this may add up to 40,000–50,000 hours for some households or be as little as 8,000 for others. Action patterns are calculated as percentages of total occupancy time. (See Appendix for sample problems in calculating occupancy time and action patterns.) There are eleven action patterns currently in use. These include:

Religion.   Behavior that has to do with worship is scored as religion action pattern. In the families this most often was scored if the family prayed at meals and bedtime. Prayer meetings and other religious meetings did not count because they were public behavior settings apart from the family.

Physical health.   Behavior that contributes to physical health (as opposed to mental health) is scored as physical health action pattern. Caring medically for children when they are sick, taking medicine, and also engaging in regular exercise, wearing trusses, and eating a diet of special foods are considered under this action pattern.

Personal appearance.   Behavior that is concerned with grooming and any aspect of personal appearance such as clothing, make-up, or adornment is scored as personal appearance action pattern. Barker (1968, 61) has a clothing scale which had to be adapted to a military base with different types of uniforms. Usually the personal appearance action pattern could be encompassed within the time it takes a person to get dressed and ready for the day in the morning. However, the time to get dressed for the outside in cold regions presents a problem. Since there was evidence that some effort was put into making parkas stylish, dressing time was added to personal appearance. Some argument could be made that the time getting dressed should also be scored for physical health.

Education.   Behavior that involves formal education where a teacher-pupil situation exists, including time spent on homework, correspondence courses, and music lessons, is scored as education action pattern. Tupperware classes, school board meetings, and other public settings are scored, however, as separate from the family. Music lessons are marginal and could be considered separate settings if they are always sequestered from other family activities.

Nutrition.   Behavior that involves the eating, preparation, or appreciation of food is scored as nutrition action pattern.

Business.   Behavior that involves the sale of goods or services is scored for business action pattern. In an ordinary store only the time spent in actually selling is scored. Time spent in socializing is scored for social action pattern.

Recreation.   Playing, taking part in sports, reading for pleasure, any activity that is considered consummatory is scored for recreation action pattern.

Aesthetics.   This action pattern concerns actions that improve the environment in any way. It is the environmental counterpart to personal appearance. Cleaning, painting, or fixing up, as well as artistic activity of any kind, is scored for aesthetics action pattern.

Government.   Behavior that has to do with the passing or enforcing of laws or with behavior attendant to these purposes is scored for government action pattern. Any carrying out of government orders or functions including attending civic affairs or hearings and listening to educational explanations of government or laws is scored as government action pattern.

Professionalism.   The person who is hired to work for wages engages in professionalism action pattern the whole time working while the person who hires the worker engages in business action pattern in the act of hiring. Any work for pay is scored for professionalism for the total hours worked.

Social contact.   Speaking, listening, communicating nonverbally, or telephoning and listening to speakers or a play is scored for social contact action pattern. The key is interpersonal relations of any kind.

Action patterns are scored as percentages of total occupancy for the family in the house for one year. If the action pattern occurred but was less than 50 percent of occupancy time it was classed as *present* in the scheme of behavior. If the percent of occupancy time went over 50 percent, it was classed as a *prominent* action pattern. Figure 9.3 shows the action patterns of the forty-two families at the four FAA stations. It can be seen that nutrition, recreation, and aesthetics were present in over 90 percent of the families' behavior over the course of a year. These three patterns form the basic behavior profiles for these families. Most families (80 percent) also had physical health and personal appearance present as action patterns.

Only 30 percent of the families had religion action pattern present, only 64 percent education, 53 percent government, and 36 percent professionalism.

Of the prominent action patterns, only recreation and social contact scored 20 percent each of total occupancy time, while nutrition, business, aesthetics, and professionalism were prominent in only 1–6 percent of the houses.

Action patterns are by no means the last word in describing family behavior but they do provide an overview of the family's behavior in these eleven content areas and these can be used as a rough life-style profile that describes both qualitative and quantitative aspects of behavior. The most frequent prominent patterns seem to be recreation and social contact but in only 20 percent of the homes.

The Fort Wainwright families provide some contrast to the FAA. Figure 9.4 shows the action pattern of the forty Fort Wainwright families covered in the behavior setting survey. The most outstanding difference between the two sets of families is the higher proportion of professionalism as a prominent and present action pattern among the Fort Wainwright families (15 percent and 76 percent) compared to the FAA families (only 6 percent and 36 percent). Another outstanding difference is the higher proportion of recreation among the FAA families compared to the Fort Wainwright families (92 percent present, 20 percent prominent vs. 76 percent and 10 percent). Education is higher for FAA (64 percent present) compared to the Fort Wainwright families. Social contact is also higher (20 percent prominent vs. 10 percent).

What do these differences mean? Taken as a whole, they define differences in life-style and in the use of the home. The army base has a smaller use of the home as a recreational site. This does not mean that the FAA families engage in recreation in the home only. Other data show they use the town facilities and their recreational building more than do the army families. They may show the very important need for more recreational space in both types of houses. The data also show the need for more educational space for the FAA personnel, who use the home as a study space, whereas the army personnel may receive more educational upgrading on the job.

One FAA station has a recreation building that is less than a block away from every house. The army base, by contrast, has many recreational buildings but these are often two or more miles away from the houses. Yet Army personnel use the homes less for recreational purposes. The explanation may be the greater "pull" of Army recreational activities, or the "push" of smaller quarters, or both. Since female adults spend more time at home at both sites, contacts between adults and children are more frequent and more disruptive of recreation. Hence, there is more of a need for separation of adult and children's functions.

The results of these data alone show that a redesign of either the houses or the community of the larger base would help. Since a redesign of the community to approximate the recreational use of the FAA station is impractical because of cost, the more workable solution is a redesign of the family residence. The design changes can include a radical new design for housing, a renovation of existing facilities, or merely a changing of furniture and remodeling of certain rooms. These proposals are listed in detail in Bechtel and Ledbetter (1976). The most significant change is to increase play space for children by remodeling the basements. The life-styles of the families as measured by action patterns alone made it clear that certain design changes can accommodate the behavior measured, but many other kinds of data were available from the behavior setting survey questionnaire that tell more about the behavior of these families.

Time Measures   Wives and husbands were measured for time spent in the house by the process of subtracting time spent away from the house. The questionnaire meticulously asked about activities that could be assigned time values.

Since the average family had not spent a full year on the base (only 308 days), data were extrapolated to a full 365-day year. The average husband spent 5,415 hours in the house a year. Wives, by contrast, spent 7,541.7 hours in the house a year. Calculated as available time to spend in the house, husbands spent 61.8 percent of their available time in the house while wives spent 86.1 percent of available time there. Looked at another way, husbands spend 24.3 percent less time at home than wives. Much of this difference is accounted for by the fact that only 32.5 percent of the wives have full or part-time jobs. On the average, a wife spent 20 hours and 35 minutes a 24-hour day, including sleeping time, in the house.

Visits to the houses by adults average 822.55 hours a year for each family, but the range extends from 14 to 3,000 hours. Visit by adolescents and children average 706 hours a year with a range of 10 to 4,500 hours.

The average family estimated that it took each person forty minutes to get suited up for the cold in winter. This was a considerable factor in deciding whether to go out or not.

Barker (1968, 70) developed a formula for calculating the "general richness index" (GRI) of a setting. GRI is used as a measure of behavioral resources available in a setting. It is high if different kinds of behavior (action patterns) are present along with different kinds of people (children, different races, different age groups). The GRI of the homes at Fort Wainwright and in the FAA areas is typically higher than for the average settings outside the home. The GRI of the homes at Fort Wainwright averaged 25.88, which is two times higher than the mean GRI for the remaining behavior settings for all of Fort Wainwright (12.06). The FAA housing shows a higher GRI of 29.8, which is probably due to the presence of more children. These numbers probably mean that the homes are the single most important behavioral resource available to persons living in these environments.

The behavior-setting methods outline fairly well the life-styles of the families living in these two cold region environments. A further comparison with a very different environment can explore the possibilities even more.

The Iran Study

In 1975, before the Ayatollah Khomeni took over in Iran and the shah was still firmly in power, the Housing Ministry of the Imperial Government contracted with Tadjer, Cohen, Shefferman and Bigelson, an engineering firm in Silver Spring, Maryland, to develop guidelines for construction of houses for Iranians in Teheran. The Maryland firm subcontracted with the Environmental Research and Development Foundation (ERDF) to undertake the user needs research on these guidelines.

The user needs research was essentially a duplication of the method developed in the Alaskan studies but adapted to Iranian culture. This adaptation involved researching the housing studies previously done by the Iranian government and the Institute for Social Studies and Research at the University of Teheran. A questionnaire based on this background information was constructed and subjected to the translation-retranslation technique. The questionnaire began in English, was translated into Farsi by people familiar with both languages, and then was retranslated back into English by another group. The final result was then pretested with Iranian residents.

The contract for developing guidelines for housing intended for application in the three lower economic groups in Teheran included 86 percent of the population. At the time of the study (May 1975), this included all those earning 2,600 U.S. dollars or less.

A decision was made to survey six housing projects that represented the best of recent government housing efforts. The sample list contained 8,980 residences from which a random sample of 149 was drawn; 95 interviews were completed. The main reason that the other 54 interviews were not completed was that residents were not at home during the times interviewers called. This may have introduced a bias toward nonworking residents.

The interviewing process itself required some innovation. Because Iran is a Moslem country, it is traditional to have male interviewers for questionnaires. Unfortunately this meant that if the male head of household were not at home, the interview had to be conducted with the woman of the house in the hallway, since it is impolite for a man to enter while the husband is away. For this project three females were recruited for the interviewing, and they were able to get inside the house and talk with the woman of the house in a more relaxed fashion.

Several questions were added to the questionnaire to accommodate the fact that customs and design concerns in Iran are different from those in the United States. For example, the daily number of people eating at the table of a house (called the *sofreh*) was not necessarily the same as the number sleeping in the house, and so the two relevant questions were asked very specifically. As it turned out, however, our urban sample showed virtually no difference in the two numbers in each household surveyed. Figures 9.5 and 9.6 show examples of Iranian housing.

Another example of a cultural difference is the fact that the kind and quantity of rugs on the floor are a possible index of economic affluence. This index also did not work out well in this study, because the more affluent householders were not included in the sample and correlations with housing quality were poor. I did note, however, that rich Iranians would have carpets worth $10,000 to $100,000 on their floors!

Action Patterns   Figure 9.7 shows the action pattern profile of the ninety-five Iranian families. The action patterns show that many patterns are *present* but few are *prominent*. The prominent patterns are nutrition, recreation, and social contact. In comparison with the Alaskan families, recreation in Iranian families is prominent in over 20 percent of the houses, and social contact is less prominent. It is significant that nutrition shows up as a prominent pattern in Iran.

Visiting is a prominent form of recreation. Visitor hours average 1,779 a year and account for 8 percent of all occupancy time. In contrast, Chapin's (1974) study of Washington, D.C., families showed only 5 percent of total occupancy time given to visiting. In the Iranian household female visitors outnumber males, and child visitors outnumber adult visitors (child visitors, 8.5, vs. adults, only 6.3 visitors).

The amount of time spent watching television is about the same in Iran and the United States. Iranians report an average of 3.44 hours a day and Robinson (1971) reported 3 hours a day for a national sample in the United States. Television watching accounts for 11 percent of total occupancy time.[1] The recreation pattern seems to be dominated in both countries by the visiting and television-watching behaviors.

It is interesting to compare the recreation action patterns of the Iranians, the Alaskans, and Barker's small-town populations. The recreation patterns in the home for all three seem almost equal but all differ from the patterns revealed in urban U.S. studies. Thus, the Iranians "act" like an isolated or rural community in these terms, even though the density of population is closer to that of the urban studies. Climate cannot explain the similarity in the Iranian and Alaskan patterns because Iran does not experience the same rigors as Alaska. One possible conclusion is that the higher recreational pattern in the home is forced by the climatic circumstances of Fort Wainwright and the FAA sites and the cultural factors of Iran.

The ideal situation for recreation might be closer to Barker's small town, or the Iranian households where recreational activities are not forced above the 30 percent level of total occupancy time. Yet, closer examination of the Iranian household brings a severe qualification. Even lower levels of recreational activity become difficult to maintain because for many of the poorer families the living room is virtually the only room of the house; 78 percent report children sleeping in the living room and 84 percent report children doing homework there, even in the more affluent apartments sampled. Custom seems to have more to do with the use of the space than does the availability of space. Seventy percent still do laundry outside even though 90 percent have kitchen areas large enough to accommodate indoor laundry facilities.

It was also observed that many older Iranians prefer charcoal braziers to modern stoves because of the taste imparted by the method of cooking. This means many modern kitchens are underutilized.

Looking at the daily life of the Iranian family as a whole, the largest difference from the American counterparts seems to be the visiting patterns and the lack of what U.S. residents would call adequate space. But the visiting patterns of the Iranian families also have a particular quality. The visitors are largely female and the visits are largely related to cooking. Thus, most visiting takes place in the kitchen.

The flavor of Iranian life is much different from that of the Alaskan families. Traffic in Iran, for example, is very heavy and there are regular rush-hour traffic jams. Clothing for men is flamboyant; women may adopt Western dress or wear the chador, a black hooded covering that may or may not include a veil. The streets are noisy, with hawkers and sellers of various goods at every corner. Mullahs calls out prayers from loud speakers. This life-style is similar to that of the next setting.

The Saudi Arabian Study

On the eastern coast of the Arabian Peninsula, the town of Dhahran has grown up like an American suburb. The families of American oil men settled here to do the work for the Arabian American Oil Company (ARAMCO). The climate is not just dry and desertlike; it is influenced by the proximity of the land to the moisture of the gulf and can be either moist and tropical or hot and dry. Which climatic effects dominate depends upon the season and whether the wind is coming from inland or over the gulf.

I can remember sitting in the dining room of the Al Gosaibi Hotel on the gulf and watching the windows stream with condensation from the coolness of the air conditioning. And once, when I was attempting to fly to Abqaiq, one of the nearby towns, the fog was so heavy it was impossible to land. Yet just a few miles away was the clear air one associates only with deserts.

Many buildings have the tropical equivalent of the arctic entrance: a large vestibule where the outer door is closed before the inner is opened. There is sometimes a grate provided in the floor to remove sand from shoes.

The living in Dhahran provides many contrasts particularly because of the influence of Arabian customs. The call to prayer can be heard, and the Arabs themselves, with their flowing white robes called *thobes* and their red-checked head coverings called *gutras* are seen everywhere. The most visible aspect of Arabian custom in housing is the outside wall. Not all houses have outside walls, but enough do to make it clear that this is not really an American suburb. Patio living is also evident, and the patios are usually well screened. Figure 9.8 shows a typical suburban house used by expatriates.

The purpose of this study was to provide ARAMCO with data on how to upgrade the housing of their employees. The Real Estate Research Corporation of Washington, D.C., contracted with ARAMCO to do the work and then subcontracted with ERDF to collect the data. Work was done in the summer of 1975.

The questionnaires were constructed from information collected in interviews with key ARAMCO personnel connected with housing and in group discussions with various population segments housed at Dhahran. They were pretested on residents.

The 2,685 workers and families of Dhahran, Abqaiq, and Ras Tanura, the three main oil towns on the eastern coast, were sampled and given the questionnaire. Of 304 sampled, 217 were found available, and 147, or 66 percent, completed the questionnaire. Completion was largely dependent on when the researchers called on the residents. Many were away during the day. Only two call backs were used. Only data from 90 families in Dhahran were used. The other families were considered too isolated and composed of too many other elements such as Europeans and Asians to allow comparisons.

Action Patterns   Figure 9.9 shows the action patterns of the ninety households in Dhahran. Nutrition, recreation, and social contact are the three prominent action patterns. The expatriates living in Saudi Arabia had nutrition more prominent than social contact, and they had recreation at nearly 40 percent, the highest level of any group.

Closer examination of the life-styles of the expatriate families living in the Saudi Arabian communities reveals that the presence of servants, chiefly cooks, adds enough occupancy time to nutrition to make it more prominent than recreation or social contact. This is an outstanding aspect of the life-style in Dhahran, and the nearby communities. The presence of the cook actually means the woman of the household spends more time in the kitchen, supervising. Note the greater than 50 percent prominence of the nutrition action pattern.

While the Saudi Arabian recreation action pattern is the most prominent action pattern of any group, the quality is different from that of either the television-watching Americans or the visiting Iranians. The most important single element is reading. The average male reports spending 8.88 hours a week reading, and the average female reports 9.34 hours. Some of this may be due to the poor quality of television available and to the relative lack of other recreational facilities.

Discussion

The findings are a curious mixture of main effect across the cultures with data particular to each culture, exactly what one would hope for in a useful cross-cultural measure. The findings are summarized in Table 9.1, which shows that although the recreation action pattern was prominent across all sites, the particular way in which it is manifested in each site dictates a different design change. Both Alaskan sites can expand the indoor play space for children by remodeling the basements. But in Iran the pattern for recreation was more concentrated on women visiting in the kitchen, so the kitchen area needs to be expanded to accommodate. The pattern also differed in the Saudi expatriate families because of the presence of hired cooks. This phenomenon led to an increase in entertainment, and so both kitchen and dining room facilities needed to be larger in the suburban homes.

In addition to the recreational action pattern, nutrition was prominent in both the Iranian and Saudi sites, and for the same reasons. The nutrition action pattern further emphasized the kitchen-centered social life of Iranian women and the expatriate women. This pattern would probably also hold for many Third World countries with heavy kitchen visiting among the lower classes and servant-centered entertainment among the upper classes.

Some other observations are necessary to illuminate these findings. By Western standards, the Iranian households, because of their extended families, are probably the "worst" for crowdedness. There is virtually no time when the housewife is alone. The reason is as much economic as it is "cultural" because housing is so expensive that several families may need to share an apartment to be able to afford the high payments. This, added to the already high density of extended-family visiting patterns accounts for the high levels of occupancy. Yet the Iranians do not perceive of the situation as crowded in the same terms as would an American expatriate in Saudi Arabia

Table 9.1
Comparison of Findings Across Study Sites

Sites	Dominant Recreational Pattern	Design Consequences
Alaska		
Fort Wainwright	TV, children's play	increase play space
FAA sites	TV, children's play	increase play space
Iran	TV, visiting	expand kitchen
Saudi Arabia	cooking, entertaining, reading	expand kitchen and dining room, provide quiet space

Major conclusion: increase recreational space across all sites

or one of the Alaskan residents. Most Iranians feel that a group of people talking in the background provides a proper environment for visiting, although many acculturated wealthy Iranians would also feel crowded in many of those circumstances.

The finding of a recreational action pattern that is not well accommodated by any of the housing designs is the most important finding of this study. It could be said that the living room at least provides a space for visiting, yet for the Iranians this does not suit the visiting in the kitchen nor does it fit the entertainment patterns of the Saudi expatriates, because much of their entertaining takes place in the dining room.

An especially important conflict arises because of television. The living room is the site of most television sets, but this interferes with visiting. The "family room" is a partial solution provided traffic does not need to pass through it. But the family room is a Western innovation and is not popular outside the U.S.

Another critical issue is the relationship between the use of the house and the community as a whole. In the FAA compounds, the proximity of recreational facilities caused a decrease in (or meant less reliance on) the use of the house as a vehicle for recreation. The larger population, the greater distance to recreation, and possibly other factors meant a higher use of the house for recreation at Fort Wainwright. All this does not necessarily mean that greater recreational use should be designed into communities in the far north. In fact, it has been found at Nanisivik (Bechtel and Ledbetter 1980) that increasing work time is a better solution to community problems than increasing recreation. Thus the management style of the community as a whole has much to do with the amount of recreational time available, and therefore, the amount of recreation that takes place in the home.

Unfortunately these data fly in the face of economic pressures which are causing smaller and smaller houses to be built (Perin 1974). In some sense, the resultant crowdedness may help to force the increasing dependence on television as a solution to a use of the space because watching television is an activity that can accommodate larger numbers with less conflict.

Lack of space is even further exacerbated by what Toffler (1980) sees as the return of cottage industry to the home as a result of the use of home computers and the electronic automation of households. Such a requirement would have to carve more space out of an already strained house design.

The only solution seems to be to add space to existing housing. Various studies show that this is already taking place spontaneously. Mangin (1970) and Lobo (1982) show it occurs naturally, over a period of time in Peruvian barriadas. Churchman (1985) details improvements in Israeli public housing, and Aksolyu (1985) describes it in Turkish *gecekondus*. Thus, a partial solution to this dilemma is already occurring worldwide. How much it will strain the already strained resources of the world remains to be seen, but as we move from using the house as a purely functional enclosure to using it as a space that must accommodate greater recreational use, and perhaps even greater work use, many more creative solutions will be needed. A workable solution now is to provide a basic dwelling that can be easily added on to after the family gains more affluence or enlists more help from other sources (Churchman 1985). This solution would certainly fit the greater pressures for space that are being experienced across cultures and climates.

Details of this study, including a copy of the questionnaire, are found in Studies and planning services to develop and apply performance specifications in procurement and evaluation of housing, 25 July 1975, data analysis report prepared for Tadjer, Cohen, Shefferman and Bigelson, Consulting Engineers, Silver Spring, Maryland.

Notes

1. The basis for calculations is only eighty families because seven did not answer the questions about television and eight replied they do not have television.

References

Aksoylu, Y. 1986. Neighborhood organizations and social change in a squatter settlement. Paper presented at EDRA 16, New York. Abstract in *Environmental and social change*, ed. S. Klein, R. Wener, and S. Lehman, 320. Washington, D.C.: Environmental Design Research Associates.

Barker, R. 1968. *Ecological psychology*. Palo Alto, Calif.: Stanford University Press.

Bechtel, R., and C. Ledbetter. 1976. *The temporary environment: Cold regions and habitability*. Hanover, N.H.: Cold Regions Research and Engineering Laboratory.

Bechtel, R., and C. Ledbetter. 1980. *Post occupancy evaluation of a planned community in arctic Canada*. Hanover, N.H.: Cold Regions Research and Engineering Laboratory.

Bechtel, R., and R. Srivastava. 1979. *Post occupancy evaluation of housing*. Washington, D.C.: U.S. Department of Housing and Urban Development.

Chapin, F. 1974. *Human activity patterns*. New York: John Wiley.

Churchman, A. 1985. Presentation on Israeli housing at EDRA 16, in the symposium "Future Trends in Participatory Decision Making." Washington, D.C.: Environmental Design Research Associates.

Festinger, L., S. Schachter, and K. Back. 1950. *Social pressures in informal groups*. New York: Harper and Bros.

Lobo, S. *A house of my own*. 1982. Tucson: University of Arizona Press.

Mangin, W., ed. 1970. *Peasants in cities: Readings in the anthropology of urbanization*. Boston: Houghton Mifflin.

Perin, C. 1974. The social order of environmental design. In *Designing for human behavior*, ed. J. Lang, C. Burnette, W. Moleski, and D. Vachon. Stroudsburg, Pa.: Dowden, Hutchinson and Ross, 31–42.

Robinson, J. 1971. Television's impact on everyday life: Some cross national evidence. In *Television and social behavior*, vol. 4. Washington, D.C.: U.S. Government Printing Office, 410–31.

Toffler, A. 1980. *The third wave*. New York: William Morrow.

Figure 9.1. FAA houses, Alaska.

Figure 9.2. Army housing, Fort Wainwright, Alaska.

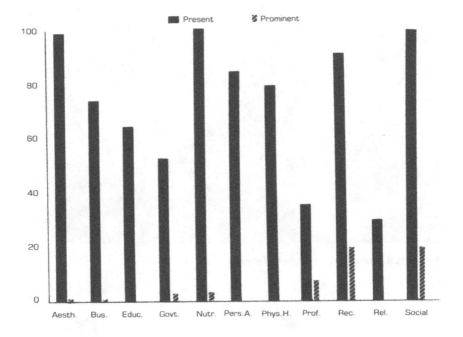

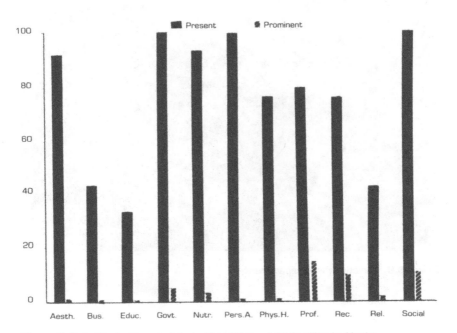

Figure 9.4. Action patterns of forty Fort Wainwright families in Alaska.

Figure 9.5. Iranian urban houses, Teheran.

Figure 9.6. Iranian high-rise apartments.

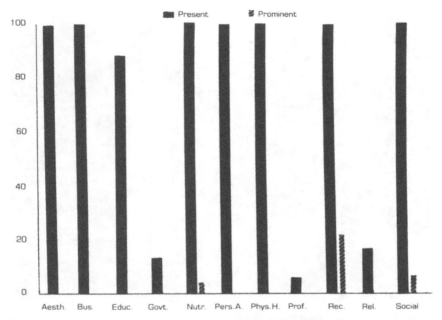

Figure 9.7. Action patterns of ninety-five Iranian families, Teheran.

Figure 9.8. Suburban-type house, Saudia Arabia.

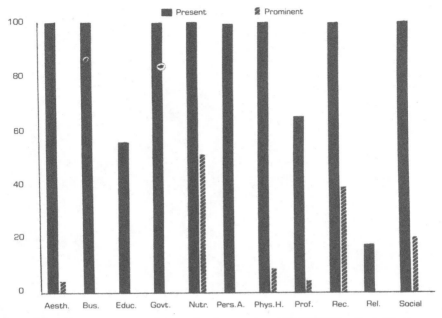

Figure 9.9. Action patterns of ninety Saudi expatriates (ARAMCO families), Dhahran.

10

RESIDENTS' AND OUTSIDERS' PERCEPTIONS OF THE ENVIRONMENT

SIDNEY BROWER

When we look at a residential environment we see what we look for, and we evaluate it in the light of our general beliefs, practices, and expectations. In this we are influenced by our national culture (low-income people in Caracas see substandard housing as a sign of hope, but in Boston they see it as a sign of despair [Peattie 1969]) and by our social class (in assessing housing quality, lower-class residents use criteria that are different from those used by their middle-class counterparts [Rainwater 1966]). Our perceptions are also influenced by our information and our interests; people who are strangers in a place see it differently from those who are thoroughly familiar with it and call it home. Residents and outsiders may look at the same environment, but, in effect, what they "see" is something different.

The fact that we see what we look for was satirized by Osbert Sitwell in his novel *Miracle on Sinai* (1933). It is a story about a group of people who went up Mount Sinai for a picnic. When they reached the top of the mountain they were enveloped in a strange cloud. There was a roaring wind, lightning, thunder, and the sound of trumpets, bells, and gongs. Then there was a flash, and two stone tablets of the Law fell to the ground.

The picnickers were the usual cast of characters that novelists bring together in doomed hotels and in planes with engine trouble. One by one, they went to inspect the tablets.

The palaeontologist was so taken with the composition of the stone he never noticed that there was an inscription, and the artist noticed the inscription but was so taken with the beauty of the calligraphy that he never read it. Each of the other members of the party, however, managed to read at least a sentence or two. The male chauvinist read, "Honor thy Father, who embodies the principal of the Dominant Male . . ."; the gossip columnist read, "Thou shalt bear false witness against thy neighbor"; the industrialist read, "Thou shalt not buy foreign goods"; the soldier read, "Thou shalt do no murder; except when dressed in uniform, issued under the War Office Regulations"; the soldier's wife, who took both sides on every issue, read, "Thou shalt not kill the beasts of the field, except for eating or for sport"; and the bishop with a genius for embracing popular causes read, "Safety first." The Arab chieftain read, "There is no God but Allah," and so he ordered his tribesmen to capture the party; they killed the men and imprisoned the women in a harem.

All of the characters saw what they were looking for. If you doubt the general truth of this premise, then try the following experiment. Take an object and tell a group of people what it is. Ask them what they think of its appearance. Then tell them it is really something else and ask them what they think of its appearance now. You will see their evaluations change. For example, show them the object shown as Figure 10.1. Tell them that the object is a celebrated ritual figure from a little-known African tribe, believed to house ancestral spirits and to possess great power, and they will look at the object as a *medium*, where every feature is charged with meaning: circles signify continuity of time, grasses represent man's link with nature, dark colors are threatening, braiding implies that lives are intertwined, and so on.

Tell them that the object is called "Composition III" and is by a young San Francisco artist, and they will look at the object as a *masterpiece*, focusing on its formal qualities and on the skill and originality of the artist: Is it well proportioned, balanced, and harmonious? Does it express the nature of the materials? Is it original and well crafted?

Tell them that the object was bought as a birthday present for a three-year-old child, and they will look at it as a *toy*, something that is amusing to look at and fun to play with: Does it make a sound when you shake it? Does anything happen when you turn it upside down? Do the rings come off? Does it stimulate the imagination?

Tell them that it is one of a new line of Magi-care industrial-strength decorator air fresheners available at most supermarkets, and they will look at it as a *tool*, something that is essentially practical: Is the decoration necessary? How much freshener does it hold? How much does it cost? Can it be refilled? Will it collect dust? Is it awkward to use?

The object shown in the picture is "really" an African doll. I have found that people rate its appearance very differently if they have been told different things about it. They tend to give it high ratings as a *medium* (it is strange and mysterious) and as a *masterpiece* (it has a simple form and nice textures), a somewhat lower rating as a *toy* (one cannot do much with it), and a low rating as a *tool* (it is very impractical). Its appearance effectively changes even though the physical elements—the composition of the object, the light, and the observers—remain constant.[1]

What we know or believe about an object, then, affects the way it looks,[2] and if we change what we know or believe about it we effectively change its appearance and its worth. Beauty is not entirely a quality of the object; it is partly in the eye (and the mind) of the beholder. If you fail to realize that, you will be taken in by Horace Rumpole's defense of an artist charged with forging a painting (Mortimer 1984, 34).

> "Mrs De Moyne. Wouldn't you agree," I asked as I rose to cross-examine, "that you bought a very beautiful picture?"
> "Yes," Mrs de Moyne admitted.
> "So beautiful you were prepared to pay sixty thousand pounds for it?"
> "Yes, I was."
> "And is it still the same beautiful picture? The picture hasn't changed since you bought it, has it Mrs De Moyne? Not by one drop of paint! Is the truth of the matter that you are not interested in art but merely in collecting autographs?"

Clearly, what we see in a painting is influenced by our knowledge of the painter and of art history and theory.[3] An original painting looks different from an identical copy because we know that it is "the real thing" and this adds something special to its appearance: the copy may capture the painting's objective appearance but it cannot capture its meaning, and meaning has a strong influence on our perceptions.[4] A small irregularity in the pattern of a handwoven rug shows the imprint of the weaver and makes the rug look more personal, but a similar irregularity in a machine-woven rug implies poor quality control and makes the rug look flawed. Japanese restaurants display startlingly realistic reproductions of food items to depict their bill of fare, but the same objects in the museum gift shop demonstrate the artist's skill, and we buy them to impress our friends. An urbanite sees a field as a peaceful and natural landscape, where a farmer sees man-made order and the application of progressive farming principles (Nassauer and Westmacott 1985). New information may change old perceptions: a string of beads bought as a fashion accessory is recognized to be a rosary, a worn decoy duck is rescued from the junkpile and displayed as an antique. Thompson (1979) writes about whole sections of London once seen as rat-infested slums, but now seen as historic treasures.

What we see reflects not only what we know but also what we look for; that is, what interests us. Like Lorelei Lee in Paris (Loos, 1963), we focus our attention on objects that interest us and ignore the rest.[5]

> When Dorothy and I went on a walk, we only walked a few blocks, but in a few
> blocks we read all of the famous historical names, like Coty and Cartier and I
> knew we were seeing something educational at last. . . . So when we stood at a
> place called the Place Vendome, if you turn your back on a monument they have
> in the middle and look up, you can see none other than Coty's sign. (78)

Education plays an important role in shaping our interests. This is especially notable in people with a visual arts education, who have been trained to
see abstract physical qualities in the landscape. In the following passage Fred-
erick Gibberd (1953) describes a town square as it is surely seen only through
the eyes of a design professional.

> We walk into the space in front of the town hall . . . and the white building be-
> comes the predominant element—a three-dimensional composition with a pleas-
> ant, curved silhouette. Our eye comes down to the normal level . . . and the
> detail design holds our attention; we are attracted by the shop fronts, the textures
> of the floors, and we unconsciously register that the snake-like kerb repeats the
> curve of the roof line. (16–17)

Perception, then, is a creative not a mechanical act: we see what we look
for and we look for things that interest us. Our perceptions are not mirror
images but interpretations of what is "out there," and it is these interpretations
of the environment rather than its objective qualities that explain our attitudes
and behaviors.[6] If our information and interests change, we see the same environment somewhat differently. This explains how it is possible for residents
and outsiders to look at the same environment and yet see it differently.

Perhaps the best way to introduce a discussion of differences in perception between residents and outsiders is to note that when an outsider changes
into a resident the environment "looks" different. Herbert Gans (1962) comments on such an experience in the West End of Boston.

> My first visit to the West End left me with the impression that I was in Europe. Its
> high buildings set on narrow, irregularly curving streets, its Italian and Jewish res-
> taurants and food stores, and the variety of people who crowded the streets when
> the weather was good—all gave the area a foreign and exotic flavor. . . . Looking
> at the area as a tourist, I noted the highly visible and divergent characteristics that
> set it off from others with which I was familiar. And while the exotic quality of the
> West End did excite me, the dilapidation and garbage were depressing. . . .
>   After a few weeks of living in the West End, my observations—and my per-
> ception of the area—changed drastically. . . . In wandering through the West
> End, and using it as a resident, I developed a kind of selective perception, in
> which my eye focused only on those parts of the area that were actually being
> used by people. The dirt and spilled-over garbage . . . were not as noticeable as

during my initial observations. . . . The exotic quality of the stores and the residents also wore off as I became used to seeing them. (11–12)

It took several weeks of living in the West End before Gans could see it as a resident. Earlier, he had seen it as the ultimate outsider—a tourist.

There are different types of tourist, but one feature that is central to the tourist experience is that of being away from home, removed from the familiar scenes and activities of the workaday environment, and cut off from the ties, commitments, and responsibilities that dominate it.[7] Tourists do not have enduring relationships with the visited environment and they do not feel responsible for what happens there. They are essentially observers rather than participants. What they know is based on first impressions, comparisons with other places, and images created by postcards, travel brochures, posters, signs, slide shows, and the like, and so, to a large extent, they see what they previously knew to be there. Tourists depend heavily on the physical environment as a source of information on their whereabouts, and they feel most comfortable in places where the features are distinctive and the orientation information is clear and vivid; that is, where there is a strong "sense of place." To intensify the feeling of being away from it all, tourists look for experiences that are new and different from those at home.

The residential experience is quite different.[8] For most residents, their home environment is the most personal of places, the setting for intimate and enduring relationships, a refuge from the world, a confirmation of self, a locus of community, and a symbol of continuity. It represents an investment and a long-term commitment, a place where one comes to recover from one's wounds and rekindle one's energies.[9] Residents look to the residential area for shelter, security, comfort, convenience, control, cleanliness, and respectability, not for adventure; and the novel, exciting, interesting places that attract tourists are often seen as undesirable to live in. In the same way, a place that looks attractive to live in does not necessarily look attractive to a visitor.

Residents acquire information about their residential area over an extended period. In the course of repeated interactions with the same people, buildings, facilities, and activities, features of the environment become embedded in the subconscious, so that residents no longer seem to be aware of them: they know they are there but they only notice them when they are changed or removed. Think, for example, of the experience of driving down a familiar road.

Familiarity with a route will cause marked differences in perception and attitude. The first time traveller, predicting only with those cues he can glean from the landscape, will be highly attentive to any information relevant to his goal. . . .

> The commuter, on the other hand, sure of his prediction, may absorb all necessary information subliminally. His active interest is aroused only by unexpected traffic movements or new changes in the environment. (Appleyard 1965, 183)

Or think of one's responses to everyday objects around the house.

> It gets to be that I become so familiar with what's on the walls, that I don't know it's there and I don't even have to see it. I *know* it's there. If you were to take it down and remove it, I would know it's gone immediately. If anything's out of place, I would know that it's out of place. (Csikszentmihalyi and Rochberg-Halton 1981, 183)

At the same time that they seem oblivious to things that outsiders find quite striking, residents notice things that escape the attention of outsiders.

> On Calvert Street the row houses stood in two endless lines. "I don't see how you knew which one was home," Luke had told him once, and Cody had been amazed. Oh, if you lived here you knew. They weren't all alike, not really. One had dozens of roses struggling in its tiny front yard, another an illuminated madonna glowing night and day in the parlor window. Some had their trim painted in astonishing colors, assertively, like people with their chins thrust out. The fact that they were *attached* didn't mean a thing. (Tyler 1982, 281–82)

Residents also see things in the environment that do not exist for outsiders: residents' interactions with the environment represent personal and collective struggles, accomplishments, responsibilities, and changes, and these become associated with the physical settings in which they occur and charge them with purely local meanings. These meanings can be so powerful that they supersede physical qualities as the dominant influence on perception; that is, residents see a place as home, birthplace, or investment, before they see it as a physical form.[10] This is apparent when residents talk about their home environment. Here, for example (Brower 1985), one resident talks about the sculpture of a nude woman in the park in front of his house, while another describes a local restaurant.

> [I] walk by there every day. . . . [A] tourist would see that . . . and say, "Oh, that's beautiful." But when I'm on my way to Peabody [Conservatory of Music] in the middle of the afternoon on a weekday, sometimes I think maybe I shouldn't be looking at this sensuous woman in the middle of the day like this . . . so sometimes as I walk by it I look the other way because I don't think I should be looking at it. But if you're a tourist, you don't go through that. You think it's all right.
>   J——'s Restaurant . . . has the best coffee because one of his old socks is in the pot. I don't know if that's true or not, but that's the rumor around the neighborhood. Wonderful coffee.

Local meanings can be positive and enhance the residents' view of the physical environment, or they can be negative and make an otherwise innocuous environment look depressing, scary, or unpleasant; but positive or negative, these meanings represent emotional linkages between objects and observers that residents feel and outsiders do not. In general, familiar environments appear more reassuring, restful, and secure than unfamiliar ones. This may be because familiar environments confirm who we are and affirm what we stand for; or it may be because we feel more competent there—we know what there is and where to find it and so we are able to pay more attention to the job at hand; or it may be that familiarity operates independently of meaning and that repeated exposure, by itself, is sufficient to give us a more positive attitude toward our environment.[11] Whatever the reason, what is important here is that familiar environments seem safer and more satisfying than unfamiliar ones. No matter what the objective circumstances, when asked to rate different environments residents tend to rate familiar ones higher than unfamiliar ones, and residents rate their own familiar environments higher than outside observers.[12] This suggests, incidentally, that in interpreting housing preference surveys we must recognize a bias in favor of environments that are familiar to the respondents.

The fact that residents prefer familiar environments does not mean that they want everything about them to be equally familiar. The effect of too much familiarity is told in Alan Jay Lerner's lyrics for the musical *Gigi*.

"Don't you marvel at the power of the mighty Eiffel tower
Knowing there it will remain evermore?
Climbing up to the sky, over ninety stories high . . ."
"How many stories?"
"Ninety!"
"How many yesterday?"
"Ninety!"
"And tomorrow?"
"Ninety!"
"It's a bore."

There are several strategies we resort to in order to prevent our home environment from becoming overly familiar. Perhaps the most common strategy is to modify (but not substantially change) the familiar image of the place. This can be done by rearranging the furniture, buying new drapes, moving the pictures around, or trying a new color on the walls (Kron 1983). Another strategy is to get away for a while: when we return there is a period during which we see things afresh. There is always the danger, however, that we will notice flaws and inadequacies that familiarity had blinded us to. This is what happened to Mole in Kenneth Grahame's *The Wind in the Willows* (1961). Mole, who had been staying with his friend Rat, had an irresistible urge to return home. His first impression, when he eventually got there, was disappointing:

> [He] saw the cheerless, deserted look of the long-neglected house, and its narrow, meager dimensions, its worn and shabby contents—and collapsed again in a hall-chair, his nose in his paws. 'O, Ratty!' he cried dismally, 'Why did I ever do it? Why did I bring you to this poor, cold little place.' (87)

But the period of fresh perception was a brief one, and features soon faded once again into the general atmosphere. By the time Mole went to bed, the familiar pattern had reestablished itself, and

> ere he closed his eyes, he let them wander around his old room, mellow in the glow of the firelight that played or rested on familiar and friendly things which had long been unconsciously a part of him, and now smilingly received him back without rancour. . . . It was good to think that he had this to come back to, this place which was all his own, these things which were so glad to see him again and could always be counted upon for the same simple welcome. (96)

Another strategy for restoring jaded perceptions is to look at the familiar environment as if through the eyes of a stranger. This is a common empathetic response to the presence of outsiders, because residents want their home environment to look good to their guests and they are upset if it does not.

> This is really one of the most pitiful things about Jersey City. There isn't anything that if someone came here from a far place, that I could say, "Oh, I want you to see this." (Lynch 1960, 29)

For residents to look at their home from the visitors' point of view does not require special talent (although some people are better at it than others), but it comes more easily in those parts of the environment that are meant to be used by outsiders, like streets, entrances, and living rooms, than in "backstage" spaces like bedrooms, basements, and attics.[13] The view as it is seen through "strange eyes" is especially important to residents who are sensitive to "appearances" (which is to say, the way things appear to outsiders) and who see the home environment as a public expression of self.

Just as residents are bored in home environments where everything is totally familiar, so outsiders are uncomfortable in environments where everything is totally unfamiliar—they feel out of place, out of control, lost. Some people like to feel at home wherever they are.

So Dorothy and I came to the Ritz [in London] and it is delightfully full of
Americans. I mean you would really think it was New York because I always think
that the most delightful thing about travelling is to always be running into Americans and to always feel at home. (Loos 1963, 57)

In order to make outsiders feel more at home, many places offer lodgings
that incorporate the features and values of the visitors' home environment;
and they offer travel agencies, group tours, guides, reception centers, and spe-
cially staged events to provide outsiders with information, interpretation, and
assistance.[14] There are those, however, who believe that the resident's experience is the only true experience of a place, and that these institutions dupe
visitors by insulating them from residents and placing them in an environment that is no more than a mirage, something that has been artificially
created.[15]

In the same way that residents sometimes look at a familiar environment
through the eyes of an outsider, so outsiders sometimes override their auto-
matic perceptions and look at a strange environment from a resident's point of
view (Brower 1985). Usually, there is little inducement for outsiders to do
this, and it requires a conscious effort; but it explains how professional designers, who seldom have any experience of living in the environments they
create, are able to act on behalf of prospective residents.

The fact that residents and outsiders both recognize the validity of the
other point of view means that if a place can incorporate elements both of
continuity and of change, it can be attractive both as a place to live and as a
place to visit. Some places achieve this through forms that are so insistent and
images that are so evocative that one does not tire of them. Others create the
effect of variety even though they may change very little, because as soon as
we become familiar with them at one level, another level opens up for exploration. Complex environments that offer the opportunity for continuity at one
level and change at another have the best potential for satisfying the need of
both residents and outsiders.

This material, in much the same form, is a chapter of Design in familiar places *(New
York: Praeger, 1988), a book on the subject of home environments: what makes them
look good and what makes us use them and care for them the way we do.*

Notes

1. In Brower (1975), I suggested these four ways of looking at objects.
2. Gregory (1968, 250) describes the process of perception as follows:

Visual perception involves "reading" from retinal images a host of characteristics of objects that are not represented directly by the images in the eyes. The image does not convey directly many important characteristics of objects; whether they are hard or soft, heavy or light, hot or cold. Nonvisual characteristics must somehow be associated with the visual image by individual learning . . . for objects to be recognized from their images. Such learning is essential for perception; without it one would have mere stimulus-response behavior.

Perception seems to be a matter of looking up information that has been stored about objects and how they behave in various situations. The retinal image does little more than select the relevant stored data. . . . Behavior is determined by the contents of the entry rather than by the stimulus that provoked the search.

For further information about the perceptual process see Gregory 1970; and Kaplan and Kaplan 1982.

3. In *The painted word* (1975, 7), Tom Wolfe discusses the way that art critics have shaped the popular perception of Modern Art: "Not 'seeing is believing,' you ninny, but 'believing is seeing' for Modern Art has become completely literary: the paintings and other works exist only to illustrate the text."

4. For a discussion about what we see when we look at paintings, and about the difference between looking at an original and looking at a reproduction, see Berger 1977, 7–33.

5. James (1950, 402) expressed it as follows: "Millions of items in the outward order are present to my senses which never properly enter into my experience. Why? Because they have no *interest* for me. *My experience is what I attend to.* Only those items which I *notice* shape my mind— without selective interest, experience is an utter chaos." Milgrim (1970) identified selective perception as a mechanism for coping with information overload.

6. Koffka (1935) distinguished between the objective or "geographical environment" and the perceived or "behavioral environment," and Chein (1954) explained it as follows:

The [geographical environment] refers to the objective physical and social environment in which the individual is immersed. The [behavioral environment] refers to the environment as it is perceived and reacted to by the behaving individual: it may bear little resemblance to the geographical environment, being an organized "interpretation" of the latter based on recollections, anticipations, perceptual distortions and omissions, and upon reasonably correct perceptions. The behavioral environment deletes from and alters, as well as adds to the geographic environment.

7. Smith (1977, 2) defines a tourist as "a temporarily leisured person who voluntarily visits a place away from home for the purpose of experiencing a change." For classifications of different types of tourists, see also U.S. Department of Commerce 1981; Pearce 1982. For discussions of the tourist experience see Appleyard 1976 and 1979a; MacCannell 1973 and 1976; Pearce 1982; Bosselman 1978; and Smith 1977.

8. For discussion of the resident experience see Lansing and Marans 1969, 197; Rapoport 1977; Lee 1973; Csikszentmihalyi and Rochberg-Halton 1981; Fried 1982; Lofland 1973; Lynch 1972; Steele 1981; Winkel 1981; Appleyard 1976 and 1979b; Becker 1977; and Birch et al. 1977.

9. Residents who perceive their home environment as threatening may not form all of these positive associations (see Rainwater 1966), but this does not mean that these associations are inappropriate or undesirable.

10. Csikszentmihalyi and Rochberg-Halton (1981, 185) did a study of objects in the home that are important to residents. They have the following to say about meanings: "The total context of artifacts in a household acts as a constant sign of familiarity, telling us who we and our kindred are, what we have done or plan to do, and in this way reduces the amount of information we have to pay attention to in order to act with ease. . . . One of the most important functions of household possessions, then, is to provide a *familiar* environment, which can reflect the order, control and significance of its inhabitants, and thus enable them to channel their psychic energy more effectively within it."

11. Zajonc (1968) cites an experiment in which nonsense words were introduced to participants as "real" words in a foreign language. Some words were shown more frequently than others. When participants were then asked to guess the meanings of the words, the more frequently heard words were said to have more positive meanings. In another experiment, participants were shown photographs of strange men; some photographs were shown more frequently than others. When asked how they might like each of the men on the photographs, participants showed a marked preference for photographs that they had seen more frequently.

12. Palmer (1983) showed residents of Syracuse, New York, twenty-eight pictures of the same house, but each picture showed a different landscape treatment of the front yard. Participants were asked to indicate how much they would like their own front yard to look like each of those in the pictures, and they were asked to identify the picture that looked most like their front yard. The findings showed that participants preferred the front yards that were most like their own.

Michelson (1976, 91), in a study of residential preferences, found that people who lived farther from their friends expressed a preference for lower density living, and that people who shopped outside their neighborhood thought of an ideal neighborhood as one without commercial uses.

Warren (1982), in a national survey of neighborhoods, found that over half of the residents interviewed rated their neighborhood at seven or more on a ten-point scale, and more than three-quarters rated their neighborhood at five or more.

One could interpret these findings to mean that people liked their present environment because they had made a careful choice in the first place, and not because it had grown familiar to them. Such an interpretation is not possible in the following study. Rosen (1971) looked at the housing preferences of residents in two public housing buildings in Baltimore, Maryland, where apartments were assigned on the basis of priority and availability rather than choice. Residents were asked to indicate how desirable it was for apartments to include certain design features, such as a balcony, a separate bedroom, a separate kitchen, and extra storage space. Some apartments already had one or more of these features while others did not. Rosen found in almost every instance that participants expressed a preference for features already present in their apartment.

The sanguinary effect of familiarity also changes people's perception of danger. In an eight-city survey of crime and fear of crime in residential areas, Hinderlang, Gottfredson, and Garofalo (1978) found that residents felt the crime problem was less severe in their neighborhood than in other areas, regardless of the objective circumstances. Familiarity may not make a dangerous neighborhood seem safe, but it makes it seem safer than other, less familiar neighborhoods. These findings are supported by other studies; see Dubow, McCabe, and Kaplan 1979, 9.

In several studies residents and outsiders were asked to rate the same environment, and the findings confirm the attachment to familiar places.

Keller (1968, 108) cites a study of housing areas in San Juan, Puerto Rico, where objective measures (developed and applied by outsiders) indicated that living conditions were shockingly inadequate. The study found, however, that residential satisfaction was high; 70 percent of the respondents rated their areas as good places to live.

Grigsby and Rosenberg (1975, 74), in a study of housing in Baltimore, Maryland, found that families tended to give their homes a higher rating than did interviewers or housing inspectors. Even among families who lived in seriously substandard housing (according to the city housing code), 50 percent were not dissatisfied with their accommodations.

Campbell, Converse, and Rogers (1976) asked resident respondents and interviewers to describe their neighborhood using twelve dimensions. They found that residents viewed their neighborhood in more pleasant terms than interviewers (243). They also found that poor respondents expressed almost as much overall satisfaction with their neighborhoods as wealthy respondents expressed with theirs (480).

In a study of three areas in Ahmedabad, Desai (1980) obtained ratings of environmental quality from residents and from independent raters: in almost all cases, the residents' ratings were higher than those of the independent raters.

Lansing and Marans (1969, 197) compared neighborhood ratings by planners and residents.

They found that 88 percent of the people living in neighborhoods judged unpleasant by the planner liked their neighborhood at least moderately well, while only 12 percent disliked theirs.

Familiarity even affects the critical eye of the professional designer. Imamoglu (1979) asked architects to rate the quality of the living rooms in sixty housing units in Ankara, Turkey, and he compared their ratings with those of the householders themselves. He found that the householders rated the rooms more positively than did the architects. Imamoglu then asked architects to evaluate living rooms belonging to other architects. He found that the architect-householders rated their rooms higher than the architect-evaluators.

13. Newcomers behave in much the same way whether they are residents or outsiders: both move with increasing confidence as routes and landmarks become more familiar. Cooper (1981), in a study of visitors at a holiday resort, found that new arrivals tended to go first to the "center," where the physical environment gave the strongest and clearest informational signals; but gradually they ventured into other areas, first paying great attention to their surroundings, and then moving with increasing confidence as routes and landmarks became more familiar. Hudson (1975) found that new residents used facilities that were near home or their place of work. As time passed, their activities extended over a wider geographical area. Aldskogins (1977) had similar findings.

For further discussions about mental images—their structure, effect on behavior, and change over time—see Devlin 1976; Appleyard 1976; Canter 1977, 67–69; Lynch 1960, 49; Downs and Stea 1977; and Evans, Marrero, and Butler 1981.

14. "I run my hotels the way I run my home," Leona M. Helmsley proclaims in an advertisement for Harley Hotels (*Ozark*, September 1985). "My home was not designed just to be beautiful. My first considerations are always comfort and convenience. And that's how I planned the rooms at every Harley Hotel."

15. Boorstin (1977) characterizes tourist environments as a cultural mirage, and events that are arranged especially for tourists as pseudo-events. He argues that in catering to tourists, host countries debase the local culture, and that "earnest, honest natives embellish their ancient rites, change, enlarge and spectacularize their festivals, so that tourists will not be disappointed" (103). For further discussions about the superficiality of tourist environments, see Mitford 1959; MacCannell 1973; and Dubos 1965, 24–25.

References

Aldskogins, H. 1977. A conceptual framework and a Swedish case study of recreational behavior and environmental cognition. *Economic Geography* 53(2):163–83.

Appleyard, D. 1965. Motion, sequence and the city. In G. Kepes, *The nature and art of motion*. New York: George Braziller.

———. 1976. *Planning a pluralist city*. Cambridge, Mass.: M.I.T. Press.

———. 1979a. Inside vs. outside: The distortions of distance. Institute of Urban and Regional Development, University of California, Berkeley, working paper no. 307, July.

———. 1979b. Home. *Architectural Association Quarterly* 11(3):4–20.

Becker, F. D. 1977. *Housing messages*. Stroudsberg, Pa.: Dowden, Hutchinson and Ross.

Berger, J. 1977. *Ways of seeing*. New York: Penguin Books.

Birch, D. L., et al. 1977. *The behavioral basis of neighborhood change*. 1977. A special report prepared for the Joint Center for Urban Studies of M.I.T. and Harvard University.

Boorstin, D. J. 1977. *The image: A guide to pseudo-events in America*. New York: Atheneum.

Bosselman, F. P. 1978. *In the wake of the tourist: Managing special places in eight countries*. Washington, D.C.: The Conservation Foundation.

Brower, S. 1975. Tools, toys, masterpieces, mediums. *Landscape* 19(2):28–32.

———. 1985. Design in familiar places: A report to the National Endowment for the Arts, University of Maryland, School of Social Work and Community Planning, Baltimore, Md., May.

————. 1988. *Design in familiar places*. New York: Praeger.

Canter, D. 1977. *The psychology of place*. London: The Architectural Press.

Campbell, A., P. E. Converse, and W. L. Rogers. 1976. *The quality of American life*. New York: Russell Sage Foundation.

Chein, I. 1954. The environment as a determinant of behavior. *Journal of Social Psychiatry* 39:115–27.

Cooper, C. P. 1981. Spatial and temporal patterns of tourist behavior. *Regional Studies* 15(5): 359–71.

Csikszentmihalyi, M., and E. Rochberg-Halton. 1981. *The meaning of things: Domestic symbols and the self*. New York: Cambridge University Press.

Desai, A. 1980. The environmental perceptions of an urban landscape: The case of Ahmedabad. *Ekistics* 47(283) (July–August):2.

Devlin, A. S. 1976. The "small town" cognitive map: Adjusting to a new environment. In *Environmental knowing: Theories, research, and methods*, ed. G. T. Moore and R. G. Golledge, 58–66. Stroudsburg, Pa.: Dowden, Hitchinson and Ross.

Downs, R. M., and D. Stea. 1977. *Maps in minds: Reflections on cognitive mapping*. New York: Harper and Row.

Dubos, R. 1965. *Man adapting*. New Haven: Yale University Press.

Dubow, A. F., E. MaCabe, and G. Kaplan. 1979. *Reactions to crime: A critical review of the literature*. A special report prepared for the U.S. Department of Justice. U.S. Government Printing Office Stock no. 027-000-00873-9.

Evans, G. W., D. G. Marrero, and P. A. Butler. 1981. Environmental learning and cognitive mapping. *Environment and Behavior* 13(1):83–104.

Fried, M. 1982. Residential attachment: Sources of residential and community of satisfaction. *Journal of Social Issues* 38(3):107–19.

Gans, H. J. 1962. *The urban villagers: Group and class in the life of Italian Americans*. New York: The Free Press.

Gibberd, F. 1953. *Town design*. London: The Architectural Press.

Grahame, K. 1961. *The wind in the willows*. New York: Charles Scribner's Sons.

Gregory, R. L. 1968. Visual illusions. *Scientific American*, November. Reprinted in *Perception: Mechanisms and models*, series of readings from *Scientific American*, 241–51. San Francisco: W. H. Freeman.

————. 1970. *The intelligent eye*. New York: McGraw Hill.

Grigsby, W. G., and L. Rosenberg. 1975. *Urban housing policy*. New Brunswick, N.J.: Transaction Books.

Hinderlang, M. J., M. R. Gottfredson, and J. Garofalo. 1978. *Victims of personal crime: An empirical foundation for a theory of personal victimization*. Cambridge, Mass.: Ballinger.

Hudson, R. 1975. Patterns of spatial search. *Transactions, The Institute of British Geographers* 65(July):141–54.

Imamoglu, V. 1979. Assessment of living rooms by householders and architects. In *Conflicting experiences of space*, ed. J. G. Simon. Louvain-la-Neuve. Also, Middle East Technical University, Department of Building Science and Environmental Design, Ankara, Turkey, research report no. 1.

James, W. [1890] 1950. *Principles of psychology*. Vol. 1. New York: Dover.

Kaplan, S., and R. Kaplan 1982. *Cognition and environment: Functioning in an uncertain world*. New York: Praeger.

Keller, S. 1968. *The urban neighborhood: A sociological perspective*. New York: Random House.

Koffka, K. 1935. *Principles of gestalt psychology*. New York: Harcourt Brace.

Kron, J. 1983. *Home-psych: The social psychology of home and decoration*. New York: Clarkson N. Potter.

Lansing, J. B., and R. W. Marans. 1969. Evaluation of neighborhood quality. *Journal of the American Institute of Planners* (May):195–99.

Lee, T. 1973. Psychology and living space. In *Image and environment: Cognitive mapping and spatial behavior*, ed. R. M. Downs and D. Stea, 87–108. Chicago: Aldine.

Lofland, L. H. 1973. *A world of strangers: Order and action in urban public space*. New York: Basic Books.

Loos, A. 1963. *Gentlemen prefer blondes*. New York: Curtis.

Lynch, K. 1960. *The image of the city*. Cambrige, Mass.: M.I.T. Press.

———. 1972. *What time is this place?* Cambridge, Mass.: M.I.T. Press.

MacCannell, 1973. Staged authenticity: Arangements of social space in tourist settings. *American Journal of Sociology* 79(1):589–603.

———. 1976. *The tourist: A new theory of the leisure class*. New York: Schocken.

Michelson, W. 1976. *Man and his urban environment: A sociological approach*. With revisions. Reading, Mass.: Addison-Wesley.

Milgrim, S. 1970. The experience of living in cities. *Science* 167(3924):1461–68.

Mitford, N. 1959. The tourist. *Encounter* 13(4):3–7.

Mortimer, J. 1984. Rumpole and the genuine article. In *Rumpole and the golden thread*. New York: Viking Penguin.

Nassauer, J., and R. Westmacott. 1985. Progressiveness as an ideal among farmers as a factor in disturbance and loss of heterogeneity in farmed landscapes. Paper presented at landscape ecology conference, University of Georgia.

Palmer, J. F. 1983. Presentation at symposium on Environmental Meaning, Fourteenth International Conference of the Environmental Design Research Association, Lincoln, Nebraska, and personal correspondence.

Pearce, P. L. 1982. *The social psychology of tourist behavior*. New York: Pergamon.

Peattie, L. R. 1969. Social issues in housing. In B. J. Frieden and W. W. Nash, Jr., *Shaping an urban future*, 15–34. Cambridge, Mass.: M.I.T. Press.

Rainwater, L. 1966. Fear and the house-as-haven in the lower class. *Journal of the American Institute of Planners* 32(1):23–31.

Rapoport, A. 1977. *Human aspects of urban form*. New York: Pergamon.

Rosen, B. F. 1971. Design criteria for hi-rise living for the elderly. Report prepared for Baltimore City Department of Housing and Community Development, 31 August. Mimeo.

Sitwell, O. 1933. *Miracle on Sinai: A satirical novel*. London: Duckworth.

Smith, V. L., ed. 1977. *Hosts and guests: The anthropology of tourism*. Philadelphia: University of Pennsylvania Press.

Steele, F. 1981. *The sense of place*. Boston: C.B.I.

Thompson, M. 1979. *Rubbish theory: The creation and destruction of value*. New York: Oxford University Press.

Tyler, A. 1982. *Dinner at the homesick restaurant*. New York: Alfred A. Knopf.

U.S. Department of Commerce. 1981. *Creating economic growth and jobs through travel and tourism*. Washington, D.C.: U.S. Government Printing Office.

Warren, D. I. 1982. *The health of American neighborhoods: A national report*. A special report prepared for the Community Effectiveness Institute. Ann Arbor, November.

Winkel, G. H. 1981. The perception of neighborhood change. In *Cognition, social behavior and the environment*, ed. J. Harvey. Hillsdale, N.J.: Laurence Erlbaum.

Wolfe, T. 1975. *The painted word*. New York: Farrar, Straus and Giroux.

Zajonc, R. B. 1968. Attitudinal effects of mere exposure. *Journal of Personality and Social Psychology Monograph Supplement* 9(2) pt. 2 (June).

Figure 10.1. Object.

PART THREE

CULTURE AS A MEANING SYSTEM

CULTURAL MEANINGS OF

HOME, HOUSE, AND FAMILY

The two parts preceding this are most concerned with the study of culture as a behavioral and cognitive system. This section emphasizes research focused on culture as a meaning system. Cultural meanings can be both expressed and studied as symbols representing human thought and behavior. The symbolic dimension of housing encodes meaning from two perspectives. First, the house can be viewed as an "outside" symbol that contains culturally meaningful domestic spaces. Or, the house can be perceived as an "inside" symbol that is contained within the culturally derived plan or representation of a larger landscape, such as a town or neighborhood, or even a nation.

In either of these symbolic dimensions of housing and culture, the concepts of human self and identity are important. Ideas that are clearly related to the symbolic expression of shelter—for example, ideas of house, home, and family—are powerful shapers of both individual and group identities and thereby influence the types of dwellings people choose. By the same token, the built environment, including houses, not only reinforces traditional group identities and expressions of self but also, when housing structures are altered, creates new symbolic expressions which mold identities, sometimes in positive ways and other times in deleterious ways.

This part begins with David Hummon's review of the literature devoted to the study of housing and identity in the contemporary United States. The intricacies of exploring the differences between *group* identity and *individual* identity as they are expressed in a complex, heterogeneous cultural environment are explored in detail. In the next chapter James Duncan explores the relation between individualism and variation in housing styles in the Kandyan Highlands of Sri Lanka. He finds that the degree to which a house is used as an expression of individual meaning, as opposed to community standards, is related to rural status and degrees of urbanization. In her contribution Julia Robinson discusses the conceptual and design problems that are inherent in moving from one kind of symbolic expression of dwelling to another—in this case describing the cultural patterns expressed in public institutions and private houses in the United States. The meanings that are attributed to these different types of dwellings may lead to design problems when the symbols are interchangeable, as they are in the design of institutional residences. The final chapter in this part is Sandra Howell and Vana Tentokali's discussion of gender and cross-cultural differences in the concepts of domestic privacy, providing insight into the ways culture-specific, gender-related concepts of identity are expressed in the design and use of housing spaces.

In sum, these chapters offer testimony to the degree to which housing may encapsulate important aspects of group identity and individual meaning. Equally important is the observation, especially apparent in Hummon's and Duncan's chapters, that the degree to which either group or individual meanings are associated with housing varies from one cultural setting to another. In this vein, the chapters also offer insight into one of the major problems in cultural analysis: How, when we begin to observe the symbolic expressions of different cultures, can we distinguish between group and idiosyncratic values? Each of the contributors to this part provides a slightly different response to this problem.

11

HOUSE, HOME, AND IDENTITY
IN CONTEMPORARY AMERICAN
CULTURE

DAVID M. HUMMON

A recently published children's book, *The Big Orange Splot*, tells the story of Mr. Plumbean, who lives happily "on a street where all the houses are the same" (Pinkwater 1977). One day, quite by accident, a seagull flying over Mr. Plumbean's house drops a can of bright orange paint on his roof, which makes a large spot on his neat olive-green roof. After several day's rumination, Mr. Plumbean paints his house a phantasmagoria of colors and images—with little orange splots, stripes, "pictures of elephants, lions and pretty girls and steam shovels." The next day, he adds a fake clock tower to his roof, re-landscapes his yard with palm and baobab trees, hangs a hammock, and grazes a pet alligator. His neighbors, outraged by his display, say he has "popped his cork, flipped his wig, blown his stack, and dropped his stopper." He responds, "My house is me and I am it. My house is where I like to be and it looks like all my dreams."

This remarkable children's story is a moral tale about the virtues and dilemmas of individualism and self-expression. What is surprising is not the book's message—a particularly suitable theme for an American fable of the late seventies—but the vehicle of its expression. No funny-looking duck, mischievous monkey, or other creature personifies the virtues of individualism, but a house. Here, the solitary man, through his actions, realizes himself against the world in the presentation of his home. Here, the proverbial American dream literally becomes his dream—a unique dwelling place that embodies the self to the limits of fantasy.

This story, I believe, underlines how much contemporary Americans have come to link dwelling place and identity. The house expresses or—as this exhortation makes clear—ought to express the person through its form,

style, interior, or exterior decoration. It is thus not surprising that both social
scientists and designers have also explored this topic with increasing frequency
during the last decade. Notable work can be found in anthropology (Perin
1977), environmental psychology (Altman and Gauvain 1981), geography
(Cooper 1974; Duncan 1982a; Relph 1976; Seamon 1979), history (Cohn
1979; Wright 1981), sociology (Csikszentmihalyi and Rochberg-Halton
1981), and the design professions (Alexander et al. 1977; Greenbie 1981; Hayden 1984; Rapoport 1982a). Only a few writers (for example, Rapoport 1982b)
have attempted to suggest what important lessons about dwelling place and
identity in contemporary American culture can be culled from this wide-
ranging work.

   This chapter begins this task, guided by several concerns. First, I will
stress research that is exemplary, representative of widely different disciplines,
and, in most instances, published during the last decade. Second, I will interpret this work through a single, though broad perspective: that of the social
and cultural construction of reality (Berger and Luckmann 1967). In general,
I will emphasize how social and cultural processes mediate the relation of
housing and identity, analyzing the many ways that dwellings, as meaningful
objects and settings, become nonverbal signs for defining and communicating
identity in modern society. Finally, after some necessary theoretical remarks,
I will address four central issues, rather than attempt a single, over-arching
synthesis of this diverse, often contradictory work. Specifically, I will explore
the role of dwelling place in the construction of personal, group, temporal,
and home identities.

Dwelling Identity:
A Theoretical Perspective

             Matters of identity involve a person's sense of self: self-
reflexive answers to that ongoing, inescapable, and quintessentially human
question, "Who am I?" Much of the time, but not always, our sense of identity is unproblematic: we know "who we are," and with little reflection, we are
able to sustain this sense of self in our interaction with others through language, dress, and other forms of nonverbal communication (Goffman 1959).
In taking on new roles, exploring new places, or coping with environmental
or social change, we may become "self-conscious" of our identity, anxiously
searching for new ways to interpret and express "who we are here and now."

   Identity can be conceptualized as consisting of three related elements
(Hewitt 1984). It involves a "positioning" of self in reality, a *symbolic placement* that situates the person "in the world," at once differentiating the indi-

vidual from some aspects of reality, affiliating the person with other aspects (Berger and Luckmann 1967). For example, I, like F. Scott Fitzgerald, know that I am different from the rich, as well as from rocks, trees, and seventeenth-century New Englanders. Conversely, I know that I belong in cities and with my piano, my family, and other people of good will. Identity also involves an interpretation of both the qualities and value of self, characterized respectively in *self-imagery* and *self-esteem*. This multifaceted nature of identity is nicely reflected in the everyday language of identity and identification. We identify ourselves *as* people of a certain type, quality, or value; we also identify ourselves *with* others or significant objects, forging a sense of belonging and attachment.

Although identity involves the individual's interpretation of self, it is a profoundly social object. Identity is predicated on the fact that people, as "symbolic animals," are engaged in an ongoing reality that is imbued with meaning by shared symbols of culture, ideational systems that distinguish gods, people, events, and ultimately selves through their patterned meanings (Becker 1962). The "repertoire of identities" (Berger 1970) embedded in culture are, moreover, socially and historically specific, the product, not of biological nature, but of the structure of social life. They are reproduced in individual consciousness through lifelong socialization and the patterned experience of everyday life.

Like identity, dwellings can be conceptualized as meaningful social and cultural objects that, in the words of Rakoff (1977), are "used to demarcate space, to express feelings, ways of thinking, and social processes, and to provide arenas for culturally defined activity as well as to provide for physical shelter." Dwellings and domestic objects are thus constituted as significant objects through culture: people become conscious of dwellings through the beliefs, values, and other taken-for-granted assumptions of their symbolic world.

Moreover, because dwellings are vested with meanings, they may, as symbols, *become* part of the knowledge of daily life, "vehicles of conception" through which people define and interpret their reality (Geertz 1973). This fundamental recognition that houses, like other material objects, may act as signs or symbols—things that "stand for" or represent other things—does not deny that houses have instrumental uses. They clearly do, and in a culture noted for its "practicality," we routinely equate such uses with the meaning of the object as a matter of "common sense." This perspective underlines the fact that human beings, as symbol makers, can and do attribute multiple meanings to the world, meanings that may reflect cultural, social, or psychological processes beyond those of instrumental use. Houses, thus, provide shelter; chairs, a comfortable place to sit; fences, protection from a neighbor's dog; yet, houses may also convey respectability or achievement; chairs, authority; and fences, independence.[1]

If one recognizes that both housing and identity are socially constructed symbolic objects, the mutual relevance of housing for identity—and identity for housing—becomes clear. On the one hand, by learning and appropriating the meanings of dwellings, the individual can use dwellings to create a sense of identity, drawing upon their meanings to locate him or herself in reality and to define self-imagery. On the other hand, given a sense of identity, the individual can use, and to some extent cultivate, the meanings of dwelling to display and communicate identity to self and other. In short, dwellings and their furnishings can, under certain conditions, speak worlds of meaning, meanings that can be used to discover, present, and maintain identity.

Personalization: Individualism, Dwelling, and Identity

The socially constructed, symbolic nature of both dwelling place and identity implies that the relation between housing and identity must also be conceptualized as a social product. The fundamental importance of this insight for contemporary American dwelling identity can be illustrated by reexamining Mr. Plumbean's action in a cross-cultural and historical perspective.

Mr. Plumbean uses his house as a medium of self-expression, a way to signify his identity as a unique person. His actions—to personalize the domestic environment—are certainly not unusual in contemporary America, though his style is not exactly middle American. Altman and Chemers (1980), for example, note how residents of middle-class suburban homes present a unique "face" to the public by adding family initials to screen doors, installing decorative lamp posts and mailboxes, painting and repainting their homes, and altering their yards with bushes and other landscaping devices. Within the private space of the house, such personalization of the environment is even more pronounced in the selection of decor, furniture, and internal differentiation of space.[2] Moreover, both Mr. Plumbean and his neighbors assume that Mr. Plumbean's house, and his actions toward it, *are* relevant to his identity as an individual. They certain disagree over the meaning of his house—he, declaring that it is his "real self"; they, that it suggests that he is a "crazy man." But neither would question that the house is a significant sign of the individual and an expression of his individuality.

Cross-cultural and historical research suggest that these assumptions about identity, individuality, and the expressive role of dwellings are socially and culturally constructed (Pratt 1982). Although routinely taken-for-granted in American society, they reflect specific historical conditions, circumstances that promote a highly individuated sense of personal identity on the one hand and that use particular material objects as signs of identity on the other. They probably do not reflect a "universal need" for dwellings that express the self as a unique individual, as Cooper (1974) and some psychologically oriented students of dwelling place and home seem to suggest (Dovey 1978; Marc 1977). Nor are they probably symptomatic of innate needs to mark and defend territory inherent in our biological nature as Greenbie (1981) and Porteous (1976) argue.

In analyzing the symbolic role of dwellings in traditional societies, for example, Rapoport (1982a) proposes that the relative use of environmental signs for identity in traditional societies is quite variable, and that other aspects of the environment—such as settlement patterns—are frequently more important than dwellings. Moreover, when dwellings are culturally significant for identity, they typically signify group identity, not the identity of the individual as a unique person.

Duncan (1982a; Duncan and Duncan 1976a; 1976b) also notes substantial cultural variation in the symbolic uses of dwelling for the presentation of identity. In Hyderabad, India, dwellings are both seen and presented as emblems of individual identity among the more westernized of elite families, but not among the "old" families who remain embedded in more traditional social relations of the walled city's neighborhoods. Within the United States, he also notes that social class may produce subcultural variation in the use of dwellings for self-presentation, with traditional working-class families less likely to conceive of and use the house as a medium of individualized self-display than middle-class families (compare Rainwater 1966; Valentine 1978; Gans 1962; and Seeley et al. 1956).

Such variation in the symbolization of identity through housing can also be documented in the historical experience of American culture. During the first generations of settlement in seventeenth-century New England, houses were conceived of not only as shelter but also as symbols of community success (Cohn 1979). Descriptions of the landscape of village communities in diaries, letters, and sermons used dwelling places as signs of civilization—signifying that communal life in the wilderness had become permanent, ordered, and viable—rather than as signs of the accomplishments of individual planters. The good society, to the extent that it was thought to involve a physical form, was primarily conceived of as village landscape, rather than an ideal home (Hayden 1984; Lockridge 1970). In this context of communal life and

values, expenditure of resources on dwellings by individuals that socially set
the individual apart, that hinted at "any pretension whatsoever" was in fact
disapproved of (Cohn 1979).

By the eighteenth century, however, people looked at the house as a sign
of the individual with growing frequency. Dwelling places were viewed as emblems of economic rank and personal prosperity, particularly in the commercial towns where the urban well-to-do sought new avenues of public and
private display (Cohn 1979). When reinforced by an increasingly explicit cultural ideology of individualism, which linked material success to both hard
work and virtue, the house also became a potent symbol in a moral landscape
of identity, signifying not only prosperity and social respectability but also dili-
gence, self-reliance, and thrift. By the eighteenth century, it had become important to "know houses" to know self and other.

Such cross-cultural, subcultural, and historical variation in the symbolic
use of the dwelling for personal identity can best be understood in terms of the
collectivism or individualism of the group or society (Duncan 1982b). In traditional societies, for example, where social relations and values are highly
collective, contribution to and participation in group consumption tends to be
rewarded by prestige, while personal consumption and display that primarily
enhance the individual tend to be stigmatized. Under these conditions, dwelling places are conceived and valued primarily as shelter and places of group
activity, and the use of the home for personal display tends to lower, not enhance, the prestige of the individual. Moreover, in traditional societies, individuals tend to be personally "known" to each other, with identities typically
embedded in such primary relations as kinship. In this case, alternative mechanisms for the presentation and definition of identity, like dwellings, have little
functional value to either the individual or the group.

This structural situation contrasts sharply with modern, industrial societies characterized by more individualistic modes of social relations. In these
societies, particularly those structured by the market relations of consumer
capitalism, individualized consumption tends to enhance prestige and self-
esteem, rather than stigmatize the individual and create a sense of shame.
(There are limits even to this display, as the collective reactions of Mr. Plumbean's neighbors suggests.)[3] Moreover, modernity, with its relative openness of
social groups, high rates of social and geographic mobility, and greater social
and cultural heterogeneity in social relations and values, makes the identification of both self and other increasingly problematic. Under such conditions,
dwelling places and household objects—as alternative means of both conveying self-identity and recognizing the identity of others—become increasingly
useful signs of identity. In contemporary American culture, where identity is
less "given" in the structure of daily life, self-expression and definition through

material objects becomes at once more possible, valued, and "necessary" (Berger et al. 1974). In short, within this logic of individualistic social relations, many contemporary Americans use dwelling places and household objects—the largest collection of personally controlled material objects—as the symbolic medium for the display of the self and its unique personhood.

Group Identities: Dwelling as Social Sign and Setting

However individualistic contemporary American life, the Plumbeans of our world also participate in the collective life of the society—a collective life that shapes the group identity of the individual. As such, identity involves a sense of location within the structure of society and a more or less developed sense of belonging to certain groups. Some such identities, including class, gender, ethnic, and racial identities, are facets of major social statuses in society and reflect fundamental social differentiation, learned through socialization, and performed through attendant roles. Other group identities are the product of smaller social worlds, generated in the informal interaction and communication of daily life.

In contemporary American society dwellings and their furnishings often play a significant role in this facet of identity either as *nonverbal signs of group identity* or as *symbolic settings* for the enactment of *socially constructed* roles and identities. Dwellings and domestic objects as nonverbal signs of group identity—like such other badges of group identity as language use, behavioral style, clothing, or formally defined membership—enable the group to differentiate itself from other groups through symbolic boundaries, and in some instances, to legitimate their claims to superiority in Veblenesque competitive display. Dwellings and household objects may also be integrative symbols that provide collective representations for group members and sustain group commitments, as in the case of the domestic display of Christian crêches, mezuzahs, patriotic flags, team trophies, or family photographs. Dwellings as symbolic settings may become an integral part of identity because they are critical to the dramaturgical realization of social identities. Whether dwellings function as nonverbal signs or symbolic settings, they enable the individual to place the self within society and to develop a more or less conscious sense of belonging. This role of dwellings in identity can be illustrated by two major areas of social organization: social rank and gender.

Dwelling, Identity, and the American Dream   Dwelling places are significant symbols of social rank and class identity in contemporary American society for two reasons. First, because dwellings and their furnishings are commodities distributed through the market, families and individuals of different classes readily translate differences in economic resources into housing of different size, quality, style, and locale. Even to the extent that housing allocation follows political, not market dynamics, the class politics of American society may further reinforce, rather than mitigate, class divisions in housing. Thus, housing—and the tenure relationships involved in housing—becomes a major vehicle for publicly defining and displaying social rank, both to self and other. Throughout the nineteenth century, public discussion of housing and class within the emerging urban industrial order elaborated and crystallized modern class connotations of housing as public symbols (Cohn 1979). Today, for example, the mansion and the shack, the restrained "Colonial" and the "budget" tract house, the luxury condominium and the public project, the penthouse and the tenement all convey associations of broad social rank, the social meanings of which are so clear that they are largely taken for granted in American society (Rapoport 1982b). Today, our sense of social rank and of "making it" in the economic system has become so closely identified with the dwellings in which we reside that the "American Dream," traditionally connoting social mobility, has become synonymous with home ownership and the single-family dwelling (Rakoff 1977).

Such differences in the economic resources of class also translate into differences in the patterns of display and group identity in interior and exterior decoration. Sixty years ago, Lynd and Lynd (1929) in their study of Muncie, Indiana, described the homes of working and middle-class Americans to demonstrate the use of material display in class identity. More recently, Lauman and House (1972) have systematically analyzed how the interior decoration of the living rooms of contemporary metropolitan homes differs substantially by class background of the household. In their study, higher-status families display sculpture and large potted plants significantly more frequently than do lower-status households, while lower-status families more often display televisions, bulky furniture, and religious paintings in their living rooms.

Second, dwellings and domestic objects become public emblems of social rank and identity in contemporary America not only because of the varied capabilities of social classes to command dwelling places in the market but also because stylized consumption and display become a significant element in the definition and differentiation of social groups within a consumer society. As Veblen (1945; compare Lindsey 1986) suggested long ago, in a society in which leisure and consumption become increasingly important mechanisms for defining and legitimating differences in social rank, housing and domestic objects become stylized, refined, and increasingly differentiated beyond simple differences of function and cost to convey increasingly complex cultural messages of social rank. For upper-middle- and upper-class Americans, for whom resources are at once less restrictive and less meaningful for group differentiation and identity, such matters of group identity move rapidly to more subtle codes of group display and definition.

Within an upper-middle-class community of Westchester County, for example, Duncan (1973) documented how two relatively elite social worlds express their group identity through different landscape taste. The older and newer elite groups were distinguished to a large degree not only by occupation, religious affiliation, and association membership but also by the way they presented themselves through house, lawn, and landscape artifacts. In this instance, the "newer" elite group symbolized itself through the cultivation of such Americana decorations as over-the-door eagles, colonial lamp posts, and visually "open," neat lawns, while the older elite group showed a distinct preference for a more "natural," enclosed, landscape design, in the studied manner of "English upper-class seedy."

Pratt (1982), in a recent study of elite families in Vancouver, has similarly documented how tastes in interior decoration differentiate and symbolize the social identities of two elite groups. In the world of the older, elite neighborhood, women decorated their homes following group standards that emphasized a traditional style of decoration, often hiring an interior decorator to help construct a "suitable" display. Women in the newer elite, who were similar in economic status but socially and geographically more mobile, decorated their homes in different modern styles to express their "individuality," either rejecting the use of interior decorators as restrictive of their "personal taste" or choosing a decorator who designs interiors as unique, "creative" displays.

"Proper Places": Dwelling and Traditional Gender Identity   The intimate connection between gender, identity, and dwelling is symbolized in the traditional American dictum: "A woman's place is in the home."[4] The social and cultural construction of the home as a peculiarly "woman's place" is recent; it emerged in the nineteenth and early twentieth centuries as a product of the urban, industrial order. The rapid separation of public life and paid employment from the home, followed by the segregation of suburban middle-class life from the city, transformed the ideal middle-class home into a place primarily devoted to privacy, domesticity, procreation, and consumption (Loyd 1982; Hayden 1984; Haddon and Barton 1979; Van de Wetering 1984). Ideal roles for women, as caretakers of the home, increasingly focused on family nurturance, housework, and the expressive symbolization of middle-class life and status through domestic consumption (Loyd 1982). Through this social assignment of women to such domestic roles, women not only became placed "in" the home but also increasingly came to *realize their identity as women* through the practical and symbolic activities of home life. Even within the dwelling place, this social and symbolic identification of women with home life, as opposed to the public world of industrial and commercial life, became symbolically reproduced in the division of interior and exterior space, with female presentation and identity assigned primarily to "interior decoration," while the outside, more visible public space became regarded as the province, role responsibility, and reflection of the male.

The social and cultural ties between women and home have become much more complex and often contradictory since World War II (Saegert 1980), particularly with the increasing mobilization of women into the paid labor force of nondomestic employment. Nevertheless, numerous studies indicate the cultural and social strength of this traditional cultural tie. In popular culture, homemaking activities are still identified primarily with women. Studies of school textbooks and prize-winning children's books indicate that little girls are more frequently portrayed within the home than little boys are and that adult homemaking activities are portrayed almost exclusively as women's work (Weitzmen and Eifler 1972; see also Saegert and Winkel 1980 for illustrations of this point). Television situation comedies and advertisements often revolve around domestic "dramas of competence" for mothers, illustrating how women can fulfill homemaking roles and traditional gender identity through consumption of advertised household products (Kirkpatrick 1981). Moreover, sociological studies indicate that these cultural scripts are still followed in actual role performance: women, even when working outside the home, still do the large majority of household tasks (Loyd 1982; Berk 1980).

Given the public cultural identification of home with women and the actual involvement of women with home-making roles and activities, it is not surprising that there is growing evidence that women's sense of identity with respect to dwelling places typically differs from that of men. First, there is some evidence to suggest that women are more likely than men to define the home as an avenue of self-expression and a reflection of self. In a recent study of the "reasons" that home buyers expressed for wanting to purchase a home, women were more likely than men to say they prefer home ownership because "it allows better expression of individuality" or because it is "a better means of achieving personal satisfaction," whereas men were more likely to note that a "man should provide a family with a home of their own" (Hempel and Tucker 1979).

Second, greater role involvement of women with the home also appears to create greater emotional investment of self in the dwelling place.

Women, for example, are more likely than men to describe their homes through emotional images (Csikszentmihalyi and Rochberg-Halton 1981). Studies of upper-middle-class women, moreover, note that women are more likely "to care about their home and to gain more satisfaction from it" (Saegert 1980; see also Saegert and Winkel 1980). Such greater emotional investment of self, however, also can generate emotional conflict in women with respect to changing women's roles and identity. Case studies of American family life, such as Rubin's *Worlds of Pain* (1976), indicate that not only do working-class couples define homemaking tasks as a woman's job but also that these women, whose traditional gender identity commits them to homemaking duties, experience considerable guilt and personal frustration as they take on paid employment outside the home.

Finally, Csikszentmihalyi and Rochberg-Halton (1981) present evidence that suggests that women and men invest domestic environments with different meanings, based on traditional gender identities. Among women and men who identify with their homes, women are more likely to interpret the house and valued domestic objects as symbols of family life, while men are more likely to interpret their attachment to dwelling places in terms of work investment or as a sign of personal accomplishment.

Dwelling, Identity, and Time

Matters of identity, as they involve a placement of the individual in reality, inevitably involve questions of time: Who am I now? Who was I then? What has one's life meant to this point? Such placement is complex and reflects both the variety of temporal processes and the multitude of cultural frameworks that organize and give them significance. Leaves falling from the trees, hair, from the head—both implicate identity in the changes of the natural world. The social rhythms of daily, weekly, monthly, and annual routines, the biographical passage of time as childhood, adulthood, and old age—both embed my actions, experiences, and ultimately identity within the myriad temporal frameworks of the social world (Wiegert 1981).

Dwellings and household objects may play a significant role in mediating time and identity to the extent they become signs of temporal processes, facilitating either the differentiation of time into socially or personally significant units, or acting as material symbols of past and future periods. In contemporary America, household rituals of holiday decorations, as well as much that "passes" for home maintenance—spring cleaning, summer mowing, fall raking—articulate the annual round into a social cycle.

In many cultures, dwellings have been used to symbolize the transition from one life stage to another, socially marking the passage from one age status to another. Often, the movement from childhood to adulthood—a major identity passage—has involved a change of dwelling place and often community. In contemporary America, the "home-leaving" of young adults, whether to a college dormitory, an army barrack, or a city apartment, involves a symbolic claim to adult identity and a ritual movement toward the autonomous self (compare Bellah et al. 1985). Moreover, if people of different ages increasingly come to live in different dwelling types (a current trend which reflects the general growth in age stratification in the United States), then housing forms may generally become defined as age-appropriate (Hochschild 1973; Steinfeld 1982). Perin (1977), for example, proposes that this is already true to a substantial degree, with the dominant cultural assumption being that movement through the life-cycle normally is accompanied by movement up a "ladder" of dwelling places, from a single-family dwelling as a child, to an apartment as a young adult, to a single-family home as an adult, and, perhaps, to an apartment, condominium, or mobile home as an elderly person.[5]

To the extent that dwellings and dwelling types have become public markers of age, status, and identity, individuals may well use dwellings to situate themselves within the life course. Owning a home for middle-aged Americans has been a sign that a person not only is "making it" financially but also is "biographically on schedule," confirming a sense of adulthood at the "appropriate time of life" (compare Rakoff 1977; Csikszentmihalyi and Rochberg-Halton 1981). In this light, the contemporary public furor and personal anxiety caused by the exclusion of many "baby-boom" Americans from the housing market may well be fueled, in part, by a crisis of identity.[6] Similarly, for elderly Americans, the public significance of the decision to stay or leave one's home upon retirement or death of a spouse may well involve a reinterpretation of identity and possible threat to self-esteem. To the extent that "giving up one's house" publicly signifies a movement to a less-valued identity, a likely outcome given the somewhat stigmatized status of the elderly in America, older Americans may rationally resist such moves to thwart the symbolic implications to self that such a move would entail (Steinfeld 1982).

Houses and dwelling objects are also important to identity as *symbols of the past*, enabling the individual to define his or her relationship to public and private worlds of former times.[7] Old homes, however rapidly disappearing from the landscape, still constitute one of the major public links to the past in everyday life. Countless ritual houses—the White House, Monticello, the Breakers, Eisenhower's boyhood home—and the many "restored" and "preserved" homes that dot the landscape may well serve as both constructions of and as links to a "valued past," providing contemporary Americans with a usable history and some sense of continuity and identity as Americans (Lynch 1972; Cohn 1979; see also Tuan 1977; and Steele 1981). In this light, concern for the "historical authenticity" of such places on the part of tourists may well reflect a desire for "real experiences" that validate self, rather than a disinterested devotion to historical veracity (compare MacCannell 1976).

In addition to symbolizing the public, collective memories of the past, houses and, more often, household objects frequently become a significant element in an individual's personal identity as symbols of past experiences and relationships. The personal memories that houses and domestic objects "store" for individuals are often very private, cultivated by the person out of significant life events, known only to individuals and family intimates (Csikszentmihalyi and Rochberg-Halton 1981). Precisely because of their highly personal nature, however, such domestic symbols may be particularly important: they have the capacity, and bear the strain, of "carrying" the individual's personal sense of self through time—of providing a symbolic lifeline to a continuous sense of identity. As mnemonic cues to past worlds, such objects may play a crucial role in defining and maintaining identity by providing a familiar, if fragmented, buoy in a sea of social change, a sense of order and continuity in one's life, and by affirming former identities lost to biological and social change (compare Rowles 1983a; 1983b).

It is in this context that research devoted to the world of elderly Americans has documented the significance of dwellings and household objects as mementoes and links to the past. Because advancing age often means loss of job, reduced community ties, fewer friends and relatives, the elderly are increasingly likely to both "find themselves" in and be dependent upon the private, symbolic world of the home to sustain their identity. At this stage in life, too, matters of identity may well involve interpretation of the meaning of life as a whole. Given such social and psychological forces, many elderly retain and value biographical objects, actively cultivating their meanings, even reinterpreting their significance, to validate past and present identities. In this sense, much of the "personalization" of domestic environments by elderly Americans is best understood not only as "self-expression" but also as "self-preservation."

The elderly are, for example, more likely than younger people to conceive of and value domestic objects as mementoes or heirlooms (Csikszentmihalyi and Rochberg-Halton 1981). Rowles (1983a) describes how a retired train man, in a small Appalachian community where the local no longer stops, has landscaped his yard with signal lights and other train equipment, actively affirming himself as he symbolically denies the passing of his era. Such preservation and cultivation of meaning and identity, moreover, underlines the very real cruelty of bureaucratic settings that routinely deny the retention of such personal, household objects to elderly residents. Such policies, by taking away the signs of past identity, may well contribute to the very "stripping" of identity from the individual (Redfoot n.d.; Steinfeld 1982; Goffman 1961).

"At Home": Dwelling, Privacy, and Identity

One significant matter remains that is certainly linked to issues of both dwelling and identity—that of "home." Common sense, that wonderful, cultural construction of the "naturally" apparent, quickly reminds us that "A house is not a home," and that "home" may refer equally well to a "home town" or a region. Yet, we can also quickly conjure images of "Home Sweet Home," dutifully embroidered and hung on a mythical living-room wall, and, by consulting our own experience, we also know that we are often, if not always, most "at home" at home. Such contradictory messages suggest, quite correctly, that the experience of home is not limited to dwelling places and that it is possible to feel out-of-place in our house or apartment. Yet, dwellings as meaningful places are often home places—significant locales that situate identity in social space, providing both a sense of attachment and a sense of being "me" here.

Writers of various perspectives have attempted to analyze the meaning and significance of home. Hayward (1982), for example, has recently argued that contemporary American families, when speaking of home, use the term to connote different meanings, ranging from the physical dwelling place, a sense of relationship with other people, of social network, and a base of activity on the one hand to conceptions of a place of refuge or continuity, a personalized place, and a symbol of self-identity on the other. These last meanings indicate that "home" is popularly used in ways closely tied to identity.

Other writers, concerned with the phenomenology of daily life, have contributed to our understanding of home by describing the experience of "at homeness" from the point of view of the individual. Seamon (1979) suggests that "at homeness" involves an often taken-for-granted experience of reality in which one is "comfortable in and familiar with the everyday world in which one lives and outside of which one is 'visiting,' 'in transit,' 'not at home,' 'out of place,' or 'traveling.'" Such relatedness to the world, some writers argue, involves several dimensions: a "centeredness" in a valued locale—a place of return and repetition (Seamon 1979); a "rootedness" in place, grounded in the familiarity of knowing and being known in a particular place (Relph 1976;

see also, Klapp 1969); a sense of being "at ease," of being "really me" here (Seamon 1979); and a sense of being "inside," of belonging "here" rather than "there" (Relph 1976; Rowles 1980; Bollnow 1967).

Finally, both popular (Packard 1972) and serious critics of modern society (Berger et al. 1974; Buttimer 1980; Klapp 1969; Relph 1976) have suggested that modernity itself, with it growing placelessness and geographic mobility, has created a rootless person, whose sense of identity is weakened by loss of a significant sense of home. Modernization, such arguments run, has eroded the social, cultural, and material distinctiveness of places, whether one examines regions, communities, neighborhoods, dwelling places, or interior rooms. Moreover, modernization, by fostering social and geographic mobility, has fundamentally altered the person's relations with place. The modern individual—confronted with a placeless, homogeneous landscape of tract housing, urban renewal, and the omnipresent McDonald's; ceaselessly moving from one dwelling place, community, and region to another—can develop neither an imagery of self based on locale nor a sense of belonging in a specific landscape of dwelling, community, or region.

These last arguments appear to be overdrawn. Recent research suggests that many of the purported effects of geographic mobility on the individual are erroneous and overly pessimistic (Shumaker and Stokols 1982), and that many contemporary Americans continue to identify with regions (Reed 1983), communities (Hummon 1986), and neighborhoods (Rivlin 1982). The continuing significance of dwellings as home places is more difficult to assess; yet, there is certainly evidence, as I have intimated above, that houses, too, continue to be a significant locus of home.

First, given that nearly half of the American populace changes housing units every five years, probably very few Americans reside in the same dwelling place throughout their lives, and therefore ancestral and childhood homes are unlikely to be centers of daily, lived experience.[8] Within the spatial framework of daily life, however, dwelling places remain a significant spatial locus, a place of return and repetition, despite daily mobility to and from work, friends, and other community activities (Seamon 1979).

Second, residential mobility also places limits on the extent to which dwellings themselves can provide a deeply rooted "territory of symbols" of past life-events. The ability to conceive of one's house as a veritable "scrapbook" of the self that affirms the particularity of one's life in its fullness is exceptional. As a result, probably few Americans experience their home and community with the strong sense of "autobiographical insideness" that Rowles (1983a; compare Coles 1967; Erikson 1976) has suggested is true for some long-term residents of an Appalachian community.

Yet, even here, two cautions are in order. First, though Americans move often, they bring with them domestic objects that continue to be symbols of the past, recreating a sense of familiarity and continuity within new surroundings. Surely, much is lost in this process; yet, the ritual installation of family pictures, favorite easy chairs, and other special objects can reconstruct a symbolic order with relatively few signs and transform a new house into an "old home." Second, it is worth emphasizing that dwelling rootedness and "familiarity" is socially distributed: as Coles (1967) has shown, the children of migrant workers have much less of it than most Americans, with tragic consequences for their identities. Yet, the elderly, who may have greatest need of such familiarity for purposes of identity, are, in fact, most likely to be rooted—they are less likely to move from their homes than people of any other age group (Taeuber 1983).

Finally, dwellings are home places for many Americans in the sense that they provide an experience of refuge, a place, where in the language of daily life, "I can best be myself," "let my hair down," "do what I like," "be more of an individual," in essence, be "at ease."[9] This experience of dwellings as home places arises because dwellings are private places in contemporary America, if not in all societies. Altman and Chemers (1980) propose that dwelling places, as territorial mechanisms for achieving privacy, psychologically enhance identity by enabling the individual to personalize the domestic environment and to bound self from others, regulating access to the self and to objects sacred to identity.

Sociologically, the house may also be experienced as a refuge for two reasons, again related to privacy. First, in contemporary America the division between public and private spheres, experienced often as the division of work and home, creates not only a differentiation of public and private roles but also divisions of experience, consciousness, and identity (Berger et al. 1974). Public life, organized around the social logic of technology, bureaucracy, and urban life, frequently provides roles that are anonymous, categorical, and functional, as well as highly segmented. Private life, in which the dwelling remains the central locus, involves the individual's particularity and relations that are less governed by formal rationality or economic interest. At home, therefore, the individual is more likely to feel "whole," "in control," more "really me."

Second, the very complexity of roles that Americans play in contemporary American society means that the "identity management" (Goffman 1954) necessary for realizing these roles becomes increasingly demanding. In public life, particularly, individuals need to "be" different people at different times and places. Dwelling places, however, because of their privacy, provide people with a "backstage," where "presented selves" can be dropped, at least temporarily, and where the individual can just be him or her "self." This private territory, however, is always a matter of time and degree: the living room, as a cultural setting for public display to guests, periodically becomes the stage, with backstage moving to the even more intimate locales of bedroom and bathroom. Some architects (Alexander et al. 1977; Greenbie 1977; compare Zeisel 1973) are sensitive to the role that housing may play in such identity management and they argue that designers should be aware of implications of built form for both culturally defined levels of intimacy and the social staging of transitions from public to private spaces.

Conclusion

In this chapter, I have suggested that the multi-disciplinary literature on housing and identity provides some important lessons for our understanding of contemporary American dwelling identity. First, I have proposed that the extent to which dwellings and related domestic objects are used as symbols of identity by a culture, particularly for the construction of the self as a unique individual, is itself a social and historical product. The readiness of contemporary middle-class Americans to interpret domestic environments for clues to identity may well be less indicative of universal psychological or biological needs than it is symptomatic of the individualism of modern American society.

Second, I have documented some of the important, culturally specific, public and private meanings that dwellings communicate—meanings that contemporary Americans use both to situate themselves in reality and to construct conceptions of self. American dwellings and domestic objects provide a nonverbal language for the differentiation, integration, and presentation of group identities, for both fundamental social statuses (class, gender, age) and smaller, social worlds. They are used to express, cultivate, and preserve more private meanings critical to personal identity, and they are the medium of highly individualized self-expression in the personalization of domestic interiors, as mnemonic clues to past identities in biographical interpretation, and as a locus and stage for the enactment of private selves.

However fruitful, this chapter raises more questions than it answers, questions that must be directly addressed by new empirical work. Our understanding of the specific cultural codes transmitted by different housing forms and styles of decoration is rudimentary, even for the dominant middle-class culture. We know even less about the meanings of dwelling place and identity within the subcultures of less powerful groups, such as children or poor urban blacks or Hispanics.

Although previous research demonstrates that contemporary Americans learn and cultivate the private and public meanings of dwellings for identity, we have little sense of how this process takes place. Certainly, much happens in the context of primary and secondary socialization, as conflicts between parent and child over writing on the walls and the efforts of the real estate and interior decoration industries testify. I expect, however, that these transactions of meaning also occur in the myriad domestic rituals of daily life. Such is often true in more traditional societies (Saile 1985); modern ritual forms—house-warmings and home-leavings, spring cleanings and handiman projects, coffee klatsches and backyard barbeques—have yet to be explored with respect to dwelling place and identity.

Although we have some sense of the integrative, world-building contributions of housing to identity, we understand less well the contradictions and conflicts that people may experience through identification with home. The significance of dwelling place in the gender identity of contemporary American women demonstrates that housing may provide a valued source of meaning and yet, at the same time, may entrap and divide the self. It is probable that stigmatized forms of housing—for example, public housing, institutionalized "homes" for dependent groups—can also engender problems of identity for their inhabitants.

Finally, we have much to learn about the implications of dwelling identity for the intelligent, humane, and socially sophisticated design of dwellings in contemporary American society. The highly mediated nature of the relation between housing and identity precludes simplistic, deterministic solutions to identity problems involving built form. Nevertheless, greater understanding and sensitivity to the way that housing and identity interact in the context of specific cultures and groups can contribute to the design of housing that nourishes rather than limits human life.

Notes

1. See Douglas and Isherwood (1979) for a provocative discussion of the nature of material commodities as signs. Rapoport (1982b) provides a useful discussion of various approaches—symbolic, semiotic, and nonverbal communication—to meanings "in" the built environment.

2. For other examples of such personalization, see, for example, Greenbie (1981); Hansen and Altman (1976); and Steele (1981). Sanders (1977) has produced a beautiful, sometimes startling photographic essay on this topic.

3. Altman and Chemers (1980) correctly suggest that the symbolic use of dwellings for individual display must always be interpreted in accord with social norms for collective restraint and group identity. This social dialectic of individual and group symbolization is certainly fundamental to all social interaction; yet, the relative significance of housing as a sign of the group or the individual differs cross-culturally—in this instance, from traditional to modern societies.

4. One could also focus on its companion proverb, "A man's home is his castle." Although the

latter certainly conveys a message of the sanctity of private space as refuge, it also suggests an image of male authority and privilege within the home.

5. This process, it might be added, seems to be increasingly refined through such popular conceptions as "student housing," "starter homes," "retirement homes."

6. In a study of families and dwelling types, Michelson (1980) noted that young families living in apartments are often satisfied with this arrangement, despite a general cultural antipathy for this arrangement, because they see their situation as necessary, appropriate, and *temporary*—to be left for a single-family-dwelling in a few years. This pattern of responses fits nicely with Perin's model, though it may have recently become an unrealistic and, thus, frustrating expectation.

7. In at least one important respect, it is possible to see dwellings as a significant sign of the future: as cultural settings for childhood socialization, they are models *for* the future selves of their younger inhabitants. Although social scientists do not routinely examine dwelling places as "role models," the care which parents devote to the decoration of the rooms of children—selecting, for example, beds, wallpaper, colors, and so on appropriate to life-long gender identities—suggests that home environments are significant in this way (Csikszentmihalyi and Rochberg-Halton 1981). Moreover, Marcus's (1978) sensitive analysis of adult memories of childhood homes suggests that early environments may well shape adult sense of place.

8. This pattern is, in all likelihood, "older" than most students of modernization and identity presume. Growing historical evidence suggests that long-term residence in the family homestead is something of a myth (Fischer and Stueve 1976).

9. These quotations are drawn from Seamon (1979); Rakoff (1977); and Silverman (1983).

References

Alexander, C., et al. 1977. *A pattern language*. New York: Oxford University Press.

Altman, I., and M. Chemers. 1980. *Culture and environment*. Monterey, Calif.: Brooks/Cole.

Altman, I., and M. Gauvain. 1981. A cross-cultural and dialectic analysis of homes. In *Spatial representation and behavior across the life span*, ed. L. Liben, A. Patterson, and N. Newcombe. New York: Academic Press.

Becker, E. 1962. *The birth and death of meaning*. New York: The Free Press.

Bellah, R., R. Madsen, W. Sullivan, A. Swidler, and S. Tipton. 1985. *Habits of the heart*. Berkeley: University of California Press.

Berger, P. 1970. "Identity as a problem in the sociology of knowledge." In *The sociology of knowledge*, ed. J. Curtis and J. Petras. New York: Praeger.

Berger, P., and T. Luckmann. 1967. *The social construction of reality*. Garden City, N.Y.: Anchor Books.

Berger, P., B. Berger, and H. Kellner. 1974. *The homeless mind: Modernization and consciousness*. New York: Vintage Books.

Berk, S. F. 1980. The household as workplace: Wives, husbands, and children. In *New space for women*, ed. G. Wekerle, R. Patterson, and D. Morley. Boulder, Colo.: Westview Press.

Bollnow, O. 1967. Lived space. In *Readings in existential phenomenology*, ed. N. Lawrence and D. O'Connor. Englewood Cliffs, N.J.: Prentice-Hall.

Buttimer, A. 1980. Home, reach, and a sense of place. In *The human experience of space and place*, ed. A. Buttimer and D. Seamon. New York: St. Martin's Press.

Cohn, J. 1979. *The palace or the poorhouse: The American house as a cultural symbol*. East Lansing: The Michigan State Press.

Coles, R. 1967. *Migrants, sharecroppers, and mountaineers*. Boston: Little, Brown and Company.

Cooper, C. 1974. The house as a symbol of self. In *Designing for human behavior*, ed. Jon Lang et al. Stroudsburg, Pa.: Dowden, Hutchinson and Ross.

———. 1978. The emotional content of house/self relationships, pt. 2. In *Priorities for Environmental Design Research: EDRA 8*, ed. R. L. Brauer. Washington, D.C.: EDRA.

Csikszentmihalyi, M., and E. Rochberg-Halton. 1981. *The meaning of things: Domestic symbols and the self.* Cambridge: Cambridge University Press.

Douglas, M., and B. Isherwood. 1979. *The worlds of goods.* New York: Basic Books.

Dovey, K. 1978. Home: An ordering principle in space. *Landscape* 22:27–30.

Duncan, J. 1973. Landscape taste as a symbol of group identity. *Geographical Review* 63: 334–55.

———. 1982a. *Housing and identity.* New York: Holmes and Meier.

———. 1982b. From container of women to status symbol: The impact of social structure on the meaning of the house. In *Housing and identity.* New York: Holmes and Meier.

Duncan, J. S., and N. G. Duncan. 1976a. Housing as a presentation of self and the structure of social networks. In *Environmental knowing,* ed. G. T. Moore and R. G. Golledge. Stroudsburg, Pa.: Dowden, Hutchinson and Ross.

———. 1976b. Social worlds, status passages, and environmental perspectives. In *Environmental knowing,* ed. G. T. Moore and R. G. Gollege. Stroudsburg, Pa.: Dowden, Hutchinson and Ross.

Erikson, K. 1976. *Everything in its path.* New York: Simon and Schuster.

Fischer, C., and A. Stueve. 1976. Why people move house. *New Society* 25:406–8.

Gans. H. 1962. *The urban villagers.* New York: The Free Press.

Geertz, C. 1973. *The interpretation of cultures.* New York: Basic Books.

Goffman, E. 1959. *The presentation of self in everyday life.* Garden City, N.Y.: Doubleday, Anchor Books.

———. 1961. *Asylums.* Garden City, N.Y.: Doubleday, Anchor Books.

Greenbie, B. 1981. *Spaces: Dimensions of the human landscape.* New Haven: Yale University Press.

Haddon, J., and J. Barton. 1979. An image that will not die: Thoughts on the history of anti-urban ideology. In *New towns and the suburban dream,* ed. I. Allen. Port Washington, N.Y.: Kennikat Press.

Hansen, W. B., and I. Altman. 1976. Decorating personal places: A descriptive analysis. *Environment and Behavior* 8:491–504.

Hayden, D. 1984. *Redesigning the American dream: The future of housing, work, and family life.* New York: W. W. Norton.

Hayward, J. 1982. The meanings of home. *Human Ecology Forum* 13:2–6.

Hempel, D. J., and L. R. Tucker, Jr. 1979. Citizen preference for housing as common social indicators. *Environment and Behavior* 11:399–428.

Hewitt, J. 1984. *Self and society.* 3d. ed. Boston: Allyn and Bacon.

Hochschild, A. 1973. *The unexpected community.* Berkeley: University of California Press.

Hummon, D. 1986. City mouse, country mouse: The persistence of community identity. *Qualitative Sociology* 9:3–25.

Kirkpatrick, J. 1981. Homes and homemakers on American TV. In *The American dimension,* 2d ed., ed. W. Arens and S. Montague. Palo Alto, Calif.: Mayfield.

Klapp, O. 1969. *Collective search for identity.* New York: Holt, Rinehart, and Winston.

Laumann, E., and J. House. 1972. Livingroom styles and social attributes: Patterning of material artifacts in an urban community. In *The logic of social hierarchies,* ed. E. Laumann, P. Siegel, and W. Hodges. Chicago: Markham.

Lindsey, S. 1986. Residential textuality and social class. Paper presented at Built Form and Culture Research Conference, Lawrence, Kans.

Lockridge, K. 1970. *A New England town.* New York: W. W. Norton.

Loyd, B. 1982. Women, home, and status. In *Housing and identity.* New York: Holmes and Meier.

Lynch, K. 1972. *What time is this place?* Cambridge, Mass.: MIT Press.

Lynd, R., and H. Lynd. 1929. *Middletown.* New York: Harcourt, Brace, and World.

MacCannell, D. 1976. *The tourist*. New York: Schocken Books.

Marc, O. 1977. *Psychology of the house*. London: Thames and Hudson.

Marcus, C. 1978. Remembrance of landscapes past. *Landscape* 22:34–43.

Michelson, W. 1980. Long and short range criteria for housing choice and environmental behavior. *Journal of Social Issues* 36:135–49.

Packard, V. 1972. *A nation of strangers*. New York: McKay.

Perin, C. 1977. *Everything in its place*. Princeton, N.J.: Princeton University Press.

Pinkwater, D. 1977. *The big orange splot*. New York: Hastings House.

Porteous, D. 1976. Home: The territorial core. *Geographical Review* 66:383–90.

Pratt, G. 1982. The house as an expression of social worlds. In *Housing and identity*. New York: Holmes and Meier.

Rainwater, L. 1966. Fear and house-as-haven in the lower class. *Journal of the American Institute of Planners* 32:23–31.

Rakoff, R. M. 1977. Ideology in everyday life: The meaning of the house. *Politics and Society* 7:85–104.

Rapoport, A. 1980. Environmental preference, habitat selection, and urban housing. *Journal of Social Issues* 36:118–34.

———. 1982a. *The meaning of the built environment*. Beverly Hills, Calif.: Sage Publications.

———. 1982b. Identity and environment. In *Housing and identity*. New York: Holmes and Meier.

Redfoot, D. N.d. Spatial reality in old age. Unpublished paper.

Reed, J. 1983. *Southerners*. Chapel Hill: University of North Carolina Press.

Relph, E. 1976. *Place and placelessness*. London: Pion Ltd.

Rivlin, L. 1982. Group membership and place meanings in an urban neighborhood. *Journal of Social Issues* 38:75–93.

Rowles, G. 1980. Growing old "inside": Aging and attachment to place in an Appalachian community. In *Transitions of aging*, ed. N. Datan and N. Lohmann. New York: Academic Press.

———. 1983a. Place and personal identity in old age: Observations from Appalachia. *Journal of Environmental Psychology* 3:299–313.

———. 1983b. Exploring the meaning of place in old age. Paper presented at the 36th Annual Meeting of the Gerontological Society of America, San Francisco, November 21.

Rubin, L. 1976. *Worlds of pain*. New York: Basic Books.

Saegert, S. 1980. Masculine cities and feminine suburbs: Polarized ideas, contradictory realities. *Signs* 5:96–111.

Saegert, S., and G. Winkel. 1980. The home: A critical problem for changing sex roles. In *New space for women*, ed. G. Wekerle, R. Patterson, and D. Morley. Boulder, Colo.: Westview Press.

Saile, D. 1985. The ritual establishment of home. In *Home environments*, ed. I. Altman and C. Werner. New York: Plenum Press.

Sanders, N. 1977. *At home*. Dobbs Ferry, N.Y.: Morgan and Morgan.

Seamon, D. 1979. *A geography of the lifeworld*. New York: St. Martin's Press.

Seeley, J. R.; R. A. Sim; and E. W. Loosley. 1956. *Crestwood Heights*. Toronto: University of Toronto Press.

Shumaker, S., and D. Stokols. 1982. Residential mobility as a social issue and research topic. *Journal of Social Issues* 38:1–19.

Silverman, C. 1983. Neighbors and nighbors: A study in negotiated claim. Ph.D. diss., Department of Sociology, University of California, Berkeley.

Sopher, D. 1979. The landscape of home. In *The intepretation of ordinary landscapes*, ed. D. W. Meinig. New York: Oxford University Press.

Steele, F. 1981. *The sense of place*. Boston: C.B.I.

Steinfeld, E. 1982. The place of old age. In *Housing and identity*. New York: Holmes and Meier.

Taeuber, C. 1983. *America in transition: An aging society*. Current Population Reports, P-23, no. 128.

Tuan, Y. 1977. *Space and place: The perspective of experience*. Minneapolis: University of Minnesota Press.

Valentine, B. 1978. *Hustling and other hard work*. New York: Free Press.

Van de Wetering, M. 1984. The popular concept of "home" in nineteenth-century America. *Journal of American Studies* 18:5–28.

Veblen, T. 1945. *Theory of the leisure class*. New York: Random House.

Weigert, A. 1981. *Sociology of everyday life*. New York: Longman.

Weitzman, L., and Eifler. 1972. Sex role socialization in picture books for children. *American Journal of Sociology* 77:1125–49.

Wright, G. 1981. *Building the dream: A social history of housing in America*. Cambridge, Mass.: M.I.T. Press.

Zeisel, J. 1973. Symbolic meaning of space and the physical dimension of social relations. In *Cities in change*, ed. J. Walton and D. Carns. Boston: Allyn and Bacon.

———. 1984. *Inquiry by design*. New York: Cambridge University Press.

12

GETTING RESPECT IN THE
KANDYAN HIGHLANDS:
THE HOUSE, THE COMMUNITY,
AND THE SELF IN A
THIRD WORLD SOCIETY

JAMES S. DUNCAN

As Robert Darnton (1984, 4) reminds us, "other people are other. They do not think the way we do. And if we want to understand their way of thinking, we should set out with the idea of capturing otherness." Nowhere is this more true than when we set out to try to understand dwellings. Precisely because we all live in them, we may be unlikely to recognize that the symbolic meaning and use of the house varies greatly, not only between different cultures, but also among different groups within a society. And yet Darnton's is a dangerous argument, for the researcher, if he is to do good social science, must tiptoe like a high-wire artist along that fine line that separates the intellectual chasm of cultural relativism on the one hand (the notion that others must be understood as utterly unique), from the even deeper chasm of universalism on the other hand (the idea that others are *au fond* no different from ourselves). The problem is that others are in fact different from us, although not utterly so. What we must do, as Geertz (1973) points out in his seminal essay entitled "Thick Description," is confront the otherness of the native's "experience-near" concepts with the familiarity of our own abstract "experience-distant" concepts that form the stock-in-trade of Western social science. In this regard, we act not so much as recorders of indisputable truths; we can leave that task, if Roland Barthes (1977) is to be believed, to the photographer, but as translators and interpreters of other world views. The act of translation is difficult, however, because as Martin (1983, 57) points out it entails trying not only to understand other cultural world views, but also to broaden our understanding of our own culture. It is interesting to note that when one studies Third World societies, the methodological problem of this hermeneutic circle of self and other dovetails with the empirical reality of Western cultural penetration into these cultures. The epistemological and the ontological aspects of the project are completely intertwined. And yet our truths are only provisional in the sense that we tend to silence incongruent voices and quote those that illustrate our interpretation of what is going on (Clifford 1986, 6–7; Crapanzano 1986, 51). One could argue that to do otherwise would be to have no argument at all, but to be overwhelmed by a babble of discordant voices clamoring for our attention. On the other hand, sensitivity to ambivalence and fascination with ambiguity may be assets during one's fieldwork. [1]

In this chapter I use such "experience-distant" concepts as "individualism" and "materialism" to try to make sense of Sri Lankan attitudes toward their dwellings. These concepts will guide my interpretation by providing the cipher that will allow me to decode a facet of their daily lives. Elsewhere, I have argued that the changes in attitudes toward housing in much of the Third World must be understood in terms of broader structural changes that are taking place within those societies (Duncan 1981, 1985). Much of what is sometimes referred to as "modernization" or "Westernization" can best be understood as an increase in the level of both individualism and materialism within the societies in question. I argue that both of these bring about a transformation of attitudes toward the house—the house becomes thought of less as a mere container of family and goods and more as a symbol of social status. This chapter is not the place to rehearse these arguments; instead my intention here is to refine them by providing a case study of the relationships between individualism, materialism, and the dwelling.

All societies are dynamic and constantly undergoing change. Over the past three centuries we have witnessed an accelerating penetration of Western, individualistic cultures into more collectivistic cultures around the world. This process has been moving with such rapidity since the end of the Second World War that the pertinent research question may no longer be, "What are the attitudes toward housing in this or that country (treated as a self-contained cultural entity)?" but "How are attitudes in that country changing in response to the impact of these foreign cultures?" [2] This widespread culture change is creating "post-traditional" societies which, despite the vast differences between them, have a certain degree of commonality based upon an incorporation, variable in degree, of individualist ideas and institutions. And yet in examining these patterns created out of the shared experience of Western cultural imperialism, it is imperative that we not fall into the trap of viewing the response within a society to the intrusion of another culture as monolithic. We must also understand that this type of culture change is not inevitable, nor does it happen in some mysterious way. There are usually pragmatic political or economic reasons for this change, which then create cultural repercussions that can no longer be explained exclusively by their political and economic origins. For example, the European cultural penetration of Sri Lanka began in the sixteenth century with the arrival of Portuguese merchants who dominated much of its maritime lowlands in their quest for spices. This process reached its height under the British, who controlled the whole of the island from 1815 until 1947.[3] A more recent political event, the election of 1977, has brought about yet another surge of Western influence. During this election, the liberal, United National party (UNP), replaced the socialist SLFP who had been in power for most of a decade. One of the principal planks of the UNP's political platform was that they would completely open a heretofore closed economy to foreign goods and greatly expand tourism. By the year 1983, when I conducted my research, many people within the intelligentsia were worried that the flood of foreign goods and tourists was having a profoundly negative cultural impact. The people, it was claimed, were becoming obsessed by material possessions and the traditional values of modesty and selflessness were being abandoned. Since its inception in the early sixteenth century, the European cultural presence has been both geographically and socially uneven. Historians have long argued (DeSilva 1977; Gooneratne 1968; Houtart 1974; Roberts 1982; Tennent 1859) that Western cultural influence was more profound in the maritime areas of Sri Lanka than in the Kandyan Highlands, in cities than in the countryside, and among elites more than among the lower classes. There have been, however, few systematic examinations of any of these alleged differences. My interest was not to test degree of Westernization, since that notion is notoriously vague and difficult to pin down empirically. Instead, I examined two of its major components, individualism and materialism, by examining attitudes toward the dwelling in the Kandyan Highlands, traditionally the most culturally conservative part of the island.

A survey was undertaken in a city and in a village in the Kandyan Highlands. A questionnaire lasting approximately forty-five mintues was administered to eighty city dwellers and sixty villagers. To be included in the sample a respondent had to have resided in the settlement for the last ten years. As Table 12.1 reveals, most had lived there for much longer than the minimum. The sample was stratified by class, age, and sex. Caste was not included as a category primarily for pragmatic reasons; it is an extremely sensitive topic among the lower castes, and it would therefore have been difficult to collect accurate information on the subject. Some informants offered information on how they would treat other castes but few volunteeered their own caste identity. It appears that caste, although still very important for planning marriages,

Table 12.1
Demography

	Poor	Low	Middle	Upper-Middle	Average
Av. # years in (village)	47.8	40.5	43.3	—	44.2
Av. # years in (city)	28.8	41.8	43.3	36.1	36.8
% Born in (village)	75% (15)	55% (11)	75% (15)	—	68% (14)
% Born in (city)	30% (6)	65% (13)	55% (11)	45% (9)	49% (10)

Note: The total sample is 140. There are 20 people in each class in the village and the city.

increasingly, in cities at least, is giving way to class as the basis for socializing. Only among some of the older villagers was any mention made of access to the house being restricted to certain castes.

The Settings

The urban interviews were conducted in Kandy, the old hill capital, with a population of one hundred thousand people. The city is nestled within hills and at its center lies a large lake constructed by the last king of Kandy in 1810. At the edge of the lake stands the *Dalada Maligawa*, the Temple of the Tooth Relic of the Buddha, one of the holiest shrines in Theravada Buddhism. Because of the city's beauty as well as its religious and historical importance, it is a center of both tourism and pilgrimage. Currently the city is both a resort and a regional service center for the hill country. In the city informants from four classes were interviewed: the poor, the lower class, the middle class, and the upper-middle class.

The poor respondents were drawn from a shanty area near the center of the city. These people are mostly pavement hawkers of inexpensive goods and dealers in illicit activities such as prostitution, illegal liquor, and the sale of drugs to tourists. This particular shanty area contains approximately seven hundred people within the space of an acre and has been in existence for twenty years. The one- and two-bedroom shanties are crowded together and constructed of wood, hardboard, tin, or whatever else is readily available. The houses have no electrical service but typically have a table, some chairs, one bed, and rest mats for the floor. Some have a radio or a cassette player, posters of film stars, and a few have a picture of the Buddha or gods decorating the walls. None of the houses has running water. They use common traps and latrines nearby.

The lower-class respondents were drawn from an area of small houses on the outskirts of the city and from row housing on one of the principal city streets. Typical occupations of the lower class are tailor, bus driver, postman, clerk, and small store owner. These people typically have one-story, white-washed brick houses, some of which have attached gardens. The houses have electricity but no running water. They all have glass in the windows and most have curtains. They have more and better quality furniture than do the poor. A typical house contains tables, chairs, beds, a picture of the Buddha, and perhaps a calendar hanging on the wall. Most have radios or cassettes and a few have televisions.

The middle-class sample was drawn from a solidly middle-class area on the outskirts of Kandy. These people include business contractors, store own-ers, school principals, and middle-ranking government officials. Their houses are larger and of better quality than those of the lower class and of no com-mon style. Unlike the houses of the village middle class, they are painted a combination of light colors both inside and out. All have flower gardens. Ap-proximately 50 percent of the houses are two-story and all have tile or asbestos roofs. All have running water, bathrooms, and electricity. The furniture is more substantial and the decorations more elaborate. Typical living rooms contain photographs, posters, batiks, potted plants, a television, cushioned furniture, and perhaps some antiques. Refrigerators, which are prestige items, are often displayed in the dining room.[4] Most of the people in this sample have a servant.

The upper-middle-class group is scattered around several "posh" neigh-borhoods in the city. Typical occupations are high government official, all-island inspector of schools, lawyer, doctor, owner of a manufacturing company, and businessman. Their houses are very large and expensively dec-orated. They are similar to the houses of the middle class except that there are more rooms and more furniture, and everything is costlier. All have tele-visions and refrigerators as well as many other appliances. In the place of posters there are original oil paintings and water colors. Sri Lankan and Brit-ish antiques are common. All have elaborate flower gardens and servants to look after the house and gardens.

The village that was surveyed lies twenty miles north of Kandy. It is sur-rounded by paddy fields and to its east are some low hills with tea lands on their brow. Between the flat paddy fields and the high tea lands, the villagers have their *Chena* homestead gardens. There are three Buddhist temples, one primary school, and several shops in the village. In this village, as in many others in the highlands, the temples own approximately 80 percent of the paddy land, which they rent to villagers. There are approximately one thou-sand people living in the village, 70 percent of whom are Goyigama, the highest-ranking caste. The Goyigama live in a separate part of the village from the Berava (drummer), Dhobi (washerman), and Batgama castes. The caste exclusiveness that was so dominant in the past is eroding now, as young people of different castes socialize even though they rarely marry. People from three classes were interviewed in the village.

The poor live interspersed throughout the village, their location depending on their caste. They have jobs such as farm laborer, watchman, servant, toddy tapper,[5] or farmer with a small, low-yielding plot in the *chena* area. Their houses, which are made of whitewashed mud daubed over a woven stick framework, with a sloped, thatched roof, are smaller than the others in the village. The interiors have mud floors plastered with cow dung, a few windows without panes or curtains and perhaps a few photographs of the occupants and a calendar or picture of the Buddha to adorn the walls. Their furniture consists of a table, a cupboard, a few chairs, a bed in the front for the husband, and mats at the back for the women and children. Typically they will have a shrine to the local gods outside the house and a small one to the Buddha somewhere inside. Approximately 25 percent have radios.

Members of the lower class have jobs such as farmer, mason, policeman, and low-level clerk. Their houses are larger than those of the poor and built of stone or brick with a sloped roof made of tile or galvanized metal. The front section of the house typically has a cement floor whereas the kitchen floor is made of hardened mud and dung. Ten or fifteen years ago it became the rage to build houses in the "American Style" with split-level roofs, and for a time there was a certain prestige attached to having such a house. Since then, however, other styles have become popular. Paint is a prestige item and nearly all the houses are painted either white and gray or white and brown. The inside walls are whitewashed and there are more and higher quality furnishings than in the houses of the poor. Normally there is more than one bed and there may be curtains or glass in some of the front windows. Very few have electricity; almost all have radios.

The middle class is principally composed of businessmen and professionals. Typical occupations include shop owner, landlord, teacher, and internal auditor for the agriculture department in a nearby town. Their houses are built of stone or brick and are sometimes two stories high. All have electricity but water taps are outside the front of the house. The exteriors are painted three to five colors with raised colored diamonds or squares being the fashion. All the windows have glass and there are curtains on both the windows and doors. The floor in the front section of the house typically has a highly polished red sheen and the rooms are well furnished. Almost everyone has a bed and there are *almirahs* (free-standing clothes closets) for clothing. The walls are decorated with pictures and wall hangings. All have radios and approximately 75 percent have televisions sets; however, none has a refrigerator or running water.

Measuring Individualism and Materialism

The survey was designed to see if individualism and materialism are at present positively correlated with two of the "experience-distant" concepts I alluded to above, urbanism and social class. I therefore intend to effect a translation of the "experience-near" data that my informants provide—comments about furniture and family, neighbors, and social obligations—into these "experience-distant" concepts of social science. Although "experience-near" and "experience-distant" concepts are distinct, they are not completely so. The point, for a social scientist, is not simply to record reality but to produce a text about it. In this sense the work of the social scientist is artisanal in that the product is at once artistic and useful.[6] The villagers may have little interest in the social scientist's "experience-distant" concepts; they realize that the social scientist's view of their furnishings and their relations with their kin is very different from their own intensely personal interest in these subjects. And this is the way that it should be, for after all, they are villagers and we are social scientists. We each have our own cultural backgrounds and occupations. An acknowledgment of that immutable difference between the language and purposes of the informant and the social scientist distinguishes a hermeneutic approach from the phenomenological one which suggests that it is possible to "become one" with one's informants, to think their thoughts. Nevertheless, the recognition of differences should not be taken as license to disregard the Kandyan's views as merely epiphenomenal.[7] The point is to transform these views into the language of social science.

In order to construct a measure of individualism, two broad areas were probed. First, interaction with kin was explored, since withdrawal from kin is a characteristic of increasing individualism. Second, the nature of involvement with other members of the community was examined. After a series of specific questions were asked about the dwelling, answers were coded and a measure of materialism constructed.

Interaction With Kin

Respondents were asked, "Who visits you more frequently at home, kin or non-kin? As Table 12.2 demonstrates, there is much greater interaction with kin in the village than in the city (57 percent against 10 percent). There is also a significant variation by class.[8] In the village inter-

Table 12.2
Interaction With Kin

	Poor	Low	Middle	Upper-Middle	Average
% Kin visit more	80%	65%	25%	—	57%
(village)	(16)	(13)	(5)		(11)
% Kin visit more	0%	10%	15%	15%	10%
(city)	(0)	(2)	(3)	(3)	(2)

action with kin decreases as one rises in social class. Among the poor, 80 percent responded that kin visited more than non-kin, while only 25 percent of the middle class answered this way. For those who claimed that kin visited more often, the following kinds of reasons were given: "My home is a family-oriented place," or "The people who live around my house are my relatives. They come most. After them, other members of my caste come to visit. People of other castes might come in an emergency, but not for a social visit." There are, however, many economic and personal rifts between kin in the village. This kind of divide was summed up by one middle-class man who in answering that he was visited more by non-kin said, "My relatives only visit me when they want something. They know better than to come too often."

The class pattern in the city is the opposite of that in the village. None of the poor said that it was kin who visited more often, whereas 15 percent of the upper-middle class answered kin. Still, these are very low figures when compared with the village. Those urbanites who answered that they saw kin more, gave reasons such as "My home is a private place for the family." More commonly city dwellers gave reasons for low interaction in the home with kin. Many different reasons were given. The urban poor who live in shanties have few relatives living in the city. They claimed that their kin who lived in villages did not visit much because "they don't like the shanty area." "If we want to visit relatives we go there" (to the village). For the urban poor, therefore, the house is not a place where one entertains kin, it is "for anyone . . . for everyone in the community." For many urbanites, in contrast to the villagers, visits from kin are not a regular occurence but take place only on ritual occasions: "Our relatives visit during festivals," or "We visit our relatives for weddings and funerals." For others, visits are infrequent because their "relatives are scattered all over the island." Wealth is another reason given for low interaction. As one upper-middle-class person said, "Some of our relatives don't come often because they are poorer than us," while another person put it even more bluntly: "Our relatives tend to stay away as they are jealous of my success."

The higher rate of interaction with kin in the village can be accounted for in part, perhaps, by the higher percentage of residents born in the village than in the city. It is likely that as much as 60 percent of the population of the village is related, whereas in the city the percentage would be insignificant.[9] Among the urban poor, to take the most extreme case, only one person in our sample has relatives other than immediate family living in the area. Within the village, the significantly lower rate of interaction among the middle class can perhaps be accounted for by their higher rate of contact with nonvillagers and jealousy within families over the upward mobility of some members. In summation then, it appears that there is greater withdrawal from kin in the city than in the village. Within the village there is a dramatic decrease in interaction with kin as one rises in social class. In the city it is the poor who are most isolated from their kin who have remained in the villages. All of the other classes in the city also have a low rate of interaction with kin.

Interaction With Community

The second measure of individualism is degree of interaction with community. Respondents were asked the following questions: "How many times do people visit you per week?" "Who visits you more frequently at home, neighbors or non-neighbors?" "What obligations, if any, do you feel you have to the community?" and "What, if anything, would happen if you didn't meet these obligations?

Within the village, the middle class stands out as being markedly different from the poor and the lower class in a comparison of amount of interaction with fellow villagers (3.6 visits a week against 5.3 visits a week) and amount of interaction with neighbors (75 percent against 95 percent). Although members of the middle class have a lower rate of interaction than the other classes, they show virtually the same degree of obligation to community and acknowledgment of community sanctions for noncompliance, as do the other classes. Within the context of the village it is difficult to separate out neighbors from kin since they are often the same. As one lower-class villager pointed out, "Nearly all of our neighbors are relatives. . . . Some are rich and some are not." The visiting that goes back and forth among neighbors and non-neighbors has to do not only with being sociable but with building ties with others and fulfilling obligations that are an integral part of village life. One of the villagers described his interaction with his fellows in the following manner: "Every man wishes to earn the good will of society." "Mutual help such as giving to the Funeral Donation Society is highly valued." A high value is placed on trying to get on well with neighbors. "All our neighbors are helpful to each other and hospitable." "We must keep pleasant relations with the neighbors." To the village poor, help from neighbors is an economic necessity. "We help each other and share our miseries together." But all, including those from the middle class, strongly believe that one must help one's neighbors during emergencies such as illness and death. Overwhelmingly they felt that strong sanctions would and should be taken against someone who failed to help people in distress. They claimed that if a person fails to help, "others won't respect him and he will be isolated"; "He will be completely cut off from the community"; "He will be rejected by people until he changes his ways"; and "When he needs people, no one will help him. . . . They will make cunning excuses." An important part of this interaction with other members of the community has to do with the degree of economic dependence that exists among villagers. This dependency is particularly strong among the poor who cannot afford the luxury of being individualistic even should they wish it. In addition to the system of paid labor, the farmers have a collective cultivation system known as *aththam* by which people help each other. Only if one helps other farmers will he be helped with his own crop. Cooperation, then, is institutionalized economically and spills over into other realms. Over 75 percent of the households have paddy fields that they work as owners or renters and the level of cooperation is great between them. The poor are also tied to others by being dependent on members of all the classes to lend them money and food when they are in need.

The village is not one big happy family: it is far from that. Caste divisions are still strong among the older generation. Here is a sampling of comments on caste. "My husband won't let low-caste people in the house." "Low-caste people should come from the back side" (of the house). "Some visitors are only fit for the compound, some can be received at the back, and others are fit to be royally received in the drawing room." "Normally women and low-caste people are received in the back. Those who are not even fit for the back are received in the compound." Among some, however, particularly the younger generation, class is intruding upon caste. "Earlier we wouldn't let low caste people in the house. But now this has changed and we let them in . . . if they are well educated." One of the most interesting cases of the conflict between caste and class took place when a girl from a Radala family (the traditional aristocracy and the highest subgroup of the Goyigama caste) married into the family of a wealthy Batgama (a low caste who traditionally were menials). One informant stated, "The girl's family dropped down to zero with the other Goyigama families. Now that family isn't proud any more; they mix with the rest of the village for the first time." There is also much jealousy in the village. This was explained by villagers as the effect of living together in close quarters. "Here we mix with each other so much that we always notice what others have." Another simply said, "We know people and gossip about them."

In the city there is less interaction than there is in the village. Although there are fewer visits a week (3.1 against 4.6) in the city, what is really striking is the vast difference in amount of visiting by class. It goes from a high of 6.8 for the poor to an average of 1 visit a week for the middle and upper-middle classes.[10] Even this is deceiving, for the poor tend to socialize on the streets around their houses, whereas the middle and upper-middle classes do not. The poor and even the lower class, therefore, have a much higher rate of socializing in the local area than do the higher classes. On the whole urbanites have fewer visitors who are neighbors than do villagers (51 percent against 88 percent). Again, the figure for the urban sample masks a vast difference in pattern of socializing by class. One hundred percent of the poor and 85 percent of the lower class interacted more with neighbors, whereas only 15 percent of the middle class and 5 percent of the upper-middle class socialized more with neighbors. Although all of the classes live in economically homogeneous neighborhoods, once again as with number of visits, there is a distinct difference between the poor and the lower class, and the middle and upper-middle class.

Many of the poor and lower-class city dwellers gave the same types of reasons for their high rate of interaction as did villagers. However, the upper classes gave many different types of reasons for their lower rate of interaction. Some explained it purely in terms of economics: "To a large extent people don't visit each other in this neighborhood. The lower class are more sociable than we middle-class people because they depend on their neighbors. We don't need our neighbors so we don't have to visit." Others tended to blame it on urbanism: "Town life is killing the spirit of the people. They want to be individuals and separate from each other. Probably the only place you find community is in the slums." Others blamed it on Westernization: "Now in Kandy we have become more Westernized and therefore less hospitable." Some simply felt that a cultural change has taken place and that people now value individual privacy more. One upper-middle-class woman described the change:

> In our area neighbors hardly have time to see each other. They don't want to intrude on each other's privacy. People are becoming much more conscious of privacy. It used to be unthinkable to send a note or phone before calling. Now it is good manners. People would look askance if you didn't inform them first. This is completely different from the village where people practically live in each other's homes. We are busy and come home tired at the end of the day. We want to be together as a family. We don't want neighbors intruding on our privacy.

For one upper-middle-class respondent the reason for the low rate of interaction is a lack of trust. "We can't take all our friends into the house. We have valuable possessions, and in these days you can't trust everyone."

There was also a clear difference between members of these classes on the issue of whether one had an obligation to other members of the community and whether sanctions would be applied if this duty was not fulfilled. One hundred percent of the poor and lower-class respondents answered yes to both questions, whereas 40 percent of the middle class answered yes to both and only 20 percent of the upper-middle-class sample felt any obligation and a mere 15 percent felt that sanctions would be applied.

The poor shanty dwellers felt most strongly about obligation and claimed to exert the strongest sanctions against those who didn't fulfill that obligation. Because of the tenuous position of the shanty settlement within the city and the illicit activities of many residents, help to others against hostile outsiders was considered a matter of survival: "Helping each other is the most important thing. How can we live without others in this area?" Among those middle- and upper-middle-class people who felt an obligation some argued that it was their duty to help the less fortunate. Others thought that one's obligation could be fulfilled by "participating in social activities like the Lions Club." Numbers alone, however, do not capture the difference in degree of obligation and sanctions felt. For example, several middle- and upper-middle-class people who claimed that they felt an obligation saw it in a completely different way from the poor. Middle- and upper-middle-class informants felt obliged to be totally independent: "As long as you leave others alone, they will think well of you"; or "Do your job well and don't depend on others"; "Minding your own business is the most important thing"; and finally, "Don't be a burden to society." Here we can see a vast gulf between the classes, for the higher classes have redefined collective responsibility in purely individualistic terms. Obligation is defined as something passive that one fulfills by being self-sufficient and making demands on no one. Some appeared to find the whole question irrelevant. "Obligation to the community? I don't feel any."

The shanty dwellers felt the most strongly about sanctions. "What if a person doesn't help others in need?" we asked. Some said, "We will not allow him to associate with us." "We will try and get rid of him." "We will drive them out." Some among the higher classes felt that one would lose the respect of others if one did not help. Others saw the repercussions in purely individualistic terms: "If someone were seriously ill we would have to help by driving them [to the hospital] in the car." "And if you didn't?" we asked. "Nothing would happen . . . well . . . we might feel a bit guilty." One man interpreted sanctions in a purely legalistic fashion, "I don't know what will happen," he said. "I suppose if a person breaks the law, he will go to jail." One man expressed a commonly held sentiment when he said, "Absolutely nothing will happen to me. *Who* is going to do something? I don't know my neighbors."

A Measure of Materialism

To assess the degree of materialism three questions were asked. (1) List what gives a person more status in rank order: (*a*) helping others in the community, (*b*) having a large house and money, (*c*) practicing religion, (*d*) helping members of your family; (2) What is the most important feature of a good home? and (3) What, if anything, can you tell about a person by looking at his house?

The villagers gave a house and money a low ranking in the status hierarchy. Only 12 percent of the villagers rated these most important in acquiring status.[11] There was variation by class, however, with 25 percent of the middle class ranking house and money first. The following are some of the typical answers given by the poor to this question. "Helping neighbors in need is what gives you status here." "People respect those who behave well and have good habits." "A house is not a symbol of status . . . it is just for shelter." "A large house won't help you be recognized by the community." A particularly interesting point of view was expressed by one poor villager: "The Radala [aristocracy] used to be very high up; now anyone can have a *walawwa* ["manor house"] if they have money." This comment indicates that there has been a shift from hereditary to achieved status that this villager has not completely accepted. He sees the Radala as having lost status and yet appears unwilling to grant high status to "anyone" who has a big house simply because he has the money to buy it. The lower class expressed similar sentiments. "Status depends upon who you entertain and how you behave." "Cooperation with the neighbors is most important." "What gives most status is giving assistance to the community without making a display, . . . that's what's recognized most." Several stressed the problematic side of materialistic status display. "My relatives won't be happy if I have a big house. They would get jealous and start talking. How can other people be happy if I have those things? Neighbors would also be jealous but wouldn't admire me. It would cause big problems for me." "The most important thing is to keep level [he made a level gesture with his hand]. It is important that everyone look the same." One woman who realized that a big house would cause problems for her nevertheless said, "I would like to show my neighbors that I have done well, even though they wouldn't like it." Many middle class people felt that material possessions did not influence status. "People respect you only when you have good habits and values but not for things like houses." Many felt, however, that there was a difference between the ideal and the reality. "The house shouldn't be a symbol of status but it has become so." Others felt that the house was in fact a status symbol. Some argued for the practical necessity of having a good house. "Having a good house will help us find good partners for our daughters." "Society accepts you as having some standing if you have a good house." There was also much ambivalence. "It is a difficult question to answer. There are certain homes which look very beautiful but which don't preserve cultural values, while there are poor homes which are very religious minded and patriotic." There was also a strong feeling that the status gained might be outweighed by the jealousy engendered. "Generally villagers look at such places with envy. Neighbors might outwardly respect you but inwardly they are full of envy." "If I had a big house people would do all kinds of things to try to bring me down."

In the city 48 percent ranked housing and money first. Again there was a difference between the classes. While only 10 percent of the poor ranked housing and money first, 30 percent of the lower class, 70 percent of the middle class, and 80 percent of the upper-middle class repondents ranked it first. Most of the urban poor felt that a house and money were not important status symbols. Typical comments were: "The house isn't a status symbol here. It is a good character which gives status"; or "Being good to people, that's the first thing." Several suggested that their group was anomalous within the city. One said, "The house is a status symbol in the present society but not in our community." Others felt that, although they themselves used other criteria to assess a person's worth, rural relatives would respect them more if they had better housing. Their typical comments were: "Village relatives admire wealth"; and "Relatives from our villages wouldn't look down on us if we had a better house." These comments are puzzling in light of the responses to this question from our village sample. Perhaps it can be accounted for by the fact that the housing of the shanty dwellers is inferior to that of poor villagers. Also the shanty dwellers own no land in the city and villagers value land very highly.

The urban lower class rated housing and money higher than did the urban lower class. Some still maintained that "neighbors won't respect or help you just because you have a good house. To get that, people must be very good to others." But this was a minority view. Some saw a large house as a social necessity. "If you live in an area where big people live, you need a big house." "I can't live in a hut." "If you do a big job, you need a big house." A few stressed the difference in attitudes between the city and the village: "In our villages caste differences are very important. But here in the city no one cares about caste. Here all people care about is economic level." Others saw it purely in terms of status. "When you have a big house, people respect you." "A large and beautiful house is a symbol of dignity. That is why everyone wants one." One person qualified this assessment by saying, "Your neighbors may respect you but they won't help you." Once again, many people also felt that a good house would be particularly admired by their relatives from the village. It is possible that some of these city dwellers no longer have close ties with their village relatives. What they might really mean is that they want their village relatives to see that they have achieved some measure of success even if this engenders jealousy, for close ties may no longer exist anyway.

The middle and upper-middle classes both rated money and housing as the most important element of status. Nearly everyone in the middle-class sample felt that "in the present society, the house is a status symbol." Many took this for granted and claimed that "here everyone has a good house." Many argued for the necessity of a big house. "We are compelled to build big houses in this society. We can't do our business otherwise." Others said, "We need big houses, otherwise how will our children be happy?" Several mentioned village relatives: "Our relatives from the village respect us very much because of our large house." It is interesting that while many of the poor and lower-class urbanites suspected that people wouldn't really respect them if they had a big house, some of the middle class had exactly the opposite impression. "People often don't want to show it but actually they respect you more if you have money and a good house."

The response of the upper-middle class were similar to those of the middle class, although unlike the latter they seemed to feel little need to justify their life-style. Their responses also seemed to indicate a more competitive attitude toward consumption. "We are oriented toward consumption," said one man. "It is a large house and money that gives you status, not charity or religion. Material things are the *only* thing." Another said, laughing, "We are very religious. We do *pooja* ["worship"] to money." For many, material goods are symbols of their success. "As soon as I made some real money I moved into this neighborhood. It showed my old friends and family that I have become a greater man." Another said, "I have a friend who has just recently made a lot of money. He bought a very large house and a huge amount of furniture. He clutters the living room and hall with expensive goods just to show that he has made it." Yet another said, "I have a china cabinet and refrigerator in my dining room and I am proud of it. I have earned it." One man summed up this kind of materialistic individualism well when he said, "To be somebody you must have your own house and property. I am proud of this. I am independent." The competitive spirit that seems to shape their desire for goods also affects relations between neighbors. As one person said, "There is a lot of comparing of people's houses in this area." The result of this is that "people get jealous of others who have larger houses." Here we can clearly see the link between materialism and withdrawal from neighbors and kin.

In the village, helping others is considered most important by 60 percent of the poor and 40 percent of the lower class. There is little agreement among the middle class; the answers are almost evenly spread among house, helping others, helping family, and practicing religion. In the city, 90 percent of the poor said that helping others is most important. Again the answers are explicable on the basis of the fact that villagers are more likely to know one another. It may be that in the village where status is largely acquired at birth and is based on family, caste, and class membership, character assessment is more important. In the more socially mobile urban setting, houses indicate income level to a community which, except in the poor shanty neighborhood, may be composed largely of strangers, who, if they are to be impressed, must be impressed by outward appearances.

We can see that among all classes of urbanites, practicing religion and helping out family members is not considered an important source of prestige. In the village, both types of activity are seen as more important in achieving respect (see Table 12.3). It is not that these are not valued, but in the city where people have indicated that their lives are more private and individualistic, those outside the house do not know about such family matters. This is most true among the middle- and upper-middle-class respondents who receive fewer visitors and are less likely to know their neighbors (see Table 12.4).

As I have argued elsewhere, there tends to be a strong correlation between social and spatial mobility and the use of housing as a symbol of social status

Table 12.3
What Gives More Status?

	Poor	Low	Middle	Upper-Middle	Average
Village					
House	5%	5%	25%	—	12%
	(1)	(1)	(5)		(2)
Give to others	60%	40%	25%	—	42%
	(12)	(8)	(5)		(8)
Family	10%	25%	20%	—	18%
	(2)	(5)	(4)		(4)
Religion	25%	30%	30%	—	28%
	(5)	(6)	(6)		(6)
City					
House	10%	30%	70%	80%	48%
	(2)	(6)	(14)	(16)	(10)
Give to others	90%	45%	10%	5%	38%
	(18)	(9)	(2)	(1)	(8)
Family	0%	5%	10%	5%	5%
	(0)	(1)	(2)	(1)	(1)
Religion	0%	20%	10%	10%	10%
	(0)	(4)	(2)	(2)	(2)

Table 12.4
Interaction With Community

	Poor	Low	Middle	Upper-Middle	Average
No. visits/week (village)	5.1	5.3	3.6	—	4.6
No. visits/week (city)	6.8	3.3	0.9	1.1	3.1
% Neighbors visit more (village)	95% (19)	95% (19)	75% (15)	—	88% (18)
% Neighbors visit more (city)	100% (20)	85% (17)	15% (3)	5% (1)	51% (10)
% Obligation to community (village)	100% (20)	100% (20)	95% (19)	—	98% (19)
% Obligation to community (city)	100% (20)	100% (20)	40% (8)	20% (4)	65% (13)
% Community sanctions (village)	100% (20)	100% (20)	95% (19)	—	98% (19)
% Community sanctions (city)	100% (20)	100% (20)	40% (8)	15% (3)	64% (13)

and personal achievement (Duncan and Duncan 1980). In other words, in a village society where most families have lived for generations, social status is largely established from birth. In a city there tends to be more social mobility, in part because, with greater spatial mobility, people's family backgrounds are not widely known.

There are many social mechanisms that restrict social mobility in the village. One is the belief that those who have always had wealth deserve it, while those who acquire it are somehow betraying poorer friends and relatives who can no longer be as close. It became clear from the interviews that jealousy is prevalent in Sri Lankan society. Those who acquire new possessions feel very susceptible to receiving the evil eye, a curse that results from jealousy. Belief in the evil eye is a widespread phenomenon in Sri Lanka as in many other societies. It is possible that this belief retards social mobility in general and the spread of materialistic value systems in particular. Materialism and individualism appear to be necessarily closely tied. If one desires to consume, it may very well be at the expense of close relations with poorer kin. Personal consumption, then, will take precedence over traditionally valued social relationships.

The question "What is the most important feature of a good home?" was asked to see whether people would offer physical features such as "good furniture" or social attributes such as "a happy family." The question was de-

Table 12.5
Most Important Features of Home

	Poor	Low	Middle	Upper-Middle	Average
Village					
Physical features	15%	30%	50%	—	32%
	(3)	(6)	(10)		(6)
Social features	60%	40%	25%	—	42%
	(12)	(8)	(5)		(8)
Cleanliness	25%	30%	25%	—	27%
	(5)	(6)	(5)		(5)
City					
Physical features	10%	55%	75%	85%	56%
	(2)	(11)	(15)	(17)	(11)
Social features	40%	30%	20%	10%	25%
	(8)	(6)	(4)	(2)	(5)
Cleanliness	50%	15%	5%	5%	19%
	(10)	(3)	(1)	(1)	(4)

liberately vague, and we took a response referring to physical features as a measure of a materialistic orientation. Only about one-third of the villagers (32 percent) mentioned a physical feature. There is, however, a marked difference between classes; 15 percent of the poor, 30 percent of the lower class, and 50 percent of the middle class mentioned physical features. While cleanliness is a physical characteristic, it does not have the same materialistic connotation as does, for example, "a large house." Therefore, cleanliness was separated out into a third category. The two-thirds who identified social attributes mentioned such things as "a happy family," "a family that helps neighbors in need," and "a religious-minded household." The other two classes answered in much the same way and gave similar reasons. They also mentioned such aspects as "cleanliness," "harmony," "good ventilation," "a beautiful and neat garden," "a home which welcomes visitors," and "living happily, not the physical things." Again, the physical aspects that were mentioned had more to do with comfort than with status display. All in all, the house was seen as a place for family and friends that ideally was both comfortable and inviting.

In contrast, a majority of the urban sample mentioned physical features. Again, there was a very large difference between the poor (10 percent), who responded more like villagers, and the other classes (55 percent, 75 percent, and 85 percent). Forty percent of the poor mentioned social attributes; many mentioned issues about morality. One person said, "Members of the family should have good characters above all else," and another said, "A good home is not one that is well arranged. A home can be said to be good only if its female members are well behaved." This was a veiled reference to the problem of prostitution in the area. Others mentioned neighborliness as the most important attribute. "It's not the physical character of the house but the people that is important. They should be helpful to their neighbors"; or "The people of a good home will treat visitors well." Only one of the poor mentioned a "beautiful, good-looking house."

A majority of the lower and three-quarters of the middle-class sample mentioned physical attributes of the house. Unlike the poor, however, they spoke about more than having basic services and perhaps a radio. They said, for example, "A good house is a big house"; or "The physical structure is very important because our status depends upon it." Only one-third mentioned social attributes such as having "good character" and being "a good neighbor." Eighty-five percent of the upper-middle class mentioned physical attributes, and their reasons were very similar to those of the middle and lower classes. They claimed that the most important thing was to have a "house that was large, beautifully built, and important looking." Interestingly, only one person mentioned relations with neighbors or the community-at-large as the most important feature.

Conclusion

Elsewhere I have argued that there is a logic to the link between individualism and materialism in general and in particular between individualism and the use of the home as a status object (Duncan 1981). The logic, I argued, is based on a common cross-cultural need to display one's identity to both oneself and others.[12] The way one has a positive identity reaffirmed in the eyes of others, however, varies greatly from group to group. I have argued that the more individualistic in orientation a person is, the more likely that he or she will use the house as an important means of achieving respect in the eyes of others. I based this hypothesis on scattered ethnographic evidence, some of which was my own. This study, however, was my first attempt to examine this relationship systematically using a moderately large sample. As I expected, there emerged a strong relationship between individualism and materialism. The village sample was less individualistic and materialistic than the urban sample, and the lower classes were less so than the higher classes. In the village, concern for one's kin, neighborhood, and community obligations are still very strong, and housing is not the basis of social status. Within the village, however, the middle class stood out as more individualistic and materialistic than the other classes. In the city, however, kinship, neighborhood, and community orientation are weak compared with those of the village, and housing is a strong determinant of status. This statement must be immediately qualified by adding that there are vast differences of opinion on most of these issues between the poor and lower class on the one hand and the middle and upper-middle class on the other. We cannot, then, explain degree of individualism or materialism in terms solely of urbanization or social class, for it seems to be correlated with both. We can suggest, however, that the study of housing is more than simply the study of shelter, for both the villagers and the urbanites saw the house as a symbol of much greater things. For them it is an important, symbolically charged object that communicates respect, success, traditional values, and how one relates to one's family and neighbors. Its symbolic power was at times so great that it literally tore extended families apart, that is, it isolated a nuclear family from its wider kin network. Only within a highly individualistic social group could this possibly be viewed with equanimity. For social scientists the study of housing is important precisely because it is so symbolically charged that it speaks to us about one of the most enduring problems in social science: the relation between the individual and the collectivity.

My research in Sri Lanka was funded by the Social Sciences and Humanities Research Council of Canada. I am grateful to Professor Gerald Pieris, head of the Department of Geography, University of Peradeniya, who invited me to be a visiting research fellow at the University of Peradeniya during 1983. I am indebted to my field assistants, Shantha Hennayake and Nalini Hennayake, and to Nancy Duncan, John Agnew, and Shantha Hennayake for criticism of earlier drafts.

Notes

1. For a fuller discussion of some of these problems of interpretation, see Marcus and Fischer (1986), especially chapter 3 entitled "Conveying Other Cultural Experience: The Person, Self, and Emotions." For an example of the complex interplay between informant, ethnographer, and reader within the so-called modernist tradition in ethnography, see Crapanzano (1980).

2. In this regard, it would be interesting to compare two former British colonies, Burma and Sri Lanka, that have chosen radically different paths since independence. The former has closed its frontiers to outside influences while the latter has since 1977 had an open-door economic policy.

3. For the impact that a British cultural model has had among North American elite groups, see Duncan and Duncan (1984).

4. This pattern of display was also common in India. See Duncan and Duncan (1980).

5. Toddy is an alcoholic beverage made from the flower of the palm. A toddy tapper climbs to the tops of palm trees to tap the toddy.

6. Williams in Clifford (1986).

7. This may seem a matter of common sense, but consciousness is often seen by social scientists as irrelevant to causal explanation. I am referring here to the structuralist project.

8. As Table 12.1 shows, city dwellers are more likely to be migrants than villagers. It is probable that city dwellers have fewer kin living in the vicinity that do villagers.

9. As Table 12.1 indicates, 69 percent of the villagers were born there. Obeyesekere (1974) notes that in the village of Madagama there was a rise in individualism accounted for in part by the increase in non-kin based outsiders who had come to live in the village. I do not have data available on what percentage of the villagers twenty years ago were born there.

10. The figure 6.8 is in fact an underrepresentation because although 1 visit daily was the maximum we coded for, several poor people indicated that they visited 6 to 8 times daily.

11. This is in line with the findings of Tambiah's (1963) survey of social status in rural central Ceylon. He found that several schemes of evaluation were in existence and that "aid to fellow villagers" and "good works" were expected of wealthy men and influenced the prestige they were accorded. The survey showed that a pious but not rich lay disciple was given a slight preference over a wealthy landlord, and a middle-income school teacher was ranked equal to a wealthy landlord but ranked higher than a wealthy shopkeeper (see Roberts 1974).

12. This theoretical position known as symbolic interactionism is worked out in Mead (1934) and Strauss (1959).

References

Barthes, R. 1977. *Image, music, text.* Trans. Stephen Heath. New York: Hill and Wang.

Clifford, J. 1986. Introduction: Partial truths. In J. Clifford and G. E. Marcus, *Writing culture: The poetics and politics of ethnography,* 1–26. Berkeley: University of California Press.

Crapanzano, V. 1980. *Tuhami: Portrait of a Moroccan.* Chicago: University of Chicago Press.

———. 1986. Hermes' dilemma: The masking of subversion in ethnographic description. In J. Clifford and G. E. Marcus, *Writing culture: The poetics and politics of ethnography,* 51–76. Berkeley: University of California Press.

Darnton, R. 1984. *The Great Cat Massacre and other episodes in French cultural history.* New York: Basic Books.

DeSilva, K. M. 1977. Historical survey. In *Sri Lanka: A survey,* ed. K. M. DeSiliva, 31–85. London: C. Hurst.

Duncan, J. S. 1981. From container of women to status symbol: The impact of social structure on the meaning of the house. In *Housing and identity: Cross-cultural perspectives,* ed. J. S. Duncan, 36–59. London: Croom Helm.

———. 1985. The house as symbol of social structure: Notes on the language of objects among collectivistic groups. In *Home environments,* vol. 8, *Human behavior and environment: Advances in theory and research,* ed. I. Altman and C. Werner, 133–151. New York: Plenum.

Duncan, J. S., and N. G. Duncan. 1980. Residential landscapes and social worlds: A case study in Hyderabad, Andrha Pradesh. In *An exploration of India: Studies in social and cultural geography,* ed. D. Sopher, 271–86. Ithaca: Cornell University Press.

———. 1984. A cultural analysis of urban residential landscapes in North America: The case of the Anglophile elite. In *The city in cultural context,* ed. J. Agnew, J. Mercer, and D. Sopher, 255–76. London: Allen and Unwin.

Geertz, C. 1973. Thick description: Toward an interpretive theory of culture. In *The interpretation of cultures,* 3–32. New York: Basic Books.

Gooneratne, M. Y. 1968. *English literature in Ceylon 1815–1878.* Colombo: Tisara Prakasakayo.

Houtart, F. 1974. *Religion and ideology in Sri Lanka.* Colombo: Hansa Publishers.

Marcus, G. E., and M. M. J. Fischer. 1986. *Anthropology as cultural critique: An experimental moment in the human sciences.* Chicago: University of Chicago Press.

Martin, R. C. 1983. Symbol, ritual, and community: An approach to Islam. In *Islam in the modern world: 1983 Paine Lectures in Religion,* ed. J. Raitt, 41–57. Columbia: University of Missouri Press.

Mead. G. H. 1934. *Mind, self and society.* Chicago: University of Chicago Press.

Obeyesekere, G. 1974. A village in Sri Lanka: Madagama. In *South Asia: Seven community profiles,* ed. C. Maloney, 42–80. New York: Holt, Rinehart and Winston.

Roberts, M. 1974. Problems of social stratification and the demarcation of national and local elites in British Ceylon. *Journal of Asian Studies* 33:549–77.

————. 1982. *Caste conflict and elite formation.* Colombo: Lake House.

Strauss, A. L. 1959. *Mirrors and masks: The search for identity.* Glencoe: The Free Press.

Tambiah, S. J. 1963. Ceylon. In *The role of savings and wealth in Southern Asia and the west,* ed. R. D. Lambert and B. F. Hoselitz, 97–112. Paris: UNESCO.

Tennent, J. E. 1859. *Ceylon,* vol. 2. London: Longman, Green, Longman, and Roberts.

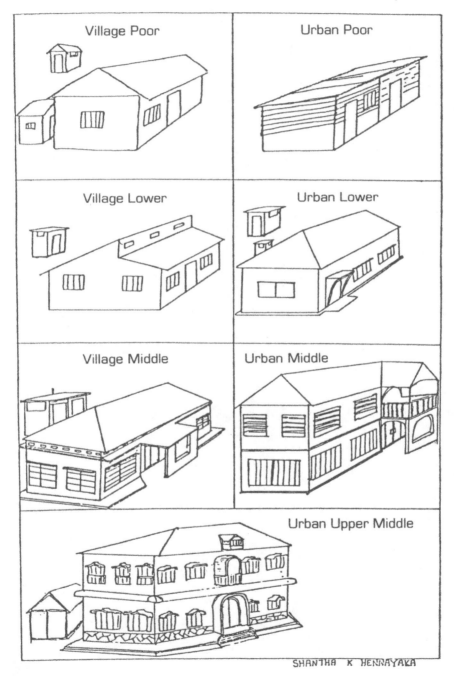

Village Poor

Urban Poor

Village Lower

Urban Lower

Village Middle

Urban Middle

Urban Upper Middle

SHANTHA K HENRAYAKA

Figure 12.1. Types of Kandyan housing.

13

ARCHITECTURE AS A
MEDIUM FOR CULTURE:
PUBLIC INSTITUTION
AND PRIVATE HOUSE

JULIA W. ROBINSON

Language is a medium of cultural interchange that provides patterns for thought and action; architecture structures activity and ways of thinking. But spoken language is a phenomenon of the moment whose influence lingers in memory, and written language, though lasting in time and space, is only influential for those who choose to read. In cultures that participate in building as an activity, the ideas manifest in built form have an ongoing influence on daily life.

The creation of built form, then, expresses a cultural pattern, and architectural forms come to stand for, communicate, and produce cultural expectations. Designers of buildings participate in the process of communicating these ideas. As members of a culture, they create the settings considered to be appropriate for the groups of people and the situations being designed for. Generally, these assumptions about what is appropriate are taken for granted, and the designer simply uses the culturally sanctioned forms and materials. Inasmuch as built forms are manifestations of what a culture deems appropriate, they are mirrors of cultural values and offer an opportunity for questioning the degree to which our cultural aspirations are matched by our cultural achievements. In this chapter I will examine societal ideas as they are expressed through public institutions and private houses.

When cultural patterns and built patterns fit, they become a strong mutual reinforcement, but this interplay may be stable or may be in flux in different ways. For example, cultural ideas may change without requiring a change in the built form (such as eating dinner in the kitchen instead of the dining room). Or, change in built form may cause restructuring of cultural expectations (reduction of the size of the kitchen may result in use of another place for eating). Changes in cultural attitudes may cause the abandonment of structures that are no longer suitable (if formal eating becomes unfashionable, the dining room may be eliminated). And new cultural ideas may engender the creation of new forms that are responsive to altered values (eating at the kitchen counter on high stools rather than at a table with chairs). Designers are often called upon to imagine new possibilities, and when that happens they may act as cultural critics and promoters of cultural change. Most often, however, they do so without understanding the relation between the proposed change and the complex pattern of existing built phenomena.

In this chapter I will explore the relation between particular architectural forms and cultural values to uncover the content of what is communicated and to consider the nature of architecture as a communicative medium. Architecture has often been referred to as a language, yet the differnce between environmental communication and language is significant and makes the analogy between the two applicable only in the broadest sense. In our culture, because environment is more fixed than language, it tends to be less subject than language to continuous manipulation by the people for whom it is a medium. Its meanings are more generalized, and the messages are communicated by redundant cues (Norberg-Schulz 1965; Rapoport 1982). The architectural or environmental messages are read and manipulated at a less explicit and conscious level than is language.

But because of the redundancy of the environmental cues, when cultural changes are taking place, the environment may begin to give off confused messages. Builders and designers who do not follow culturally prescribed patterns may communicate unintended messages. It is not enough to bring together a group of the architectural features that are historically linked to a certain type of environment. Since some features are more powerful communicators than others, one potent cue out of place (for example, an exit sign in an otherwise ordinary living room) may subvert the intended meaning. This is the problem faced by designers who try to alter environments. Certain architectural features express the fundamental structure of the decision-making process (an exit sign signifies fire safety regulations), while others have been associated less strongly (sofas of the kind found in institutions, for example, are also sometimes found in private houses), or have been subject to changing associations (smoke alarms are now found in private dwellings). For this reason, it becomes important, when describing to designers how individual types of settings communicate, to provide a very complete description that allows both general and specific understanding of the relation between the message and the cues.

The idea of architecture as a medium for culture implies an underlying structure for communication. The nature of this structure has been debated at length (for example, Rapoport 1982; Doxtater 1980), but using Saussure's sense as applied in Barthes (1964) and Eco (1979) that semiotic structure is not necessarily linguistic, but that linguistic structure is one sign system among others (including architecture), we shall call this structure of communication semiotic. It is not, however, only the semiotic structure of architecture that communicates. It is the link between built form and cultural attitudes that enables architecture to be a powerful medium. When the cultural context is not known, architecture only provides indications, since the associations with other elements are not available. In that instance architecture is experienced primarily at the level of the senses, or is incorrectly interpreted with reference to inapplicable cultural experience, and the communicative power of the built form is much reduced or negated. Architectural messages are thus profoundly embedded in their cultural context, and they must be studied in context. It is therefore reasonable to be an informant on one's own culture, using introspection and observation balanced by validation with other methods.

The association between architectural forms and particular social expectations builds up and causes difficulty when cultural ideas change. Formal attributes originally directly related to a purpose (the bell to call parishoners to worship) are often retained in symbolic association long after the functional tie has vanished. Nevertheless, these associations may continue to be considered necessary parts of the formal structure of an ideal type. This ideal type defines the cultural standards for an underlying set of values. With the passing of time, insight into the inability of certain standards to reflect values leads to the need for change. This results in a tension between (1) the architectural form as symbol of values and set of standards and (2) the altered values and standards. The old architectural forms may cease to characterize the ideas of a society in flux. But the investment economically and psychologically of a society in its architecture makes alterations or elimination of the built structures difficult. The discrepancy between new standards and old forms must be widely seen as negative before change can be politically viable. And it may not be enough that an ideal type ought to be eliminated; the development of an alternative ideal type may be required for the old forms to be actually removed. Moreover, when a new type is being designed, the features of the existing one must be carefully understood, as past forms become the context in which new ones are read.

Intepreting the attitudes of one's own culture may seem to be a search into the obvious, for we know our culture so well, that once stated, we recognize both the message and the device for communicating the message. On the other hand, it is a challenge to learn to see one's views afresh and to be self-critical. In this interpretation, then, it is not simply the message that is important, nor is it individual devices for communicating, but it is understanding the operation of communication in its broadest sense and the match of the ideas represented in architectural forms to our societal aspirations. By such critique we may better understand how to create settings that match our ideals rather than our history.

The Study

    The body of this chapter is an interpretation of the differences between institutional housing and vernacular (see Rapoport 1969, 23) single-family detached housing as found in a Midwest urban area of the United States. It is based on an exploratory study of ten housing environments: four residences for mentally retarded people and six other settings for nondisabled people (a hospital, a dormitory, two apartment buildings, two single-family dwellings). The original investigation focused on the needs of severely and profoundly mentally retarded adults (Robinson, Thompson, Emmons, and Graff, 1984).

    The research on settings was done to define the architectural parameters of deinstitutionalization or normalization (providing social and physical environments as close as possible to everyday settings: Nirje 1969, 181). The normalization principle implies a polar relation between institutional and ordinary (normal) ways of living. However, the architectural character of the settings associated with these two living styles, while assumed to be an important support mechanism, is only beginning to be carefully described (for example, Wolfensberger and Glenn 1975; Wolfensberger and Thomas 1983). This study used the concept of ideal building types, seen as a culturally defined idea, as the basis for a comparison between these contrasting residential settings.

    The use of ideal types as one method for the creation of architecture is a commonly accepted process (see Broadbent's discussion of iconic design: 1973, 30, 418–19). Type links the act of perceiving and categorization with the act of recreating or designing. Rapoport (forthcoming) discusses the way settings are categorized and points out that the clear-cut case represents a central tendency within a class of things. Artifacts located within such a class are characterized by having some but not necessarily all of a group of salient characteristics. He argues for using "extreme" examples as a starting point and then moving to more subtle examples. In this chapter, I am comparing two extreme examples in order to identify characteristics associated with the two classes.

The research of the ten settings resulted in an architectural definition (described in detail below) that is framed as 48 pairs of illustrations representing the two poles institutionlike and homelike for architectural categories of housing aspects. The drawing pairs are supplemented with annotations, and a 224-item architectural checklist of associated features. To validate the interpretation, drawing pairs were separated and individual drawings were assessed by a self-selected group of psychology students who rated each illustration using a five-point semantic differential format with the poles "institutionlike" and "homelike." The drawings were then reassembled in pairs, and within each pair, evaluated using the Student T test. Ratings were found almost consistently to represent the two poles (of 32 pairs, 27 [83 percent] were found contrasting at the level of $P \leq 0.001$, and the others, all plans, had evaluations of 0.005, 0.007, 0.041, 0.044, and 0.118, perhaps suggesting more about the illegibility of plans than about the researchers' conclusions). Slides of the ten settings were rated at the same time according to the same semantic differential scale, and the ratings supported a hypothesized continuum of housing between the two poles institutionlike and homelike (see Figure 13.1).

The interpretation presented here derives from the definition of architecture described above, but the pole homelike is revised to describe the single-family residence only, rather than to incorporate apartment dwellings as in the original definition. By doing this, the opposition becomes more extreme and visible.

The primary challenge of analysis within one's own culture is to develop perspective. Everyday life can be seen as a figure-ground relationship in which the culture is ground, and the action of the moment is figure. To be able to see the nature of the ground, habitual thinking patterns must be called into question. It is primarily through dissonance with our expectations that we notice the environment (we trip on the stair, the door is an unusual color, a building is altered). The dissonance may be accidental or contrived (for example, current artistic modes and high architecture often use dissonance to make the viewer notice particular attributes). In a critique of one's culture of origin, the concept of contrived dissonance is thus essential.

For this inquiry, dissonance is used to study the cultural ground of architectural setting in three dimensions: (1) contrasting disciplinary approaches to the same subject matter, (2) comparison between two building types, and (3) contrasting descriptive approaches. In the first dimension, the principal investigator, trained in two fields, architecture and anthropology, has taken advantage of these two contrasting perspectives on the environment, that of making the environment (conception) and that of interpreting the environment (perception/cognition). The act of making the environment requires identification of the features or the categories of features that form the physical setting.

Interpreting the environment requires identification of the physical features that are relevant to the culturally anticipated action. The notion of behavior setting (Barker 1968) links these two ideas. The advantage of using both perspectives simultaneously is that each focuses on different elements. The production mode provides a listing of the myriad features that go together to create a place. And the interpretive mode allows a categorization and evaluation of the interpretive relevance and importance of features that is not possible in a mere listing of features. The final description responds to both approaches. The perceptual characteristics are described graphically and interpreted verbally. For the designer, specific features are identified in a checklist, and their integration is illustrated in pictures and the hypothesized behavioral outcome is described in the annotations.

The second dimension of the study is a comparison between settings. Building type as defined here is a fundamental category common to both the conceptual and perceptional approaches to understanding architecture, although each approach defines it differently (in architecture, building type is primarily defined by its formal characteristics whereas in anthropology it is primarily defined by activity or behavioral expectations). Documentation of the four institutional settings for mentally retarded people (a 15-person cottage in a state hospital for 1,500 people, a dormitory for 80, an apartment residence for 14, and a family group residence for 8) led to the development of the premise that housing for mentally retarded people (and by extension other housing) falls on a continuum between the two opposing poles of housing implied by the normalization principle.

The use of bipolar opposites as a way of understanding culture has a longstanding tradition in anthropology (for example, Lévi-Strauss 1971). Bipolarity as used here clarifies issues through constructing dissonance. In this study, the words used for the opposing poles evolved as the points of comparison were developed. Although the term *institutional* has continued to stand for the one pole because of its validity for both lay people (Robinson 1981) and professionals (for example, Rivlin et al. 1981; Rotegard et al. 1982), the term designating its opposite has been changed. During the investigation, *normal*, selected to stand for the ideas of the normalization principle, was rejected as not being a term ordinarily applied to housing, and was replaced with *homelike*, adopted from Rotegard et al. (1982). In this chapter, the term selected to oppose *institutional* is *vernacular*, chosen as the other extreme on the housing continuum.

The terms *vernacular* and *institutional*, applied to housing, differ from what have been used as opposites by others. Rapoport for example has developed process and product criteria that define the two categories vernacular and high style (forthcoming). His criteria for vernacular essentially match those of the category we call vernacular here. Institutional design, however, differs from high style in that the model of ideal type is seen as singular rather than multiple, and that there is a tradition of institutional buildings. On the other hand, the concept institutional expresses an idea that transcends time and could be applied to such buildings as temples which could only be called high style if one is stretching a point. In other words, the polarity proposed here is a political one. Vernacular design arises from the populace; it is generated by the user. Institutional design is imposed by the group, or by leaders, and thus stands for the dominance of group value over individual values. The contrasting settings are seen as being based in the contrasting values held by Western society for decisions made in the public as opposed to the private realm.

The last dimension of the study is that of the nature of the description, which combines use of holistic and atomistic approaches. The two categories of housing were broadly compared using architectural designations for parts of the environment: site, exterior building form, interior building organization, and room or space design. Specifically the buildings were compared using categories of spaces such as parking, front yard, backyard, entry, living room, hallways, staircases, and so on. Slides of the specific spaces in buildings which represented the two poles in the study (hospital and dormitory for institutionlike, apartments and single-family home for homelike) were compared. Architectural categories of features were used to create an inventory of features (for example, dimension; wall, ceiling, or floor characteristics; window and door openings; lighting; furniture). These were compared with behaviors found in the settings through observation, to elicit relationships between features and behavior. And last, the culturally derived categories and expectations of the investigators were probed.

The probing of investigator categories and expectations happened unintentionally but became an important investigative device. When the researchers began to communicate the findings from the observation and inventory by drawing idealized settings, they uncovered new features. The architects' conceptual category for "institutional corridor," for example (assumed to be culturally derived based on personal experience with building, literature, television, and so on) could be drawn without reference to documented places, and in the act of drawing, features apparently embedded in visual memory were elicited which had not been thought of before (for example, metal handrails in institutional fire stairs). Interestingly many of these features were in the slides but were only noticed after the drawing process called them to the researchers' attention. These new features were incorporated into three categories of description: drawings (holistic description of setting), annotations (description of hypothesized relations between setting and behavior), and a checklist of features (atomistic description of environmental features hypothesized to be relevant to behavioral differences in the two settings) (see Figure 13.2).

The parameters of this study are very limited. It took place in the early 1980s within the city limits of Minneapolis with ten selected examples of housing. Nonetheless, the American culture is assumed to be broadly shared because of cultural dissemination through the written and televised media, and so even though details about specific materials or furniture may be different in other regions of the country, or in other examples of the building types selected for study, the broad characteristics of comparison are assumed to be similar. The extent to which an investigation takes place within a narrow cultural and temporal context must be taken into account when generalizing to other contexts, but for description and analysis within the cultural confines selected, it is not a problem.

What may also be a problem for this study is the possibility of the tautological nature of study of one's own culture. The study undertaken was a biased one. Using the normalization principle, institutional housing is seen as negative and homelike settings are seen as positive. The behaviors associated with institutional settings in work by Goffman and others, and observed in our investigation were assumed to be linked in some way to the environment, as were the normal behaviors assumed to be linked to homelike setting (Thompson and Carey 1981), and those links were the basis for interpretation of the relation between setting and behavior. However, the validity of the resulting interpretation of homelike and institutionlike of both the drawings and the slides is supported by both the ability of the psychology students to evaluate them and the consistency of their assessment. The evaluations of the slides also support the existence of the hypothesized continuum between institutional and homelike.

The validity of the research now completed is being further challenged by ongoing study of thirty housing settings in which free-sort and open-ended questioning techniques are challenging the names of categories, the notion of bipolar opposition, and the particulars of the description of housing types.

Institutional and Homelike Setting: Interpretation

The underlying theme in the polarity of housing is that of control. At one end of the continuum, the institutional, control is retained by an organization of people other than residents. At the vernacular end, represented by the owner-occupied single family detached house, control is in the hands of the residents. In between lie such hybrids as multifamily dwellings, public housing, hotels, and group homes. The specific examples of built form that are used to exemplify the extreme points of the polarity are the large, isolated, traditional self-contained institution and the owner-occupied single-family detached vernacular house. Some of the salient characteristics of the traditional institution are:

1 An organization of people who are not residents owns and maintains the housing as a public service

2 The residence is a work domain for representatives of the responsible organization

3 The residents are assumed to be requiring care, thus are dependent and are served as members of a particular group with similar care requirements

4 A large number of residents are served (over 20)

The single-family detached vernacular house has the following parallel characteristics:

1 The house is owned and maintained by its inhabitants

2 Habitation is the primary purpose for the housing structure

3 The residents are a functionally independent group of individuals

4 The residence houses a small number of people (usually 1–6)

These contrasting constituent features of the two housing types are visible in the architectural forms they take and represent attitudes about the people they house.

Vernacular housing derives from ideas about habitation and community that have evolved over a long period of time. The detached house, which we see as the ultimate expression of ideal housing in American culture, is generally found as one part of an integrated community, accessible to employment, recreational, commercial, and other activities. The residence is the psychological locus of activity but is not the only physical place encountered by its occupants, who must participate in the larger community to meet their daily needs. The house design responds to the desire for maximum control by the residents. It is a domain for expression of the individual needs and desires. Its form and character are not static but can be altered to meet the changing needs of the resident.

The institution, on the other hand, came about as a result of the perceived need to isolate certain people from the established community. The needs of the group—isolated in a place designed to be inhabited twenty-four hours a day by its residents—were met by creating a self-contained community. The community was planned and controlled by some organizing group. The design of the traditional institution responds to the need to regulate groups of people, and thus to control by the organization, instead of by the individual residents. Group needs are more important than individual needs, and the decisions about what is done lie in the hands of staff. The design of the building tends to reflect staff needs as much as or more than residents' needs. The building that houses the community is designed to serve many people, thus to be durable. As a result, the form of the institution, once built, tends to resist change.

The vernacular and traditional institutional housing settings thus represent contrasting values which are assumed to be manifest in the built forms that they exhibit. These values are interdependent but for the purposes of analysis can be described as four sets of attitudes: resident control versus organizational control, autonomy versus dependence, individual orientation versus group orientation, and use of subjective versus objective criteria for environmental decisions. Overall, these may be seen as two contrasting overriding categories, that of the organization which sees itself as responsible for the care and support of a dependent group of people, and that of the individual responsible for himself or herself.

Within the context of the principle of normalization, these two poles tend to be associated with negative (institutional) and positive (noninstitutional) values, but in the larger context of society, they may be seen as neutral or reversed in value depending on the circumstance. It may, for example, be seen as more appropriate for very ill people to be cared for by an institution than to require them to be self-sufficient. On the other hand, there may be intermediate options which fall between the two polarities, or which are out of the bounds of this conceptual structure. This interpretation is therefore not *the* interpretation but *an* interpretation.

In the following abbreviated analysis of the housing forms, the elements are discussed as if they were able to be isolated. Each aspect, however, is linked to the others so that it cannot be fully understood if seen as unrelated to the whole. For example, the number of rooms and their size inevitably affect the scale of the building. The discussion is organized by formal attributes from large to small scale. This scalar relation does not reflect any sense of relative importance, but simply convenience. As suggested by Norberg-Schulz (1965, 151) and Rapoport (1982, 51), redundancy is an important part of environmental communication, and the message may be found at all scales. But as with scientific inquiry (Popper 1967) it often takes only one item out of place, such as an exit sign in an apparently typical family living room, to confuse (disprove) the message (conjecture). In sum, it is not only the content of the message that is of concern in this interpretation but also the way architectural form both carries and produces attitude by organization of space, use of materials, and furnishings.

Scale   The first noticeable difference between vernacular detached houses and traditional institutions is that of size. The typical house is designed to serve no more than six to eight people at maximum, whereas the institution, responding to economy of scale, may serve up to several thousand people, subdivided into groups of twelve to forty. The institutional building is also occupied by administrators, direct care staff, and support staff who may provide janitorial, cooking, and laundry services. But the number of people who occupy the building does not alone account for the difference in size. In general spaces are larger (for example, bedrooms in vernacular settings have 72–80 square feet per person, while institutions have 82–180 square feet per person) because of the public orientation.

Materials   Materials in a house respond first to criteria of comfort, then aesthetics, and last, durability. Although it is desirable to have things that will not wear out immediately, things such as wall and floor materials are selected as much for their ability to enhance the quality of life of the resident as for their practicality. There is likely to be choice of materials based on the use of the space. Rooms where there is likely to be water on the floor, for example, may have ceramic, linoleum, or vinyl tile. Rooms that support quiet activities may have wood or carpet flooring. If the house is small, simple materials, such as wood frame in Minnesota, are used to create the structure: the outside may be wood, stucco, or aluminum. The size of the building allows quick egress, and therefore fire safety is not a primary concern.

   The primary criteria in selection of materials for an institution are durability and safety. The building surfaces must stand up to use by large numbers of people and to standards of hygiene that require the use of harsh cleaning processes. Traditional flooring materials have been stone, ceramic tile, various forms of concrete (such as terrazzo), linoleum tile, or vinyl, or, more recently, industrial-weight carpet. With the exception of bathrooms, or places where a high level of water use is expected, the same type and color of flooring is used throughout the structure; similarly, wall, ceiling, and other materials are consistently used throughout the building. The large number of people housed in an institution makes safety considerations dominate the choice of materials. The fact that the structure must be as noncombustible as possible dictates masonry or metal construction, and noncombustible materials for ceilings and floors. Institutional buildings are thus built of brick or concrete or, more recently, metal frame and panel construction.

Context and Image   The vernacular detached dwelling in America is generally located on a street with other similar residences, sometimes including other housing types (double houses, low-rise apartments). Associated with the house is likely to be a garage accessible by a driveway either from the street or from an alley at the back. Visitors park their cars on the street in front of the house or park in the driveway. The house is most often separated from the street by a lawn which is adorned by at least one tree, different plants, and a lamp or other sculptural objects arranged primarily for aesthetic and expressive reasons. The house itself shows the many functions within it by its variety of window size and placement. The roof form may be pitched to indicate its residential nature. The image is one of general conformity in scale with the context, but with an expression of individuality in the character of the structure and the arrangement of the site materials.

Traditional institutions are typically found in isolated rural areas. But whether rural or urban, the facility is set in parklike grounds with formal entrance. One enters by car on a long driveway ending in parking lots. The building is usually visible and recognizable as a public building from a great distance, appearing like a workplace rather than a residence because of its scale, uniform size, and placement of windows and its flat roof.

Arrangement of Spaces   In the vernacular dwelling, spaces are arranged from most public to most private. There is a front of the building which houses entry and living room, and successively, depending on the floor plan, dining room, kitchen, den, recreation room, bedroom, and bathroom. The front door is the place of exchange between the public world and the private interior of the house. On the outside, as we have described, there is a differentiation of territory from the street to the front door, elaborated by distance, level changes, or changes in direction of the path. On the exterior of the front door is an area defined visually by a roof of some sort and a platform, where the visitor may ring a bell or knock and be received. Here too is where the mail may be left. The front door is assumed to be locked, or unlocked, by a resident.

On the inside, the house entry is usually defined as partially separate from the rest of the house, arranged so that the visitor cannot see directly into the house, or at least into the most private bedroom and bathroom areas. Directly accessible to the entry is the living room, which is adjacent to the dining room, which in turn is adjacent to the kitchen. These are the main public spaces. Often associated with them is a toilet closet that does not have bathing facilities. Additional public spaces may include a recreation room or den, which is typically easily accessible to the entrance but removed by level from the other spaces. Bedrooms and bathrooms are grouped and are separated from the rest of the house by level change, by distance, or by change in hallway configuration (such as narrowing of width or lowering of the ceiling).

All rooms in a house have exterior walls and windows. It is common for one or more of the public rooms to open directly onto the exterior to allow for outdoor living, generally at the back of the building. The outdoor area at the rear is set up for specific activities depending on the interests of the residents. There may be a deck or patio where barbequing is done, a vegetable garden, a swing set, a sandbox, a place for badminton, or a flower bed. The ground plane may be covered with a lawn or paved or covered with shrubs. Frequently the territory at the back of the lot is surrounded by a fence or a hedge.

In an institution, the rooms are not arranged by level of privacy but by room size (structural bay) and for fire egress (relation to circulation), and by needs for equipment (plumbing, ventilation) and control of access. As building costs are assumed to be very high, the organization of rooms is designed to enclose the required spaces within the smallest viable building volume. Required activities are designated and provided with discrete spaces (generally rooms). Circulation is defined as a separate activity (and therefore space) whose role it is to link the rooms and provide the required distance to fire egress. The best arrangement has the least amount of circulation space, the smallest amount of equipment, the smallest exterior surface, and the greatest volume for the particular site and context characteristics.

When the institutional structure is several stories high, the result is generally a plan in which the horizontal circulation spaces (corridors) are at the interior of the building, the main vertical circulation space (elevator) is at the center, and fire egress spaces (fire stairs) are at the ends of corridors, at the building edge. The entrance does not demarcate the public from the private area. As the institution itself is public in function, it is simply the territory of the institution that is demarcated by the entrance. A person at the reception desk or counter is used to filter the building users; the building itself limits use only by having access routes not apparent from the front. As the elevator is usually located in a place invisible from the entrance, a stranger can be immediately identified as the one who is confused about where to go. Since there is most likely no legible map, one must ask directions from the person at the reception desk.

The lobby in the institution, which is frequently located at the entrance, is not equivalent to a living room. It is actually a public waiting room. Equivalent to the living-room areas in a private residence, where people entertain visitors, are the lounges on the individual floor, ward, department, cottage, unit, or whatever the subdivision of space happens to be called. The route from entry to space subdivision is not usually direct and often requires traversing another subdivision. At the point of access to the subdivision is an office or desk where once again one must receive instructions or permission to enter. The organization of the subdivision is tied to the location of the elevator and the plumbing cores, which are placed centrally, always along the public circulation space. Bedrooms, offices, and other spaces that are similar in size and require windows are grouped together at the building edge.

Staff spaces, inaccessible to the resident, are not only located at the main entry point but also are dispersed according to the size and character of the available area. Lounges, which are larger than other rooms, are frequently located at the corners, often distant from the access points, which means a visitor must pass several spaces (including the bedroom and bathroom) to be received in the resident's living room. Alternatively, lounges are enlargements of the public corridor in which seating has been placed. The bedrooms are located directly off the corridor. As the need for surveillance of residents is held in high priority—the corridor design permits this—the bedroom cannot be locked from the inside, and often regulations call for the bedroom door to remain open. The bedroom is almost always shared; in traditional institutions for mentally retarded people, it is shared by three or more people.

In large institutions, access to the out-of-doors is very indirect and requires passage through corridors and elevators or fire stairs and fire doors. The outdoor areas are not designed for specific people's use as in a house, but for generalized use, with paths, benches, and possibly courts for organized group games as in a public park. Spontaneous, individual-directed use of the outdoors is thus inhibited.

Circulation In a vernacular dwelling, circulation takes place in a diffuse manner through spaces and rooms as well as in areas designated only for that purpose. In the public part of the house, there is often no defined corridor, but the entry, living room, dining room, and kitchen spaces are laid out to permit movement between and through them. In the private areas, discrete bedrooms and bathrooms usually lie along a corridor, but when a bathroom is associated with a particular bedroom, the bedroom is traversed to get to it. Similarly, access to the out-of-doors is as frequently directly from a room as from a corridor. When there is more then one level, a staircase is used for access. Because a house is small, the staircase is near all of the rooms in the house; it is usually open and creates a link between levels which unites the house. Halls and stairs are considered rooms and often contain furniture and decorations such as pictures and curtains.

An institution has designated circulation areas. In response to fire regulations, each space is designed as discrete and is located along a corridor. Where there are several levels, the main circulation device is an elevator, which is usually located in the center of the building, distant from the entry. Staircases are provided for fire safety and are located at the sides or ends of the building.

These fire stairs are enclosed by heavy doors and are designed to be noncombustible. As they are enclosed by doors which are difficult to open, they do not unite levels as do stairs in a house, but instead act as barriers between levels. Since all rooms in an institution need to have access to corridors, the overall organization of such a large number of spaces requires the use of many levels, the use of long corridors, the creation of spaces that are entirely interior (thus with no outside wall), or some combination of these. Access to the out-of-doors takes place through the designated circulation areas, most often through the front entry or else by way of a back exit off a corridor or through the fire stairs. Because the rooms are not organized by the level of privacy or by proximity of use, there are long distances between the spaces that in a house are close. To get from bedroom to bath, for example, may require going past elevators, offices, or living rooms.

Rooms In a private residence, the names of the spaces do not necessarily describe all the activities that take place there, but the nature of the space determines what happens. Therefore, the living room, which typically has delicate materials and valuable objects, is likely to house quiet activities, whereas the kitchen, finished with waterproof flooring, is likely to house more lively activities. The dining room, which has a table surface, may be used for writing or sewing. The recreation room or den, which are optional spaces, will be furnished with durable flooring, wall materials, and furniture conducive to informal and active recreation. The bedroom is not simply a place to sleep but is the private domain of its occupants, and thus will contain furniture and objects related to their interests such as books, magazines, posters, stuffed animals, radios, and stereos.

Each room in a house has a distinctive shape, is oriented in a different direction, and has windows of particular shape and placement. In addition, each room may have unique floor covering, wall covering, window treatment, light fixtures, furniture, and upholstery. For example, bedrooms, which may have the same type of furniture (bed, dresser, table, chair) are easily identifiable because the style and materials will be special. They, like other rooms in a house, are designed for maximum light and ventilation and to allow for various furniture arrangements. Thus they are usually square with a lot of exterior wall area and are frequently located at a corner to allow for cross-ventilation.

In a private dwelling, the bedroom, and sometimes a particular bathroom or den, is the territory of the individual and is under the control of its occupants, but the rest of the house is accessible to all. All residents are entitled to use all the spaces. At any time, the entire house is territory under their control.

Spaces in an institution have names that tend to represent and limit the activities they are designed for and that are supposed to take place there. There may be an activity room, a television room, a game room, and a lounge. In the bedroom, for example, the resident is only supposed to sleep. A group activity takes place in the activity room or other area depending on the particular nomenclature of the organization. As the activity designation is carried in the name, the character of the rooms may be generalized. Therefore, typically, all spaces will have similar flooring, ceiling, window shape, and window treatment, room lighting, color, and furniture style, although the room size and particular furniture (table and sink in a craft room, couch in an activity room) will vary. All the rooms are very large and of easy-to-clean materials. With the possible exception of the rooms designed for group use by residents, the rooms are long and thin with the windows and corridor at opposite ends. This is typically true for bedrooms, where the beds are placed along one of the long sides.

There are, in an institution, areas that are designated only for direct care and support staff. While the staff has access to all of the spaces, the residents are denied access to staff areas. Within the facility may be offices and meeting rooms, and in large institutions, commercial-sized laundry and kitchen areas, and special janitor's rooms.

Furnishings   The furnishings of a vernacular dwelling are selected by the inhabitants; they are not selected all at once but are accumulated gradually and answer specific needs. For this reason, few of the objects in a house may match, but each object is acquired in relation to the existing context so that it nonetheless is part of a whole. For this reason, too, objects do not wear out all at the same time but are replaced when necessary. Such things as furniture, light fixtures, curtains, and carpeting are bought for a specific place within the house and for a designated purpose. Depending on the situation, criteria of comfort, beauty, or durability will be stressed, but all must be met, and the item is judged by the people who will be using it. The flooring, lighting, window treatment, and furniture are different for each room in the house in response to the purpose, users, and physical conditions of the space.

Furniture is selected and arranged by the people who inhabit a house and is constantly in a state of flux. Residential furniture is designed to be easily manipulated. For example, the living-room furniture is most often upholstered in soft fabric and consists of a sofa, which is heavy and essentially stationary, and one to three side chairs, which may be pushed around into various positions for activities such as reading (near a lamp), watching television (all facing one direction), or holding a conversation (facing the sofa). If there are more people than these pieces of furniture can hold, less comfortable chairs may be brought in from the dining room or elsewhere in the house. The furniture also may be used to symbolize certain values, such as the importance of social interaction. In some houses, where the living room is used primarily for formal entertainment, the furniture is most often set up for conversation, in a perpetual state of expectation. Commonly there is a coffee table in the middle of the living room between the chairs, which may be used for food, magazines, or other items. If the room is large, the chairs are placed within a circle of about ten feet in diameter and stand away from the walls. This arrangement, with the limited diameter of the circle, the chairs facing one another, the coffee table in the middle, is designed to invite social interchange. That it makes cleaning difficult, or that it must be arranged at times to accommodate other functions, is incidental to the social and aesthetic role played by the arrangement.

Institutional furniture is purchased in large quantities. Because it must stand up to use by large numbers of people, it must be very strong and made with durable materials. It is purchased by the administration for the use of residents. As a rule, the furniture throughout the facility is similar, if not identical, in style. The generalized acquisition of furniture extends even to the bedroom, where each person is provided an identical bed, night table, and armoire. In the traditional institution, even bedspreads, blankets, and curtains are identical. Each resident is provided for, and all are treated alike.

Although institutional rooms are conceived of as serving particular purposes and are furnished to accommodate that purpose, the range of options is constrained because the furniture is generally very limited. For non-bedroom furniture there is a choice of one or two sizes of table, one or two kinds of easy chair, one or two kinds of sofa, and folding chairs. The style of items is similar, and the colors limited in number. Wood, which is the most common structural material for furniture in a house, is not considered strong enough for most institutional purposes and is generally supplanted by metal. Fabric for the same reason is replaced by vinyl. There is a uniformity of furniture within the institution that is in direct contrast to the individual home.

Floor, wall, and ceiling surfaces are, like furniture, treated similarly throughout the institutional building, and so the same colors and materials are found within each space. It is not unusual for lighting to be handled in the same way, with general fluorescent ceiling lighting serving all spaces.

Arrangement of furniture in an institution accommodates the designated purpose of a space as well as the need for hygiene. Each room is furnished to serve the maximum possible number of people expected to use that room at any time. It is considered undesirable to have to move furniture between spaces, and the furniture is difficult to move because of its design. Each room, therefore, has large quantities of furniture. But since it is important that the janitors can easily clean the rooms, the furniture is arranged in a regular pattern. In the space equivalent to a living room, for example, there will be a seat for each resident (unlike in a house where it is not anticipated that everyone will frequently use the living room all at once), and the seats will be lined up along the walls so that janitors do not have to move them to clean. The outcome in this type of space is that the furniture is arranged as in a lobby where the intention is to allow strangers to sit together without making eye contact. In the dining room, which is used only at specific times, the furniture may even be folded up between meals so that the floor can be cleaned after each use.

Conclusions

From this description of the relation between form and cultural values we can see that the institutional framework, once set in place, creates a structure for behavior that is compelling at a fundamental level. A place set up to be primarily a workplace and designed for supervision creates what Foucault calls "a therapeutic operator" in that it is an architecture that is designed "to transform individuals: to act on those it shelters, to provide a hold on their conduct, to carry the effects of power right to them, to make it possible to know them, to alter them" (1979 [1975], 172). Originally conceived of as benevolent, the institutional residence no longer seems so.

Society is nonetheless obliged to deal with the dependent and the sick. If the institutional setting as it now stands is no longer appropriate, what can be done? To whatever extent possible we can use the domestic setting, even though this will not properly serve every situation. It is clear, however, that mere modification of our institutional buildings will not be able to alter the basic flaws they contain which result from the housing of numerous people simultaneously, the primacy of the setting as work environment, and the control of a supervising group. These flaws—scale, organization of spaces, and materials—are embedded in the buildings. While the furnishings and the lighting may be changed, the operational aspects of the building will remain indomitable. The power of a building to delimit behavior thus creates a self-perpetuating communicative message, one that may be modified, perhaps, but not basically altered.

Building type, as elaborated here, has at least two levels of physical characteristics by which it communicates. One level is that of appearance, which by association with the more profound level, that of operative container, communicates purpose and attitude; this idea is related to Broadbent's idea of deep structures (1980 [1974]). Supporting change in the behavioral patterns associated with a building type requires more than a change in building appearance; there must be a break with past behavior and a creation of an altogether new building type.

Rapoport has differentiated between monumental buildings, which are consciously designed to impress, and vernacular architecture which is "the direct and unself-conscious translation into physical form of a culture, its needs and values" (1969, 2). In our culture, the monumental building is almost invariably a public building expressing the power of society over the individual. Instead of embodying a positive attitude about a shared and communal life, these buildings simply represent what is nonprivate.

The single-family detached house, in contrast, permits expression of individual identity and at the same time a relationship to the group. We have seen how the domain itself is organized as an elaborate transition between the public street and the most private bedroom and bathroom. The very existence of an identifiable place of habitation controlled by its residents proclaims the importance of the individual occupants. It spacially represents their place within society. The elaboration of the individual's identity takes place through the provision of quarters for special activities (carpentry, sewing, playing, gardening), and through the furnishing of space. The evolution of identity over time is recorded in the objects within the house. Virtually every object has a specific identity and a remembered individual history. The particularization of the house that takes place within the context of its expressed relation to society enables inhabiting. Additionally, personae of the residents are made manifest to themselves and to others in the act of inhabiting.

What is architecturally peculiar about institutions as housing settings is that they are designed not as communal buildings but as public edifices. Their scale, the types of materials used, the arrangement of the interior spaces, and the character of the setting are those of monumental buildings. These characteristics create a residential setting that resists the imprint of the individual and thereby precluded inhabiting the structure and organization. The arrangement of spaces, the furnishing of spaces, even the durability of the materials create an environment inflexible and uniform throughout.

People who are seen as unhealthy or deviant in this culture have traditionally been hospitalized or placed in other segregated institutional forms of housing such as prisons, old people's homes, or schools for delinquents. Unlike the house that is accessible to work and shopping settings, and requires participation of the residents beyond the residential area, the institution is a self-contained community where a resident's biological needs are provided for twenty-four hours a day. Goffman (1961) and others have described how these social and physical institutions tend to create patterns of behavior special to them and maladaptive in an ordinary community setting.

For nondeviant members of society, institutions are seen as suitable for temporary habitation only (dormitories, barracks, hospitals), because the institutional setting is basically contrary to the development of the sense of individual identity so valued for functioning in our society. The dwelling in American culture is the place of manifesting and creating identity of self, and between self and the community, and therefore, by housing people permanently in institutions that deny this activity, we are denying them their personhood, their rights to a full existence.

While consciously designed to impress, the institution as a form of housing seems to communicate unconscious messages of repression. Fundamental to the normalization principle is the awareness that every individual has the right to the development of an identity. That the institution which is inherently public and traditionally monumental negates this possibility condemns it as an appropriate form for housing.

An examination of the institution and the private dwelling draws attention to the contrast between the embellishment of the latter and the starkness of the former. Whereas the private dwelling has layers of privacy and is furbished in different ways within its spaces, each place having a definite character discernible from the others, the public building is generalized. This generalization expresses no specific message about what a community of residents might be and only alienates its occupants instead of fostering a sense of shared purpose for them.

There are many people who require care and must be looked after in ways not possible in the home. A new building type must therefore be developed to supplant the institution; it must foster the idea of community as well as individuality. Such a building type is emerging—the community residence (see Architecture, Research, Construction 1985; Robinson 1988). It is essential in developing this alternative not to unconsciously recreate the structural characteristics of the institution while only decorating it with elements associated with the private house. In the long run that would subvert the home associations and negate the original intention. The new type must emerge from a concrete understanding of how the physical environment may support individuals as members of a dynamic, mutually supportive group.

The designer, who normally unconsciously uses architecture to create "appropriate" places, is faced with the challenge of understanding not only *what* different architectural features communicate but also *how* they do so. The selection of configurations and materials must correspond to new attitudes. The complexity of the task is reinforced by an understanding that certain decisions play a key role in determining later ones, and that one dissonant feature may subvert the intended response. However, design done with an awareness of the behavioral implications of specific structural and supplementary features, combined with a concern to evaluate designs once constructed, may allow the creation of another building type which can replace the institution without reproducing its inherent problems.

Built form as artifact not only expresses the ideas held by a culture but also communicates and perpetuates them. Insofar as there are different kinds of buildings or building types in a culture, architecture can be used to indicate that there are different kinds of places—places for which different kinds of behavior may be expected, behavior settings (Barker 1968). The power of the building type as a subject of analysis thus derives from its embeddedness in culture. Unlike style, which is understood only by the formally educated, building type communicates meaning to all societal members. If building types are studied by being compared to each other, as in this study, or by being examined for change over time (King 1980), the values represented in them may be elucidated and related to formal attributes. Identifying the elements and the meanings they convey enables productive building upon or modifying of existing cultural values by means of architecture. The incompatibility between public buildings and their function as habitation calls into question the whole idea of public building as it has evolved in our culture. This suggests the need for further exploration into the nature of public buildings, not just for habitation, but for general use in a democratic society.

This chapter is based on research from two projects. "Architectural Planning of Residences for Mentally Retarded People" was supported by grants from the following University of Minnesota units: the Center for Urban and Regional Affairs, the Graduate School, the School of Architecture and Landscape Architecture, and the Department of Psychology. Participants on this project included, in addition to the author, Travis Thompson, Paul Emmons, Myles Graff, and Evelyn Franklin. "Housing Form: Empirical Description" was supported by the National Endowment for the Arts and the University of Minnesota School of Architecture and Institute of Technology. Participants on this project included, in addition to the author, Travis Thompson, Myles Graff, Julio Bermudez, Michelle Johannes, and Jan Greenberg. With the exception of the graph, made by Travis Thompson, the chapter illustrations are by Richard Laffin.

This chapter is a revised and updated version of the following: "Architectural factors in housing developmentally disabled adults" (paper presented at a symposium of the American Psychological Association, Toronto, 1984); "Cultural values in institutional and vernacular American housing" (paper presented at the International Confer-

ence on Built Form and Culture Research, Lawrence, Kans., 1984); Humanitarian
architecture: Some issues and directions *(paper presented at the University of Min-
nesota College of Liberal Arts Colloquium, Minneapolis, 1985), and published in* The
Paradigm Exchange II, *University of Minnesota Faculty and Students Colloquium
(Minneapolis: Center for Humanistic Studies, University of Minnesota, 1987); and
"Architectural settings and the housing of developmentally disabled persons," in* Aging
and developmental disabilities, *by M. P. Janicki and H. K. Wisniewski (Baltimore:
Brookes, 1985).*

References

Altman, I., and M. Chemers. 1980. *Culture and environment.* Monterey, Calif.: Brooks/Cole.
Architecture, Research, Construction, Inc. 1985. *Community group homes.* New York: Van
    Nostrand Reinhold.
Barker, R. C. 1968. *Ecological psychology.* Palo Alto, Calif.: Stanford University Press.
Becker, F. D. 1977. *Housing messages.* Stroudsburg, Pa.: Dowden, Hutchinson and Ross.
Broadbent, G. 1973. *Design in architecture.* New York: John Wiley and Sons.
———. [1974] 1980. The deep structures of architecture. In *Signs, symbols, and architecture,*
    ed. G. Broadbent, R. Bunt, and C. Jencks.
Canter, C., and S. Canter, eds. 1979. *Designing for therapeutic environments.* New York: John
    Wiley and Sons.
Cooper, C. 1974. The house as symbol of the self. In *Designing for human behavior,* ed. J. Lang,
    C. Burnette, and W. Moleski. Stroudsburg, Pa.: Dowden, Hutchinson and Ross.
Doxtater, D. 1980. The non-language of architecture. In *Language in architecture: Proceedings
    of the ACSA 68th Annual Meeting,* ed. V. Meunier. Washington, D.C.: Association of
    Collegiate Schools of Architecture.
Eco, U. 1979. *A theory of semiotics.* Bloomington, Ind.: Indiana University Press.
Environment Design Group. 1976. *Design standards: Intermediate care facilities.* Boston: Mas-
    sachusetts Department of Mental Health.
Foucault, M. [1975] 1979. *Discipline and punish: The birth of the prison.* New York: Vintage
    Books.
Goffman, E. 1961. *Asylums.* Chicago: Aldine.
Gunzburg, H. C. 1973. The physical environment of the mentally handicapped: 39 steps toward
    normalizing living practices in living units for the mentally retarded. *British Journal of
    Mental Subnormality* 10:90–99.
King, A. D., ed. 1980. *Building and society.* London: Routledge and Kegan Paul.
Lévi-Strauss, C. 1971. *L'homme nu.* Paris: Plon.
Nirje, B. 1969. The normalization principle. In *Changing patterns in residential services for the
    mentally retarded,* ed. R. B. Kugel and W. Wolfensberger. Washington, D.C.: President's
    Committee on Mental Retardation.
Norbert-Schultz, C. 1965. *Intentions in architecture.* Cambridge, Mass.: M.I.T. Press.
Popper, K. R. 1962. *Conjecture and refutations.* New York: Basic Books.
Rapoport, A. 1969. *House form and culture.* Englewood Cliffs, N.J.: Prentice-Hall.
———. 1982. *The meaning of the built environment.* Beverly Hills, Calif.: Sage Publications.
———. Forthcoming. Defining vernacular design. In *On vernacular architecture: A collection of
    essays,* ed. M. Turan.
Rivlin, L. G., V. Bogert, and R. Cirillo. 1981. "Uncoupling institutional indicators." Paper pre-
    sented to the Environment Design Research Association Conference, Ames, Iowa.
Robinson, J. W. 1980. Image of housing Minneapolis: A limited study of urban residents' atti-
    tudes and preferences. Master's thesis, University of Minnesota.

————. 1988. Design: Architectural considerations. In *Here to stay: Operating community residences*, ed. M. P. Janicki, M. W. Krauss, and M. M. Seltzer. Baltimore: Brookes.

————. 1988. Design of housing for developmentally disabled adults. In *Here to stay: Operating community residences*, ed. M. P. Janicki, M. W. Kraus, and M. M. Seltzer. Baltimore: Brookes.

Robinson, J. W., T. Thompson, P. Emmons, and M. Graff. 1984. *Towards an architectural definition of normalization: Housing for severely and profoundly mentally retarded adults*. Minneapolis: University of Minnesota Center for Urban and Regional Affairs and School of Architecture and Landscape Architecture.

Rotegard, L. L., B. K. Hill, and R. H. Bruininks. 1962. *Environmental characteristics of residential facilities for mentally retarded people in the United States*. Minneapolis: University of Minnesota, Department of Psychoeducational Studies.

Thompson, T., and A. Carey. 1981. Structured normalization: Intellectual and behavior change in a residential setting. *Mental Retardation* 18:193–97.

Wolfensberger, W. 1972. *The principle of normalization in human services*. Toronto: National Institute on Mental Retardation.

Wolfensberger, W., and L. Glenn. 1975. *Program analysis of service systems (PASS): A method for the qualitative evaluation of human services*. 3d. ed. *Handbook and field manual*. Toronto: National Institute on Mental Retardation.

Wolfensberger, W., and S. Thomas. 1983. *PASSING: Program analysis of service systems' implementation of normalization goals, normalization criteria and ratings manual*. 2d ed. Toronto: Canadian National Institute on Mental Retardation.

ALL RESIDENCES

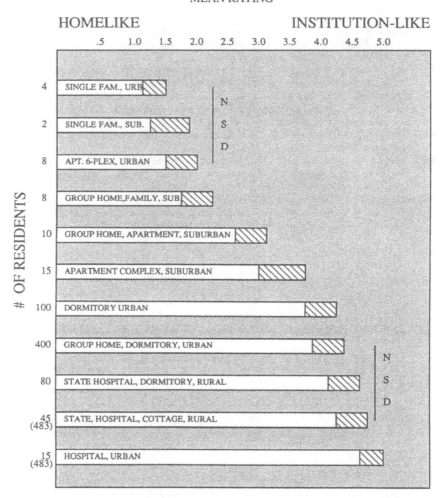

Figure 13.1. Homelike or institutionlike: mean ratings of eleven housing settings.

Institutional   Homelike

LIVING ROOM - FURNITURE ARRANGEMENT   C-7

A lounge is a room in a public building where strangers must wait together without a reason for interaction. Thus the seating is placed at the perimeter of the room to prevent eye contact and for ease of cleaning. Seating for eight or more people is generally provided in the form of several sofas and a number of individual chairs.

In living rooms, the furniture is set up to seat four or five people. The furniture is grouped for easy conversation with all chairs within a 10-foot diameter. The sofa is the focus of the room, and the other chairs are arranged around it. When there is a large number of people, furniture is brought from other rooms, or cushions are used and people sit on the floor.

	ROOM/SPACE FEATURE	INSTITUTIONAL	HOMELIKE
115.	Windows are operable in living room	no	yes
116.	Habitually, living room will seat	more than five people	five people or less
117.	There is a sofa, loveseat or couch in living room	no	yes
118.	There are more than two sofas, loveseats, or couches in living room	yes	no
119.	Seating is	placed against walls	placed variously within the room
120.	Living room seating is covered with vinyl	yes	no
121.	Living room seating is	all one color	a variety of colors and patterns
122.	Living room chairs are	all one style	in varying styles
123.	Windows in living room have	no covering or metal shades	fabric curtains or shades

Figure 13.2. Three forms of description: drawings, annotations, and architectural checklist.

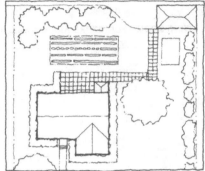
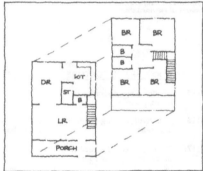

Figure 13.3. Site.

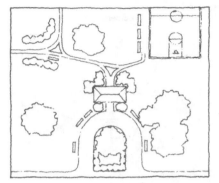
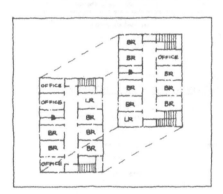

Figure 13.4. Organization of space.

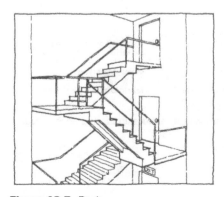

Figure 13.5. Stair.

Figure 13.6. Bedroom.

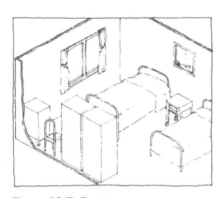
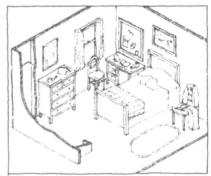

Figure 13.7. Furniture.

Figure 13.8. Living room.

14

DOMESTIC PRIVACY:
GENDER, CULTURE, AND
DEVELOPMENT ISSUES

SANDRA C. HOWELL
VANA TENTOKALI

Studies of domestic space allocations across different societies strongly suggest that applications of the concept of privacy, as formulated for Western urbanized populations, may be irrelevant, nonsalient, or ambiguous to non-Western household groups and to populations functioning according to pre-industrial rules of social organization.

Of particular interest is the current feminist literature on privacy constraints for the woman in households and dwellings (Wright 1981). Depending upon whether privacy is defined as "the ability to control information about one's self" or "the ability to create physical boundaries that exclude others" (Altman 1975), the situation in many non-Western household settings may be ambiguous. Control of information is not necessarily related to physical boundary delineation nor is the class of information to be controlled at all consistent cross-culturally. Further, the absence of boundary labels for woman's individual space could be related to the more salient need for individuals to bond with gender, in order better to access and control information relevant to themselves and the multi-age, cross-gender household in which they reside and participate in collective economic and socialization activities.

Where, in North American and European households, property ownership is available to the individual woman, albeit often jointly with spouse, privacy appears to be tightly linked with perceived proprietorship. In stem family households, which were customary in Japan and persist in many agrarian cultures, privacy of separate subgroup quarters also is associated with property inheritance (Yanagisako 1984).

Temporal factors, rather than spatial identity, may also be more salient to perceptions of spatial privacy for the individual in the home (Werner, Altman, and Oxley 1985). In the United States, the ability of a woman singularly to utilize, organize, or regulate the entire domestic space for dominant waking periods and for key domestic behaviors seems, perceptually, to offset the requirement that she share particular spaces for certain periods of the day or week (that is, sublimate her assumed preference for privacy). Such temporal gender control, however, may be a collective rather than an individual expectation in certain cultures.

This chapter discusses these new and less simplistic insights into domestic privacy with illustrations primarily from the United States, Japan, and a Muslim village in Greece.

Habitation in Cross-Cultural Perspective

Particularly in the contemporary world, culture and stage of economic development interact uniquely to influence forms of habitation. To understand the transactions of co-residents in domestic space, it is necessary to differentiate behaviors that reflect socioeconomic (or productive) status from those that appear as persistent rituals of habitation holding consistently across economic groups within a society. This is not an easy differentiation because in contemporary industrial societies the accessibility of consumer goods often penetrates the domestic environments of many socioeconomic classes.

Attention must focus on the habits of daily living within the household. Daily living consists of primary activities in which household members function transactionally. Daily living also, and importantly, contains the regularized interpersonal transactions in space that form a household's expectations. The presence of spaces within the home that appear to allow definition for these primary activities, from the researcher's perspective, may be defined in very different functional or intentional ways by households and their members. Household definitions may relate to a particular household dynamic or may reflect an underlying cultural imperative (Kantor and Lehr 1975).

In the United States, we are accustomed to viewing these differences in space use either as signs of life-style variation across families within society or as a reflection of a particular household constellation in relation to the available space (for example: the multiple uses for space necessitated by the transient presence of secondary kin such as grandparents or nephews). In other societies what may be being demonstrated is a persistent cultural pattern that is more a deeply rooted belief in how relationships and roles within a household should be conducted. Imbedded in the belief system are fast-held attitudes toward gender and age. These belief systems change with the developmental stages of the household and are also pressed by exogenous forces.

For example, an urban Japanese white-collar family asserts that they use a second "bedroom" for storage of toys and television viewing, and that the young children (four and six years old) sleep in another room beside the parents. The American researcher may hear this as a family-specific pattern and view it as an inappropriate or idiosyncratic use of available space (that is, as an undervaluing of the need for "privacy" for parents and children). Further probing within this same family may reveal that when the son is about ten or twelve, the second "bedroom" will be allocated to him for his need to study. Cross-family research of similar socioeconomic status and house plan, within the same society, shows ten- (plus or minus) year-old sons having separate spaces for sleep and study. Moving up the socioeconomic scale provides evidence that girls, once over twelve, are also provided separate spaces from parents in the Japanese home (*Shogakusei Now* 1984). The persistence of the conjoint parent-child sleeping pattern (Caudill and Plath 1974) is still in evidence across socioeconomic classes and thus suggests a cultural attitude toward socialization of children rather than a class or unique family behavior. In one professional family in Tblisi, USSR, the fourteen-year-old musician daughter was provided the second bedroom in a small apartment in order for her to have privacy to practice her piano, while the eight-year-old son slept on a sofa in the living room, opposite his grandmother, whose bed was screened by curtains. This differential valuing of privacy, in an industrialized socialist society, provides case evidence of transition from a more gender-biased cultural pattern that still pervades even "post-industrial" societies. In other daily life domains, in Japan, the Soviet Union, and the United States, such as food preparation, the woman still dominates the function and its space.

The United States and Japan can be defined as roughly at the same level of economic development. By contrast, at the more agrarian stage of economic development of a Muslim village in northern Greece, the gender and generational roles within domestic space have been differently defined. Here the emphasis is placed on domestic space in its broadly productive and economic uses. Collective, not individual, activities dominate gender and generational roles. Household production becomes an integral part of the socialization process and dominates the uses of spaces in the dwelling.

Each society interprets household transactions within space according to a cultural heritage of expectancies. At times, this cultural heritage is confronted with new models of space and expected behaviors which may be tested and accepted or rejected. The implications for current Westernizations of the

Japanese house are a case in point to be discussed later. The role of the mother (and grandmother) in socialization of children traditionally required a rather continuous monitoring of behaviors and the application of varied verbal and non-verbal reinforcements. Such socializaiton (modeling) implies, architecturally, both proximity and visual access to children's activities. Whereas an American parent might correct the child's behavior *after* discovering a malfeasance in a not visible space (child's room), a Japanese parent is most typically able to respond immediately, because of the penetrability of partitions and the small size of the household spaces.

The Household Construct

This chapter explores the relation of household function to domestic space in three distinctive societies. The term *household* has been chosen instead of *family*, because of our primary interest in the dwelling in transition, across culture. As discussed by Netting, Wilk, and Arnould (1984), the term *family* tends to preserve conceptual norms or ideal types within a given society in the face of changing values and increasingly heterogeneous behaviors across households. This structural "metaphor" seems more persistent in urban industrial societies and is heard in the wide debates in the United States about the "breakdown of the family," despite the evidently accepted and actual variations in household composition and function. Furthermore, the particular language of family definition may vary across cultures and in relation to context. The term *kazoku*, which is translated as "family" from Japanese to English, referred originally to co-residing stem structures but, in immigrant second-generation households, may refer to co-residing daughters' families or to non-co-residing children and grandchildren (Yanagisako 1984).

Households will be discussed by case; this method is considered to be the best grounded one for deriving insights about internal household decisions over time. (See Appendix for a detailed discussion of case-study methods.) The "functional elements" that determine co-residence groups, and will provide the basis for our analysis, are borrowed from Wilk and Netting (1984): (1) a common residence, (2) economic cooperation, and (3) socialization of children.

Some clarifications are needed in the use of these criteria. *Common residence* may include, at any given time, and by respondents' definition of the situation, both of the other functional elements taking place on the same site but under a separate roof. This qualificaiton will allow the inclusion of the various traditional and contemporary housing forms in many different societies. *Economic cooperation* is not limited to productive activity (as in the agrarian case in Organi, Greece), but may include more contemporary in-home business or professional activities being pursued among a growing number of urban couples in the United States and Japan (the other case societies). Productive activities also include household maintenance and rules about task roles. Household economic cooperation now more dominantly also refers to consumption decisions. *Socialization of children*, and particularly with regard to gender role, a main focus in these cases, restricted our choice of households to parenting ones. In the United States this does not necessarily limit us to the ideal "nuclear family" but may include divorced, single, widowed, or remarried-parent households. In these cases we may see intermittent co-resident children or nonrelated adults, for whom spatial and task reorganizations take place. In Japan we are, similarly, not limited to the ideal stem family where the married eldest son and his family dwell with one or both seniors. In Organi, the agrarian Muslim case, the households are, most typically, patrilineal multiple families (all married sons, their wives and children, unmarried children of both sexes, and grandparents).

Case Study Method

    The current *dwelling form*, given by plan, is the fundamental document that establishes the physical boundaries of the household for the purpose of the case study. The plan may incorporate enclosed areas surrounding the dwelling, if activities of householders are regularized in the space. The *housing history* provides a background to each household case study. Such histories are collected, both retrospectively and sequentially, during repeated visits. The information sought is about the changing composition of the household and specifically its effect on space allocations. Thus, for example, a village household reports making a one-room addition each time a newly married son brings a bride into the dwelling.

    Since the focus is on the case dwelling unit over time, former dwellings of household members are not, in this context, of particular relevance. The housing history dominantly focuses on the transactions of residents and space for a particular dwelling and household. It is an ideographic rather than a nomothetic (normative) documentation (at least until cases within a society are cumulated).

    A most complex example of such a history for one United States suburban household involved a twenty-year flow of people in and out of the three-floor dwelling with accompanying shifts in sleeping arrangements. The flow included the half-year in-residence of a frail paternal grandmother who occupied the downstairs dining room; the exit of the father due to divorce; the construction of sleeping quarters for teenage twin sons in the basement; the marriage of the daughter and subsequent two-year inclusion of the couple in the household before the birth of a child; the two-year absence of a son for military service, and his return for three years to attend college, his subsequent marriage and move to another residence; the departure of first one and then the other twin son to separate dwellings over a three- to four-year period; the resident illness and subsequent death of the youngest son at age twenty-one. The five-bedroom house is now occupied by the mother, alone, with approximately monthly overnight or longer visits by adult children or infant grandchild. The proper documentation of this history would include annotated floor plans of the dwelling at each stage of household development.

Activity sampling, in which the household members report on past and current daily practices in relation to space use is a key part of the method. Members are encouraged to expand on particular interactions within the dwelling that involve such activities as food preparation and meals, agreements and disagreements over bathroom use, television viewing, children's play space, locations for entertaining guests, and work and leisure use of dwelling space. Key celebrations and special events in space are also recorded. *Observations and incident recording* involves participant engagement by the researcher in different household activities. In one Japanese case, the resident grandmother performed a tea ceremony in her own space and subsequently assisted her daughter-in-law in preparing a small box-lunch in the kitchen for the departing guests. During the latter activity the researcher was told about and shown the kitchen-bathroom additions. In one visit to a Muslim village house the women, during the men's absence, replicated their fashion show for the researcher in the courtyard enclosure.

A *household tour* is an important source of information collected at the initial visit to the home and is subsequently used as a basis for discussing change and constancy of spatial use. Furniture mapping and photographic records are completed at this time. The household tour provides insights into attitudes toward spaces, if the researcher is attentive to comments by household members and skillfully probes on emerging issues thought to be either household-specific or culturally reflective. One example of this language of space occurred when the women of the village household politely but persistently refused to show the woman researcher the food preparation area on the ground floor of the dwelling, commenting, "You don't want to see that, it is nothing." Determining if the place where animals are kept and meats are prepared is considered unclean in this culture, or whether this reticence represented a status consciousness relative to the researcher, needed to be validated by probes of the activities specific to the space in the life of the household. By contrast, several Japanese took great pride in showing the bathing room and describing the household patterns of sequential and joint use. This is an issue that typically would have to be probed in an American household because of inhibitions about body care.

While it is technically difficult to tape-record conversations in motion, during a tour, a recapitulation of the topics that emerged during the tour can be conducted afterward in a tape-recorded, informal focused interview. "Let me understand how [or where] people usually sleep in the house" and "Tell me again, why is that the arrangement?" "You said sharing the upstairs study caused problems. Did you ever consider using any other space as a study-office? Why [or why not]?" (This last issue was probed because of the presence of an underutilized tatami room in the dwelling of a Japanese professional couple.)

The household tour is, selectively, repeated on subsequent visits to record changes made in the dwelling or changes made in the use of space, or to verify and expand on incomplete information. For example, information would be recorded about the storage of different household items, the addition of new items such as a refrigerator or second television set, and the implications of these for changing household interactions.

Case Studies

Village Households in Organi   *Oda* (room) is the primary designation for a multipurpose space in all of the household dwellings in Organi, a Muslim community of Thrace, northern Greece. The households have common characteristics, reflected in their compositon, houseform, and use patterns.

Governed by Islamic rules of household privacy, the Organi house is uniformly tucked behind a wall of nondescript and impenetrable building facade and a courtyard which is entered without visual access to the house entry.

The Organi house has two floors with four to six rooms each, depending on the number of married sons. The first floor (above ground) rooms are allotted one to each nuclear family. The ground floor rooms are rarely used as residential quarters for members of the household; they are used principally for animals, storage, and certain food preparation activities. The nonfamily rooms are occupied for various productive tasks (weaving, food preparation) but never for sleeping. When the son of family S. married, an *oda* was added and the daughter-in-law and, later, their children, considered that enclosed space as their sleeping domain and the place where their possessions were stored and displayed. Household members slept on the multirugged floor or the conjugal couple slept on a bed (a recent popular furniture item), each in their particular *oda*. When asked to explain the persistence of the practice of having children of all ages sleeping in the parents' space, the repeated response was, "This is how it is and should be." The bed, if present, is always placed tightly against the walls of a corner and, during the day, can be sat upon by any members of the household for various activities and social interaction, mainly of the women. In this sense, these spaces are not at all "private" (Figure 14.1).

Also on the main floor is a smaller space called *satzak* (life). Never used for sleeping, the *satzak* is a transition space betweeen inside and outside, closed and open, private and semipublic. This space, as well as the sleeping *oda*, contains many activities. During one visit to the S. home, the researcher was invited to join the household for dinner in the *satzak*. All members of the household (male-female, child-adult) participated, seated on floor rugs around a low table, sharing the single bowl, each with his or her own spoon.

Men are rarely on the main floor of the house during the day. The major social space for the village men is a local coffee house/general store, where women are not allowed. Children are sent to purchase needed items from the store. Men work in the fields surrounding the houses (where women also participate) and in the courtyard or ground floor performing some of the maintenance and animal care tasks (although women dominate these). The courtyard is an outside accessible space where the women may come and go without veil.

There is no word for "privacy" in the vocabulary of the Organi household. In response to persistent probing by the researcher, the women were alternately puzzled or amused by the alien idea of being alone, having time to oneself, having a place to be away from others. Conversations among the women, and with the researcher, were predominantly about men, family, and clothes (the wearing of Western clothes, only within the residential compound, is a joyful recreational activity among Organi women). Regular participation by male and female children in assigned gender-specific tasks is referred to as "play" by the women. Daughters learn the crafts of embroidery and rug and pillow making for the household and their own dowries.

The clear impression given to the architect-researcher was of the meaningfulness of collective use of space among the women. Isolation from the group seemed to imply rejection or distance from significant activities and information. Even the daughter-in-law, whose tasks were clearly subordinated to the will of the mother-in-law, and who spoke little in that household, revealed, on a visit to her family of origin, her acceptance of the delegated role within the marital household.

The important fact emerging from this case is that in this multifamily enclave no consideration has been given to conversion or expansion of spaces in order to provide more separate quarters for individuals, including, particularly, unmarried adolescents or adult children. The issue of spatial privacy is clearly not salient in this culture and not relevant to the activity patterns that dominate daily life. Temporal factors also heavily dominated the activities and the uses of both inside and outside spaces.

The Changing Face of Privacy by Gender and Generation   Mr. and Mrs. Nomura[1] designed and built a house in a Japanese suburb in 1983. In their discussions about how the house plan works for the family, several issues emerged. First is the importance of Mr. Nomura's own separate study space and its relation to the rest of the house. Mr. Nomura, a college professor, wanted to be physically insulated from household activities but still visually connected. His bedroom-study was located across from the living-dining-kitchen area. An interior window garden (*nakaniwa*) allowed visual access from his study to family activity. Mrs. Nomura, also a professional, required space for her computer and books, but she felt it necessary to be near their thirteen-year-old daughter in order to superivse her schoolwork. The daughter had been following, with her school friends, the monthly issues of the magazine *My Private Room*, and she decided it was time for her to have a completely closed room with a real door she could lock. One of her friends had such a "Western-type" room and was able to be alone and away from family surveillance more of the time. The daughter wanted her whole room decorated in pink, including a real bed with a frilly bedspread, instead of a *futon* (floor mattress). Mrs. Nomura discussed the daughter's desires with her husband and friends and read several conflicting articles about the effects on Japanese children's behavior of this "Western" separation of spaces in newer Japanese homes. The parents decided they would compromise slightly but essentially adhere to the more traditional pattern of *fusuma* (movable screens) between daughter's and mother's spaces. They also told their daughter that "for reasons of economy" in a six-*tatami*-sized room (3' × 6' grass mat) a Western bed was not possible, but carpet and curtains could be selected in pink and she could further decorate her space as she wished.

While the daily life of the Nomura family, a dual-professional couple, is in many ways different from the more typical urban Japanese household, elements of the "traditional" expectations of role and relationships remain. Atypically, the parents tend to sleep separately in their respective space: his is downstairs, hers is upstairs. This is explained as more congruent with their different schedules; he works late and she rises early to prepare the daughter's lunch and meet her morning work schedule, and his snoring disrupts her sleep. Also atypical, Mr. Nomura is a frequent participant in food preparation and post-meal cleanup. Mrs. Nomura still assumes most of the housekeeping responsibilities, however, which include daily vacuuming, dusting, and cleaning bathrooms. Each person hangs out his or her own *futon* in the morning (Figure 14.2).

Dilemmas of Space   Mr. and Mrs. Okuyama, another dual-professional couple, bought a townhouse in Kyoto in about 1980. They had one infant daughter at the time. Mrs. Okuyama was completing her graduate education, Mr. Okuyama was just becoming established in a university position.

Unlike the Nomuras, who designed their own home, the Okuyamas had to fit their emerging life-style (which is a mixture of traditional, technological, and Western) into a prebuilt setting.

The two outstanding examples of Japanese tradition in the Okuyama life-style are (1) their persistence in sleeping, on floor *futons*, with their young child(ren) and (2) bathing with their child in a deep tub. In many other ways their daily lives deviate from traditional patterns, and this is reflected in their furnishings, which are largely Western-type, including couch, cabinets, and a round dining table and chairs (located in the kitchen). They are particularly proud of a vibrating lounge chair that sits prominently in the living room, and a massive three-piece set of oak storage pieces, given to them as a wedding present by grandparents.

The Okuyamas have hung a bamboo screen between the kitchen and living room area (half-level up). They speak, somewhat uncomfortably, about the fact that the kitchen faces onto the street, where neighbors might see in during their family mealtime. In traditional Japanese houses the cooking area is at the side-back, and dining areas are invisible from the street, often visually accessing a small enclosed garden (Figure 14.3).

The Okuyamas express considerable frustration at having to share a study space. They have crowded a very small second bedroom on the upper floor with two desks, chairs, and a bookcase. A formal *tatami* space on the ground floor is described in the developer's promotional literature as "a fully independent room facing the private garden. A Japanese-type room, where you might even hear the rustling of the leaves from the common-green. It may be used as a reception room or a bedroom." In addition to its actual use as a guest bedroom and furniture storage place, the Okuyamas use it as a child's indoor play space. It had not occurred to them (as of 1982) to deploy this space as a separate, private, second office-study. In 1984 the Okuyamas had a second daughter. The reallocation of space and reformulation of household tasks were explored again in 1987. The couple still shares a study.

Family Dynamics   Before the 1978 interview the Tanaka household included the young married couple, the husband's elderly parents, and the husband's sister and her husband. They lived in a two-bedroom unit (in an apartment complex) they were purchasing from the Japan Housing Corporation.

Mr. Tanaka is a management trainee with a large Japanese firm which partially subsidizes his housing and transportation costs to the ex-urban new town in which they reside. Mrs. Tanaka is pregnant. Before her pregnancy she cared for her mother-in-law, who was disabled and restricted to a *futon* on the floor of the *tatami* room in the unit. During the period of her disability, and until the mother-in-law's death, the Tanakas slept in the living-room space of the dwelling. The husband's sister and her psychologically disabled husband occupied the second bedroom. After the death of the mother-in-law, the father-in-law agreed to sleep, on a *futon*, in the living-room area and the couple took over the *tatami* room. Subsequently the sister and her husband were separated and they both moved out. The bedroom they had occupied was then used for storage. The Tanakas have purchased a baby crib for their anticipated child. It was placed in the entry hall and is to be used as a daytime proximate controlled space for the infant, who will sleep on *futon* with them at night.

Mrs. Tanaka expressed much resentment toward the requirement that she attend to the needs of her in-laws and her husband's relatives. She had expectations for nuclear autonomy which were expressed in comments about the father-in-law and by the purchase and placement of Western dining furnishings and modern stereo equipment installed in bookshelves. A family altar in the living room memorializes the deceased mother-in-law and is juxtaposed with the Western appurtenances.

Property as Privacy and Control   Mrs. Carabini is the widow of a skilled worker. She is in her early sixties and lives with a twenty-one-year-old employed son, in an East Boston house she and her husband purchased in 1948 (Figure 14.4). Her parents and several siblings lived nearby then, and two of her other children and their families now live in the neighborhood. Her description of the house's history (as tape-recorded) included the following comments (Yokouchi 1980):

> There are three floors, all one family, all mine. This house was nothing when we bought it—we modernized everything over thirty-one years. We did it all little by little (we're not rich). Put in oil heat (was all coal) there was nothing here. He [her late husband] did a lot of everything himself, plumbing, electrical connections. I had no closets, I had this put in. We had ceiling lowered last year and I will continue repairs [started by her husband].

The woman remembers the original house:

> . . . like a dungeon; nobody took care of it; they closed doors off—we opened them. Three thousand six hundred dollars bought the house thirty-one years ago. [They added bathroom tiles and aluminum siding.] We're an average family, just working people. I live out of my kitchen—only go upstairs to do beds; kitchen is more important than living room with TV. For coffee you have to sit at a table with people. Besides, I am a baker [she used to run a bakery]. People say, "You should get an apartment now your husband's gone." No, this is all I want. Then I got the boy home.

She has three children, eight grandchildren, and three great-grand-children.

> I have plenty of room for them. It's my own, that's all I care about. At my age, where would I go? My husband's gone, where would I be? In an apartment, no, after all these years, I couldn't live somewhere else and pay the high rent. At least I put everything in this and it's mine. I put everything in this house. The house is paid for, fifty dollars a month for taxes. This is my home, I love it, I worked all these years, I wouldn't give it up for nothing. When I go down, the house goes with me. If you work hard for something, you want to hold on to it.

Theoretical Issues in Domestic Privacy

Three theoretical issues need to be further explored in future cultural research on habitation: (1) the changing and varied expressions and meanings of privacy as "control" in relation to domestic space; (2) the interactions between gender and generation as an evolutionary process relative to perceptions and occupancy of domestic space; and (3) the dynamics of "vernacular" dwelling; within-culture changes interacting with cross-cultural seepage.

The concept of "control" has referred, in Western psychological literature, to the domain of the individual. Thus, when control is used to connote an essence of privacy within the home, it is to the individual's perceptions and behaviors that attention is paid.

That this individualistic rendering of the concept of control may be culturally biased toward Western socialization patterns is argued in recent discussions between Japanese and American psychologists (Weisz et al. 1984; Azuma 1984). The Japanese severely criticize the designations of primary and secondary control as governing principles and psychosocial determinants of behavior. The Japanese claim that North American psychologists are driven by Western psychoanalytic and ego-oriented theory, which places personal gratification and reinforcement of self-identity at the core of behavior mechanisms. Socialization of the child, in Japan, stresses identity as contingent on reciprocal support and reinforcement of family and primary reference group goals (Doi 1962). The very methods for assessing "locus of control" are seen as imposing an alien value system on the Japanese respondent.

The differential domestic sleeping and bathing behaviors in Japanese and American households illustrate a significant and persistent disparity in socialization to space use. It is not so clear, however, to what extent Japanese and American households currently practice or expect gender or generational territorial control within the domestic environment. For both adolescents and the elderly, the situation appears ambiguous but decidedly relevant, judging from frequent public and private discussions.

Religion, law, and architectural rules govern privacy regulation in most Islamic cultures. Privacy is directed toward the insulation of the whole household from outside, non-kin exposure. According to Salem Al Hathout (1980) in a study of Islamic domestic law:

> The concern for privacy was reflected in the physical *plans* in several ways. Among these are the placement of doors within the street, absence of windows or the architectural treatment of them [to prevent visual penetration from the street], and the limit on building heights throughout the city.
>
> The Maliki scholars did not allow the opening of a door in front of another door or near to it. The reason given by Ibn al-Quasim (d. 191/807) was that the neighbor who owns the existing door has the right to say, "I benefit from the place in front of my door in which you want to open yours. I open my door with no one intervening on my privacy, and I bring my loads near my door without causing inconvenience to anyone. Thus, I would not let you open a door in front of mine or near to it since you may use it as a reception and entertainment area or for comparable matters."
>
> Intrusion into the private life of the residents, as we have seen, is considered to be a great damage, and if the placement of doors in front of each other was considered an intrusion that was not tolerated, then it is obvious that the residents would not tolerate being under the constant view of others.

The issue of individual control of space, within the Islamic agrarian households studied, appears to be nonsalient. But there is also an ambiguous link to either religious proscriptions on gender separation or perpetuation of socialization to gender roles, dominantly by senior females of the household. Janet Abu-Lughod (1980) suggests this ambiguity in her comments about the regulation over male-female conduct and the architectural controls to "assure female modesty" that are differently manifest in Muslim and Hindu societies. Traditional Hindu households segregate within the dwelling to secure the women from male kin. "In Islam, maximum segregation between the sexes is required outside the kin group. . . . Private (household) space is safe and secure."

A further ambiguity, which was not specifically explored in the Organi study, is that of the temporal aspects of dwelling use, and particularly of time-defined domination of interior space and decisions about appointing that space by the women in the household.

In case studies of household privacy and control in the United States, the issues are becoming particularly varied and complicated by interpretations that confound gender, class, and generational issues (Howell 1983a).

Urban working and middle-class homeowners tend to view the dwelling as truly conjoint property between spouses and to address spatial decisions within the household in the course of one or another interpersonal dynamic. Kantor and Lehr (1975) specifically address the uses of domestic space in American family transactions as a protolanguage. Perhaps because of the generosity of space and the activity-specific designations given to "rooms" (by producers and users of dwellings), household members are enabled to act out (and work out) the often ambiguous socialization rules unevenly transmitted in American society.

Gender and generational theories on the meaning of domestic space have certainly begun to emerge in the United States literature. Gelfond (1986) argues that for American suburban, not-otherwise-employed women, the perception of privacy in the home is a defense, through isolation, against the unknown threats of the commercial world. Howell (1983b), and others close to the field of aging, perceive attachment to dwelling and privacy definitions within the dwelling more as expressions of *competence* or *mastery* and to have particular relevance in the face of social and physiological losses.

There has been little theoretical discussion of how the evidently changing behaviors of American (and Japanese) women toward acquisition and retention of a dwelling are affected by employment, divorce, or widowhood.

Lebra (1979) analyzes the changing face of gender-generation interactions in Japan in terms of the exogenous social and economic forces at play against a "long-cycled reciprocity" which the tradition of filial piety requires. These forces, which include increasing employment mobility among sons and growing autonomy among younger women, pose severe conflicts in expectations among elderly women about their potential dependency and future occupancy of their own domestic space. Lebra's research shows the development of "strategies toward autonomy" among older women which include retention of economic control over the late husband's property, partly in order to assure the hiring of care inside her home if she needs it, and the assumption of the role of preserver of the "ancestral" home. Research by Lebra and others also suggests that there is a greater congeniality and reciprocity expressed between women in alternating than in adjacent generations, that is, grandmother to granddaughter. Important to our theme are the changing intra-domestic strategies of aging Japanese women, where activities within the inter-generational households are becoming more reciprocally vaired (for example, alternating responsibility for food preparation and child care tasks, where such prior household rules would have laid them fully upon daughters-in-law).[2]

The prevailing American pattern of providing adolescent daughters with their own separate space and the increasing incidence of this pattern in urban Japan may modify the perceptions and actions of future generations of Japa-nese women. One might speculate that the kitchen, in both the American and Japanese households, is already becoming less female gender-linked and that spatial separation may extend to sleeping and in-house work areas, not only due to changes in gender issues but also due to increased freedom to express performance requirements by individual members of a household.

All of these speculations are contingent on the responsiveness of housing producers to social change and to the design sensitivity of social planners to continuity and change within their culture. At present the dominant produc-tions of housing forms reflect vernacular stereotypes, stereotypic conceptions of household behaviors, or the short-term economics of multiplying dwelling units for underhoused populations. The dynamics of and variabilities in household behaviors are not now accepted as information relevant to design.

One is reminded of the Peter Eisenman house, to which design an upper-income North American couple, uninterested in children, acceded. Neither the implications of entertaining nor the process of child development was ini-tially programmed. The owners got a sociofugal dining area interrupted by an obtrusive column and a loft-sleeping area whose edge and stair created mobil-ity hazards for their later arriving toddler (Goldberger 1977).

On a broader, cross-cultural scale, the seepage of Western design and modern construction technologies already challenges household behaviors in many newly urbanizing societies. It is important that we find new ways to monitor and analyze this simultaneous change in households and habitat.

Appendix: Notes on Case Studies

The case-study method developed for this research is adapted from the principles for good qualitative research set down by Patton (1980). Fragments of case studies have been selected to represent the issues of concern in this chapter and to illustrate the content, implicit and explicit, emerging from this work. Some of the cases are the product of repeated visits (most desirable); others are in-depth retrospectives from a single visit.

Because of the difference in approach between the architect-researcher in

Organi and the psychologist-researcher in Japan and the United States, parallel formats had to be synthesized from the Organi field notes. In most of the Japanese and American cases, men as well as women are interviewed. In the Organi cases, men were not accessible to interview. In several past and in future case studies, children's perceptions at grammar school age and adolescence were and will be included. A more formal protocol is now being prepared for ongoing fieldwork in the U.S. and Japan.

Notes

1. All names are changed to respect anonymity.
2. These are sources of increasing reports of conflict in intergenerational households.

References

Abu-Lughod, J. 1980. Urban form in Arab-Muslim cities: Contemporary relevance of Islamic urban principles. *Ekistics* 280:6.

Al Hathout, S. 1980. Urban forms in Arab-Muslim cities: The concern for privacy and the shaping of the Muslim house. *Ekistics* 280:15.

Altman, I. 1975. *The environment and social behavior.* Monterey, Calif.: Brooks-Cole.

Azuma, H. 1984. Secondary control as a heterogeneous category. *American Psychologist* 19: 970–72.

Caudill W., and D. W. Plath. 1974. Who sleeps by whom? Parent-child involvement in urban Japanese families. In *Japanese culture and behavior,* ed. T. S. Lebra and W. P. Lebra. Hono, Hawaii: The University Press (East-West Center).

Doi, T. M. C. 1977. *The anatomy of dependence* (*Amae no Kozo*). Trans. John Bester. Tokyo: Kodansha International Ltd.

Gelfond, M. 1982. Agoraphobia in women and the meaning of home. In *Proceedings of EDRA* 13:348–53.

Goldberger, P. 1977. The house as cultural object. *The New York Times Magazine* (March) 20:74–78, 84.

Howell, S. C. 1983a. Women, housing and habitability. Paper presented at Symposium on Gender-Related Issues: Women in Housing, University of Washington.

———. 1983b. The meaning of place in old age. In *Aging and milieu,* ed. G. D. Rowles and R. J. Ohta, 97–107. New York: Academic Press.

Kantor, D., and W. Lehr. 1975. *Inside the family.* San Francisco: Jossey-Bass.

Lebra, T. S. 1979. The dilemma and strategies of aging among contemporary Japanese women. *Ethnology* 18:337–53.

Netting, R. M., R. R. Wilk, and E. J. Arnould, eds. 1984. *Households: Comparative and historical studies of the domestic group.* Berkeley: University of California Press.

Patton, M. Q. 1980. *Qualitative evaluation methods.* Beverley Hills, Calif.: Sage.

Shogakusei Now (*Elementary School Students Now*). 1984. Japan: Fukutake Shoten 4:8–41. (Survey of Children 10–12.)

Watashi No Koshitsu (*My Private Room*). 1984. No. 8 (October 1). Tokyo: Shofu to Seikatsu SHA.

Weisz, J. R., F. M. Rothbaum, and T. C. Blackburn. 1984. Standing out and standing in: The psychology of control in America and Japan. *American Psychologist* 19:1955–69.

Werner, C. M., I. Altman, and D. Oxley. 1985. Temporal aspects of home. In *Home Environments* 8, ed. I. Altman and C. M. Werner, 1–32. New York: Plenum.

Wilk, R. R., and R. M. Netting. 1984. Households: Changing forms and functions. In *House-holds: Comparative and historical studies of the domestic group*, ed. R. M. Netting, R. R. Wilk, and E. J. Arnould, 1–28. Berkeley: University of California Press.

Wright, G. 1981. *Building the dream: A social history of housing in America*. Cambridge, Mass.: MIT Press.

Yanagisako, S. J. 1984. Explicating residence: A cultural analysis of changing households among Japanese-Americans. In *Households: Comparative and historical studies of the domestic group*, ed. R. M. Netting, R. R. Wilk, and E. J. Arnould, 330–52. Berkeley: University of California Press.

Yokouchi, T. 1980. A study of housing modification in East Boston. Master of Science thesis, Massachusetts Institute of Technology.

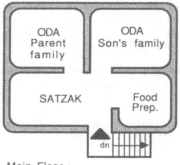

Main Floor

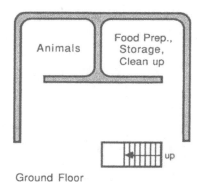

Ground Floor

Figure 14.1. Organi (Greece) generic village house.

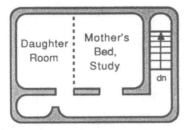

Second Floor

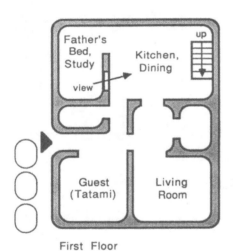

First Floor

Figure 14.2. Japanese owner-designed house (Nomura).

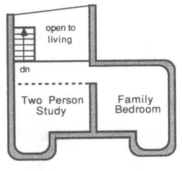

Second Floor

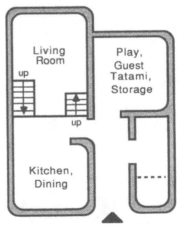

First Floor

Figure 14.3. Japanese developer townhouse (Okuyama).

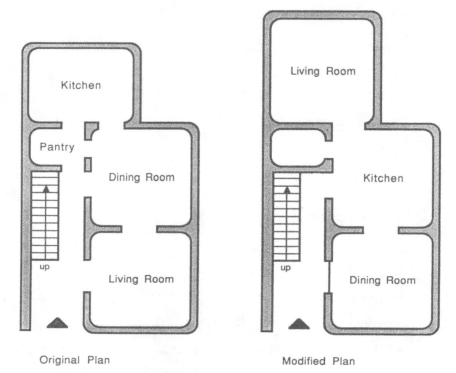

Original Plan · Modified Plan

Figure 14.4. East Boston house (Carabini).

PART FOUR

CULTURE AS INTERPRETATION

TRADITION,

HOUSING DEVELOPMENT,

AND DESIGN

Culture as interpretation refers to the interaction of the social structural, historical, and cultural meanings of the designed environment. People read and respond to space and spatial arrangements in culturally appropriate ways, using cues from the past, the present, and their perceptions of the future. From the designers' point of view, the interpretive process draws on social, cognitive, and symbolic information to create a design which emerges from the cultural setting but also adds a personal sense of "artistic" style to the cultural form. From the researchers' point of view, the interpretive process represents a new kind of analysis which moves away from positivist measurement of the environment and instead attempts to weave social, historical, and cultural elements into a sensitive understanding of a particular place within the constraints of a period of time, cultural setting, and sociopolitical reality.

This final set of chapters demonstrates how design principles can be drawn from interpretations of cultural meaning and context. Each chapter illustrates that culturally appropriate design is not simply a matter of drawing on our knowledge of the traditional; it also requires sensitivity to social and cultural change and the generation of new form and design theory. In this light, Peter Rowe demonstrates how the development of new housing in Saudi Arabia might incorporate an appreciation of the old and an accommodation of the new. He calls for a creative rather than strictly emulative approach to resolving the duality between traditional and modern approaches to design. William Bechhoefer's study of the evolution of housing in Kabul, Afghanistan, presents an example of how housing built by one cultural group can be reused and adapted by subsequent residents from different cultural traditions. His chapter also demonstrates the remarkable degree to which housing adaptations might occur without professional design intervention. Eleftherios Pavlides and Jana Hesser derive vernacular architectural principles from their sociolinguistic fieldwork on social change in a Greek village. Their chapter, which attributes changes in traditional housing form and style to distinct historical periods, reveals a part of the diversity to be found within single cultural traditions of design. Jon Lang provides a review of the cultural pluralism, colonial traditions, and syncretic processes that characterize Indian housing as a basis for his critique of the limitations of current housing policy and architectural development. This part concludes with Mario Noriega, Wren Rogers, and Ignacio Restrepo's case example from Bogotá, Colombia. Their argument is that the culturally appropriate design of housing must begin with an appreciation of the larger urban environment.

These studies all link cultural housing traditions to the development of house form, urban design, and development policies. Although they employ distinct research methods and theoretical frameworks, their conclusions reinforce one another and support the contention that successful culturally appropriate design solutions are informed by an understanding of the cultural context but also require the creative interpretation of the researcher, designer, and policy maker.

In different ways, each of the chapters in this part point to what might be an appropriate conclusion for this book. They demonstrate that simply understanding cultural differences and how these have been manifest in design principles, though an important first step, is not enough to insure effective design in the future. Culture is not static; it is represented by a process into which various interpretations might be offered, negotiated, and realized. Adherence to principles of culturally appropriate design need not inhibit the designer; indeed, these authors argue that such principles call forth the need for imaginative and dynamic solutions to design problems.

15

DUAL ASPECTS OF TRADITION
IN SAUDI ARABIAN URBAN
HOUSING DEVELOPMENT

PETER G. ROWE

Contemporary urban housing development in the Kingdom of Saudi Arabia presents a paradox and offers interesting insights into both the role of tradition in shaping settlements and the appropriateness of methods for transforming and assimilating foreign design influences. On the one hand there is a deeply felt need to reaffirm traditional values and a sense of national identity continually. On the other hand, there is a strong continuing commitment to the use of modern Western technology. So far, both public policy and private entrepreneurial investment have been weighted heavily in favor of modern development, and as a result there have been profound transformations of the city away from traditional urban-architectural conventions.

Apart from presenting an overview of housing and urban development in Saudi Arabia, I will argue that this paradox becomes pronounced only at moments when both traditional practice and strivings toward modernism operate in reduced and stereotypical forms. To survive, tradition must cope with the inherent dualism presented by the paradox and provide direction for contemporary circumstances as well as continuity with the past. Furthermore, this is a situation where matters of urban and architectural expression and design become important. Rather than adopting building processes which seek to merge or accommodate the old with the new, approaches must be found that transcend such differences in origin.

Discussion proceeds from a brief outline of the geographical and historical context of Saudi Arabia to an examination of the surface physical features of traditional settlement patterns. Beneath this surface reading is an attempt to uncover relevant culturally based principles and conventions which structure the urban landscape. The processes of modern urban development mark a sharp break with the past and draw heavily on post–World War II Western models of planning and architecture. Instead of undergoing critical temperance as they did in the West, such models have been maintained largely in their original form. Several explanations for this rejection of traditional practice can be advanced and are central to discussion of the role of tradition as it copes with the apparent dualism of modern progressive aspirations and established values.

Throughout this chapter, the level of discrimination of housing populations, urban issues, and so on remains general because of problems with the availability of reliable data and because of the shortage of space here. Certain biases of a foreign observer are no doubt included, although attempts have been made to search for alternative interpretations on more speculative points.

The Context

The Kingdom of Saudi Arabia covers most of a large peninsula between the African and Asian continents. With a land area of about one million square miles, the kingdom is roughly 30 percent of the size of the continental United States. It is predominantly an arid region, transected by four climatic zones, ranging through hot-dry, hot-humid, composite, and upland (Talib 1984). The country is dominated by mountainous regions in the west, which form a backdrop to the coastal plains along the Red Sea and then graduate down in the east to flat coastal areas beside the Arabian Gulf (Bindagji 1980). The desert area of the Rhub al Khalil, or "empty quarter," occupies much of the country's southeast and accounts for about one-third of the total land area. Having emerged through the mountains from relatively verdant plains and *wadis* in the west, ancient travelers trekked east, in a manner similar to their modern counterparts, along desolate caravan routes from one oasis to the next. Contrary to much popular fiction, such respites took place in large and extensively cultivated areas, such as Al-Hasa and Al-Yamama, with grove upon grove of date palms and assorted gardens (Lawrence 1983). The population of Saudi Arabia is concentrated in major cities, towns, and habitable agricultural areas. Estimates vary, although reliable sources place the population at about 7–7.5 million nationals, with an additional several million expatriots (El Mallakh 1982). The natural growth rate appears to be about 2 percent a year, moderate by comparison to many other developing countries (El Mallakh 1982; Davis 1971). Migration from rural to urban areas has been extensive and accelerating over the past few decades. This has resulted in sizable urban concentrations around Mecca, Medina,

Jeddah, and Taif in the west, Riyadh in the center, and the Dammam, Dhahran, Al-Khobar metropolitan area in the east. In 1974, according to one source, approximately sixteen towns had populations in excess of 30,000 people (Al-Madani and Al-Fayez 1976). However, about 20 percent of the population, harkening back to earlier tribal beginnings, remain largely nomadic (El Mallakh 1982). In fact, until recently, certain tribal qualities of the population in the form of tight kinship patterns, domains of influence, and autonomy were more common than not.

The history of Arabia is long, varied, and rich in its dynastic development (Ochsenwald 1984). However, a significant watershed for the modern era occurred in about A.D. 1901–2 (A.H. 1318–19) with the onset of battles between the rival Houses of Saud and Rahseed that culminated, in 1932, with the unification of the kingdom under Abdul Azziz Ibn Saud (Lacey 1981; Almana 1982). This period of armed conflict, taking place when it did, can be described as a civil war, as a war of unification, and as the ouster of the Ottoman regime and its remnants.

Prior to the hegemony of the House of Saud, there was little to no urban development in what is now Saudi Arabia, with the exceptions of the holy cities of Mecca and Medina and the seaport of Jeddah (Al-Farsy 1982). In Mecca and Medina, the *Haj*, or pilgrimage to the holy shrines of Islam, also resulted in a variation in annual population, which has now grown to the level of about 1 million people. Historically, Jeddah has been the principal seaport and place of embarkation for the *Haji* (Pesce 1977). The population in other centers, such as Al-Hasa, although large, was dispersed in smaller towns and villages. For example, some estimates as far back as the eleventh century (A.D.) place the population of the Al-Hasa area between 120,000 and 150,000. However, in the account of Nasiri Khusrau, a Persian traveler of the time, "Al Hasa refers at one and the same time to a town, a region, villages and a fortress" (Lawrence 1981; Al-Farsy 1982).

The impeteus for modern development and a different kind of international prominence came to Saudi Arabia with the discovery of oil in the Eastern Province by Standard Oil of New Jersey (now ARAMCO) in 1932–33 (Lacey 1981; Al-Farsy 1982). However, it was not really until the 1950s and 1960s that development pressures began to be exerted. Crown Prince Faisal Ibn Abdul Azziz took the throne in 1958 following the death of his father Abdul Azziz Ibn Saud in 1953 and the diffident reign of his brother Saud Ibn Abdul Azziz. He then embarked on a strong and at times delicate campaign to redirect the kingdom's modest though developing resources toward a program of modernization. It was a program aimed principally at improving the welfare of his subjects, although it was also aimed at coaxing many of them into the twentieth century (Lacey 1981). One fairly immediate consequence of successful oil exploration and its associated economic development was rapid urbanization. In any context the rates of change brought about by this process are very high. For example, the settlement of Riyadh, which was barely several hundred meters across during the war of unification, emerged as a city of 600,000 by the early 1970s (El Mallakh 1982). Dammam, near the locus of the oil activity, sprang from a small sleepy town on the Arabian Gulf to a prominent city in the same time period. In fact about 90 percent of all the housing in Dammam is now only twenty years old and roughly 35 percent was built in the last five years or so (CH2M Hill Int. 1976). Al-Khobar is now a modern city where only a small coast guard station once stood. Generally, the rate of urbanization has been running at from 10 to 12 percent a year (Boon 1981), and even during the current downturn of oil prices it has hardly slowed.

Traditional Patterns of Settlement

In common with other cultures, the spatial domain of traditional Arab-Islamic settlements provides an elaborate "text" of formal and figural expressions. Throughout, exceptional features embellish and intermingle with more invariant and prosaic elements. Both conspire to create and qualify urban sensibilities of home, place, and community.

A surface reading, as it were, of this "text" material reveals several outward manifestations and expressions of these sensibilities. Highly decorated surfaces are often found around doorways both to mark the place of entrance and to welcome visitors. Especially in confined urban settings, there is a prolific use of screening devices (*shish* or *rawashin*) over windows that intrude into the street (Figure 15.1). Although the primary purpose of these devices is the preservation of a sense of privacy and seclusion from the outside world, the traditional screened bay window, or *mashrabiya* (Earls 1981), also once served the purpose of shading a large water vessel and allowing breezes to cool its contents.

A use of indigenous materials, such as mud brick and stucco, combined with a practical yet inventive reckoning with climate, gives the architecture a uniform yet distinctive appearance. For example, in the mountainous Asir region of Saudi Arabia, sloped walls formed of mass mud-brick construction are intersected by horizontal bands of flat stone pieces projecting from the surface. In an area prone to violent storm events these bands serve to deflect precipitation and thus protect the wall from erosion (Talib 1984). By contrast, the prominent wind towers and ventilating wall systems, once commonly found in the hot-humid coastal regions along the Arabian Gulf, captured sea breezes in an attempt to moderate the interior conditions of the house (Figure 15.1). The predominant urban use of compact, closely spaced mass forms is a response to diurnal fluctuations in temperature and minimizes the amount of unshaded surface area (Talib 1984).

Urbanization is typically marked by aggregation of small public and semi-public spaces intricately woven together. There is a consistent use of private courtyards and gardens, with an emphasis on enclosure and a precious use of water and natural vegetation. Public buildings, such as markets (*suqs*) and mosques, often employ a repetitive use of distinctive arch forms. The mosques are marked by towers or minarets. Throughout, there is a strong sense of enfolding and protection which simultaneously sets the community apart and integrates its inhabitants more closely together (Hakim 1986a).

When viewed from the distance of time, settlements exhibit a seemingly organic record of growth and change which might be sharply contrasted during many epochs with the more rational urban order of the West (Figure 15.2). Invariably, there is at least a tri-fold division of space, ranging from very private, through controlled semiprivate, to public (Alohali 1983). Again this characteristic can be contrasted with the common Western proclivity toward a bi-fold division of space. Finally, there is a lack of differentiation of urban form into separate and distinct land uses. On the contrary, a community is usually a highly despecialized dwelling environment (Hakim 1982).

However, as Abu-Lughod and others have noted, one cannot speak of Islamic cities in the same sense as modern new towns or colonial towns of one regime or another (Grube 1978; Abu-Lughod 1983). There was no such thing as a standing "blueprint" that could be imposed on an indigenous population. Instead, Islam expanded into otherwise culturally heterogeneous areas with different social traditions and forms of architecture (Abu-Lughod 1983). As described earlier, even within the relatively homogeneous cultural confines of the Arabian peninsula, factors such as climate and material availability can produce significant differences in architectural expression. Furthermore, like other great religious and philosophical movements, the hegemony of Islam was absolute across moral, ethical, and related social dimensions of life but allowed looser interpretations to be made elsewhere (Hakim and Rowe 1983). The result has been a considerable diversity and wide regional variation in local urban-architectural idioms. On the other hand, however, amid all this diversity and variation, one is always somehow aware of being in an "Islamic city." There seems to be something distinctive about the experience that suggests fundamental principles are at work, giving rise to common urban-architectural conventions (Abu-Lughod 1983).

Without doubt the common sense of social contract founded in Islam makes itself felt in the built environment (Abu-Lughod 1983; Akbar 1984). Interpretations of specific injunctions from the *Qur'an* and *Sunnah*, such as the respect of privacy and the concept of unselfish interdependence among people, into modes of development, property rights, building regulations, and architectural conventions are clearly evident (Hakim 1982). As Hakim notes, the *Fiqh*, or science of law based on the *Qur'an*, had developed by the year A.D. 900 into a comprehensive literature, a branch of which dealt specifically with damages prescribed by building activities (Hakim and Rowe 1983). *Fiqh* manuscripts from the fourteenth century (A.D.) were often extremely elaborate in the guidelines they provided to master masons and builders. For example, the maintenance of exterior walls of dwellings in sound structural condition and well-preserved appearance was directly equated with the encouragement of individuals to behave in a responsible manner on matters affecting community well-being. In short, basic questions of settlement responsibility were addressed leading to the codification of building conventions and preferred practices (Hakim 1986a).

The traditional mode of subdivision granted space to a tribe, or kinship group, and allowed the group autonomy within the space on most matters of further land subdivision and building development. A clear manifestation of this practice is the cellular form of additive development in an Arab-Islamic settlement where each cell, so to speak, contains a distinctive social domain (*hara*), the extent of which might vary. Nevertheless, according to the *Hadith* (sayings of the Prophet) the sense of responsibility and special relationship between proximate neighbors extends to at least seven on either side. On the matter of finding a place to live, one is also directed to find ten or more friends and then to settle (Talib 1984).

Another consequence of this mode of development is the overall primacy that is given to the residential district within the urban landscape. Public buildings are often located in residual spaces between and among communities. Major roadways are of secondary significance and frequently respect the irregular edges of residential enclaves (Alohali 1983; Abu-Lughod 1983). Vehicular transportation was far less pronounced and influential on the space required for circulation than it is today. However, these passages between community domains were also regarded as a kind of "frontier" on the one hand and a "neutral turf" on the other. They were clearly the edges of the community but also the places of broader social interaction, exchange, and marketing (Abu-Lughod 1983).

Unlike the West with its strong emphasis on "freehold" forms of property tenure, Arab-Islamic settlements typically incorporate complex and highly refined divisions of property rights (Akbar 1984). There are usually many versions of the "right of easement" and rental tenure. There is extensive use of the concept of a usufruct, whereby one has the right to enjoy another's property short of its destruction, and there are the pecularities of trusteeship (*waqf*). Furthermore, buildings, rooms, and furniture are subject alike to the same treatment (Akbar 1984).

Underlying these practical conventions can be perceived strong tendencies toward the sharing of space and other resources, a nonproliferation of nuisance, and a basic respect for local concerns. Nowhere are there attempts to engage and interfere in the life and circumstances of distant co-residents of a settlement or urban area. Consequently, Western-style notions of zoning, whereby decisions about the distribution of uses are made by residents on everyone's behalf, were not generally practiced. Fundamentally, public health, safety, and welfare was considered a local issue under the general guidance of a common yet tacit form of social contract (Al-Hathloul 1981a; Akbar 1984).

Perhaps the most significant set of conventions at work in Arab-Islamic settlements derive from the pervasive sense of privacy for family and related matters of gender separation. Anywhere other than in the most private realm, at least the visual aspect of gender separation is absolute. In Saudi Arabia, women appear in public fully veiled and are usually escorted. As we shall see later on, the private dwelling is sharply divided into male entertainment quarters (*majlis*) and the family living area. In traditional settlements, the transition between the living quarters of the dwelling and the larger community domain is both subtle and practical. Typically, semiprivate urban spaces, often consisting of short cul-de-sacs (*atfa*), provide a zone that affords a family the opportunity of avoiding unwanted contact (Al-Hathloul 1981a; Talib 1984). It also provides space for unencumbered children's play and warranted social interaction. More often than not these spaces are intricate networks conforming to age-old irregularities in property lines and radiate out from the center of a community to public streets. The strict adherence to visual privacy for the family also precludes any overlooking of a neighbor's property. Thus the uniform building height that is so characteristic of Arab-Islamic towns is as much the outcome of social conventions as it is the outcome of technological limitations and pressures for development.

In summary, behind the flourishing of regional diversity can be seen the "guiding hand," as it were, of urban-architectural conventions and building practices which are direct expressions of fundamental interpretations of social responsibility. Although these conventions and practices were often codified from specific decisions made for specific cases, they also involved tacit dimensions that avoided the necessity for such explicit arbitration (Hakim and Rowe 1983). Throughout, administrative procedures of community building concentrated on localized events and opportunities. Rarely were requirements promulgated "across the board."

Similar principles and conventions can also be seen at work in the conformation of dwelling units. In the Kingdom of Saudi Arabia there are at least four traditional housing typologies (Al-Hathloul 1981b). They are: (1) the rural house, which has sometimes become incorporated into urbanized areas; (2) the "Medina House" with its centrally placed open courtyard and relatively high rise; (3) the "Qa'ah House" with a covered courtyard reception area at its center; and (4) the "Mashrabiyah House" with its row-house configuration and distinctive projecting screens. The Mashrabiyah House is sometimes referred to as the "Makkan House" from the city of its origin (Fadan 1983a). Throughout there is a practical reckoning with available materials and climate. For example, the organization of rooms in the Medina House, around the tall column of space which forms the interior courtyard, enhances air circulation through the stack of adjacent rooms. By wetting the surface at the base of the courtyard even higher levels of comfort can be provided (Talib 1984). In most parts of the kingdom the solid construction exploits properties of heat gain and re-radiation.

Nevertheless, the spatial organization of the house also strongly reflects social customs, especially the matter of privacy and gender separation (Figure 15.3). The predominantly male quarters for reception and entertainment, or *maq'ad* and *majlis*, are entered directly from the street through a door or gateway vestibule, adjacent to which is provided a bathroom area for performing ablutions. The main room of the *majlis* is furnished around the walls in a manner which allows face-to-face contact for all. Consequently, it has a central orientation although it may be well lit from surrounding exterior walls. Some reception areas incorporate dining areas off the main sitting area and, in all cases, there is a fairly direct private relationship to a kitchen or food preparation area. The family quarters usually share the same building as the *maq'ad* and *majlis* but are largely separate and distinct. Included within this realm are all the other rooms of the house such as bedrooms, bathrooms, kitchen, storage areas for provisions and family living rooms. Most often the courtyard, where present, is part of this configuration, and outdoor sleeping areas can be found within screened roof terraces for use during summer months. As mentioned earlier, the family quarters have a separate entry and entry vestibule usually opening on to a minor cul-de-sac or small passage within the community (*atfa*) and thence into the public realm of the street.

The responsibility for insuring privacy can also be seen in the exterior configuration and embellishment of dwelling units. Doorways are deliberately placed so as to avoid direct confrontation with dwellers from neighboring units across a street or passageway (Al-Hathloul 1981b; Akbar 1984). Orna-mented screening devices are similarly employed to surround windows and open-roof terraces, particularly where the rough equivalence in building height is transgressed for other reasons of accommodation.

Addition and renovation of dwelling units within a community typically take place in an incremental, shared-wall fashion. During periods of early de-velopment, such practices are economical and climatically responsive, be-cause they take advantage of existing structures to form part of a dwelling's enclosure and to provide needed relief from direct isolation. Within more ma-ture communities the practice also allows the need for expansion and the pe-culiarities of property ownership to be flexibly accommodated, particularly under such a broad mandate of neighborly responsibility. Complete bridging between buildings across a street is not uncommon, nor is the interstitial sub-division of blocks, although easements for public rights-of-way are usually preserved in place or substituted by a closely approximate route (Akbar 1984). Throughout, however, the topology of the spatial organization of dwelling units is maintained, regardless of site irregularities (Talib 1984). This com-pliance further underlines the role of custom, rather than local technical con-straints, in shaping the dwelling environment.

Finally, the underlying urban-architectural conventions that facilitate prevailing concepts of social contract, together with indigenous technological considerations, give rise to an urban landscape of considerable complexity, beauty, social harmony, and cohesiveness (Pesce 1977). Typically, simple overall formal compositions are animated by variegated patterns of fenestra-tion, screened balconies, and other ornamentation (Figure 15.4). This is par-ticularly apparent in the Syrian Quarter of Jeddah, for example, and in the notable residences of other towns (Figure 15.5). A bustling street life brings with it a multiplicity of uses, a comfortable sense of community, and an al-most timeless quality to daily experience.

Modern Developments

As mentioned earlier, modern housing and urban de-velopment in Saudi Arabia has been dramatic and conspicuously marked by an importation and transposition of Western practices. The consequences, however, for traditional settlement have not always been positive, despite the great strides that have been made in other dimensions of life.

During the late 1940s and early 1950s several events gave strong direction to the modernization of housing and urban development in Saudi Arabia (Al-Hathloul 1981a; Fadan 1983b). In 1947 the government of the Eastern

Province, in Al-Hasa, requested the assistance of the Arabian American Oil Company (ARAMCO) for the planned expansion of the neighboring towns of Dammam and Al-Khobar (Al-Hathloul 1981a). Subdivision plats were prepared by ARAMCO surveyors and engineers in the form of a uniform gridiron layout coterminus with the old settlements (Figure 15.6). By 1952 Dammam had become the provincial capital, incorporating about one thousand acres of development and a population of about twenty-five thousand people. Almost half of these totals resulted from the cooperative development between the local municipality and ARAMCO (Hakim (1986b).

Al-Khobar was the first community in the kingdom to be totally planned from the outset. An orthogonal gridiron plan was layed out, again with the assistance of ARAMCO surveyors, running parallel to the shoreline of the Arabian Gulf. Several major axes were incorporated in the form of broad tree-lined boulevards, and a Western hierarchy of commercial and neighborhood streets was defined to accommodate the exigencies of rational traffic movement (CH2M Hill Int. 1976). On the whole, the development of Al-Khobar incorporated much of current Western planning thought and was widely regarded within the kingdom as a model of "modern planning" (Figure 15.7).

Another such model development was prepared in 1953 for the capital city of Riyadh (Fadan 1983b). Following a decision to move government agencies from Mecca and to locate them along the airport road, the need arose to provide housing for government employees. The resulting community of Al-Malaz was located 4.5 km from the center of Riyadh and, by the time the transfer took place in 1957, included about one thousand dwelling units, of which about 20 percent were in the form of apartment blocks. The development plan incorporated a public garden, a municipal hall, and several other public facilities including the first buildings of the university (Fadan 1983b). Again a uniform grid of rectangular blocks (100m × 50m) was platted across the five hundred hectares of land, with typical housing lots in the order of 25m × 25m. The overall density of development by traditional standards was extremely low (20 percent) and once again reflected in all respects the modern town planning idiom of the time (Hakim 1986b).

The profound effect that these planned modern communities were to have on the kingdom's development can be attributed to several causes. First, the projects were sponsored by government authorities as explicit statements about how modern residential neighborhoods should be planned. Furthermore, in Al-Malaz, the desirability of the modern proposal was reinforced through the housing of government employees, an emerging elite within the social structure (Fadan 1983b; Hakim 1986b). Second, a conspicuous effort was made to incorporate new building techniques, materials, and practices as a demonstration of what could be accomplished within the kingdom in keeping with international trends (Hakim 1986b). In short, the communities offered an alternative vision that was entirely consistent with other parallel efforts to modernize various aspects of Saudi life.

Another series of events that gave strong direction to modern urban development were instrumental accompaniments and extensions of these physical models. In 1951 the ARAMCO Home Ownership Plan was initiated to provide loans for employees to build housing (Arabian-American Oil Company 1968). Specifically, under this program ARAMCO provided interest-free loans for use within cooperatively planned and developed communities, such as those in the Eastern Province. The employees could then acquire sites and select their own architects and contractors. However, the relative lack of professional expertise within the kingdom resulted in the development of a catalog of standardized designs for single-family houses, largely by foreign architects (Hakim 1986b). These practices, although with increasing Saudi Arabian professional participation, were to continue. By 1974 the Real Estate Development Fund (REDF) had been created by royal decree. Its explicit purpose was to "encourage the private sector to build for residential and commercial purposes" (El Mallakh 1982, 308). Under this program loans of up to 50 and 70 percent of development costs could be advanced, subject to the approval of building site, purpose, and so on.

The fund has subsequently become the largest grantor of loans among the institutions dealing with specialized credit within the kingdom, so much so that in the Third Plan for national development (1980–85) the REDF is scheduled to finance about 50 percent of all new housing construction (El Mallakh 1982). Again, the parallels with Western financial and adminstrative control mechanisms are apparent.

A further manifestation of modern planning was the wholesale adoption by municipalities of comprehensive zoning plans and related ordinances as the primary means for directing urban growth. Often prepared with extensive participation by foreign consultants, these plans imitate Western counterparts in almost all respects. Land uses, subdivision layouts, lot sizes, and building setbacks are firmly established and gauged to produce housing environments that coincide with a modern suburban and urban view of development. For example, most single-family housing has setback requirements insuring detachment of units and a singularity of land use. Contrary to many earlier practices, the ordinances hold for entire urban areas, thus extending the role of responsibility from one's immediate neighbors to the entire city populace.

The final set of events that have shaped the urban development of Saudi Arabia are perhaps the most inclusive and pervasive. By the late 1960s and early 1970s, massive rural to urban migration produced rather severe shortages of adequate housing. These shortages were further exacerbated by infrastructural deficiencies which caused supply bottlenecks, and by the consequences of economic inflation (El Mallakh 1982). The onset of shortages also coincided with a rise in general expectations about standards of modern living.

The magnitude of these shortages is amply illustrated by statistics from the national five-year development plans (El Mallakh 1982). They also further emphasize the rapid rates of urban development in a comparatively small country. For the period of the First Plan (1970–75) some 75,000 dwelling units were produced against an estimated demand of 154,000. During the second period (1975–80) the rate increased dramatically to about 40,000 units a year, although it fell well short of the demand estimate for a total of 338,000 units. For the Third Plan (1980 and on) the target has been increased still further.

The distribution of housing units among the population also appears to have been problematic. One report cites substandard housing conditions at as much as 50 percent, the rule rather than the exception for lower-income families (El Mallakh 1982). After a period of stable prices between 1964 and 1972, annual inflation rose from 2.4 percent a year to 18.9 percent for the period 1973 to 1978. Although this trajectory was turned around in 1978, the negative impact on lower-income development was considerable (El Mallakh 1982). Furthermore, particular inadequacies in supply produced an inflation rate of about 25 percent in the housing sector during this time of rapid urbanization, significantly higher than for a general "basket of goods" (El Mallakh 1982). Recently the public sector has responded with an emphasis on the provision of lower-income housing, including high-density developments and "serviced lots" (Ministry of Planning 1980). However, the supply of housing remains a national problem.

Modern housing and urban development in Saudi Arabia has taken on many forms, including high-rise apartment and commercial buildings, independent institutional building complexes, mid-rise apartments, public housing projects of various forms, single-family villa subdivisions, and even some informal "shack settlements" (Rowe (1984). As mentioned, the layout of contemporary urban settlements is invariably regular, usually incorporating a grid-iron pattern of streets with a distinct vehicular orientation. In comparison to traditional settlements, typically there is less land coverage. Housing densities, especially in residential subdivisions, are significantly diminished. Generally, open space within the urban fabric is more abundant, although far less well differentiated. The distribution of land use tends toward singular designations and is less mixed in any given area than earlier counterparts, while remaining in the aggregate much the same. In short, the urban landscape is distinctly modern and Western (Figure 15.8).

Villa subdivisions, reminiscent of single-family tract housing in the West, is popular and occupies a prominent position in both public and private residential developments. During the past fifteen years, probably 75 to 80 percent of housing development has been of this general form. The density of typical villa subdivisions is on the order of fifteen to seventeen dwelling units a hectare, or roughly half the density of traditional settlements (Boon 1981; Rowe 1984).

Despite the modernity of these developments, many of the traditional urban-architectural conventions have been sustained. Requirements for family privacy are preserved through the two-part division of the unit into *majlis* and family quarters and through the provision of separate means for entry and egress. Similarly, exterior gardens and terraces are also subdivided and screened by the use of walls. Building heights are generally uniform and the exterior fenestration is screened by the use of shutters or equivalent devices. In keeping with the traditional figural treatment of facades, decoration is abundant around main entrances and other openings. However, in contrast to the relative uniformity of earlier forms of architectural expression, styling is often idiosyncratic, profuse, and opulent. It seems to have become more a matter of individual taste and a demonstration of personal status and well-being than an expression of modesty and community cohesiveness (Figure 15.9).

In certain other regards, villa developments also diverge markedly from the usual conventions of traditional building. Under the ambit of subdivision regulations prevailing height and set-back restrictions effectively deny the formation of connected forms of housing and thus cause some loss for both passive climate control and the visual vitality of the street. This pattern of development also tends to discourage any despecialization of the residential land use over time; a transformation that has often done much to improve the retail convenience and amenity of neighborhoods. The dominance of the roadway system, rationalized from the outset to carry vehicular traffic, practically reverses the traditional morphology of building and street. Here it is not automobile use as such, but its deliberate and untempered use that undermines traditional conventions (Hakim and Rowe 1983). However, one might also argue that one of the consequences of modern development and its technology is an upward change in scale that still affords much the same convenience and relations among uses as before. From this point of view the traditional residential domain, with its surrounding commercial areas and marketplaces, is maintained, but with a larger grain appropriate to automobile use and more extensive overall urban development.

Another significant departure from traditional patterns of urbanization is the process by which villa developments unfold. A consequence of the regular subdivision of land into serviced lots is that it allows a random configuration of residential building, where one unit is often isolated from its nearest neighbor (Hakim and Rowe 1984). This pattern is in direct contrast to the organic and additive processes of traditional settlement and the local allowances that could be made for changing circumstances.

Mid-rise apartment dwelling is also commonplace, and again certain traditional elements can be seen at work. Privacy is maintained on the exterior through conventional means. Multiple use is often accommodated at the ground-floor level and communal semiprivate facilities are frequently provided. However, the unit layout of many of these buildings is strongly influenced by Western prototypes and is thus not amenable to the integration of a Saudi life-style. Here the requirement for two distinct realms within the dwelling unit sometimes necessitates the use of two adjoining apartment units.

However, it is with contemporary forms of public "Crash" or "Rush" housing that the most blatant departures from traditional practice seem to have occurred (Boon 1981; Rowe 1984). In an apparent effort to efficiently satisfy a burgeoning housing demand, Western-style multistory tower blocks have been constructed in vast developments of five thousand or more units on the outskirts of cities like Dammam and Al Khobar (Boon 1981; Talib 1984). Although the overall density is relatively high, at about forty-five dwelling units a hectare, it is not significantly greater than traditional forms of settlement. With a site coverage of only about 20 percent, the open space between the tower buildings, far from creating an opportunity for outdoor activity as it might have in other cultural contexts, is inhospitable and alien (Rowe 1984). Questions about appropriate orientation and use of building forms for privacy and climate control were seemingly ignored. Furthermore, functional dependence upon sophisticated technologies tends to outstrip present capacities for adequate service and maintenance (Figures 15.8 and 15.10).

Within the overall framework of housing production the "Crash Housing" accounts for a relatively small percentage of supply (Boon 1981). However, the lower-income tenants, originally envisaged for these developments, make the problems with such a drastic departure from tradition all the more poignant. By and large this group is unaccustomed to living in towers above the ground. They are used to privacy in their dwelling environments mediated along the lines of traditional conventions. Typically, they are large families that prove difficult to accommodate in rather minimal standardized room arrangements. Furthermore, the mass housing image, as it has at times in the West, segregates one income class from another in a social context that otherwise tends to ignore such distinctions (Rowe 1984). Ultimately this form of dwelling environment is alienating and has been abandoned, although reasons for the lack of occupancy point in another direction as well. Even under conditions of large overall deficits in supply, a sudden flooding of the housing market with these units could have had the effect of disabling private-sector initiatives.

Apparent Rejection of Tradition

In Saudi Arabia the apparent rejection of tradition in a culture that also shows a strong, even rising adherence to established social conventions is perhaps surprising. Several authors have speculated that such a rejection is precipitated by the way the host tradition has been undervalued (Payne 1977; Boon 1981). They argue that, with the superimposition of modern technology, old practices and building forms are regarded as being "substandard." Alternatively, new building conventions passed on by way of new technologies are perceived of as being "super standard." In either case a rejection of tradition seems to be the consequence. Furthermore, it is an outcome that derives from valuation of past practices in "all or nothing" terms against other opportunities and tends to exclude selective consideration of how these opportunities might be tempered according to established conventions (Hakim and Rowe 1983).

One might also regard the rejection of traditional practices in favor of modern technical approaches as being a form of colonialism common in many parts of the world. However, in the realm of the closely held social and business dealings characteristic of the Saudis, colonialism in a strict sense seems inapplicable (Rowe 1984). A more compelling argument can be made for adherence by many Saudis to an international technocracy; one in which problems are defined in universal terms and for which solutions appear largely as matters of capital and technique. This orientation is further reinforced by current curricula in education, modeled after American and European schools and through the practical necessity of the wholesale training of graduate students, overseas in Western centers of learning (Rowe 1984).

From another vantage point, rejection might be seen more as a kind of oversight than one of conscious dismissal. Contrary to the prominence of art and architecture as forms of cultural expression in the West, in Saudi Arabia such a prominence is rarely enjoyed. Instead, other modes, such as literature and religious writing, are where tradition is most conspicuously celebrated. Consequently, the matter of building and urban-architectural expression is regarded as being of secondary importance, if it is an issue at all.

A plausible alternative explanation for extensive rejection of traditional practices may also be preferred, however, in the light of the sheer difficulty of relating past practices and institutional processes to practical exigencies of modern building (Hakim and Rowe 1983). They simply do not fit. A disparity of development conditions has occurred in which past practices have been rendered irrelevant and inappropriate for those involved. At the center of this disparity is a shift in the distribution of uncertainty within society through the change in status of land and buildings to fixed, identifiable commodities defining a market and circuit of capital. Those in positions of ownership and control exercise their options, limited only by their entrepreneurial capacities. Those without such positions no longer enjoy quite the same security as they might have had in earlier times. The concomitant simplification of real estate transactions away from the diversity of traditional forms of tenure only reinforces the trend toward commodification. Furthermore, in Saudi Arabia, decisions about the configuration of large-scale developments are made by a very small group on behalf of many, or in the absence of an identifiable indigenous user group. Such decision making effectively rules out the "moral suasion," negotiation, and arbitration that took place with collective participation under a system of inherited norms and habitual ways of doing things that was characteristic of earlier patterns of settlement.

In addition to their metaphysical qualities, traditions are usually highly pragmatic, incorporating what might be called commonsense views of public health, safety, and welfare set within the ecology and available resources of the time. For example, the careful reticulation of water as a common property resource and the equally careful consideration given to the passive modification of climate in the building environment can be seen as practical means of survival, as much as they are responses to the dictates of cultural ideology per se. However, when perceived, if not real, terms of survival became shifted by the opportunities prescribed by new resources and modern technology, prior norms justifiably became open to question and the result was often revision and even rejection (Rowe 1984).

Throughout, the morphology of earlier settlements anticipated, accommodated, and was shaped by a particular and predominant process of urban development. The rate of growth and change was comparatively slow, often spanning generations. The resulting physical pattern of settlements was usually incremental, additive, and irregular in form, and the settlements were largely similar in building type. Functions, although highly mixed, reflected interdependencies among activities that were relatively small in magnitude and simple enough in structure to be intelligible to most inhabitants. With contemporary development, both the magnitude and structural order of urban development has increased dramatically, diffusing so-called traditional practices. The resulting physical patterns of development are no longer incremental and irregular, at least as they were before, but rationalized to the exigencies of a new technological order.

Resolving the Dualism

In redressing the situation, a common approach is to effect something of a "middle-ground merger" of traditional practice with the modern progressive impetus. In some versions, otherwise contemporary architectural and urban design principles become overlayed with traditional organizational patterns and iconography. The problem with this approach is that it becomes invariably confined to the treatment of what might be called "symptoms" and only results in urban-architectural renderings that are superficial. They look like traditional buildings but that is all. Likewise, attempts to modernize traditional settlements often result in certain technical refinements. However, such technical integration is typically inefficient and difficult to achieve without wholesale reconstruction. In either case there is really no structural change in the fundamental conception of settlement patterns. One form is overlayed upon the other, fixed as it were by the differences in origin.

Perhaps a more fruitful version of the "middle-ground merger" attempts to redress "the root cause" of settlement problems through the use of participatory processes. Here efforts are made to devolve matters of habitation, provision of shelter, and design of communities to the inhabitants. Effectively such a posture assumes user sovereignty, with all the necessary information about available choices being at hand. Implicitly, however, the guidance that might be expected to come from tradition is regarded as being either weak or suspect, and as requiring explicit reinforcement and intervention. Logically speaking, it also tends to disregard, or gloss over, very real limitations about the range of available choices occasioned by prevailing frames of reference. Those making the choice are guided only by their immediate experience. Furthermore, in many participatory planning efforts, little rearrangement of institutional structures and roles is achieved, particularly on a more comprehensive scale where the effects can be more long lasting. As a practical matter, contemporary Saudi development, with its highly centralized decision-making processes and often the absence of a "community" to work with, also makes participatory forms of intervention that are much more difficult to achieve.

One might also ask, however, about how such arguments are advanced and whether the apparent paradox, with its implicit frames of reference about the modern and the traditional, does not obscure a deeper and more critical issue. After all, the matter of tradition is as much of the moment as it is of the past. The word itself carries with it the concept of "bringing across," or "delivery." Knowledge is transmitted from the past to enable present-day experience and place it in perspective. In short, the role of tradition and its conventions establishes both continuity and a source of guidance, in this case, for settlement. It might thus be expected to cope with the dual conditions of lore and future aspirations. One might also argue that the matter of tradition itself becomes an issue only when such a dualism is present. Further, such a dualism only really occurs when a community is confronted with the perception of sufficiently reduced renditions of those things that are of the past and those that are of the present and future. Otherwise such distinctions could not be made and the matter of tradition, or its absence, would not be raised.

In the Kingdom of Saudi Arabia the dualism is very much in evidence. As described earlier, many organizational principles and urban-architectural conventions of the past have been abandoned for a modern way of city building. The models for new development are unmistakably Western and of the immediate post–World War II era. However, they do not seem to have progressed or become transformed as they have in their originating cultures. The prevailing paradigm is still very closely aligned with a doctrine of "form follows function" and a rather reduced version at that. Professional practice seems to have been oblivious to any critique of "modernism" in either planning or architectural thought and has generally disdained anything but isolated attempts at reconciliation with an alternative view of the host culture.

The question then remains, Is it possible to overcome the current dualism and establish a vital role for tradition? Or, to put it another way, Along what lines might one approach this problem? In principle, the answer seems to lie in somehow enlarging the scope of each of the dual aspects that tradition hopes to cover to a point where both are transcended. Put less abstractly, the urban-architectural conventions of city building require critical appraisal and, therefore, disentanglement from the reduced and stereotypical views that presently hold them captive. Discovery rather than emulation is required in an effort to extend and authenticate relevant conventions and practices. However, the form of discovery cannot simply be seen as a matter of appropriation directed solely toward establishing continuity with the past. Resolving the dualism also requires continuity in the present. Neither should discovery be seen as design invention anew. Many of the institutional processes that gave shape to earlier settlements are still at work in shaping the rule structure for the social contracts involved in city building. Furthermore, there is a considerable and developing discourse around fundamental differences between the form of Arab-Islamic settlements and cross-cultural counterparts that also goes a long way in explaining the surface structure of traditional urban landscapes. Instead, a more radical reinterpretation of institutional practices used to provide habitation, such as concepts of tenure, building, and use regulation, should be undertaken; one that acknowledges both earlier and modern models as frameworks but regards neither as being necessary and sufficient for contemporary urban development. In addition, architectural and urban design must begin to provide similar reinterpretations. Tangible alternative models are needed for both their experimental and their symbolic value. In view of the power such models appear to have exerted in the past, the latter purpose is particularly important. Surprisingly perhaps, formal design explorations seem very much to be required—surprising insofar as it is an area where such investigations were typically shunned as being irresponsible and irrelevant, or where there was little to interest designers.

As an example of a very modest step in this direction, explorations of alternative housing environments can be made in the form of basic typological exercises. In one such study, a more or less square site, typical of blocks in a city grid, was assumed with an area of one hectare. It was also assumed, in keeping with typical patterns, that the site was surrounded on all four sides by public streets, one or more of which could be of more major importance. The program of uses for the site called for the provision of about fifty dwelling units and about twelve hundred square meters of retail commercial space. All dwelling units were to have modern space standards, averaging about two hundred square meters a unit, and to be constructed using modern fabrication technologies. An emphasis was placed, in the general form of development, on a medium-density low-rise pattern, somewhat reminiscent of both traditional settlements and contemporary higher-density villa developments. The form of tenure for the residential development was assumed to be both "freehold" and "rental," with similar arrangements for the distribution of commercial space between spaces with a resident owner and a renter (Figure 15.11).

Several urban-architectural conventions, or organizing principles, were assumed to be appropriately operating at the level of the block, or residential domain. The surrounding streets were considered as functioning simultaneously as "neutral turf," "frontier," public meeting place, and place for market transactions. They also coincided with relatively constant automobile use. Each dwelling unit was to be served by a local street allowing for comfortable entry and egress. These areas were seen as being semiprivate domains, obtaining to a small cluster of from five to ten houses. They were also to function as small community areas for children's play, small social gatherings, and so on.

Where possible, such streets or semipublic zones should be discontinuous, to allow the privacy of the serviced dwelling units to be preserved and gradually mediated from surrounding public zones. Development within the residential district was considered as occurring in either a contiguous or discontinuous fashion. However, advantage was to be taken where possible of "shared-wall" situations and "rights of common easements" (such as access or shading). Car parking for each unit was also to be provided on site.

All external openings to dwelling units were to be arranged to avoid directly confronting or intruding on a neighbor. Similarly, the visual privacy of rooftop terraces and interior courtyard was to be protected. The dwelling units themselves divided into the traditional two-part arrangement of male reception and meeting areas (*majlis*) together with the family living quarters. Within each of these major divisions traditional arrangements of spaces were followed. For example, the major entrance to the dwelling unit and the *majlis* was adjoined by a washroom facility to allow guests to take off their shoes, as is customary, and "wash-up" if necessary, before entering the house. Throughout, special emphasis was placed on conditions of entry and egress within the house and between the house and neighboring units to preserve appropriate contact between family members and others. Less basic accommodations, such as additional rooms and suites for relatives or servants, were sometimes incorporated, together with additional family outdoor areas. The resulting design explorations are neither wholly traditional in appearance and layout nor entirely modern. They are a different typology (Figure 15.11).

Such investigations, however, can only be regarded as first steps. Typology, concerned as it is with matters of conformation, remains reduced in expressive architectural terms. Further advances will thus require a more self-conscious grappling with appearances and their meaning that moves beyond the principles of organization discussed here. The next contributions to tradition must come by symbolic representation.

In summary, contemporary urban development in the Kingdom of Saudi Arabia takes place against the backdrop of a distinctive Arab-Islamic tradition and yet is strongly inclined toward modern Western models. The resulting dualism that the tradition of settlement must cope with is not solely of the past or of the present and future. Likewise, resolution of the dualism is unlikely to be found by favoring either the old or the new. Nor do mergers of past and present building practices and institutional arrangements hold out much hope, unless they can be counted on to sustain development toward new systems of spatial conventions and urban-architectural typologies: systems and typologies that shake loose from the fixity of their origins. In these respects the situation in Saudi Arabia is not unique. Instead it is one that is clear even to the point of exaggeration and one that very much reflects contemporary circumstances about the role of tradition.

References

Abu-Lughod, J. 1983. Contemporary relevance of Islamic urban principles. In *Islamic architecture and urbanism*, ed. A. Germen, 64–70. Dammam: King Faisal University.

Al-Farsy, F. 1982. *Saudi Arabia: A case study in development*. Boston: Kegan Paul International.

Al-Hathloul, S. A. 1981a. Tradition, continuity and change in the physical environment of the Arab-Muslim city. Ph.D. diss., M.I.T.

———. 1981b. Urban forms in Arab-Muslim cities: Physical elements or themes and principles. *Al-Faisal Architecture and Planning Journal* 1 (1):24–28.

Akbar, J. A. 1984. *Responsibility and the traditional Muslim built environment*. Ph.D. diss., M.I.T.

Al-Madani, R., and M. Al-Fayez. 1976. *Population Bulletin of the United Nations Commission for Western Asia*. Nos. 10 & 11, p. 186.

Almana, M. 1982. *Arabia unified: A portrait of Ibn Saud*. London: Hutchinson Benham.

Alohali, Y. N. 1983. *Urban dwelling environments in rapidly growing cities: Anayzah, Saudi Arabia*. Monograph, School of Architecture and Planning, M.I.T.

Arabian-American Oil Company. 1968. *Aramco handbook*. Dhahran, Saudi Arabia.

Bindagji, H. H. 1980. *Atlas of Saudi Arabia*. Oxford: Oxford University Press.

Boon, J. J. 1981. An overview of dwelling forms and residential patterns in Saudi Arabia. *Al Faisal Architecture and Planning Journal* 1 (1):8–9.

CH2M Hill International. 1976. *Dammam Action Master Plan, Technical Report 5: Existing conditions*. Riyadh: Ministry of Municipal and Rural Affairs, Kingdom of Saudi Arabia.

Davis, K. 1971. World urbanization 1950–1970: Volume 1. *Population Monograph*, ser. 4, University of California, Berkeley.

Earls, M. W. 1981. In support of conservation in traditional cities. *Al-Faisal Architecture and Planning Journal* 1 (1):16–17.

El Mallakh, R. 1982. *Saudi Arabia: Rush to development*. Baltimore: The Johns Hopkins University Press.

El Sadek, S., ed. 1980. *International symposium on Islamic architecture and urbanism*. Dammam: King Faisal University.

Fadan, Y. M. O. 1983a. Traditional houses of Makka: The influence of socio-cultural themes upon Arab-Muslim dwellings. In *Islamic architecture and urbanism*, ed. A. Germen, 295–323. Dammam: King Faisal University.

———. 1983b. The development of contemporary housing in Saudi Arabia (1950–1983): A study in cross-cultural influence under conditions of rapid change. Ph.D. diss., M.I.T.

De Gaury, G. 1975. Memories and impressions of the Arabia of Ibn Saud. *Arabian Studies* 2: 19–32.

Grube, E. 1978. What is Islamic architecture? In *Architecture of the Islamic world*, ed. G. Mitchell.

Hakim. B. S. 1982. Arab-Islamic urban structure. *The Arabian Journal of Science and Engineering* 7 (2).

———. 1986a. *Arab-Islamic cities: Building and planning principles*. London: Routledge and Kegan Paul.

———. 1986b. Islamic architecture: Building and urbanism in Islamic culture. In *Encyclopedia of World Architecture*. New York: John Wiley.

Hakim, B. S., and P. G. Rowe. 1983. The representation of values in traditional and contemporary Islamic cities. *Journal of Architectural Education* 36 (4):22–28.

Lacey, R. 1981. *The kingdom: Arabia and the House of Sa'ud*. New York: Avon.

Lawrence, M. 1983. A traveller in the Eastern Province. *Ahlan Wasahlan* 7 (5):28.

Ministry of Planning, Kingdom of Saudi Arabia. 1980. *The Third Development Plan, 1400–1404/1980–1985.*

Ochsenwald, W. 1984. *Religion, society and the state in Arabia: The Hijaz under Ottoman control, 1840–1908.* Columbus, Ohio: Ohio State University Press.

Payne, G. K. 1977. *Urban housing in the Third World.* London: Leonard Hill.

Pesce, A. 1977. *Jiddah: Portrait of an Arabian city.* London: Falcon Press.

Rowe, P. G. 1984. Problems of coping with tradition in shaping settlements. In *Architectural values and world issues,* ed. W. G. Gillard and D. Woodcock, 67–74. Silver Spring, Md.: Information Dynamics.

Talib, K. 1984. *Shelter in Saudi Arabia.* New York: St. Martin's Press.

Figure 15.1. Traditional house in Al-Hasa (photo by author).

Figure 15.2. Traditional pattern of urbanization (El Sadek 1980, 1).

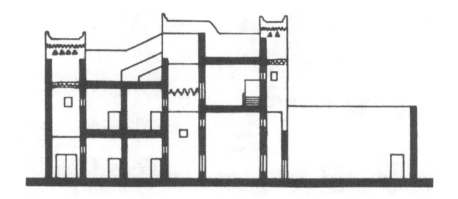

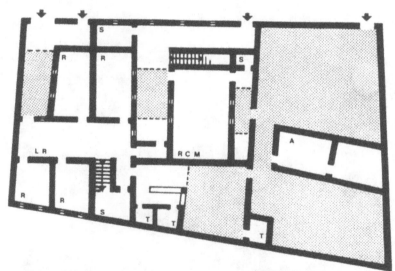

Figure 15.3. Plan and section of a traditional house (Alohali 1983, 77).

Figure 15.4. Urban landscape of Jeddah (Pesce 1977, 27).

Figure 15.5. A palace in Al-Hasa (photo by author).

Figure 15.6. Old town of Dammam and early subdivision developments (Archive, municipality of Dammam).

Figure 15.7. Modern pattern of urbanization (photo by author).

Figure 15.8. High-rise "crash" housing near Al-Khobar (photo by author).

Figure 15.9. Typical villa development (photo by author).

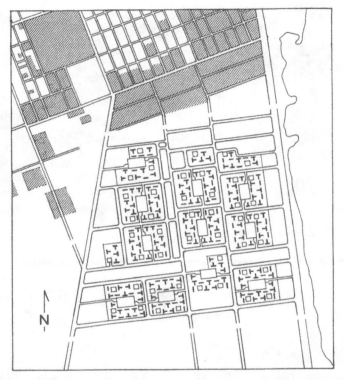

Figure 15.10. "Crash" housing and the gridiron of Al-Khobar (after Boon 1981, 8).

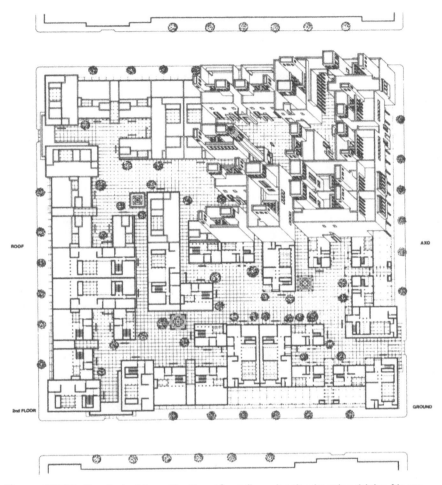

ROOF

AXO

2nd FLOOR

GROUND

Figure 15.11. Typological investigation of medium density housing (John Neary, School of Architecture, Rice University, 1984).

16

CONTEXTUAL
TRANSFORMATIONS
OF TRADITIONAL HOUSING
IN KABUL, AFGHANISTAN
WILLIAM B. BECHHOEFER

Traditional housing in Afghanistan represents appropriate responses to different living conditions. Two case studies in Kabul, the capital of Afghanistan, will illustrate the process of response. The forms of the past are still viable because Afghan society remains substantially traditional in outlook, and new housing built by people for themselves conforms in most respects to the patterns of older dwellings. Similarity of available materials and construction techniques in specific areas of the country and similarity of family needs have resulted in a relatively limited vocabulary of house types in any given region.

These houses, however, are enormously flexible. Housing that was generated in one cultural and geographic context has been reused and transformed by different cultural groups. Each transformation is based on specific cultural requirements and, to a lesser degree, on resource availability. While the original model is always clear, the new model has its own independent identity.

The first of these case studies is of Serai Lahori, which is one of the few remaining fine examples of housing in Kabul from the nineteenth century. The enclave was built by an Indian minority in a predominately Muslim population. Traditional Islamic house types have been employed, but with specific alterations because of cultural imperatives. In particular, attitudes toward family and community privacy generate design decisions that are reflected in the organization of houses and urban spaces.

The second case study examines new squatter housing built by several cultural groups who have migrated to Kabul. Whereas Serai Lahori was built by an urban population, the squatter housing was built by people for whom the experience of a major urban center is largely unknown. Village architecture is brought from the countryside to create "urban villages" within the city. The scale, density, and expanded economic opportunity of the new urban cultural setting have an effect on traditional village building through connections to a larger urban fabric.

During the 1970s the growth of Kabul was a natural response to movements of populations seeking the real or apparent advantages of an urban environment. The occupation of the country by the Soviets in 1979, however, has severely altered life-styles and institutions that have been in existence for centuries. The population of Kabul has swelled with refugees from the countryside seeking the relative safety of the capital. This accelerated migration must necessarily distort the long-established patterns of urban life and growth that are described here and that represent instances of success in solving problems of urbanization.

Methodology

Documentation of the housing in Kabul took place in 1974. Architecture students from Kabul University and the University of Maryland collaborated in the preparation of drawings based upon field measurements. Surveys of residents of Serai Lahori were made to determine how houses were built and how they are used; additional oral history was provided by neighboring residents of the old city of Kabul. The squatter houses were occupied by owner-builders, who were proud to share their achievements. The results were compared with housing documentation by other researchers to corroborate findings.

Kabul

Kabul is situated in the fertile valley of the Kabul River at an altitude of 6,600 feet. Mountains that create excellent defensive barriers and the climate have recommended Kabul at least since the time of Alexander the Great as an urban site. The first defensive walls which were constructed in the fifth century have been rebuilt many times since and can still be seen. At the beginning of the sixteenth century, Babur, who was later to found the Moghul Dynasty of India, made Kabul his capital, and upon his death was buried there. In his writings he often expressed his love for the gardens and fine climate of Kabul, which he compared to the lowland plains of India.

Through much of its history, Kabul had been exceeded in wealth and culture by many cities in Afghanistan—Kandahar, Ghazni, and Herat, among them—but the growth of Kabul truly began in the late eighteenth century. In 1776 Kabul became the capital of the region, at which time the city was very densely built and confined within fortifications. In the nineteenth century the outlines of what is now called the "old city" were clear. On the north is the Kabul River; on the south is Sher Darwaza Mountain, with the fortified wall on its crest, which joins Bala Hissar citadel on the east (Figure 16.1). A wall—now destroyed—ran from Bala Hissar north to the river to complete the defenses.

Surrounding villages were already considered suburbs and were incorporated into the city in the twentieth century. Since about 1930 there has been a continuous growth of single-family residential development both east and west of the old city. Migrations from the countryside to Kabul became significant in the 1950s but grew enormously in the 1960s. It is not, therefore, a coincidence that growth of squatter housing on the slopes of Koh-i-Asmai, the mountain west of the old city, corresponded to those migrations. There are areas of the city with their own distinct character, like villages in the coherence of their boundaries and the relative homogeneity of their residents.

The Old City

The physical character of the old city was determined by three major factors: economics, defense, and socioreligious custom. Because of the desirability of building within the protective confines of the city walls, land was extremely expensive. The bazaar streets were crowded by the maximum number of shops, and peddlers worked on foot or with carts or animals. Commercial areas demanded direct access to the street level for selling and servicing and were therefore generally built with one or two stories. Residential construction, however, rose to three and sometimes four stories, cantilevered over the streets to gain needed floor area. The demand for space and for pedestrian and animal traffic circulation resulted in narrow, dark, winding streets.

The bazaar was and, despite modern incursions, to a large extent still is the social, political, and economic forum of the city and the nation. It determines the organization of the old city; each bazaar gave its name to the section of the city that it served. Shor Bazaar, one of the major bazaars, refers to a major street of stores and workshops, public baths and mosques, and also to a grouping of perhaps fifty thousand residents. These residential areas were broken into smaller neighborhoods, defined by local mosques and shrines and by a few tea shops and stores.

Open shop fronts and a variety of activities enrich the bazaar experience.

There is opportunity for all sorts of interaction: merchandise is sold, items are manufactured, and services are provided in a manner that is highly visible to the passerby. The variety of activities presents a visual contrast to the relatively uniform rhythms of the shop structures.

Secondary streets occur off the bazaar street and are passageways that link the public bazaar with private residences. Few windows open onto these streets and very little social activity occurs there, since they are used primarily for circulation. Because of the scarcity of land in the city, these passageways are very narrow. Because of the upper floors that cantilever out to maximize building space, many houses completely span the street and turn it into a tunnel.

Whereas defense of the city from the outside was a major factor in shaping the old city, within the city it was also necessary to protect people and goods from family and tribal feuds and from the prevailing lawlessness. All buildings turn an essentially blank face to public streets. For example, the *serai*, an open space surrounded by rooms, is a typical building type in that its access is always at one guarded point, and its activity is oriented to the space within. Housing also turns inward to a court or to a compound surrounded by a wall. There are some houses with major facades on the street or on a semi-public space; these houses belong to one related group and their common area can itself be closed.

Socioreligious custom is a fundamental influence on the form of the old city in that it defines privacy needs among the various ethnic groups in Kabul. A primary determinant of form in traditional Islamic houses has been *purdah*, the institution of secluding women. Although *purdah* is nowhere defined as a religious precept of Islam, it is nonetheless associated with Muslim society, to which it may have been adapted from Byzantine Christian practice. The court, or compound, of the traditional house provides a space where women of the family may live and work unobserved by strangers. Entries to houses are arranged so that a view into the house from the street is impossible. A room for male guests is generally found at the entry in order to avoid contact with the rest of the house.

Characteristic massive construction has provided an effective accommodation to the dry climate of Kabul, as well as to social requirements. The narrow streets are shaded from the summer sun and keep out the heavy winter snows; walls of mud or brick insulate from the heat or cold; courtyards provide sinks of cool air and shade in the summer; and, whenever possible, rooms are arranged with a north or south orientation, to be used in summer or winter, respectively. The problem of the winter snow on the buildings has never been successfully resolved. Although snow does not fall in the streets because of their narrowness, the flat mud roofs of the buildings must be shoveled continuously to avoid leaks and collapse; the only space for the snow is in the streets. For much of the winter, then, the streets become a practically impassable morass of mud, because there is no way to drain off the water. So far no economical system of roof construction to support snow loads and prevent leaks has been introduced into Afghanistan.

Another feature of the architecture has been the use of elaborately carved wood facades. They are lightweight and beautiful, and they admit air and light into rooms; they require resources, however, that are now lacking in Afghanistan: suitable wood and trained craftsmen. Poplar trees were used, as they still are, for structural members, and it is said that holly trees once grew in the Kabul valley and were used for the facades. While poplar grows fast and is grown now as a crop, the holly grows very slowly. Once the original holly trees were cut, therefore, hardwood from India would have been the only appropriate substitute for facade construction. Kabuli families were wealthy indeed to have afforded the wood suitable for carving and the craftsmen needed to build these facades.

Economic pressure, the need for internal and external defense within the city, and socioreligious custom are the prime determinants of the form of the old city of Kabul. Traditional methods of construction have served the Afghans well, and though the elaborate facades of the past are no longer built, they are being replaced with simpler versions or with modern window systems.

The flexibility and responsiveness of traditional urban organization and of traditional house forms and building systems can be demonstrated through examination of housing for a minority group. While the population of Afghanistan is overwhelmingly Muslim, there is a sizable minority with Indian origins. Their Sikh and Hindu cultures differ in one fundamental respect from that of their Muslim neighbors; they do not require *purdah*. This one factor transforms the architecture of their community and establishes its separate identity. Factors of economics, defense, and resource availability shape their buildings much as they do those of the Muslims. The Indians, however, have built housing that demonstrates a fundamentally different attitude about the privacy of the individual family and the community, and it is this attitude which motivates the transformation.

Serai Lahori

History and Development   The *serai* is an important functional adjunct to the bazaar. There are two kinds of urban *serai*: the work-storage *serai* and the residential *serai*. In the former, traditionally the bottom level was used for shops, work space, or storage, and the top floor for living space. Frequently the interior facade of the *serai* is composed of upper and lower galleries, which act as a formalized transition zone between the more public open space and private areas. The residential *serai* is an adaptation of this configuration; its use, however, is entirely residential, and the houses that surround it rise to three, and often four, stories. In both kinds of *serai*, thick walls keep out much of the bazaar's noise and heighten the illusion that these spaces are far removed from the bazaar.

The development of a residential *serai* and its functional relationship to the rest of the city can be explained by examining the evolution of the form of a *serai* from the form of a secondary street or passageway. As noted before, the main purpose of a passageway is circulation. If, for reasons of defense, a gate is built at each end of the passage, the street can be blocked off at certain times and places and thus become more private and easily defended. Such gates are still found in the old city. The next step in the evolution of a *serai* is to permanently close one end of the street and use it only for access to houses on that street. Eventually, widening the passage creates a useful open space, as illustrated in the site plan of Serai Lahori (Figure 16.2).

Serai Lahori, the first case study, is a residential *serai*, a group of houses arranged around an open space off Shor Bazaar at its eastern extremity. In the nineteenth century, access to this part of the city from the outside was through the Lahore gate, now destroyed, which took its name from that major Indian city, which is now in Pakistan.

Serai Lahori is in a part of the old city where many Indian groups have settled. Most of its residents are Sikhs; some are Hindus or Muslims. The narrow guarded entrance to the *serai* is by a kind of tunnel. The tunnel passes under the Sikh temple, which is the religious and social center of the community. The temple thus takes on considerable architectural significance by its placement at the entry where its presence increases consciousness of its central role in the life of the *serai*.

According to tradition, the temple elders estimate the temple site to be more than six hundred years old. Assuming the accuracy of this figure, the site would have to have been Hindu, since it was not until the middle of the fifteenth century that Sikh beliefs developed out of both Hindu and Muslim traditions. It is also possible to assume the existence of an Indian community around the temple and houses grouped around a defensible community street-space, since both of these patterns are typical and traditional in the old city of Kabul. Historically, Muslim groups also lived in the area. The existing temple and most of the house structures are one hundred or more years old; additions and changes have been made continuously. It is impossible to determine whether there is any correspondence between what now exists and earlier communities on the site.

The impact of India on Afghanistan has been significant throughout its history. In the fourth to third centuries B.C., Buddhism came from India to Afghanistan. In the fourth and fifth centuries A.D., and again in the eighth to tenth centuries, Indian dynasties controlled parts of the country, while Afghan rulers at various times have dominated Delhi and regions of northwest India.

In the nineteenth century, the towns and cities of Afghanistan were largely populated by ethnic groups other than the ruling indigenous Pushtun tribes. Mountstuart Elphinstone, in *The Kingdom of Caubul*, which was originally published in 1815, remarks that the greater part of the residents of Kabul were Tajiks, who kept shops and engaged in handcraft trades, and Indians, who were bankers and traders. A few Pushtuns who lived in cities followed commerce, but most were the important men at court, soldiers, and religious leaders. As in most nations, the poor also gathered in the city and became laborers. Elphinstone concludes that the ruling Pushtuns viewed city life as essentially degrading and preferred the freer existence of the countryside. Even today there is a large, mostly Pushtun, nomadic population.

At the time of this study about twenty-five thousand Afghans of Indian origin were living in the cities of Afghanistan. They typically engage in a variety of commercial activities, such as money changing and selling textiles or other goods. The Hindu and Sikh religions are practiced, but Sikhs are in the majority. Hindi and Punjabi are the primary languages of these groups; Dari, or Afghan Farsi, is generally the most useful second language and is used by the disparate peoples of Afghanistan as a common language.

Architectural Organization   Before looking in detail at Serai Lahori, there are four general characteristics of the complex to be noted. First, the organization of these houses around a defensible closed street reinforces the sense of a distinct community within the old city of Kabul and represents one of the most typical patterns of housing to be found. Indeed, a person who was found outside his community late at night was highly suspect unless he carried a light to indicate his honesty of intention.

Second, the houses of Serai Lahori are not the traditional Islamic type, with the interior courtyard as the major focus. Instead, houses look directly on the community street, reflecting the freedom of Sikh and Hindu women from seclusion in the immediate family; the courtyard becomes secondary or nonexistent.

Third, when constructed in the nineteenth century, these houses belonged to the wealthy, and evidence of rich embellishments is seen everywhere. In particular, the wood panels are of exceptional quality. The houses are now rented and have been allowed to deteriorate.

Finally, whereas the interiors of the houses are kept clean, the community street has become a repository for raw sewage and garbage. In the past local farmers would have removed wastes to use as fertilizer; with the growth of Kabul, farms are now too far away to make the system feasible. Without a modern system of waste disposal, these urban spaces, which once were used intensively, have become spoiled. Nonetheless, the community space at Serai Lahori allows women to socialize with one another across it from the upper levels of the houses. It is also the place where the primary water source for the community is found and it is a play area for children (Figure 16.3).

The Houses of Serai Lahori   The house type most characteristic of the old city demonstrates traditional organization around a central zone, which consists of a courtyard and the stairs to other levels. The visual axis from the entry of the house to the stairs is broken to increase privacy. The side walls adjoin other houses and thus have no openings. The major living rooms are in the front and back (Figure 16.4).

Each house is composed of a series of rectangular volumes that define the functional and structural zones of the house. The volumes are usually stacked up to a height of three stories. The basic structural system is one of mud- or brick-bearing walls with poplar joists and beams; walls are reinforced against earth tremors by horizontal, vertical, and diagonal wood members.

A series of wood panels acts as a curtain wall, effectively reducing the dead load on the cantilevered parts as well as providing light and ventilation to the interior. The basic panel is composed of a frontal element, often an arch, with three vertically sliding shutters behind. The top stationary piece is often punctured with openings to insure some ventilation even when all the shutters are closed. Panels and shutters are highly decorated with carvings and moldings (Figure 16.5).

Room shapes are generally not dependent upon function. Uses of rooms are generalized. Essentially there are living-sleeping rooms and storage rooms, in addition to toilet and kitchen facilities. The main living room is usually the main sleeping room. Guests stay in a room near the entry to minimize interference with the family privacy. Room use is often rotated because of season or immediate need. For example, in the summer the rooms toward the front of the house are used because they ventilate better.

This flexibility is reinforced by simplicity of furnishing. Floors are generally covered with rugs, and walls are lined with mattresses or cushions, and the center of the room is left free. Usually there is at least one bed in the main sleeping-eating room; but, if there is space, the cushions are used as seats in preference to the bed. A cloth on the floor becomes a table. Such simplicity of room shapes and furnishing contributes to the adaptability of the houses to various patterns of usage.

Basements, when built, are generally storage spaces. However, there is often a heating system in the basement; a fire is built at one end of the house, and hot air is circulated in air spaces beneath the stone floor above on its way to the chimney. Thus the rooms directly above are heated by a radiant floor and are comfortable in the winter.

The walled roof is one of the spaces most used by the family. It is a utility area where the kitchen and toilet are often located. A bakery is a common feature, recognizable by its pitched, open-ended roof which allows smoke to escape. In good weather, meals are cooked and clothes are washed on the roof; when the weather is very hot, it becomes the evening sleeping area. The addition of living rooms on the roof level is comparatively recent and is to be found on the majority of houses in the old city. Many of the roofs of Serai Lahori connect with each other to provide an upper-level, private link between houses. Openings are left in the roof walls so that people may look down upon the community street or communicate across it.

The foregoing description defines a generic house type in Kabul. Sikh and Hindu residents of Serai Lahori have modified this basic house for their own purposes. If the house had been built by Muslims, rooms would open only to the courtyard, which would be the major work area for the women; however, in Serai Lahori the living rooms open directly to the outside communal space as well as to the interior courtyard. As a consequence, courtyards are typically deep and narrow and are used more for light and ventilation, and sometimes for a well, than for any specific activity. This simple, but fundamental, modification transforms the sensation of the house from introverted and isolated to extroverted and communal. Differing attitudes toward privacy and the seclusion of women are, therefore, accurately reflected.

Variations on the Serai Lahori house type occur in response to difficult or unusual building sites and to specific needs of residents. One variation is the location of stairs. Whereas a courtyard is preferred in the middle of the house, stairs may be more easily moved. For example, the placement of stairs in the rear corner of a house assures privacy from the street and allows the courtyard to be bigger.

The second variation in the houses of Serai Lahori is the elimination of the courtyard to provide increased enclosed living space or to accommodate narrow building sites, where an interior open space would not be feasible; rear living rooms in these conditions characteristically have small windows to a passageway or open space. Such houses can be very comfortably occupied by Sikh or Hindu families, where *purdah* is not a requirement; for these groups the interior courtyard has lost much of its functional necessity.

Additions and alterations have been made to the houses, such as the construction of extra rooms on the roof, the construction of new floors, the closing of courtyards, and the rearrangement of doors and windows. Innumerable repairs have altered or destroyed original features of the buildings. And yet these changes and repairs reveal that the houses continue to be expressions of the changing life-style of the old city of Kabul.

The Settlement of Koh-i-Asmai

The second case study of adaptation of traditional housing forms is the squatter housing on the base of the hills around Kabul. The term *squatter housing* evokes images of the dilapidated construction and unwholesomeness typical of such settlements in many parts of the world. In Kabul, however, the phenomenon must be viewed differently because of the unique set of physical and social circumstances that have brought this kind of housing into being there. In fact, the squatter housing of Kabul is solidly built and well-designed, and it satisfies many of the needs and aspirations of a population whose income has already risen considerably above a subsistence level. The only aspect this housing has in common with other squatter developments is its illegal occupation of the land and its construction by the owners. As many Afghans possess the ability to build, it is useful to see what people will provide for themselves when given the opportunity and to study how these constructive energies affect the urban organization of Kabul.

Kabul offers a unique combination of attractions for people seeking urban life in Afghanistan. By virtue of being the political, administrative, and commercial center of the country, it has the greatest concentration of goods and services. Because Afghanistan's economy remains overwhelmingly agricultural, employment in rural areas is very often sporadic, and many find their way to the capital in search of jobs, improved status, and excitement.

Typically, a man will come to Kabul looking for seasonal or permanent work. Upon arrival he will stay with others related to him through family, clan, or tribe. Considerable internal solidarity characterizes such communities, which provide an immediate social milieu for the newcomer. Usually, these communities are in the older, over-crowded areas of Kabul, especially in the old city. In time, if there is some financial success, the man's family or other relatives may be brought from the country. Their arrival creates pressure to find new housing. Shunning modern apartments with their lack of privacy and space, and unable to afford land on the valley floor, they appropriate mountain slopes such as Koh-i-Asmai as sites for building their own homes. The pattern thus emerges of migration from the countryside to an established poor neighborhood of Kabul, where the whys and wherefores of city life are learned, and thence to new self-built homes.

Although the residents of the mountain generally are thought of as among the poorer segments of Afghan society, a closer look reveals that their industriousness and their inclination to pool family resources have paid off in the financial success that has enabled them to build substantial dwellings. Their success in the private sector is paralleled in the aggressive and individualistic way they have "squatted" on the mountainsides and thereby affected the look of the entire city in a major way.

Functionally, however, Kabul remains a grouping of coexisting insular communities. The internal solidarity of individual communities is an effective mechanism for initiating the newcomer into city life in general, but at the same time perpetuates groups that owe little allegiance to the city at large. The new housing developments on the hills around the city are an extension of the old communities and are, therefore, no more integrated into the life of the city as a whole than were the older communities from which they emerged. Indeed, the local bazaar at the base of the hill is the only real connection to the rest of the city, and citizens protest the incursions of roads and other municipal services which—albeit desirable—might imply taxation or threaten homes.

Housing covers a substantial part of the southern slopes of Koh-i-Asmai. The south side is preferred for its favorable solar orientation in both winter and summer. Typically, there will be a bazaar at the base of the hill, where trucks or hand-drawn carts can easily service the shops. Because access to the slopes is by foot or pack animal, the highest density of residential construction is also at the base of the hill. Here, the houses, and often some rental apartments, are tightly packed. Further up the mountain, houses are more spread out and may be free-standing. The main paths of circulation tend to be straight up the slope, which gives a certain clarity to the development, but which is not necessarily the most convenient for ease of movement. Indeed, the angle of ascent reaches as much as forty degrees, which is particularly difficult to climb in winter when there is snow and ice (Figure 16.6).

Municipal services are virtually nonexistent. Water is the major problem; it must be carried in goat skins or metal cans on the backs of men or animals. Unless the family carries its own water, the cost to a household half way up the mountain can be as much as 10 percent of its income, and the price rises in proportion to the distance climbed. Consequently, the small gardens in many of the houses are a source of enormous pride. Plumbing is not used and septic systems are not feasible on the rocky slope: sewage is discharged into the streets to become a source of filth and disease. Almost all homes have electricity, and there are some telephones.

Houses are built of stone from the hillside and sun-dried or baked brick and are often covered with plaster. Poplar poles support roofs of mud reinforced with straw. All materials are inexpensive and readily available, except window glass which is usually the last item to be afforded. A consistency in the use of available materials gives a remarkable visual cohesion to the housing clusters (Figure 16.7).

Since the owner-builders originally come from the countryside and since the climate, site conditions, and construction materials are similar to those found in mountain villages, the resemblance of the architecture to villages is not coincidental (Figure 16.8). Certain architectural elements are common to virtually all of the houses on Koh-i-Asmai and, indeed, to housing throughout the country. A south-facing courtyard or compound and roof terraces provide outdoor living spaces with excellent light and views. Except for the kitchen and the latrine, which are isolated to the courtyard to keep odors out of the living areas, rooms are nonspecific in their functions and may be used for all activities of the family.

For ease of construction and adaptation to the slopes, houses tend to be simple one- or two-story blocks, divided into the number of rooms required. Nevertheless, many houses have become complex to a point of apparent disorganization, having been built over several years, as money has become available and as the family has grown or has enlarged because of new arrivals. The "typical" house, therefore, is not so much a specific form, but instead the result of a process of building in which pragmatic accommodations are made to site, economy, and family need.

While the housing resembles village housing at neighborhood scale, the extent of building required for Kabul's large population implies an overall scale of development unprecedented in village counterparts. Villages have a limited population and relatively coherent and closed economic and social structures, which are reflected in a clear definition of architectural boundaries and form. In the city, on the other hand, cultural life and opportunity are expanded through concentration of human and economic resources. Housing developed in mountain villages is used successfully by individual families as a prototype for construction on slopes in the city. That same housing, though, collectively is transformed by the scale of its application and by its open-ended quality, which signifies the beginnings of its connection to a larger urban context.

Conclusion

Serai Lahori and the housing on Koh-i-Asmai represent two aspects of contextual transformation. The significance of Serai Lahori is to be found in the manner in which its forms accurately reflect its historical and cultural precedents. Transformations of prototypical housing types by a minority group to reflect an outlook radically different from that of its Muslim neighbors demonstrates a response to cultural context. The motivation of the residents has been to modify an existing viable pattern of urban living.

On the other hand, the "villages" of Koh-i-Asmai are transformations of rural prototypes which are imported to an existing urban situation. An architecture that is familiar to its builders is brought into contact with a context of urban culture. The intimate and relatively closed system of the traditional village now must connect to the larger urban fabric, and a continuing process of transformation begins.

The housing types described in Serai Lahori and in the mountain villages are found throughout the Islamic world and in other cultures as well. Both examples illustrate the flexibility and adaptability of traditional architecture to changing requirements. The studies further suggest that identification of prototypical housing types can be the basis for comparative analysis of many kinds of housing and that localized analysis can define specific transformations that have taken place. Contextual determinants of housing and urban form are requisite data for housing design if it is to contribute to cultural identity and regional character. .

References

Dupree, L. 1973. *Afghanistan.* Princeton: Princeton University Press.

Dupree, L., and L. Albert, ed. 1974. *Afghanistan in the 1970s.* New York: Praeger.

Dupree, N. H. 1975. *Kabul city.* New York: The Afghanistan Council of the Asia Society.

————. 1972. *Kabul.* Kabul: Afghan Tourist Organization.

————. 1970. *A historical guide to Afghanistan.* Kabul: Afghan Tourist Organization.

Elphinstone, M. 1972. *An account of the Kingdom of Caubul.* Karachi: Oxford University Press. Reprint of first edition of 1815.

Hallet, S. I., and R. Samizay. 1980. *Traditional architecture of Afghanistan.* New York: Garland STPM Press.

Katz, T. B. 1974. Report on housing on Koh-i-Asmai, prepared for School of Architecture, University of Maryland.

Samizay, M. R. 1974. Urban growth and residential prototypes in Kabul, Afghanistan. Master's thesis, MIT.

Shairzay, A. 1973. Report on housing in Kart-i-Sakhi, prepared for Department of Architecture, Faculty of Engineering, Kabul University.

Szabo, A., and B. Dyer. 1978. *Preliminary notes on the indigenous architecture of Afghanistan.* Cambridge: Harvard University, Graduate School of Design.

Wilber, D. N. 1962. *Afghanistan, its people, its society, its culture.* New Haven: Human Relations Area Files Press.

Area Handbook for Afghanistan. 1973. 4th ed. Washington, D.C.: Foreign Area Studies of the American University.

Figure 16.1. View of Kabul, looking northeast from Sher Darwaza mountain (1974). A modern commercial street bisects the old city.

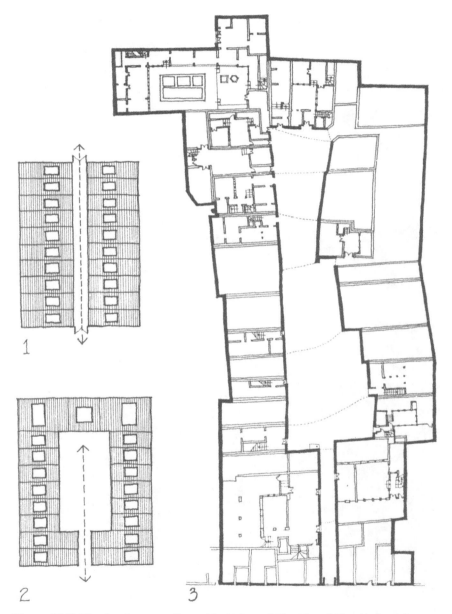

Figure 16.2. The development of a residential *serai*. The plan of Serai Lahori shows entry through the bazaar and the Sikh temple and houses grouped around a common space.

1

2

3

Figure 16.3. View of Serai Lahori (1974).

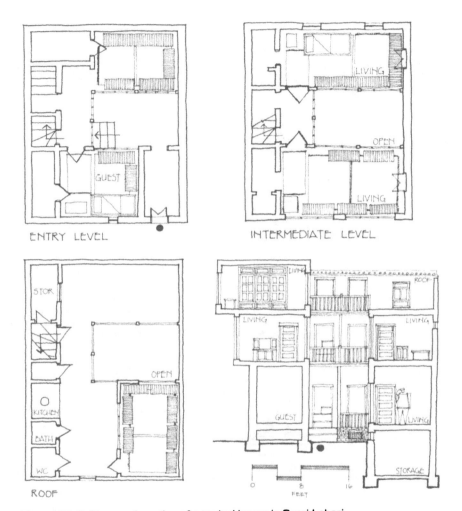

Figure 16.4. Plans and section of a typical house in Serai Lahori.

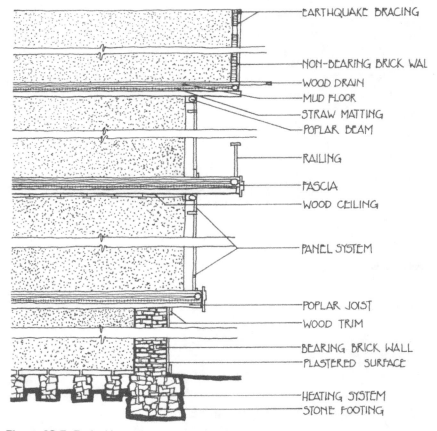

EARTHQUAKE BRACING

NON-BEARING BRICK WAL

WOOD DRAIN
MUD FLOOR
STRAW MATTING
POPLAR BEAM

RAILING

FASCIA
WOOD CEILING

PANEL SYSTEM

POPLAR JOIST
WOOD TRIM

BEARING BRICK WALL
PLASTERED SURFACE

HEATING SYSTEM
STONE FOOTING

Figure 16.5. Typical house construction in Serai Lahori.

Figure 16.6. View of Koh-i-Asmai (1974). Commercial activity takes place at the base of the hill and houses are built on the slopes.

Figure 16.7. Housing construction shows considerable care and skill. The angle of ascent is as much as forty degrees.

Figure 16.8. A typical mountain village to the north of Kabul (1974).

17

VERNACULAR ARCHITECTURE
AS AN EXPRESSION
OF ITS SOCIAL CONTEXT
IN ERESSOS, GREECE

ELEFTHERIOS PAVLIDES

JANA E. HESSER

Anecdotes abound of architect-designed buildings in culturally foreign contexts that have gone unused, or that have been used in surprising and "unconventional" ways, or that have been extensively transformed by the inhabitants. Why does this happen? It is presumed that an understanding of the local cultural context, the local patterns of space use, or the local meaning attached to the visual forms of built objects could have prevented or ameliorated some of these architectural misadventures. We believe such understanding is possible and with this premise in mind, we set about to examine the built environment of a Greek island village. Our objective was to "see" that environment through the eyes of its inhabitants and to arrive at an understanding of its use and meaning as defined by those inhabitants.

We believe that the approach we adopted in studying this vernacular architectural setting represents a significant departure from much previous work. Most important, we sought to define significant visual categories and to understand the meaning attached to visual variation, as defined and understood by the inhabitants. We visually documented the environment as it appeared to us only as a necessary take-off point into this other reality. Second, we made an effort to document how the village architecture had changed through time, in a departure from many earlier studies which attribute a timeless quality to vernacular built form. Third, we collected detailed comparative data on a sample of buildings in order to describe variation, instead of describing a representative archetype as is often done. This chapter discusses the results of this study and identifies how these results can be of value to designers.

Cultural Setting: Eressos, Lesbos

The island of Lesbos lies seven miles from the west coast of Asia Minor (Turkey). Eressos is located on the northern side of a fertile valley on the slopes of three hills which command a view of the Aegean Sea to the south. Like other settlements on Aegean islands, Eressos is located several miles inland from the sea which, in the past, was a source of pillagers. Most of its fifteen hundred inhabitants engage in pastoralism and agriculture and produce primarily for commercial markets but also for partial subsistence. A small percentage of men are in white-collar occupations (for example, the civil service or teaching), and some run small businesses (for example, stores, taxi services, coffeeshops, or metalworks).

The village is ninety kilometers from Mytilini, the major port and city of Lesbos, and is connected to it by a road paved in the early 1970s. Taxis make frequent trips to Mytilini and there is a daily bus between the two places. Electricity was introduced into most homes in the 1960s, although some houses still exist without this amenity. Although interior plumbing is now being installed, most houses still obtain water either from a neighborhood spigot or from a spigot in the yard.

The village forms a compact settlement with well-defined borders and is surrounded by open fields and pasturage. Houses and yards, located immediately adjacent to one another, are clustered in residential islands separated by narrow cobblestone streets. Tall walls surround these residential islands and subdivide them into lots containing a yard and one of more buildings. Each lot with its yard and buildings belongs to a nuclear family, or a nuclear family and one set of grandparents.

The house, the yard, and the street in front of the house are the domain of women, their female friends, the elderly, and children. They are places of work, socializing, and child rearing. With the exception of going to work in the fields and going to church, women spend most of their time in their own homes and neighborhoods. By contrast, men spend little time at home or in their neighborhoods. For them, the house is a place to wash, eat, change clothes, sleep, and receive company. Only on formal occasions such as their namedays, an engagement, or a marriage will men stay home to participate in the celebration.

The residential islands surround a large open space, the central public square. While the public square is the heart, or nucleus, of the village which spreads out around it, there are other smaller squares and open spaces distributed throughout the village. Each one is a focal point for a neighborhood where neighbors (usually women and older people) may gather during the day. These neighborhoods are named and their general boundaries are known by the villagers.

The central square provides the focus for the men's primary place of social interaction. A large part of the central square is shaded by an enormous plane tree during the summer. The edges of this space are occupied by shops and public offices and by cafes that serve their customers on outdoor tables when the weather is good. The public square is occupied almost solely by men, and at times by children at play, usually boys. When not working, men spend as much of their time as possible in the public square and in the cafes. There they find entertainment, exchange information, conduct deals, seek employment, or hire laborers.

Women only timidly venture into this public space and only if they must. They recognize the public square as the domain of men. Rather than enter the public square themselves, women will send children to do errands or deliver messages to their husbands. If they must enter a shop or office on the public square, they will not cross the street to reach it, but will approach it by way of the skirting streets. Only when public events or festivities such as a wedding celebration are held in the public square do women freely enter it, but then, only accompanied by their husbands and families.

While recently there has been some "loosening" of this separation of public and private, male and female domains, in certain rural villages, by and large it characterizes the social structure of Greek village life.[1] It meant that we spent much of our time in those areas that are primarily the domain of women, and that women became our most numerous and most important informants.

Methods

Theoretical Approach Our theoretical approach was based on a sociolinguistic model. We considered this an appropriate model because our basic premise was that built form constitutes a system that depicts and conveys information for its community of users—it is a kind of communication system, or a kind of "language."

Sociolinguists strive for a study of language that depicts the full complexity of its actual use in society (Hymes 1974, 19). Sociolinguists examine language in the context of a speech community which shares rules for the conduct and interpretation of speech (Hymes 1974, 31). To understand the meaning of language in a particular community, it is studied in the context of actual communicative events (Hymes 1974, 16, 133).

Sociolinguistic research utilizes ethnographic methods and constructs both "emic" and "etic" accounts of speech events. In anthropology, emic accounts of behavioral events are defined as those representing the insider's or actor's point of view, and etic ones represent an outsider's point of view. The etic account is considered useful as a preliminary grid which can be related to emic accounts and which can provide a framework for comparing different emic accounts. It is the emic account, however, that validates information by revealing, for example, how phonological features are relevant to the identification of cultural behavior (Hymes 1974, 11, 22).

To obtain the insider's point of view the sociolinguist conducts ethnographic research of speech events which includes simultaneous study of the circumstances of their occurrence, identity of participants, and features of the utterances themselves (Hymes 1974, 199). Sociolinguists also value a diachronic study of language, in the belief that understanding the way language has changed through time is an important aspect of understanding an existing speech community.

Sociolinguistics, or what might also be termed "socio-semiotics," provides a paradigm for combining ethnographic fieldwork with a detailed study of the form of meaningful sound (morphemes) in its social context. The same approach, when applied to a study of architectural form, generates "architectural semiotics," in the original sense of the word. As initially defined by De Saussure, semiotics meant the "empirical study of systems of signs within systems of use in actual communities," in contrast to its more common recent usage as the "study of systems of signs as codes alone" (Hymes 1974, 6).[2]

Taking the same approach that the sociolinguist takes to the study of language, we hypothesized that when vernacular architecture is examined from the point of view of an insider (the emic account), socially significant information known and shared by the inhabitants will be revealed. The etic account of a house (i.e., a description of its appearance, features, construction, and so on), though constituting necessary preliminary information, can only be assigned meaning through the collection of emic data.

To test the hypothesis, detailed documentation of house features and their variation (the etic account) had to be supplemented with information on how the members of the community perceive, categorize, and value house features. To achieve these objectives the anthropological methodology of participant observation and interview was combined with traditional architectural visual documentation of houses through measured drawings and extensive photography, and with interviews that included the use of slides as an eliciting device.

Drawing on the sociolinguistic model, we also felt it was vital to add a historical dimension to our study. In our view, social pressures are continually operating upon vernacular architectural form and decoration, not from some remote point in the past, but as an immanent social force acting in the living present (to paraphrase Labov [1983]), and so the meaning of architectural form for its inhabitants is also a dynamic changing one. As a result we added a diachronic element to our data collection to discover how the present built environment was created.

Data Collection   We studied Eressos during a continuous residence in the village from October 1977 to August 1978.[3] We spent the first three months obtaining census data and walking through the entire village identifying and making notes on a map about the visual diversity of houses. We frequently encountered residents and solicited from them information about village life and social structure, building practices, and the history of particular buildings and people. We documented visual observations with photographs and sketches, and we recorded and later transcribed the conversations and interviews we had with people who invited us into their homes. We became familiar with the local dialect which proved to be invaluable for our work. Using certain words from the local dialect indicated to informants that we did not have the prejudice against village life that is common among urban Greeks.

During the next five months of our stay, we studied thirty houses intensively. Although the sample was gathered by convenience, we attempted to include in it the full range of visual variation identified in our preliminary work. (In a subsequent survey of house types in the village, we found that our sample did contain representatives of each type in roughly the same proportion as they occurred in the village.) We systematically documented these houses with photographs, sketches, and drawings based on detailed measurements of all features of the house, including, for example, the dimensions of grooved moldings around wall cavities, the components of windows, and the size of door hinges. It usually took us two days to complete documentation of a single house. Throughout these months, we continued collecting information through unstructured interviews and participant observation, especially with the families whose houses we measured.

During our last months in Eressos, we conducted systematic interviews with the owners and residents of those houses we had measured. Using slides to elicit information, we showed each family pictures of its own house, as well as of the variety of house types and features found in the village. These interviews provided information about past and present construction practices, uses of the house, and village history; they also elicited revealing value-laden responses.

In this way we obtained explicit information about the use and meaning of particular spaces or architectural features for a particular group, in the present as well as in the past. At other times inferences about use and meaning could be made by relating characteristics of the people being interviewed, such as age, socioeconomic standing, gender, or gender of offspring, to their responses. The focus of our interest in these interviews was the respondent's familiarity with and associations elicited by the presented images; ability to name features, rooms, or elements; and definition of appropriate uses or activities associated with the space. We reconstructed the present and past meaning of house form and decoration, and variations thereof, by looking for consistencies between reactions of respondents.[4]

Results

In considering the results of our study, which are described below, we want to emphasize that these are findings that emerged from analysis of the data and which became accessible only because we approached our study of the built environment through the eyes of its inhabitants. We did not anticipate these results. We set out to determine only if the built environment possessed meaning for its users and if so, what that meaning was.

Time and Change   While vernacular architecture has most commonly been regarded as having a timeless, unchanging quality (Glassie 1968, 33; Dorson 1973, 13), the diachronic emphasis of our study revealed constant transformation through time in the architecture of Eressos. The existing buildings, and the memories of the inhabitants, allowed us to reconstruct the changing form and meaning of the village's architecture over the past 130 years. Within this time, we discerned three periods salient for the inhabitants which were also manifest in house form and decoration. We did not specify the periods according to our knowledge of history; instead, they emerged from the data and reflect the inhabitants' sense of time. These periods provide the context for other findings to be discussed.

Period I, from 1850 to 1889, is the earliest time for which we can decipher any information about houses, either from oral accounts or from securely dated existing buildings. During that time Eressos was part of the Ottoman Empire, and a small Turkish minority lived harmoniously with the predominantly Greek population of the village. A great earthquake in 1889 caused considerable destruction in Eressos and stimulated extensive construction and renovation. The earthquake now serves as a convenient marker of time: the villagers still refer to it in their conversations by pinpointing events as having occurred before or after it. They also identify houses that pre- and post-date the earthquake.

Period II bridges the time between the great earthquake of 1889 and the end of World War II in 1945. This was a time of rising nationalism as well as increasing identification with the Western world. During the last decade of the nineteenth century and the first decade of the twentieth, the idea that Greek political authority should replace Ottoman rule spread through the Greek populations of the Ottoman Empire including Lesbos. In 1912, the idea was realized and Lesbos became part of Greece. In the Balkan Exchange of 1922, an agreement was made between Greece and Turkey to exchange the Greek and Turkish populations within their borders. The Turkish minority of Eressos left and was replaced by Greek refugees from Asia Minor.

Period III extends from the end of World War II to the present. After the civil war, which was fought at the conclusion of World War II and which ended in 1949, there began a massive exodus from many rural areas of Greece, including Eressos, to major urban centers. A changing national economy has supported this abandonment of rural villages which has only now begun to wane. In the past thirty years Eressos has dwindled from 3,500 to its present size of 1,500 people.

Sensitivity to Distant Influences   Most commonly, the stylistic inspiration for vernacular architecture has been said to derive from strictly indigeneous sources (Jenkins 1973, 505; Evans 1973, 530).

However, we found primarily nonlocal sources inspiring or stimulating stylistic change in Eressos. The village has not existed in a vacuum—it has experienced the currents of social, political, economic, and architectural developments occurring elsewhere. While the loci generating these currents and the nature and degree of their impact on Eressos have changed over time, their influence has been persistent and significant.

During Period II, the source of influences upon Eressos shifted from the East to the West. Inspiration for prestigious visual form was derived more and more from the Greek mainland and Western Europe and less from Asia Minor, where economic and cultural ties had been maintained for centuries. These stylistic influences and changes anticipated and accommodated the new political, economic, and cultural order that followed the incorporation of Lesbos into the Greek state in 1912.

These new stylistic elements were derived from the neoclassic architecture of Athens and other mainland cities influenced by nineteenth-century European Greek revival architecture.[5] For example, plaster decorations of the fireplace and sacred corner began to incorporate neoclassical motifs such as triglyphs, corinthian columns, and dentines. Eastern decorative motifs, such as the heart shape, or Byzantine floral and leaf shapes, were eliminated. Neoclassic influences were also evident on the house exterior. Triglyphs and den-tile decorations appeared under the eaves of some houses,[6] and allusions to a pediment on the frontal facade of other houses were suggested by the framing of the tiled roof to form a triangle. In one house, the stucco on the exterior corners was etched to resemble pilasters. Creating precise symmetry on the facade, rarely seen in earlier buildings, was another expression of this new sensibility.

The iconography of women's handiwork changed too, paralleling changes in the architecture. Patterns reflecting Greek national identity began to appear in carpets and other textiles. Figurative subjects depicting Greek folk tales, and the meander motif of ancient Greece, replaced abstract Eastern designs.

In Period III buildings have been modernized according to standards set by the architecture and life-style of Athens and other large cities. In earlier times, distant influences inspired new forms and decorative motifs in already existing elements (such as fireplaces). Now totally new elements and new spatial arrangements are being introduced as well, and old elements eliminated.

The new stylistic criteria adopted are largely derived from international modernist architecture, which rejected both interior and exterior decoration. This movement has heavily influenced architecture in Athens and through Athens, all of Greece. In the context of Eressos it translates into a desire to simplify and smooth the house surfaces, often by using concrete; to remove features considered old fashioned such as narrow rectangular windows, wall protrusions, and cavities. "Modernity" also means furnishing the interior with appliances and furniture, and decorating walls with paint and patterned paper or plastic.

The Expression of Status Consciousness   Although vernacular architecture has often been presumed to be vigorously utilitarian (Roberts 1973, 282–83) and totally unselfconscious (Megas 1968, 3–12), we found evidence to the contrary. The inhabitants of Eressos, far from being unselfconscious about their houses, interpret small differences in house form and decoration as important status indicators.

In Period I, Eressos had a highly stratified society based on a system of ascribed status dependent on one's family of birth. The highest status members of this society were referred to as "aristocracy." The only way of bettering one's status in society was through the system of arranged marriage. This social stratification in Periods I and II was expressed architecturally by the overall type of house (there were seven house types) (Pavlides 1985, 158–96) and by particulars of its features which were always congruent with the status expressed by the house type. Specific dimensions of spaces, combinations of features, and degree of decoration could also indicate status. Small houses were simple and had few relatively unadorned wall elements, while larger houses were more complex and had more spaces, more wall elements, and more elaborate decoration. Wood was particularly scarce and its interior use was prestigious. Degree of elaborateness was another criterion used to identify status. The more elaborate and complex a decoration, the greater its prestige. The adjective *vari* (heavy) was used to describe a highly elaborate plaster mantel (*phari*) or icon corner (*iconostassi*). Dimensions could also indicate status. The larger the dimension, the better, whether of an entire house, of a room, of a wall cavity, or of a window. Dimensions were not continuous, however, but instead were clustered around a few standard dimensions for the particular feature. For example, in all the rooms we measured in our thirty-house sample there were only five room heights: 180, 255, 290, 310, and 350 centimeters.

Eressos houses continue to express status in Period III, but it is through degree of modernization rather than through a well-defined hierarchical system of size and features as in Periods I and II. House type, size, and features have become secondary to the use of modern materials such as cement and paint, the presence of furniture and appliances, the removal of old-fashioned features, the piping of water, and electrification. Status is determined by the extent of modernization and smaller, fully modernized houses are more highly valued than larger, nonmodernized ones.

Dowry as a Stimulus for Construction and Renovation   In any society, house construction and renovation do not happen randomly. In Eressos, the need to provide daughters with a house and its furnishings as part of their dowry has been and remains the primary stimulus for house construction and renovation.[7] The changing expression of status in the Eressos house, throughout the three periods, has been due to changing perceptions of what constitutes an appropriate dowry.

In Period I, the erection of a new house or the renovation of an older one was undertaken to make up part of a dowry. Although young women and men had some say in spouse selection, family negotiations (*proxenio*) were primary. A girl's dowry figured prominently in these negotiations and its size and quality were vital factors in attracting a desirable husband. Providing a dowry house was accomplished either by constructing a new one or by renovating the family house and securing another smaller one for the parents. A family was often aided in its task by other villagers in exchange for produce or labor. Only wealthy villagers had cash to pay for labor to construct grand houses for their daughters.

The preparation of a house entailed not only building the walls, roof, ceilings, doors and windows, and built-in benches and cupboards but also producing furnishings for it. The design and size of a house were decisively influenced by the need for storage and display of the "furnishings," which included the material accoutrements of daily life (clothing, bedding, food, utensils, rugs) as well as prestige and decorative items (embroidery and crochet work, photographs, rugs). All of these material and decorative accoutrements, except for food utensils, were exclusively produced by women as part of their dowry. In Period I, these furnishings defined the appearance of the house interior, and anything of value in a house, especially in the less affluent ones, was the result of women's labor.[8]

During Period II, a fully equipped house remained a primary part of the dowry. House construction and renovation continued to be stimulated by the presence of a daughter approaching marriageable age. The introduction of neoclassical stylistic elements in architecture (especially among the wealthier villagers) and in furnishings reflected changing tastes and ideas about the type of dowry most likely to attract potential grooms.

In Period III the institution of dowry has remained strong and is still the primary factor stimulating renovation and stylistic modification of existing buildings, and the occasional construction of new ones. There is pressure to provide a totally modernized house in Eressos even though the possibility exists that the house will not be lived in, or might be abandoned after several years, when the young family emigrates to Athens. An even better dowry is considered to be a condominium apartment in Athens.

The Distinction Between Furniture and Furnishings In discussions of the house interior, furniture is commonly subsumed under the heading "furnishings." It became clear to us, however, that furniture and furnishings ought to be treated as two distinct categories when considering their meaning for the house interior and its users in Eressos.

All houses on Lesbos during Periods I and II lacked furniture. The absence of furniture, and the multiple uses of space characteristic of this period (see "Division of the House into Rooms," below), had important implications. Without furniture it was necessary for all activities to take place on the floor or on built-in benches. Various portable items were used for activities which today call for relatively immovable furniture. For example, a thin mattress was used for sleeping, a small low table was used for preparing food and for eating. These were stored after use. Since the floors were used for both sitting and sleeping, they had to be well covered with carpets for protection and insulation, and since they were highly visible without furniture, they also became a significant visual element of the house.

The absence of furniture also affected the appearance of the walls. All storage was accommodated in niches and other cavities embedded in them or on protrusions from them. All the house was in some sense public and all areas were "on display." Consequently wall cavities were frequently "closed" with a diaphanous cloth drape, not only to protect the objects stored inside from dust and sunlight, but also to visually enhance them and sometimes to attract attention to their contents. Horizontal surfaces of wall protrusions and cavities were invariably draped with a decorative cloth and shelves edged with crochet-work *dandeles*. The process of covering and decorating the floor and wall surfaces was referred to as "dressing" the house (*to spiti ine dimeno*) and constituted the total furnishing of it.[9]

In Period III the house interior has been radically redefined with the use of relatively immovable furniture and appliances. Beds, tables, chairs, sofas, a refrigerator, and a bottled-gas stove are crowded into the small rooms of houses built for use with a few small movable objects. Since storage functions of built-in cupboards and niches are now served by furniture, they are no longer needed. Their removal also frees up wall surface and makes furniture placement easier. Hairline cracks provide evidence of where these wall elements used to be. The only wall element not removed in the process of a complete modernization is the *iconostassi* in the sacred corner of the house.

Division of the House into Rooms   We are accustomed to dividing the interior space of houses into function-specific rooms or areas, but Eressos houses during Periods I and II were not divided this way. Instead, they were divided into "formal" and "informal" areas. Any given activity could take place in various parts of the house, depending on the character of the activity or the status of its participants. For example, entertaining a guest could take place in any one of several rooms depending on the status of the visitor or the formality of the occasion. By the same token many different activities could take place in the same space, as circumstances dictated. Thus, for example, the same room could be used for informal socializing, women's craft activities, eating, sleeping for the whole family, and food preparation exclusive of cooking, or it could be turned into a "formal" area by the use of appropriate carpets and other furnishings.

The introduction of furniture, which became widespread in Period III, has resulted in the function-specific naming of rooms. In the modernized house, tables, chairs, and sofas define "dining rooms" (*trapezeria*) and "living rooms" (*salone*), rooms specifically associated with entertaining. The introduction of beds define one or two rooms as "bedrooms" (*krevatokamera*). The desire to have rooms for particular activities often led to the building of additions or the subdividing of an existing room to create a house with a room assigned for each activity. The subdivision of existing spaces into more rooms, combined with the introduction of furniture, has resulted in extremely crowded interior spaces. The resulting inconvenience is well tolerated, however, because of the symbolic value of the newly created and furnished rooms.

Paradoxically, actual patterns of space use have changed only modestly. Sitting still occurs on the floor during informal events, and sleeping can still occur in various places in the house or in the yard. The modern "kitchen" (*kouzina*), while still used for many activities previously associated with the renovated space, is rarely used for cooking or dishwashing. These activities still take place in the yard or in a utility room separated from the rest of the house.

Age of Occupants, House Features, and Decoration Two factors affect house features in such a way that they signify the age of the occupants. The first factor is the continuous stylistic change that has characterized house form and appearance over the last 130 years. A house prepared as dowry at a particular time reflects the style in vogue at that time and thus the age of the occupants. The second factor is the custom of passing on to a new couple, as dowry, any valuables or decorative items, such as carpets or embroideries, owned by the parents. With this transference of material goods, the interior of older couples' houses takes on an impoverished look. In the past, this impoverished look was reinforced by the custom of using black coverings over all interior surfaces of the house for a prolonged period after a family death, more likely to be experienced by older people. Although in Period III this dramatic altering of interior decor is no longer practiced during mourning, avoidance of decoration is considered appropriate. Thus, because older people have given their best as dowry and because they express mourning by avoiding decoration, rather stark house interiors were correctly identified during the slide interviews as belonging to older people.

House Form and Gender of Offspring In Period III, the extent to which a house has been modernized is commonly related to the presence of a daughter in the family. A house that still has the stigmatized features of plaster decorations over the fireplace, wall cavities and protrusions, uncovered ceiling beams, and unplastered exterior surfaces is likely to be the house of a daughterless family. In some instances, such houses are not even provided with electricity or piped water. Without a daughter who requires a dowry, there is less incentive to spend money and expend effort to change the house.

Summary of Findings The following major points emerged from our study of the architecture of Eressos: (1) There is a sense of time and change that is specific to the locality. (2) Local styles are sensitive to distant influences and are composed of elements gathered from diverse sources. Local architecture is sensitive and responsive to social, political, and economic pressures, and to architectural developments occurring elsewhere. (3) There is a high degree of status consciousness expressed in the built environment, in contradiction to the notion of a "natural" or "unselfconscious" architecture. (4) The primary stimulus for construction of new houses or renovation of old ones is the need for families to provide dowry for their daughters. (5) A distinction can be made between furniture and furnishings of a house, and these have important implications for the use of space in the house interior. (6) Interior space is not divided according to function specificity, but instead according to the formal or informal character of an activity. (7) Age of the occupants is expressed in stylistic features of the house and its interior decoration. (8) The gender of offspring is expressed in the degree of modernization a house exhibits.

Design and Planning Implications

The type of research reported here can be useful to architectural practice and education and is relevant to establishing appropriate governmental policy on the preservation of vernacular architecture.

Designing for the Newly Urbanized   The rapidity of urbanization experienced everywhere in the world today annually uproots millions of people who leave their vernacular built habitats to seek new shelter in architect designed housing. Knowing something about the newly urbanized—their original habitats, patterns of space use, and reading of visual form—could prove useful to the planners and designers of new housing. Anecdotes about new housing being inappropriately used by its new inhabitants are sometimes amusing, often tragic, in the misallocation of the limited resources available to impoverished people. They also point to the great need to understand the cultural background of migrants to urban centers.

The division of the Eressos house into "formal," "everyday," and "utility" zones according to the character of activity is an example of information about the social context of architecture that could be useful to designers. This information provides insight into the way activities are structured in the house. It sheds light on why fully equipped kitchens are not used as such in Eressos and has implications for the way these people are likely to perceive their surroundings when they move to urban areas. Kitchens in Eressos are zoned as "everyday" zones, and there is a strong taboo against the presence of food odors generated by cooking in areas used for socializing. Modern apartments and houses that we are accustomed to, with cooking areas often integrated into the living areas, would be unacceptable to Eressiotes. It is of interest that some Athenian housewives explicitly express the importance of physically separating the cooking area from the living areas of a house or apartment.

Designing in Vernacular Settings   A second possible application of studies like ours is to the design of new structures in vernacular settings. Not knowing local codes of social meaning—for example, whether and how social stratification is expressed—could elicit unexpected reactions from local people. This point can be illustrated by the example of a house built in Eressos that was an architect's interpretation of the local vernacular. While this house was very successful from an outsider's point of view, local residents were ambivalent since its prototype was one of the least prestigious local house types. In this particular case local reaction mattered little to the Athenian who built the house. However, use of local vernacular for its visual qualities without understanding its social connotations could present difficulties if the building being constructed were for local use. Knowledge of the code could help, either to observe it, for example, through the conscious use of prestigious design elements or avoidance of stigmatized building types, or to anticipate and offset confusion through appropriate public education.

Defining Government Policy on Historic Preservation   In many countries, including Greece, governmental regulations provide guidelines for architectural preservation and for the construction of new buildings in vernacular settings. Government policy and the definition of appropriate regulations for new construction could benefit from social contextual studies of vernacular architecture. We witnessed an example during our stay in Eressos. A traveling exhibit of drawings and models of vernacular architecture was brought to Eressos, sponsored by the Ministry of Housing. Regional architectural stereotypes were presented in an effort to reeducate the peasants to build in the old vernacular. There was one type which supposedly represented the entire island of Lesbos. It was an artificial construct based on some building features found on Lesbos but had nothing to do with the houses of Eressos, or with the actual houses found in other villages.

Another example is provided by the following experience we had while doing research in Eressos. While there we sometimes expressed our views on the value of preserving the old buildings and tried to convince people not to destroy them. In one particular instance a local man asked for drawings for a modern cinder block building to replace a lovely (in our view) older stone house. In spite of persuasive reasons for saving the old building and renovating it, he was fixed in his plans to destroy it. Perplexed by our persistence and concern, he finally inquired whether we knew someone who would be a good husband for his daughter who preferred old-fashioned houses. We were ignoring the supreme social function of the house in Eressos, which is to serve as dowry. What mattered was not cost or practicality, but the image of modernity that would most likely attract a desirable groom for his daughter. The old house was torn down and its stone walls used to construct the foundation for a new cinder-block house. Local perceptions like these clearly can block efforts to preserve vernacular environments. Preservation efforts can be most effective when they address local needs, perceptions, and concerns.

Conclusions

In examining the architecture of Eressos over the last 130 years, we documented continuous changes in architectural form involving extensive renovations, and dramatic alterations in furnishing the house interior. These changes were related to social contextual factors including political authority, economy, means of production, and social stratification. During all three periods the primary stimulus to change remained the need to provide appropriate dowry. Often architectural changes served no purpose other than to satisfy changing perceptions of acceptable and desirable architecture used to express the social position and aspirations of house owners. Functional or utilitarian concerns served by these architectural changes were secondary. Changes in the architecture of Eressos occurred primarily as a response to its changing social meaning.

The kind of anthropological research that coincided with our collection of visual data requires lengthy stays in a community. The collection of etic and emic data is costly and takes a lot of time and effort. A priori there is no obvious reason for expending the extra energy that is needed to study the visual environment in its social context in this way. However, a purely visual approach to the architecture of Eressos would never have revealed the richness of information that the inhabitants read in it. Coherent patterns of meaning emerged only by understanding the inhabitants' point of view.

Further studies of this nature involving anthropologists as well as architects are essential for our understanding of vernacular environments. They can also provide information relevant for our schools of architecture, which are seeking ways to sensitize students to the social aspects of design; for environmental designers who increasingly are confronted with designing for users who are both geographically and culturally far removed from themselves; for governments interested in passing regulations and laws to help preserve their national architectural heritage.

Notes

1. A similar division between male and female domains and places of activity has been described as existing in other parts of Greece, for example, in Vasilika (Freidl 1962, 12), in northern Greece (du Boulay 1974, 31), on Tinos (Dubisch 1976, 321–22), on Ios (Currier, 1976, 309–10), and on Kalymnos (Bernard 1976, 295). It has been the subject of extensive analysis and a film by Hoffman working on Thira (1976, 331–82).

2. Amos Rapoport (1982, 43) also raises this point:

In linguistics itself, there has been increasing criticism of the neglect of pragmatics (see Bates, 1976)—the "cultural premises about the world in which speech takes place" (Keesing 1979, 14). The development of sociolinguistics is part of this reevaluation; the point is made that the nature of any given speech event may vary depending on the nature of the participants, the social setting, the situation—in a word the context (see Gumprerz and Hymes, 1972; Giglioli, 1972). In any event, it appears that the neglect of pragmatics and the concentration on syntactics almost to the exclusion of everything else are serious shortcomings of the semiotic approach.

3. One of the authors (Pavlides) is a native Greek and has maternal relatives residing in Eressos. Linguistic fluency and established ties with inhabitants through the network of kinship greatly facilitated entry into the village, access into people's houses, and flow of comunication.

4. Much of the preceding description of setting and methods is drawn from a previously published work by the authors (Pavlides and Hesser 1986, 68–71) and is used here by permission of Princeton University Press.

5. Radford and Clark (1974, 67), who have documented a similar shift in motif to neoclassicism on Thira at this time, also see it as the introduction of forms "not direct from ancient Greece, but by way of Genoa, Venice and Germany."

6. Tzakou (1974) has documented a similar transformation of the house exterior on the island of Siphnos.

7. The process of arranging marriage contracts and the role played by dowry in Eressos is similar to that described for other areas of Greece. The father everywhere bears the primary responsibility, but he is aided by his wife and sons. The wife's major contribution is the weaving and decoration of carpets and linens for the house interior (Papaharalambos 1968, 43; Friedl 1962, 53–54; du Boulay 1974, 95–96; Bialor 1976, 232). However, the house is not invariably a part of the dowry. It is mandatory in other villages on Lesbos (Zourou 1974, 85) and is mentioned as a common part of the dowry by Peristiany (1976, 217), Hoffman (1976, 332), Dubisch (1976, 321), Bernard (1976, 296), Allen (1976, 185–86), Kenna (1976, 349), and Pasadaiou (1973, 12). However, on Cyprus (Papaharalambos 1968, 5) and on Chios (personal communication) it was customary for the groom to build the house. In Karpofora, inclusion of a house in the dowry is a recent phenomenon (Aschenbrenner 1976, 214). In Vasilika, the family house goes to the sons of the family (Friedl 1962, 214).

8. Sinos (1976, 15) reports that in simple houses on Cyprus the only items of value were those made by the women for their dowries. These items were used not only in daily life but also for decoration of the walls and doorways.

9. These storage areas also have been noted by Papaharalambos (1968, 44) in the houses on Cyprus and by du Boulay (1974, 23–26). Our experience in other parts of Greece suggests that the building of houses with a similar variety of storage features was typical in rural areas and probably reflected an absence of furniture. That people today, even when they have furniture, commonly sit on the floor for informal gatherings or for work is indicative of the significance of furniture as objects of prestige and show, rather than as totally utilitarian and necessary parts of the house.

10. The same pattern of use and equipping of the house described here is described, with some variations, by du Boulay for a contemporary village in northern Greece (1974, 23–24).

References

Allen, P. S. 1976. Aspida: A depopulated Maniat community. In *Regional variation in modern Greece and Cyprus: Towards a perspective on the ethnography of Greece*, ed. M. Dimen and E. Friedl, 168–98. New York: New York Academy of Science.

Aschenbrenner, S. E. 1976. Karpofora: Reluctant farmers on a fertile land. In *Regional variation in modern Greece and Cyprus*, 207–21. *See* Allen 1976.

Bates, E. 1976. *Language and context: The acquisition of pragmatics.* New York: Academic.

Bernard, H. R. 1976. Kalymnos: This island of the sponge. In *Regional variation in modern Greece and Cyprus*, 291–307. *See* Allen 1976.

Bialor, P. A. 1976. The northwestern corner of the Peloponnesos: Mavrikion and its region. In *Regional variation in modern Greece and Cyprus*, 222–31. *See* Allen 1976.

Currier, R. 1976. Social interaction and social structure in a Greek island village. In *Regional variation in modern Greece and Cyprus*, 308–13. *See* Allen 1976.

Dorson, R. M. 1973. Concepts of folklore and folklife studies. In *Folklore and folklife: An introduction*, ed. R. M. Dorson, 1–50. Chicago and London: The University of Chicago Press.

Dubisch, J. 1976. The ethnography of the islands: Tinos. In *Regional variation in modern Greece and Cyprus*, 314–27. *See* Allen 1976.

du Boulay, J. 1974. *Portrait of a Greek mountain village.* Oxford: Clarendon Press.

Evans, E. E. 1973. The cultural geographer and folklife research. In *Folklore and folklife*, 517–32. *See* Dorson 1973.

Friedl, E. 1962. *Vasilika: A village in modern Greece.* New York: Holt, Rinehart and Winston.

Gigliolo, P. P., ed. 1972. *Language and social context.* New York: Penguin.

Glassie, H. 1968. *Patterns in the material folk culture of the Eastern United States.* Philadelphia: University of Pennsylvania Press.

Gumpertz, J. J., and D. Hymes. 1972. *Directions in sociolinguistics: The ethnography of communication.* New York: Holt, Rinehart and Winston.

Hoffman, S. M. 1976. The ethnography of the islands: Thira. In *Regional variation in modern Greece and Cyprus*, 328–40. *See* Allen 1976.

Hymes, D. 1974. *Foundations in sociolinguistics.* Philadelphia: University of Pennsylvania Press.

Jenkins, J. G. 1973. The use of artifacts and folk art in the folk museum. In *Folklore and folklife*, 497–516. *See* Dorson 1973.

Keesing, R. M. 1979. Linguistic knowledge and cultural knowledge: Some doubts and speculation. *American Anthropologist* 81:14–34.

Kenna, M. 1976. Houses, fields, and graves: Property and ritual obligation on a Greek island. *Ethnology* 15:21–34.

Labov, W. 1973. *Sociolinguistic patterns.* Philadelphia: University of Pennsylvania Press.

Megas, G. A. 1968. Skopoi kai methododia tin erevnan tis Laikis Oikodomis: Horotaxia, poleodomia, architectoniki. *Laographia* 16:3–12.

Papaharalambos, G. H. 1968. *I Kypriaki Oikia, Leukosia.*

Pasadaiou, A. 1973. *I Laiki architectoniki tis Imbrou.* Athens: Academia Athinon.

Pavlides, E. 1985. Vernacular architecture in its social context: A case study of Eressos, Greece. Ph.D. diss., University of Pennsylvania.

Pavlides, E., and J. E. Hesser. 1986. Women's roles and house form and decoration in Eressos, Greece. In *Gender and power in rural Greece*, ed. J. Dubisch, 68–96. Princeton: Princeton University Press.

Peristiany, J. G. ed. 1965. *Honor and shame: The values of Mediterranean society.* London: Weidenfeld and Nicolson.

Radford, A., and G. Clark. 1974. Cyclades: Studies of a vernacular environment. In *Shelter in Greece*, ed. B. Dourmanis and P. Oliver, 431–44. Greece: Architecture in Greece Press.

Rapoport, A. 1969. *House form and culture.* Englewood Cliffs, N.J.: Prentice-Hall.

————. 1982. *The meaning of the built environment*. Beverly Hills, Calif.: Sage.

Roberts. W. E. 1973. Folk architecture. In *Folklore and folklife*, 281–94. *See* Dorson 1973.

Sinos, S. 1976. *Anadromi sti Laiki architektoniki tis Kyprou*. Athens.

Tzakou, A. 1974. *Central settlements on the Island of Siphnos: Form and evolution in a traditional system*. Athens.

Zourou, F. M. 1974. *O gamos sti Voria Lesbo*. Mytiline.

18

CULTURAL IMPLICATIONS OF
HOUSING DESIGN POLICY IN INDIA

JON LANG

Since World War II many countries have made valiant efforts to meet the housing needs of their populations through public policies involving the design and construction of housing units and residential areas. India is such a country. The results have drawn both praise and criticism—praise for the intention and criticism of the results. Much of the criticism has focused on the process of housing delivery—on the economic structure of society, on the nature of the market, or on the nature of governmental agencies responsible for overseeing the process. This chapter is more narrowly focused on the thinking of architects, as building and urban designers, that has informed and become embedded in the housing programs of India. It is about architects' images of good environments and the problems with these images. It also suggests a way of responding to the slippage between intentions and results. Although this chapter focuses on India, the observations I make here apply to many countries especially those having a diversity of cultures.

I will describe the basic relations between the patterns of culture and the patterns of housing areas in India. This description is biased by my concern with understanding those variables of importance in determining good housing design. My study differs from an anthropological study of the same topic by asking the questions: "Why are housing and house forms in this pattern?" and "What does this mean for the design of housing programs?" instead of dealing with traditional anthropological issues. I begin by describing what is perceived by social scientists, architects themselves, and lay observers as wrong with present housing policies, particularly public sector housing design. They all suggest that much housing design is culturally inappropriate. I then go on to describe the variables that enable an architect to ask questions about the interrelationship between the cultures of India and the housing areas and the house forms associated with them. I will argue that the process of design implicit in the housing programs of India must change from a mimetic one to a problem-solving one if culturally appropriate housing is to be achieved.

The Criticism of Design in the Housing Programs in India

The design process for most architects and urban designers involves the mimetic adaptation of particular patterns to the situation at hand. The set of patterns used by an architect is referred to as his or her style. National housing programs usually have sets of prototypes embedded within them. In India these are mainly for flats, detached houses, and a hierarchy of roads and services to accompany them. The design of a particular project thus involves the application by the designer of his or her patterns to a set of prototypes. The suitability of the design to the resources and requirements of its ultimate residents depends on the cultural suitability of both prototypes used and the designer's own patterns.

Many of the housing programs in India are funded and administered from New Delhi and are aimed at many income levels. The designs that result from their application tend to be based on a limited set of models that are applied throughout the country from the Himalayas to Cape Comorin. Decentralization of decision making alone would be unlikely to change this. The models are powerful ones—they capture the imagination and have a high degree of internal logic. The question is, "How externally valid are they?"

The models on which the prototypes of housing design in much housing policy in India are based include the cantonment, which worked well for the (British) Indian Army in the nineteenth century; the related Garden City model as originally promulgated by Ebenezer Howard (1902) as a response to the housing and environmental conditions of industrial England; the Neighborhood Unit Concept of Clarence Perry (1927) devised as part of the New York Regional Plan, and the Radiant City of Le Corbusier (1934), which was a response to the unsalubrious conditions of European cities and the development of new technologies, especially the automobile and building construction techniques, and which was used in India to break the "shackles of the past." In addition, the British presence in India is reflected in the bylaws and building codes which dictate such things as location of plumbing, and side and front set-back requirements in plotted housing. Thus many housing design programs are based on international precedents rather than indigenous ones. The application of these models is clearly seen in the new residential

Table 18.1
Percentage of Population Living in One-Room Units

Ahmedabad	65.3
Bangalore	55.9
Bombay	72.3
Calcutta	71.4
Delhi	63.0
Madras	67.5

developments outside the major cities of the country and the large number of new towns built since Independence. The results indicate that substantial opportunities for fulfilling the needs of housing residents have been lost because of the lack of understanding by policy makers, planners, and architects of how culture and house form are interrelated, and their lack of knowledge about the many cultures that exist in the country and their implications for housing.

Analyses of what has been built show repeated misfits between house form and culture as it is. There has been a failure to deal adequately with private open space (Payne 1977), to relate house type to family type (Brolin 1976), to recognize the nature of transportation systems (Nagendra 1979) and the relation between home and school (N. K. Bose 1968), to deal adquately with the needs of women (A. M. Singh 1978), to deal with the nature of ablutions (Vastu-Shilpu Foundation 1983), to understand the differences between the fronts and backs of buildings (Rapoport 1977), to recognize the climatic impact of new materials (Nilsson 1975), to recognize the cultural use of materials (A. K. Singh 1984), to deal sensitively with aesthetic issues (Bhoosan and Misra 1979), to consider how houses evolve (Das 1983), to recognize the interrelationship between home and work (Das 1983; Greer 1984) and the nature of population integration and segregation (Grenell 1972; Gupta 1974; Rapoport 1977), and, more generally, simply to meet the life-style needs of the population (King 1974; A. K. Singh 1984). This criticism is leveled at housing areas designed by both local and foreign architects. Often this criticism seems to be aimed at both the housing and the culture of India. This chapter focuses on the first.

India is an extraordinarily diverse country in climate, peoples, and cultures. It is a federation of states under one central government. "Indians are a minority in India" is a trite political observation recognizing the diversity of peoples in the country yet it can be argued that there is a typical urban house throughout India. More than half of the population of Indian cities live in single-room units as Table 18.1 indicates. An analysis of these units and the adaptations people have made to them gives some inkling of how people wish to live and the interrelationship between house form and culture in India, but

a much more fruitful line of information is yielded by looking at the house
forms of those who have the resources to do better than just survive and who
have the capability of living in house types that fit life-styles closer to their
"ideals" derived from cultural values.

Built Form Determinants

At any time, the design of housing does reflect the sum
of the cultural forces that exist in a society—the values of those in power who
make decisions and those responsible for designing the public policies, programs, and processes of delivering housing to the population. This does not
mean, however, that the housing is appropriate for the culture—the life-styles
and values—of those people who inhabit it.

It is possible to argue that the housing policies of India are aimed at producing an egalitarian, casteless society. There are two observations that can be
made about this. First, the support of ethnic-based societies and diversity of
house sizes clearly shows that this is not true; second, we now are fully aware
of the foolhardiness of believing that housing form will determine culture although it can impose many restrictions on behavioral possibilities. Thus,
assuming that one of the goals of housing policies is to design culturally congruent environments—ones with which people are happy and in which they
wish to live given their resources—an understanding of the past and present
uses and abuses of housing areas suggests how the housing design should be
done and the general direction in which housing policy goals should trend.

Looking at traditional housing which has emerged through a long process
of trial and error helps architects and anthropologists alike understand the important variables that should be considered in designing the layout of the built
environment. In such housing, adjustments have been made to house types
over the generations so that the house forms fit basic cultural patterns. Thus
architects have been looking at Shahjahanabad (Old Delhi) (Fonesca 1969),
the *stores* of Tiruchirapelli (Patel 1976), the *pols* of Ahmedabad (Doshi 1974),
the aesthetics of Jaisalmer (K. Jain 1982) and the self-built *bustees* of Indian
cities (Payne 1977; Das 1983). The danger, as Grover (1967) and A. M. Singh
(1978) warn, is that these patterns will be incorporated into public policies for
housing design with all their deficiencies and will be applied in contexts in
which they are not valid in much the same manner as the patterns that are
being used now. What is important is to understand the set of the variables
linking house form and environment (see Rapoport 1977).

These variables include the nature of the physical environment—what it
affords for climate and for natural resources to be used as building materials—

and the nature of the sociocultural environment—the basic cultural ethos, the nature of behavior patterns, the nature of the family unit and aesthetic values. The variables of the built environment that are of concern include patterns of built form and open space and land uses; "neighborhood patterns"; the more detailed relations of buildings to each other and to open spaces, including roads and communal settings; and the internal organization of buildings, their rooms and their furnishings.

The relations between patterns of the environment and culture are not deterministic except in a negative sense. If the built environment does not afford an activity it cannot be carried out. If it does afford an activity, it could but not necessarily would be carried out. Any particular pattern of the environment affords many activities and aesthetic interpretations and, except for some activities, any pattern of behavior can be afforded by many different environmental patterns. The behaviors that will occur will depend on the *predispositions* of the population, its perceptions of cultural norms, and its perceptions of the consequences of the behavior. What the patterns of the environment afford a population or individuals also depends on their *competencies* and *resources* (see Lang 1980). Poorly designed public policies and thus housing environments can eliminate or make difficult the possibility of behaviors that are part of the culture of a people. Good housing design enhances these. One of the problems of design is to decide on what is an appropriate model of culture to be used as a basis for design.

Traditional Patterns of Culture and House

One of the major determinants of house form in traditional India was the canonical texts on architecture. These texts are based on images of what the culture should be, and so they are, by definition, highly normative (Acharaya 1927). The application of these design principles is more observable in middle- and upper-income housing than in housing for the poor. There are many such texts, the best known of which are the *Shilpa Shastras*, and the *Manasara*. These canons of design were inculcated in the minds of masons and carpenters through the master-apprentice form of artisan training. Even today, builders follow these precepts in many parts of India, although the purpose they serve is largely unknown by those who employ them. They are simply "the way things are done." Historically these canons reflected a series of religious beliefs—the *broad cultural ethos* because Hinduism is as much a way of life as a religion. The canons provided instructions for very practical ends, such as coolness on hot summer days, and for symbolic aesthetic ends.

The *Shilpa Shastras* and *Manasara* are Hindu in origin, the *Jatakas* and *Pali* are Buddhist and the *Mania Adi Sastram* are Tamil (Coomaraswamy 1938). There are similar edicts for the design of Moslem housing.

The *Shilpa Shastras* not only specify city and village forms in a number of geometric patterns and the location of temples, tanks, and land uses but also the design of forty-eight building types from palaces to cow sheds (Raz 1832). The layout of houses is based on the *Vastu-purusa* and the *Vastu-mandalas*. The former is based on the symbolism associated with the various parts of the body of Vishnu pressed to the ground, and the latter specify a number of proportional schemata based on the *Vastu-purusa* (Shastri 1968). Few urban places or houses fit specifically with these canons of design. Jaipur is the only city still observably laid out according to a mandala—a three-by-three schema—but the canons of house form are reflected in housing as diverse as the eighteenth-century *havelis* (merchants' mansions) of Jaisalmer in Rajasthan and the present-day mason-built houses in Trivandrum, Kerala. The implicit use of the *Shastras* is particularly strong in the southern Indian states of Tamil Nadu and Kerala, where traditions hold considerable sway.

More typically, traditional urban residential patterns reflect the means of livelihood of their occupants, the relationships between one group and another and the relationships of people within caste, occupational, and ethnic groups and between such groups. This is clearest in such settings as *mohallas*, *pols*, *paras* and *stores*. All of these are groupings of people based on ethnicity, clan, or occupation. The *pols* and *mohallas* and *stores* are essentially cul-de-sacs which are gated against outsiders. The pols of Ahmedabad were originally developed for defense against outsiders and still withstand communal rioting successfully (Kuhlar 1981). They are also organized to provide shade from the sun and to channel breezes through the streets and into and through the houses. They are true sociospatial schemata in which the members of the group have both formal and informal obligations to each other (Doshi 1974). They provide a sense of identity to their residents. Each such neighborhood will have its own temple reflecting the religious affiliations of the group with a particular god or aspect of Hinduism or Jainism.

In the traditional city there is still a clear hierarchy of streets from the major to the most intimate (Solanki 1968) based on territorial controls and uses. In Old Delhi, for example, there is a five-level hierarchy. Most important are the main commercial streets which act as spines and are the main channels for pedestrian and wheeled traffic. The second-level streets are narrower, with shops closer together and often a concentration of a single type of shop—of silversmiths or leather workers, for example—based on the historical development of the streets. The third-level streets are local shopping streets with residences intruding on the ground level. The fourth and fifth levels are the *mohallas* or *pols*. The smallest streets are deadends with family and community open spaces (the *chowks*) in which elders gather and children play. They may contain a tea or *pan* shop. The communal spaces are paved; often a tree provides shade. This affords shelter for the gathering of groups of people, the composition of the group depending on the time of day. This type of arrangement can also be seen in the *bustees* of cities although on a smaller scale and with a greater amount of life spilling out into the *chowks*. Modern housing policies also decree a hierarchy of streets but these are based narrowly, almost entirely on levels of automobile traffic flow.

The *pols* were typically Hindu. Moslem areas were more along the open streets; their mosques are accessible to all who pass by. There is likely to be a single mosque that dominates the others. The Moslem house, on the other hand, stresses internal privacy more than the Hindu, but this is not always as obvious in house plan as one might suspect.

The single-family detached-home residential area is not typical of the Indian city historically. Today set-back and side requirements often decree such housing in suburban areas. The detached home in its compound is, however, characteristic of the Bengali village, but this was a homestead rather than simply a house. This is also true of traditional Nair houses in Kerala where the house, again really a homestead, stood within a walled compound. In Kerala there was very little nucleation of such units until recently (Bhoosan and Misra 1979). The general pattern of home in a walled compound persists in even the smallest of single-family detached houses of cities such as Cochin and Trivandrum. The purely single-family-home residential area is, however, largely a product of the British era. It is also the house type to which many middle-class Indians aspire despite the criticism that it receives from many architects.

Traditional residential areas of cities are more than simply places for houses. They are highly active, with a variety of additional land uses, commercial, religious and often light manufacturing, in a highly dense environment. There is, nevertheless, a considerable amount of open space because most of the traditional houses were the type that had a courtyard. These areas reflect the close integration of the different aspects of life, the importance of the spiritual and the material in Hindu culture, attitudes toward privacy and communality in Indian life, and attitudes toward the ownership and control of land. Most housing programs in India have failed to recognize this and advocate separation of uses. Designing for the traditional patterns will not, however, result in good housing for the future. What we can learn, however, is the nature of the key variables to consider in design.

Key Variables of Form and Culture in Traditional Housing

House forms are shaped by many factors. These include family organization and the pattern of basic activities—who carries them out, the role of servants, attitudes toward which activities are private and which are communal, which are sacred and which are profane, and which involve ritual pollution. These activities include everyday activities such as food preparation, cooking and eating, sleeping and ablutions, and less frequent activities such as the receiving of guests. Cooking is the most sacred activity other than purely religious ones; defecating, which requires bathing afterwards, is the most polluting. Religious practices are particularly important in many Hindu homes with space being allocated to a *puja* room where possible and a *tulsa* bush in the center of the courtyard. Where there is not enough space for a puja room, at least a corner is allocated for this purpose. Gender roles and norms of accepted interaction between men and women and between adults and children and status differences within the household are all reflected in house form.

In many parts of India, house form is also dictated by the means of livelihood of the family because these were often fulfilled within what was basically the residential-cum-working unit. Space is required for looms; shops have to be accessible to the street so they come between the verandah and courtyard. The details of house form are affected by such things as attitudes toward women during menstruation; ceremonies associated with rites of passage; and aesthetic values, craft traditions, and attitudes toward the display of wealth and status. The role of animals is often important even in the most urban areas and the attitude toward nature dictates the use of vegetation as a part of the house and its surroundings. The climate was always something with which to contend, although often sacrifices of comfort were made for sociocultural purposes. *Chajjas, jharookhas* (screen-enclosed balconies), and flat roofs in hot, arid areas, and pitched roofs where rainfall is higher are all responses to climatic needs although the specific form they take is also dependent on traditional patterns. Where people have migrated they have taken these patterns with them and employed them in the new situation even though the patterns may not be the most appropriate for the climate (K. Jain 1982).

In orthodox Hindu homes, menstruating women are regarded as unclean and either a special room in the backyard or a corner of a room in the main house is available for them to retire to. The way births, marriages, and deaths are handled vary in different parts of India and with different religious beliefs within regions. Some of these attitudes are reflected in house form. In Lakshadweep, there are special houses for giving birth and for dying (Chandoke 1983).

A part of Brahmin houses in Kerala do not have ceilings; this is where the dying are laid. Servants and often women had separate entrances to *havelis*. Craftsmen traditions are reflected in the *havelis* of Jaisalmer. The stone masons were, reputedly, Moslems trained in Medina and their work in Jaisalmer is unique to it although similar carvings can be found in Udaipur and other Rajasthan cities (see K. Jain 1982).

The most common family type in India was and is the extended family, although there are some major deviations from this, particularly in tribal areas. The extended family takes many forms. The most common form consists of a couple, their sons and their sons' wives and children. Here too there are some notable exceptions with the Nairs of Kerala being matrilineal and matrilocal, with the daughters remaining in the household with their children and their brothers. Husbands mainly visited the house for conjugal visits (Hazra 1984). The most typical house for upper- and middle-level castes was, nevertheless, the courtyard house. It was not, however, the universal house form.

The courtyard layout affords many things. It meets the climatic needs of many parts of India by acting as a channel for breezes. It affords outdoor space for household activities such as the drying of pulses. It affords space for ceremonies. Perhaps most important, it acted and acts as outdoor space for women in households where they spend most of their lives within the house. This is true of orthodox Hindu families as well as Moslem households. Flat roofs in hot, arid areas provide spaces for sleeping during the summer months. The form of fenestration depends not only on climatic requirements but also on privacy requirements, often being designed to allow women to see out while remaining unseen from without. For economic reasons, the courtyard house is not a prototype in housing programs. With the changing role of women and the use of electric fans maybe it need not be, but there are substantial losses, nevertheless.

The plan form of the courtyard house also reflects the zones of penetration of people—visitors and kin and servants—from the outside. There are strong norms of behavior specifying how far each can approach the house and who can enter onto the verandah, which is the seating area for men of the family and others of equal status. Close associates may enter the front hall, but only the most intimate kin can penetrate the house beyond the courtyard. In some areas of the country the internal organization of the plan also reflects canons of design from the *Shilpa Shastras*—the courtyard is in the center and the kitchen is often in the northeast corner, for examples. The proportional schema for both plans and facades also often follow the dictates of the *Shastras* (Shastri 1968).

Typical across all income levels in India historically has been the extension of the house to accommodate new members as the family grows. This may involve horizontal growth in areas where there is sufficient room for it or vertical growth in denser areas (see Chaterjee 1977; Das 1983). The recognition of this has become part of housing programs in recent years in many parts of the world as well as in India. There comes a time, however, when houses have been developed to the full extent possible within space and technological constraints.

In traditional housing, the materials used for building are often local ones, but where populations have migrated the materials are likely to be those of their original habitat or materials which have some symbolic value. Thus, much of the highly decorated work on columns and beams in the traditional *pol* houses in Ahmedabad is in wood, but this necessitates the importation of timber from long distances (M. Jain 1982). The decoration, either carved on beams and columns or painted on walls, is very much locality and group specific and thus gives a sense of identity to people (Kanhere 1982). The clearest distinction is between the geometric patterns employed by Moslems and the more representational art of the Hindus. The specific rooms that are highly decorated are usually those where socializing, either within the household or with visitors, takes place. The size of house, proportional schemata used, the placement of doors and windows, the nature of doors and windows, the nature of decorations, items decorated, and colors used provided a family with a symbol of place regionally—or place of origin— and place in the social/caste structure of that region.

Furniture was simple. People slept on mats on the floor. These could be rolled up during the day and the room used for different purposes. Food preparation took place with the women squatting on the floor and cooking took place in hearths on the floor. Window placements recognized that many household activities took place with people sitting or squatting on the floor or on *palatas*. Swinging benches—known as *zoola, hindolo, hinchako* or *jholoo*—allowed the person sitting in them to create a breeze (Shah 1976).

The Breakdown of Traditions

Many traditions still persist. This is particularly true of the rural areas of India but much about urban life also reflects traditional patterns of household organization. There have been, however, major forces for change. These include colonial influences, particularly of the British and to a lesser extent, the Portuguese; the impact of the industrial revolution with its new life-styles and its demand for workers and the need to house them; and the impact of architectural movements often guided by social and philanthropic ideals. Political forces have also led to changes in the power structure of society and thus age-old patterns of relationships between people. Recently the consumer boom is altering patterns of obtaining information, recreation, and dependence on servants for the middle class.

The British introduced the grid-iron plan, which was also advocated by the *Shilpa Shastras*, and the bungalow adopted and adapted from its rural Bengal prototype. George Town in Madras was founded in 1640, only a year later than Shahjahanabad. Its street pattern persists. In cities such as Bangalore the areas of bungalow residences were extensive (Staley 1981). They still exist and are continuing to be built, although in a more cramped form, because they are favored by the middle class. In the bungalow the traditional courtyard house is turned inside out with the open space surrounding the house rather than the other way around. The British along with the French, Portuguese, and Danes also introduced a new aesthetic based on the classical orders of Europe (Nilsson 1968).

With the industrial revolution came new housing forms: the chawl and the tenement. Chawls consist of a single room plus verandah, in back-to-back row house units. Latrines and water sources were located in common areas. The smallest chawl in Madras is 100 square feet; the largest is 400 square feet. Much of life takes place in the narrow alleys between the rows of units. In 1961, it was estimated that 21 percent of the population of Ahmedabad lived in chawls originally built to house textile workers (Bhoosan and Misra 1979). Tenements are similar but the units are located in flats, but again with common latrines. Over the years considerable extensions were made to chawls with additions being built into the narrow alleys. There have also been considerable changes in the internal organization of units in tenements. Efforts were initiated to improve chawls through public action with the founding of the Bombay Improvement Trust in 1898, and the Calcutta Improvement Trust in 1911. The building of chawls is now prohibited.

Chawls and tenements were built by industrialists. From the beginning of the twentieth century, municipal corporations took a greater and greater initiative in providing better housing. New building types such as flats were introduced, not only for British civil servants, but also, as the century progressed, for social housing. The results were and are very mixed because the building type requires considerable adaptation of life-styles on the part of the inhabitants. Accompanying this were sets of rules and regulations designed to provide a more salubrious environment, but these were designed more as a response to the appalling conditions of the European industrial cities of the late nineteenth century rather than the specific needs of India. In the 1930s the ideas of the Modern Movement in architecture as well as the Garden Cities Movement began to be felt. They have made many Indian cities more spacious, and their influences persist even though, as mentioned at the outset of this chapter, the results have drawn considerable criticism because they have made the close-knit communal life-style of many Indian populations difficult to pursue. Also influential was the eclecticism of palace design, but this was on privately built houses of the middle class (Gaekwad 1980). From this emerged the style of house now known as the "modern vernacular," which draws on a variety of Indian and Western motifs. Government-built housing has been largely unaffected by such patterns.

The internal organization of houses today reflects the growing nucleation of Indian families, the use of tables and chairs for dining, and changing attitudes toward gender roles and the place of children in the household. To some extent these changes are strongly influenced by the nature of housing types available. It is difficult for a middle-class family to maintain a traditional extended family household in a 750-square-foot apartment. Other changes in house form have led to changes in the way activities are carried out. Some of these are for the better. Water-borne sewage has reduced the reliance on low-caste sweepers to clean latrines. Platforms have been introduced for cooking; bottled gas has replaced traditional fuels. Electricity extends the day and reduces privacy. Technological changes have made life easier for people, but questions are being raised about the accompanying social changes. Social changes resulting from changing values and attitudes toward life have and are changing traditional roles in society. India searches for an egalitarian, casteless, prosperous society. The degree to which it succeeds will be reflected in housing design, but changes in housing design alone are not enough.

Revival Movements in Indian Domestic Architecture

When Western education was introduced under Thomas Babington Macauley, artists and craftsmen in India began to receive Western classical training. Workmen, the *silpins*, lost the patronage of their former clients under the political policies of the East India Company and later the British government, so there was a loss of contact by workmen and designers with their Indian heritage. From the beginning of the twentieth century there were systematic efforts to respond to the aesthetic philosophies of the British through an examination of Asian traditions. This was most noticeable with the emergence of the Bengal school of art. In architecture there were two Bengal-based movements that had influence on the thinking about the nature of architecture but had little sustained impact at the domestic level. These were the Oriental Eclecticism Movement and the Modern Indian Architectural Movement (Hathi 1981). The political and philosophical stance of the former was one of being for an eclecticism of a united Asia as against Western civilization. It can be exemplified in domestic architecture by the houses of Rabindranath Tagore—the Uttarayana complex of houses at Shantininken. The houses have elements which are Buddhist, Japanese, Moghul as well as local decorations of the Santal tribes. The influence of the British bungalow still underlies the site layouts, perhaps justified by its Bengal origins.

The Modern Indian Architectural Movement began in the 1930s and is most closely associated with Sris Chandra Chaterjee but similar attitudes were displayed at the Sir J. J. School in Bombay under Claude Batley. Chaterjee was a member of the Congress party and served on its national Planning Committee under Nehru before Independence. His attitude toward architecture was radically different from that of Nehru, who was a staunch supporter of the Modern Movement as it is understood in the West. Chaterjee's intent was to establish an architecture based on "principles of Indian architectural composition and construction." This involved the study of the application of the Indian orders of architecture rather than Western ones. There was, however, no change in basic attitudes toward housing or the problem-solving process of architects, only toward certain symbolic issues. This was also true of the Post-Independence Revival Movements which arose under the sponsorships of the states after 1947. This movement represented a continuing search for identity. This was manifested more in government buildings than in public domestic architecture. It is very much represented in the modern vernacular designs.

The Modern Movement and Housing Design in India

With Independence came a major effort to expand existing social, or public, housing through major construction programs. The designs chosen show the major impact of the Modern Movement in architecture and urban design on architectural thought and on public policies. The application of the ideas of the movement were given considerable impetus by Nehru, who sought a symbol of India's effort to build up a major industrial infrastructure, and a secular and socialist society. Chandigarh is a product of this transition in Indian thinking.

The design of Chandigarh has been so heavily reviewed that there is no need to extend this discussion here (see, for example, Evenson 1966; Nilsson 1975; Thukral 1984). Suffice to say here that the city was designed as the capital for Indian Punjab under the leadership of Le Corbusier. It is based on elements of his radiant city idea, the garden city concept, and the neighborhood unit on a grand scale. It is an exemplar of the application of the tenets of Modern Movement architecture. Two things, however, are important to bear in mind. First, the ideas behind the planning and design of Chandigarh still shape much of thinking in the planning and design of housing in India today. Second, the search for an appropriate symbolic aesthetic for housing in India still remains. Opinions on Chandigarh differ. Charles Correa states, "[Le Corbusier's] aesthetic is more real India, an India of Bazaars, sprawling, cruel, raucous colour, with a grandeur all its own. His aesthetic evokes our history." It has also been described as boring and irrelevant to India. It has certainly had an impact on the designs of a whole generation of Indian architects and it continues to reflect and be reflected in Indian housing programs.

Accompanying all this have been major changes in the life-styles of upper- and middle-income people in cities. Upper-income families tend to be nuclear ones, often, however, with at least one member of a third generation present. The families are small; the children attend private schools often associated with the Roman Catholic church. A high premium is placed on receiving a good education. Gender roles are still very distinct, with men going out to work and the women organizing the household. Marriages are still arranged. The household members will own a car if they are wealthy, a scooter if they are middle class. In the house children will have their own bedrooms, each with its own bathroom. The house will have a separate dining room and the living room will be near the entrance so that the women of the household do not have to be present to receive male guests. There will be a separate entrance for servants. The house may have unplastered walls, exposed concrete, deep-recessed French windows, and landscaped gardens in front if the family is of the old elite. It will probably be in the "modern vernacular" rather than in modern architecture if the family is noveau riche. It will have refrigerators and pressure cookers and other modern appliances.

The middle class will follow suit to the extent they can. The lower-middle class are under extreme pressure. Space is at a premium for them, and so privacy norms are much lower. They are likely to live in flats often as small as 500 square feet. The unit is likely to be a tenement with communal bathrooms. Open space outside becomes an important place to play for children and the life of the family spills out into corridors. The local area is important for recreation, shopping, and entertainment. Cinemas are important. Neighbors help each other more; pujas are an important community function. Life is more boisterous and louder than for the upper-middle class and wealthy families. Certain patterns of life are still highly traditional. For example, when guests visit, men and women separate, but one old taboo has been abandoned—all of the women gather in the kitchens, outsiders and family members alike (Chakrabati 1975). The kitchen has lost some of its traditional sacrosanctity.

For the poor, hunger and discomfort rule. There is little privacy in life. There is little space and families are large. There is a desire for privacy for bathing and defecating and for couples to sleep together. Common latrines do not offer privacy. Much of life takes places in the open: cooking, sleeping in the summer, keeping hens and goats, active and passive playing, having morning tea, breakfast, bathing. However difficult to achieve, certain behaviors are very important: washing before cooking and after eating, for example. The dwelling unit will be a hutment built by the inhabitants themselves. It is unlikely to have electricity, and water will have to be obtained from a communal tap. There will be no drainage so the area will be muddy, and waste will be dumped next to the house. There will be mosquitoes (P. Bose 1983). Educational opportunities will be lacking and community services will be poor. Community life is important. There will be a heavy reliance on neighbors in times of trouble; there will be no way of avoiding them in day-to-day life. The patterns of life are congruent with patterns of housing. Neither is regarded as desirable. The resources available to improve the situation in India are very limited.

Conclusion: The Development of Public Policies

In one sense there is always a congruence between a culture and its architecture. The architecture reflects how things are done. In another sense there is a major gap between what is being done in housing design and the desired cultural patterns of people who move into the housing produced. Yet, with little alternative people accept their position.

Domestic architecture will always be open to criticism on one dimension or another. Life-styles change, the relationship between peoples change, and aesthetic values change. The provision of housing units and residential areas which meet people's aspirations is difficult in a situation of limited resources. The policy maker and designer ultimately have to ask the question: What is the model of culture which should be the basis for housing design? In India no single model will suffice if one accepts the current cultural diversity of the country.

Instead of relying on a relatively few prototypes drawn from the ideologies developed in societies with very different cultures for the design of residential areas, urban designers and architects need to be able to address the specific issues at hand. Thus what is needed in housing programs are not prototypical solutions but prototypical design processes. Architects and urban designers need to be more flexible in their thinking and need to be able to look at the environment in a much sharper way than at present. This is also true of policy makers. Architects need to be educators. To be this they need a broad understanding of the relation between housing form and culture and of the patterns that do exist and how they are changing. An aesthetic will emerge from this, too.

There are many architects in India very concerned with improving housing design in their country, as the references in this chapter attest, but they are hampered by their own entrenched was of designing housing areas, outmoded bylaws, and the prototypes specified in housing programs. The design professions and social scientists need to organize themselves politically to take a leadership role in getting the process of design implicit in public policies changed. Currently they are reluctant to do this.

References

Acharaya, P. K. [1927] 1979. *Indian architecture according to the Manasara-Silpasastra.* Patna: Indian India.

Aggarwal, S. 1984. Urban habitat: The evolution of pattern in Delhi. Student paper, School of Planning and Architecture, Delhi.

Bhoosan B. S., and R. P. Misra. 1979. *Habitat Asia: Issues and responses.* Vol. 1, India. New Delhi: Concept Publishing.

Bose, N. K. 1968. *Calcutta 1964: A social survey.* Bombay: Lalvani.

Bose, P. 1983. Interrelationship of the built environment (shelter) and the life style of the poor. Ph.D. thesis, Indian Institute of Technology, Kharagpur.

Brolin, B. 1976. *The failure of modern architecture.* Princeton: Van Nostrand.

Chakrabati, C. L. 1975. The impact of social pollution on the form of the urban habitat: Case study Calcutta. Master's thesis, Indian Institute of Technology, Kharagpur.

Chandoke, S. K. 1983. The human environment: Role of socio-cultural factors in man's adaptation to the physical environment—with special reference to habitat. Paper presented at the XIth World Congress of the Anthropological and Ethnological Sciences, Quebec City, P.Q. and Vancouver, B.C. Mimeo.

Chaterjee, A. K. 1977. *Contemporary urban architecture.* Delhi: MacMillan.

Coomaraswamy, A. K. 1938. Symbolism of domes. *Indian Historical Quarterly* 14:1–56.

Das, N. C. 1983. Neighborhood design in India—self-generated vis-à-vis planned environments. In *Housing for the masses*, ed. S. V. Singh. Indian Institute of Technology, Kharagpur.

Doshi. H. 1974. *Traditional neighborhoods in a modern city.* New Delhi: Abhinav Publications.

Evenson, N. 1966. *Chandigarh.* Berkeley and Los Angeles: University of California Press.

Fonesca, R. 1969. The walled city of Old Delhi. *Landscape* 18 (3) (fall): 12–25.

Gaekwad, F. 1980. *Palaces of India.* London: Collins.

Greer, G. 1984. *Sex and destiny: The politics of human fertility.* London: Secker and Warburg.

Grenell, P. 1972. Planning for invisible people: Some consequences of bureaucratic values and practices. In *Freedom to build*, ed. J. F. C. Turner and R. Fitcher, 95–121. New York: MacMillan.

Grover, S. 1967. Housing for slum dwellers. In *Jantar: A souvenir publication of the School of Planning and Architecture, Delhi*, 90–91.

Gupta, S. K. 1974. "Chandigarh: A study of sociological issues and urban development in India. *Architectural Design* 44(June): 350–51.

Hathi, R. 1981. Indian architecture: From traditional to contemporary: A study of the turbulent phases. Master's thesis, School of Architecture, Ahmedabad.

Hazra, A. 1984. House: A socio-cultural reality: An analysis of Koya built form. Master's thesis, School of Architecture, Ahmedabad.

Howard, E. 1902. *Garden cities of tomorrow*. 2d ed. London: S. Sonnenschein and Co.

Jain, K. 1982. Haveli facades: Concepts of embellishment. In *The impulse to adorn*, ed. J. Pieper and G. Michell, 43–54. Bombay: MARG Publications.

Jain, M. 1982. Eclectic elements: Bohra houses of Sidhpur. In *Impulse to adorn*, 91–98. *See* Jain, K.

Kanhere, G. K. 1982. Traditional motifs in house ornamentation. In *Impulse to adorn*, 55–62. *See* Jain, K.

King, A. D. 1974. The colonial bungalow-compound complex: A study in the cultural use of space. *Sociology* 8(1): 81–110.

Kuhlar, A. 1981. Riots: The dynamics of physical spaces. Master's thesis, Indian Institute of Technology, Kharagpur.

Lang, J. 1980. The built environment and social behavior: Architectural determinism re-examined. In *VIA 4*, 146–53. Cambridge, Mass.: MIT Press.

Le Corbusier. 1934. *La ville radieuse* (The radiant city). Trans. P. Knight and E. Levieux. New York: Orion Press.

Nagendra, M. 1979. Organization of activity spaces in an urban neighbourhood: Case—a para of Midnapore City. Master's thesis, Indian Institute of Technology, Kharagpur.

Nilsson, S. 1968. *European architecture in India, 1750–1850*. London: Faber and Faber.

———. 1975. *The new capitals of India, Pakistan and Bangladesh*. London: Curzon Press.

Payne, G. 1977. *Urban housing in the Third World*. London: Leonard Hill.

Patel, G. 1976. Dwelling clusters in South India. Master's thesis, School of Architecture, Ahmedabad.

Perry, C. [1927] 1966. The neighborhood unit formula. Reprinted in *Urban housing*, ed. W. L. C. Wheaton, et al., 94–109. New York: The Free Press of Glencoe.

Rapoport, A. 1977. *Human aspects of urban form*. New York: Pergamon.

Raz, R. [1832] 1972. *Architecture of the Hindus*. Veranasi: Ideological Book House.

Shah, K. P. 1976. Organizational patterns, social and physical. Master's thesis, School of Architecture, Ahmedabad.

Shastri, S. K. 1968. A study in the methodology of design as described in the ancient Indian texts on architecture (dwelling houses). Master's thesis, School of Architecture, Ahmedabad.

Singh, A. K. 1984. *Tribal development in India*. Delhi: Amar Prakashan.

Singh, A. M. 1978. Women in Delhi Bastis. In *The Indian city: Poverty, ecology and urban developments*, ed. A. de Souza. New Delhi: Manohar.

Solanki, B. N. 1968. Urban spaces in Indian cities. Master's thesis, School of Architecture, Ahmedabad.

Staley, E. 1981. *Monkey tops: Old buildings in Bangalore cantonment*. Bangalore: Tara.

Thomas, P. 1975. *Hindu religion, custom and manners*. Bombay: Taraporevala Sons.

Thukral, G. 1984. Chandigarh: Broken promises. *India Today* 9: 140–41.

Vastu-Shilpu Foundation. 1983. *Low cost housing: Indore*. Ahmedabad.

19

PROGRESSIVE DEVELOPMENT AND CULTURAL FACTORS IN LOW-COST HOUSING IN BOGOTÁ, COLOMBIA

MARIO NORIEGA

WREN ROGERS

IGNACIO RESTREPO

Project Context

Solving the problem of housing in the sprawling, poverty-ridden cities of the Third World cannot be viewed as the quantitative problem of putting x number of roofs over the heads of the homeless. The solution must be based not only on discovering and analyzing the special needs inherent in this type of housing according to cultural, social, and physical contexts but also on the facts that the shape of cities everywhere must be controlled and that the need for quality in the home and urban environment is as pressing a problem as that of providing statistically required housing units.

This chapter describes an investigation of the priorities in low-cost spontaneous housing and two projects for the design of low-cost housing units and neighborhoods based on the conclusions derived from that investigation. The two design projects were undertaken in Colombia. Mere observation suffices to show that one of the outstanding characteristics of Colombian cities, and Latin American cities in general, is their state of permanent change. Literally from one day to the next the urban physiognomy varies: streets are transformed, buildings disappear, neighborhoods spring up while others are swallowed up. The lack of resources and infrastructure necessary to withstand this permanent pressure of rapid change has resulted in widespread deterioration of the urban fabric.

The situation of uncontrolled change in most Colombian cities is critical. In larger cities, the majority of the population lives in poverty, and the housing shortage is acute; statistics show more than half the population living in illegal settlements. Those who live in low-income projects built by the government and the private sector must contend with home and urban environments often hostile to their specific cultural, social, and economic needs.

The projects presented here are concerned with detecting and helping to control, through planning and design principles, the processes of architectural and urban change in low-income housing settlements. These settlements and neighborhoods were of interest to us for several reasons. First, in Colombia, "shelter" for families in the low-income bracket is not just a place to live. The house is a vital factor in family income (for example, rooms are rented out, stores and workshops are located within), and in family economic security. Thus solving the problem of the "house" is as important in Colombia as is seeing to questions of health and welfare. Second, despite the fact that the majority of the population lives in this type of settlement, almost nothing is known about its essential characteristics, those spatial aspects of change and the cultural influences and priorities on which its development depends. This lack of qualitative information exists both on the architectural scale of the house and, to a much more serious degree, on the urban scale of its physical environment and context.

Nonspontaneous low-income settlements (that is, ones designed and built by someone other than the user) tend to concentrate on the isolated concept of the single-family unit. To reduce construction costs, the area per unit is reduced, and the result is a miniaturized version of a typical—and totally inappropriate—middle-class house. The conception of these same units on an urban level is even more dismal. Identical housing units are endlessly repeated, and the definition of urban spaces and services is carried out intuitively, as an afterthought, if at all. With the lower cost of land used as justification, developments are located beyond city limits, thus indiscriminately extending the urban network and raising the costs of services and transportation. The importance of the urban environment, the fact that the success of the house itself as a place to live depends not only on its internal design but also on its location, on its relation with its surroundings, and thus on the nature of those surroundings, is overlooked.

The resulting low-quality housing and the destruction of the urban environment and culture have never been more evident in Colombia than in recent years. Well-intentioned but poorly oriented government policies, based exclusively on fulfilling the immediate need for half a million low-cost units, fomented this class of construction through special credit systems for developers, the creation of new city planning codes, and government building programs. The result has been large-scale, uncontrolled urban sprawl and instant slums.

Project Description

Investigation and Method   Spontaneous low-income settlements in Colombia are divided into two general categories: squatter neighborhoods, where private or government land is "invaded" and settled, and pirate neighborhoods, built on land outside city limits that is sold cheaply to settlers and that lacks such basic services as water, sewage, electricity, and transportation. Both are illegal and outside the control of city planning authorities.

The house in these settlements is built by the family over an extended period of time, according to available resources, and almost always without a specific plan. This gradual construction process is known as "progressive development."

The Barrio Pablo Neruda, a pirate settlement outside of Bogotá, was chosen in 1974 as the basis for a small-scale, pilot investigation of the influences (cultural, economical, social, spatial, and so on) and criteria in the progressive development of low-income housing. Seven houses were chosen as case studies. The specific objective of this stage of the investigation was to detect, based on different families' hierarchies of investment and the physical process of construction, fundamental priorities in this type of progressive development.

This investigation was continued five years later, because the very nature of progressive development required follow-up work to define clearly the inherent priorities, characteristic elements, and determinant factors. A new objective at this stage was to arrive at a method including a standard graphic format that could be used to record and analyze the process of change in this and similar larger-scale projects.

The 1979 follow-up investigation was one of the projects in which we began to develop and implement the methodology and general structure we apply to all our work, including investigation, architectural and urban design, and urban planning. This structure or diagram, which is adapted to the specific needs of each project, is based on six steps or chapters: (1) collection and organization of data, (2) analysis and investigation, (3) definition of project parameters and goals, (4) development of alternative solutions, (5) evaluation of alternatives and subsequent project development, and (6) project follow-up. Our insistence on the use of this general method and apparently simple diagram is a response to what we see as the enormously complex problems of contemporary architecture and urbanism, which frequently demand—but do not necessarily receive—the simultaneous manipulation of several variables (such as cultural, spatial, technological, social, economical, and administrative). We are concerned that architects and urban designers, in recent years more than ever, tend to view the solutions to the problems that confront them as almost exclusively formal; we try, especially in urban design and housing projects, to use the six-step method to develop projects with a marked emphasis on an urban structure or system combined with architectural typologies, which can then evolve into specific forms according to the tastes and needs of owners and users.

The seven case studies in the Pablo Neruda neighborhood were recorded in drawings and photographs in both 1974 and 1979. Data were accumulated on the family (number and ages, wage-earning activities, origins, and so on), on the characteristics of the construction (materials, methods, costs, labor, stages), and on equipment, furnishing, and decoration.

The graphic records (made in 1979 according to the above-mentioned standard format) recorded the physical development of the house (Figures 19.1 and 19.3) and compared aspects ranging from the quantitative discrimination of investment according to zones of the house to the more qualitative aspects of choice of materials, colors, furnishing, and the process of "expression." In the 1979 investigation, these aspects were organized into three basic groups and analyzed space by space. These groups were: physical development of the house; furnishing and decoration; and organization and use of space (Figures 19.2 and 19.4). These aspects were further crossed, by the use of a matrix that allowed us to both quantify and qualify conclusions with seven factors considered crucial in the process of change, in order to arrive at a definition of the stages through which the house has passed in its development, and to identify the hierarchy and priorities in these stages (Figure 19.5). The factors taken into account were context, territoriality, privacy, security, identity, comfort, and income generation.

The four stages that emerged clearly as common to the houses in their process of development were as follows, in chronological order and thus order of importance:

1 Definition of territory and expression of identity through the demarcation of property with facade (even if there was no house behind)
2 Beginnings of spatial organization, with the construction of at most two multi-use areas or rooms
3 Expansion, subdivision, and specialization of spaces
4 Extroversion of the house, or manifestation of interest and participation in the urban context: the house's progress and the owner's interest in investing his limited resources become intimately related to the development of the neighborhood as a whole (services, schools, transportation, the furnishing of public space, and so on)

Design   In 1981 a private developer commissioned us to design housing prototypes for a 166-unit low-income project, the Gran Yomasa II Housing Project in Usme, an area on the outskirts of Bogotá surrounded by illegal settlements. The site had already been parceled when we began work on the design of the units. As a basis for the project we translated the conclusions arrived at in the Pablo Neruda investigations into the following design principles (Figure 19.6):

1 The consolidation of the urban spaces and street profile implied by existing lot divisions

2 Emphasis on the street as the basic design unit, through facade treatment and an internal organization of the house that placed circulation and service areas along the public zones of the project

3 Insistence on the importance of the facade, not only as a space-defining element, but as an expression of owners' identity and territory

4 The provision for future expansion of the house ("progressive development") implied in both the structural system and the spatial organization

5 The dimensioning of spaces to allow their use for multiple activities

6 A spatial and functional organization of the unit that would facilitate its use as a source of income (for example, areas easily converted to workshops or stores, circulation designed to permit easy subdivision of the house for the purpose of renting out rooms)

7 The concentration of services and circulation in a central, naturally lighted area of the house, both to lower building costs and to improve spatial and functional qualities

The fact that the Yomasa site had already been divided into lots when we entered the project prevented us from controlling the urban "system" as much as we would have liked; because the project was never built, neither were we able to judge how well we had been able to translate the priorities we had detected in progressive development into valid and workable design principles. Our first opportunity to do both these things came in 1986, when we were commissioned by Red Cross of Colombia to design a thirty-unit low-income neighborhood in Lerida, the town that is being used as the base for rebuilding Armero, which was destroyed by the eruption of the Ruiz Volcano in 1985. (This project forms part of our commission by the Colombian government to plan and design the entire city of Lerida, Regional Center. Both the city and this neighborhood are currently under construction, with a projected completion date of November 1987.)

The basis for the planning and design of Lerida was the structuring and control of urban space, using a "web," which integrates a hierarchy of vehicular and pedestrian circulation with plazas, parks, and a system of green space conformed by existing creeks and wooded areas, and which is punctuated by special projects and services (Figure 19.7). This attitude toward the structuring of urban space was taken as a means of orienting growth and controlling both short- and long-term architectural projects: that is, of creating the best possible conditions for the city to grow by itself. Emphasis was put on the use of urban and architectural typologies existing in the region, the creation of generous public areas, the planting of trees to define space, and the proportioning of an infrastructure of basic services, all in the belief that a sound urban structure can better resist indifferent architecture than vice versa.

The most important item in the new design is the *calle mayor* or main street, a loop whose profile of pergolas and arcades is derived from the existing commercial avenue of which it is a continuation. This boulevard is marked by a series of important plazas and glorietas, which in turn relate it to housing neighborhoods and special projects such as the hospital, market place, and government center.

The Red Cross housing is located on the western portion of this loop or boulevard, near the main plaza (Figure 19.8). In designing this neighborhood we used the same seven principles we had established for the Yomasa project, with the difference that the consolidation of urban space contemplated in the first point was a result of our own urban design, and not of existing lot divisions. An additional important point in this project was the application of commonsense design principles derived from existing architectural typologies in the region, specifically the use of an arcade to protect pedestrian circulation along the sidewalk from the tropical sun and foster the use of the front spaces on the first floor of the units for commercial activities.

Project Conclusion

Low-cost housing and high-quality, culturally appropriate architectural and urban environments cannot continue to be mutually exclusive. The solution to the housing problem in Colombian and other Third World cities must take into account the vital role played by public spaces and community services in the development of these settlements. It has been proved time and time again that low-income units stressing the individual unit at the expense of the urban environment, no matter how well-intentioned, fail miserably as livable places. Both the design of the house and its urban context must go beyond mere considerations of cost and form and take into account special cultural, social, and spatial aspects. Above all, it is our conviction that if planners and designers concentrate on providing the appropriate urban environment and services, the housing unit will tend to take care of itself. A good house on a bad street is at best a lonely gesture; a bad house on a good street tends to slip by unnoticed. To combine the best of both is not too much to be hoped for.

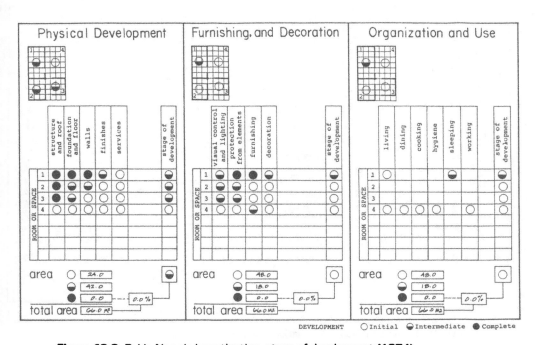

Figure 19.1. Pablo Neruda investigation, general information (1974).

1. LOCATION
   city _Bogotá (Usme)_
   neighborhood _Pablo Neruda_
   address

2. TYPE _2_

3. VALUE
   lot _3 000_
   building _19 700_
   financing _Banco Popular_

4. RESIDENTS
   ownership _Property 1_
   length of residence _8 months_
   location of former residence _Toca_
   1 year
   Family composition and income

	age	productive activity	monthly income
Father	32	shop employee	
Mother	28	shop in house	
Son	9		
Son	7		
Son	3		
Son	1		
		total	

5. DESIGN AND CONSTRUCTION
   design _Provivienda_
   construction _Contracted construction worker_
   Starting date _February 1974_

0 5 1 2 3 4 5 6 7m

Physical Development

	structure and roof	foundation and floor	walls	finishes	services		stage of development
ROOM OR SPACE 1	●	●	●	◐	○		◐
2	●	●	◐	○	○		◐
3	●	◐	○	○	○		◐
4	○	◐	○	○	○		◐

area ○ 24.0
◐ 42.0
● 0.0 ---- 0.0%
total area 66.0 m2   ◐

Furnishing, and Decoration

	visual control and lighting	protection from elements	furnishing	decoration		stage of development
ROOM OR SPACE 1	●	◐	●	◐		○
2	●	◐	○	○		○
3	◐	◐	○	○		○
4	◐	◐	○	○		○

area ○ 48.0
◐ 18.0
● 0.0 ---- 0.0%
total area 66.0 m2   ○

Organization and Use

	living	dining	cooking	hygiene	sleeping	working		stage of development
ROOM OR SPACE 1	○				◐			○
2								○
3								○
4	◐		○	○	○			○

area ○ 48.0
◐ 18.0
● 0.0 ---- 0.0%
total area 66.0 m2   ○

DEVELOPMENT   ○ Initial   ◐ Intermediate   ● Complete

Figure 19.2. Pablo Neruda investigation, stage of development (1974).

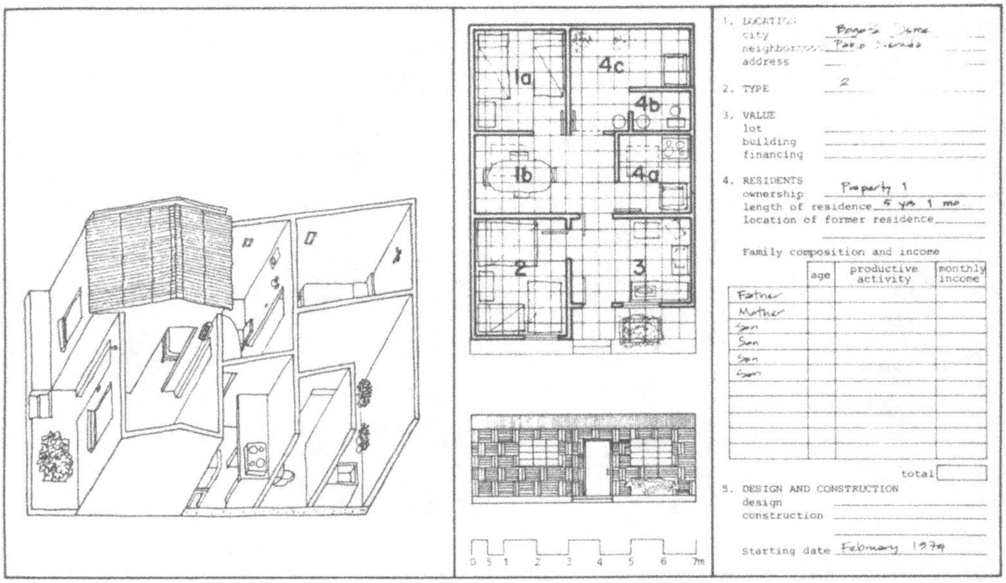

Figure 19.3. Pablo Neruda investigation, general information (1979).

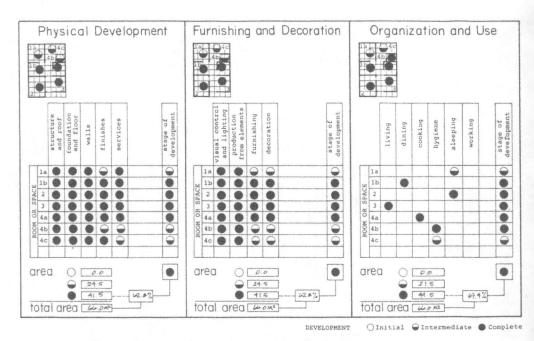

Figure 19.4. Pablo Neruda investigation, stage of development (1979).

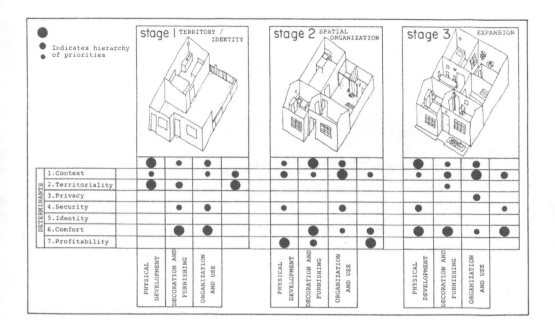

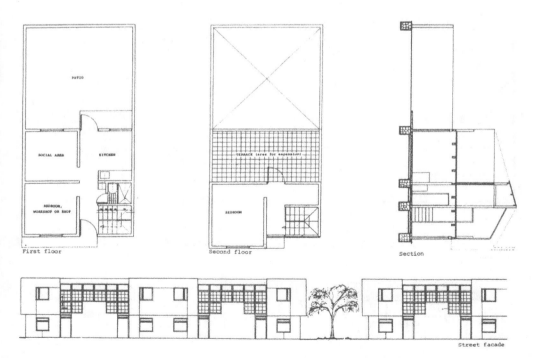

Figure 19.6. Gran Yomasa II housing project, Usme: plans for a typical unit (1981).

Figure 19.7. Lerida, regional center: overall plan (1986).

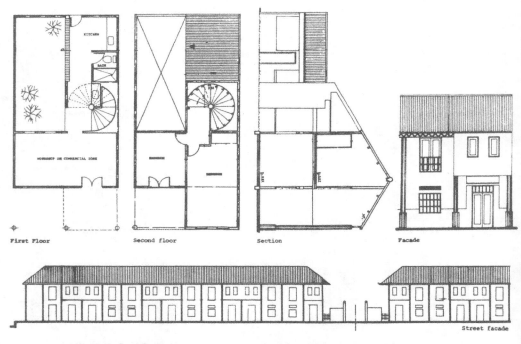

First Floor   Second floor   Section   Facade

Street facade

Figure 19.8. Red Cross housing, Lerida: plans for a typical unit (1986).

CONTRIBUTORS

William B. Bechhoefer is Associate Professor of Architecture at the University of Maryland School of Architecture. A graduate of the Harvard Graduate School of Design, he was recipient of the Fulbright-Hays Senior Lectureship in Architecture for teaching in Afghanistan in 1973–74. As a Peace Corps Volunteer he was Professor of Architecture at the Ecole des Beaux-Arts in Tunisia in 1968–69. He currently directs the graduate degree concentration Design for Developing Countries at the University of Maryland and leads research and student programs in Sri Lanka and Turkey. He maintains a private architectural practice.

Robert B. Bechtel is Professor of Environmental Psychology at the University of Arizona and Director of the environmental section of the cognitive program. He received his doctorate in Psychology from the University of Kansas in 1967, and his research background is in ecological psychology. Bechtel's books are *Enclosing Behavior* (1979) and *Research Methods in Environmental and Behavioral Research* (1987). His current design projects involve cross-cultural housing and buildings (Japan, Peru, Canada) and research in extreme climates.

Sidney Brower is Associate Professor in the Community Planning program at the University of Maryland at Baltimore. He holds a bachelor's degree in Architecture from the University of Cape Town, South Africa, and a master's degree in City Planning from the Massachusetts Institute of Technology. His chapter was extracted from *Design in Familiar Places* (1988), which is about residents' perceptions of the environment and implications for urban design.

Erve Chambers is Associate Professor of Anthropology at the University of Maryland, College Park. He is President of the Society for Applied Anthropology (1987–89) and founding editor of *Practicing Anthropology*, a career-oriented publication of the SfAA. He received his doctorate in Anthropology at the University of Oregon. Chambers has conducted research on housing and community development in the United States for fifteen years and has served as a member of the Urban Planning and Development Council of the Tampa Chamber of Commerce. He is author of *Applied Anthropology: A Practical Guide* (1985) and is currently working on a history of early American anthropology.

Richard J. Dent is currently Assistant Professor in the Department of Anthropology at the University of Maryland, College Park. He earned his doctorate in Anthropology at The American University in Washington, D.C. Dent is involved in a number of archaeological projects in the Middle Atlantic area and has recently completed a manuscript on the prehistory of the Chesapeake Bay region. In addition, he has long-term interests in cultural resources management and the uses of the past by contemporary society. Dent's research on the gentrification process is an outgrowth of these last two interests.

Dennis Doxtater received his Bachelor of Architecture and master's in Cultural Anthropology from the University of Washington and his doctorate in Architecture from the University of Michigan. He has taught at the Universities of Michigan, Idaho, and Washington and is currently Associate Professor of Architecture at the University of Arizona in Tucson. His research interests are in the symbolism of primitive/traditional architecture (Scandinavia, S.W. Pueblo, and Andalucia), in contemporary office buildings in Sweden, and in a continuum of social science theory of environment.

James S. Duncan is Associate Professor of Geography at Syracuse University. He is a graduate of Dartmouth College and received his doctorate at Syracuse University. His major research interests are in housing and identity, and the social psychology of the urban built environment. He has conducted fieldwork in Canada, the United States, India, and Sri Lanka. He is the editor of *Housing and Identity: Cross-Cultural Perspectives* (1981) and *The Power of Place: Integrating the Sociological and Geographical Imaginations* (1988) and the author of several geography journal articles and a forthcoming book entitled *The City as Text: The Politics of Landscape Interpretation in Nineteenth-Century Kandy*.

Graeme Hardie is Director of Research at the School of Design, North Carolina State University. At the time of undertaking the research for this chapter he was head of the Environmental Studies Division of the National Institute for Personnel Research, Human Sciences Research Council, Johannesburg, Republic of South Africa. He has a Bachelor of Architecture from the University of Arizona and a doctorate in Anthropology from Boston University. His research has focused on the impact of cultural continuities and changes on the built form; developing ways of involving users in the design process, particularly in relation to house and settlement issues; and understanding government housing policies from the perspective of those affected.

Timothy Hart is the acting head of the Environmental Studies Division of the National Institute for Personnel Research, Human Sciences Research Council, Johannesburg, Republic of South Africa. He is also coordinator of the national research program entitled Human Needs, Resources and the Environment. He has a master's degree in Human Geography from the University of the Witwatersrand, Johannesburg, and for several years has been engaged in research on development and housing in low-income communities. His research topics have included state-sanctioned self-help housing and the privatization of low-cost mass housing.

Jana Hesser is an anthropologist trained in the field of medical anthropology who has also worked closely with her husband, Eleftherios Pavlides, in examining social and cultural aspects of the built environment. Hesser holds a degree from the University of Pennsylvania and has taught Anthropology at Case Western Reserve University and Kansas State University. She is currently Research Director for Kansas State University's Division of Continuing Education.

Sandra C. Howell is Associate Professor of Behavioral Science in the Department of Architecture at the Massachusetts Institute of Technology. She received her doctorate in Life Span Developmental Psychology from Washington University in St. Louis. Howell is the author of *Designing for Aging: Patterns of Use* (1980) and many book chapters and journal articles. She was the recipient of the 1982 Senior Research Fellowship from the National Endowment for the Arts which allowed her to return to Japan. Howell is a Fellow of the American Gerontological Society and a former Member of the Board of Directors of the Environment Design Research Association. She is currently completing a book, *Habit and Habitability*, which enlarges on her studies of Japanese and American households.

David M. Hummon is Associate Professor of Sociology at Holy Cross College, Worcester, Massachusetts. He received his doctorate from the University of California, Berkeley, where he specialized in urban sociology, the sociology of culture, and social theory. His research addresses the way contemporary Americans interpret places and, in doing so, use place meanings to construct a sense of identity and reality. Recent publications include "Place Identity: Localities of the Self," in *Purposes in Built Form and Culture Research* (1986), and articles in *Sociological Quarterly, Qualitative Sociology, Urban Life,* and the *Journal of Cultural Geography.*

Delmos J. Jones is Professor of Anthropology at the Graduate School and University Center of the City University of New York. He received his doctorate from Cornell University in 1967. He has conducted research and published articles on native Americans, the tribal people of Northern Thailand, Australian Aborigines, and the United States.

Jon Lang is Chairman of the Urban Design Program at the University of Pennsylvania. He received his early education in India, England, and South Africa and was graduated from the University of the Witwatersrand, Johannesburg, with a Bachelor of Architecture. His graduate studies were at Cornell University. The research on which his chapter is based was conducted in 1984 while he was sponsored by the Indo-American Subcommission on Culture and Education. He is the author of *Creating Architectural Theory: The Role of the Behavioral Sciences in Environmental Design* (1987).

Roderick J. Lawrence was graduated in Architecture from the University of Adelaide, South Australia, in 1972. After two years' work in professional practice in Sydney, he began a postgraduate research fellowship at St. John's College, Cambridge, England. He has a master's degree and a doctorate. From 1978 to 1984 he worked at the Ecole Polytechnique Fédérale de Lausanne in Switzerland. Since then he has been Consultant to the Committee for Housing, Building, and Planning of the Economic Commission for Europe and Visiting Lecturer and Researcher at the School of Architecture at the University of Geneva. In 1985 he was a Visiting Research Fellow at the School of Social Sciences at the Flinders University of South Australia and guest Lecturer and Studio Master at the University of Adelaide. Lawrence is currently appointed to the Centre for Human Ecology and Environmental Sciences at the University of Geneva. He has written many articles and contributed chapters to books concerning the reciprocal relations between architectural and behavioral parameters in house planning from cross-cultural, societal, and psychological perspectives that address historical processes. He is also the author of two books, *Le Seuil franchi: Logement populaire et vie quotidienne en Suisse romande, 1860–1960* (1986) and *Housing, Dwellings, and Homes: Design Theory, Research and Practice* (1987).

Setha Low is Professor of Environmental Psychology and Anthropology at the Graduate School and University Center of the City University of New York (1987–89) and Associate Professor of Landscape Architecture and Regional Planning at the University of Pennsylvania. She received her master's and doctorate in Anthropology from the University of California, Berkeley. She is the Chair of the Environmental Design Research Association and founding organizer and editor of the Cultural Aspects of Design Network. Low has conducted research on low-income housing programs in Guatemala, cultural landscape preservation in the United States, and urban public space in Costa Rica and Spain, and has served as a consultant on various landscape design projects. She is author of *Culture, Politics and Medicine in Costa Rica* (1985) and is currently working on a comparative study of the cultural significance of the *plaza*, funded by a Fulbright Research Fellowship and a grant from the Wenner-Gren Foundation for Anthropological Research.

Kenneth McDowell began his university education as an Architecture major at the University of California, Berkeley, and completed his undergraduate work with a Bachelor of Science in Psychology from the University of Utah. He received his master's degree and doctorate from the University of California at Riverside in Psychology. Since 1969 he has been teaching social and environmental psychology at the University of Saskatchewan and has recently opened a consulting business in environmental and architectural psychology. McDowell's research interests, publications, and consulting and supervisory activities have focused on the built environment and have ranged from studies of institutional settings to residential environments. A dominant theme of these efforts continues to be the design of environments that facilitate the productivity and well-being of those who live and work in Canadian communities.

Mario Noriega received degrees in Architecture and Urban Design and Planning from the University of Los Andes, Bogotá, in 1972 and Rice University in 1976. Before becoming managing partner of the firm Noriega, Restrepo, and Asociados LTDA in 1981, he was both the founding Director of Bogotá's Cultural Institute and Assistant Director of City Planning in charge of the Department of Urban Studies and Investigation. Noriega is the specialist in urban design and planning at his firm.

Eleftherios Pavlides holds a master's degree in Architecture from Yale University, where he studied under Charles Moore. He has worked as an architect in both Greece and the United States, incorporating visual elements of local architectures into his design. In his doctoral dissertation for the University of Pennsylvania, and in subsequent publications, he has explored the social significance that visual elements of local architectures hold for their inhabitants. Pavlides has worked in architectural socio-semiotics, an approach to the study of architecture in its social context, which combines rich visual documentation with ethnographic methods. He has organized several field courses in the United States and Greece in which faculty and students of architecture and anthropology work together to identify the social meaning of architectural form for its users and to incorporate that meaning into the design process. He is currently a member of the Architecture faculty at Roger Williams College, Bristol, Rhode Island.

Labelle Prussin received her bachelor's and master's degrees in Architecture from the University of California, Berkeley, and completed her graduate studies in Anthropology and Art History at Yale University. She has published and taught widely and is currently Professor of Architecture at the City College of New York at CUNY. Her research interests are focused on Islamic architecture; nomadic architecture and gender-discrete creative processes; and Afro-American and Caribbean architectural continuities. Prussin's current academic commitment includes the development of a concentration in developing world architecture, and her current nonacademic commitment involves the preliminary planning for an exhibition titled "African Nomads: Transformations in Space," to be held at the National Museum of African Art, Smithsonian Institution, in 1991.

Amos Rapoport is one of the founders of the new field of environment-behavior studies. His work concerns the role of cultural variables, cross-cultural studies, lessons of traditional design, synthesis and theory development, urban design, and Third World design. He is currently Distinguished Professor of Architecture at the University of Wisconsin-Milwaukee. He has been a teacher, visiting professor, and lecturer at universities and conferences in America and many other countries, including Israel, Turkey, Argentina, Brazil, Canada, India, Indonesia, and New Zealand. His research is widely published and translated, and books he has written or edited include *House, Form, and Culture*; *Human Aspects of Urban Form*; and *The Meaning of the Built Environment*. Rapoport was editor-in-chief of *Urban Ecology* and is on the editorial boards of a number of other journals, in addition to having acted as consultant to *Encyclopedia Britannica*, the United Nations, and World Bank. He is a Fellow of the Royal Australian Institute of Architects and an Associate of the Royal Institute of British Architects. During 1982–83 and again in 1985 he was a Visiting Fellow of Clare Hall, Cambridge.

Ignacio Restrepo received his degrees in Architecture and Design from the University of Los Andes, Bogotá, in 1973 and Rice University in 1980. He is the partner in charge of architectural design and construction at Noriega, Restrepo, and Asociados LTDA, as well as being the firm's specialist in computer-related activities.

Edward Robbins received his doctorate from the University of Michigan. He is Lecturer in Social Studies at Harvard University and Lecturer in Architecture at the Massachusetts Institute of Technology. His researches have focused on the relationships between culture, social production, and architecture. Robbins has published in the *Journal of Architectural Education, Open House, Architectural Review, Spazio e Societa,* and others. He was coeditor of the August 1985 *Architectural Review* issue on the problem of Third World housing. He is currently working on a monograph about drawing and its role in the social production of architecture.

Julia W. Robinson, Associate Professor at the University of Minnesota, is a registered architect with a master's degree in Anthropology. Her interest in the relationship between anthropology and architecture has been pursued not only in her research on housing, which is the basis for her chapter in this book, but also in her work in architectural theory, research, and design methods. Titles of some of the articles she has authored illustrate this: "Premises, Premises: Architecture as Cultural Medium," "Design as Exploration," and "A Role for the Architect in Environmental-Behavior Research."

Wren Rogers received her bachelor's degree in Architecture from Yale University in 1975. In addition to her work directing production as partner at Noriega, Restrepo, and Asociados LTDA, she is Curator of Architecture at the Museum of Modern Art of Bogotá and member of the editorial board of the magazine *HITO.* Before joining the firm she was Assistant Dean of Architecture at the University of Los Andes in Bogotá.

Peter G. Rowe is Raymond Garbe Professor of Architecture and Urban Design at the Graduate School of Design, Harvard University, where he holds the administrative appointment of Director of the Urban Design Programs. Formerly the Director of the School of Architecture at Rice University, Houston, and Vice President of Rice Center, Rowe is the author of numerous research projects and publications, including the books *Principles for Local Environmental Management* (1978) and *Design Thinking* (1986).

Vana Tentokali is Assistant Professor in the Department of Architecture, Aristotle University of Thessaloniki, Greece, from which she received her Bachelor of Architecture and, recently, a doctorate. From 1983 to 1986 she was a Visiting Research Associate in the Department of Architecture at the Massachusetts Institute of Technology, where she continued her studies of housing and family life. She has recently contributed a curriculum covering women and housing to the design program in her university.

Joan Turner received her doctorate from the Graduate School and University Center of the City University of New York in 1984. Her dissertation, "Building Boundaries," was a study of ethnic conflict over housing on the Lower East Side of New York City. She has written articles on the topics of ethnicity and class and local-level organizations. She is currently employed by AT&T as a manager of their Health Promotion Program.

INDEX

CPSIA information can be obtained
at www.ICGtesting.com
Printed in the USA
BVHW051646150323
660520BV00002B/63